AF564607

BUSINESS ETHICS AND GLOBAL VALUES

For Management Courses

Focus on

INDIAN ETHOS • ETHICS IN PROFESSIONS • CORPORATE GOVERNANCE • MNCs VALUES

S.K. BHATIA

Director
Human Resource Management Foundation, New Delhi

and

Senior Faculty,
Business Management Institutes

Formerly:
- Director (Personnel), Oil India Ltd.
- Director (Pers. and PR), Mekaster Group Co's.
- Add. General Manager (Pers. and Admn.) Bharat Heavy Electricals India Ltd.

Foreword by

DR. ABAD AHMAD

Professor of Management,
and Former Pro-Vice-Chancellor,
University of Delhi, Delhi.

DEEP & DEEP PUBLICATIONS PVT. LTD.

F-159, Rajouri Garden, New Delhi-110027

BUSINESS ETHICS AND GLOBAL VALUES
For Management Courses

ISBN 978-81-8450-097-4

Typeset by S.S. COMPOSERS,
3190, Mohindra Park, Shakur Basti, Delhi-110034.

Printed in India at SARAS GRAPHICS PVT. LTD.
8, Rai Industrial Area, Sonepat (Haryana)

Published by DEEP & DEEP PUBLICATIONS PVT. LTD.,
F-159, Rajouri Garden, New Delhi-110027.
Phones: 25435369, 25440916
e-mail: ddpbooks@yahoo.co.in • ddpubs@gmail.com
Sales Showroom:
2/13, Ansari Road, Daryaganj, New Delhi-110002 • Telefax: 23245122

Dedicated to my wife

KUSUM

for her infinite patience,

understanding and inspiration

and

my elder brother (late) **VED VYAS BHATIA**

for wise counsel

Contents

PART III

VALUES AND CULTURE

PART IV

INDIAN ETHOS IN MANAGEMENT

PART V

BUSINESS ETHICS IN PROFESSIONS

PART VIII

GLOBAL VALUES

PART IX

SPECIFIC COURSE REQUIREMENTS

PART X

ANNEXURES

Foreword

There are, at present, three approaches having a similar focus in protecting various interests, i.e. corporate social responsibility, business ethics and corporate governance. These subjects have, however, developed separately during different periods.

The first approach, CORPORATE SOCIAL RESPONSIBILITY has its origin in USA about seven decades ago. It is an obligation of decision-makers to take actions which protect and improve the welfare of society as a whole along with their own interests. Such decisions may affect environment, consumers and community. It was Peter Drucker who later emphatically argued that management should assume social responsibility. Management should consider the impact of every business policy and action upon society. It has to consider the actions that are likely to promote the public good and to advance the basic beliefs of society, and to contribute to its stability, strength and harmony. He laid emphasis on "Quality of product and customer service".

Later on Sandra Holmes in her study of 540 top executives emphasised that in addition to making profit, business should help solve special problems whether or not business creates these problems.

The second concept, BUSINESS ETHICS with its social values and social concerns came to focus in 1970's in USA, which forced companies to abstain their policies that violate consumer protection and environmental problems. Business ethics safeguards business practices relating to different stakeholders or constituencies (i.e. internal and external constituencies). Business ethics are rules of business conduct, by which propriety of business activities may be judged. Business ethics equally relates to the behaviour and responsibilities of managers and ethical obligations of business professionals. Here focus is on people, how individuals should conduct themselves in fulfilling the ethical requirements of business. There is a growing realisation all over the world that ethics is vitally important for any business and for progress of any society. Ethical leadership can attain this by standing the test of environmental performance and development of corporate social performance (CSP) as recently highlighted by Clarkson. Ethics and profits go together in the long-run and it can protect the society. In fact, experience convincingly shows that good ethics is the foundation of good business.

The third approach is CORPORATE GOVERNANCE which advocates enhancing the accountability of the board of directors to shareholders, more transparent auditing and more responsibilities of independent directors, and a division of roles of chairman and chief executive, etc. The importance of good corporate governance can hardly be over-emphasised, specially after witnessing the shocking corporate failures like that of Enron recently, and many such crises caused earlier by inadequacies and malpractices in corporate governance.

I am happy to note that Shri Bhatia has exhaustively covered all these approaches in his book. Another aspect of vital importance is the role of ethical leadership in providing direction and communicating the values and beliefs that influence and shape the organisation culture and behavioural norms. The moral environment of an organisation depends on the moral calibre and integrity of the leader. The author has touched this aspect in great detail in chapters highlighting critical role of leadership. In addition, chapters have been specifically devoted to protection of stakeholders' interests.

In my opinion the book, besides being educative on various concepts, practices and dilemmas, will provide a thrust on practical implementation and development of ethical practices in organisations. It is a practical tool for enhancing integrity in the organisations. The book has been written in simple and easily understandable language.

I am confident this will be a valuable addition to the management literature in India. It will serve as a teaching and learning resource for corporate managers and students of business ethics and corporate governance who want to improve reputation, image and enhance competitive advantage of their organisations by following a principled approach with awareness of duties and obligations.

Delhi

DR. ABAD AHMAD
Professor of Management, and
Former Pro-Vice-Chancellor,
University of Delhi, Delhi

Preface

1. This is my third book on this evolving and vital subject of business ethics. My earlier two books are as under:

(i) The first book titled as "Business Ethics and Managerial Values" was released in 2002. At that time subject of business ethics was hardly introduced in some institutions/universities as part of their curriculum.
(ii) The second volume titled as "Business Ethics and Corporate Governance" was published in 2005. By then this subject got great importance in corporate sector, political and personal lives in our country. Ethical values of leadership are rated high in their image. All universities have now started teaching this subject as part of syllabus.
(iii) The present volume named as "Business Ethics and Global Values" 2008 is specially designed to cover the curriculum of MBA, BBA and other post-graduate courses in Indian universities and institutions.

2. Aim of the Book

Business ethics now occupies a centre stage in management education in India and is a topic of public concern. The objective of this book is to:

(a) *Share knowledge, build skills* and *develop minds* of the young entrepreneurial managers of tomorrow,
(b) *Provide clarity and insights* into concepts of business ethics and corporate governance so that young managers avoid business misconduct,
(c) *Inculcate high level of integrity* and create moral and social awareness so that they can decide when faced with business dilemma,
(d) Help in fostering *ability to reason* when applying ethical principles,
(e) Help realise their *social responsibility* and values, wisdom and way of life, and
(f) Provide upcoming students' managers with comprehensive knowledge of the subject to enable them do excellently in their examinations.

3. Highlights of Special Coverage in this Volume

The volume covers all major emerging concepts and approaches in the field as mentioned below:

- Business Ethics: Emerging Issues.

- Leader's Role in Building Ethical Organisation.
- Emerging Values of Corporates.
- Values of Indian Culture.
- Indian Ancient Ethos in Management.
- Concepts of Mahatma Gandhi.
- Business Ethics in various Professions—such as Marketing, Media, HRM, Computers, Production, etc.
- Corporate Governance and Concept of Whistle Blowing.
- Corporate Ethical Role Towards Society.
- Environmental Problems—Global Warming (UN Meet on Climate Change, December 2007 at Bali).
- Ethics in Global Business (MNC's Role).
- Personal Values of Children.
- Committee on Ethics, Rajya Sabha.
- Understanding Hinduism.
- A Specific Section containing 10 Chapters on Topics covered in Universities Syllabi.

4. Plan of the Book

The book contains over seventy-two chapters which are conceptually arranged in ten parts. Part ten contains fourteen annexures which covers corporate practices.

- Several ethical tests/case studies provide grasp of the subject.
- At the start of each chapter, details of topics covered are mentioned to facilitate the readers.
- Up-to-date and recent developments on topics are included. It reflects contemporary and emerging developments in the field.

5. I hope this volume in your hands "Business Ethics and Global Values" will fulfil the need of the students in:

(a) Preparing for the examinations including viva,
(b) Preparing their assignments for university courses comfortably, and
(c) Equip them to apply these concepts in work situations and discussions.

I am confident readers—students, faculties, as well as practicing managers will find this volume comprehensive and useful to them in adopting innovative solutions.

Suggestions for improvement of this text, will be highly appreciated.

New Delhi S.K. BHATIA

Acknowledgements

Text books for educational purpose are a team project. While my name is on the cover of this book, literally, it is combined contribution of the writings of so many scholars and authors from whose distinguished works, ideas and valuable contributions have enabled me in completion of this book. As far as possible, I have tried to include their names and publication in each chapter and list of references. Every effort has been made to gratefully acknowledge them, but if any have been inadvertently overlooked, I crave their indulgence. I shall make necessary arrangement to acknowledge at the first opportunity.

Some articles were collected from various sources—newspapers, seminars, magazines and text books, during long years of service and used as teaching material. Unfortunately, these sources were not noted and it is impractical to offer acknowledgements. I express my thanks to those who contributed anonymously to this book.

I am immensely grateful to my son, Neeraj and daughter-in-law Pulkit, in USA, who not only arranged my study visit to USA, but also helped in arranging the literature on the subject, from various sources such as Libraries, Bookstores and Internet, etc. Company of little Arunika and playful Arjun made my study tours more lively and interesting. I thank my wife for her unfailing support and encouragement throughout this project.

My gratefulness to Dr. Abad Ahmad, former Pro-Vice-Chancellor and Professor of Manangement, University of Delhi, Delhi for writing a brilliant and encouraging foreword.

Finally and most important my daughter's family Namita, her husband Atul, loving children Malvika (in USA) and Geetka (in Bangalore) for learning, inspiration and joy.

I thank energetic team of M/s Deep & Deep Publications Pvt. Ltd. for managing the book into its final form.

New Delhi — S.K. BHATIA

PART I

BUSINESS ETHICS—AN OVERVIEW

CHAPTER

1

Business Ethics: Conceptual Approach

There is no agreement as to what the term business ethics means. Let us remember story of a boy who went to a priest and said, "I will give you an apple if you tell me where God is!"? Priest replied, "But I will give you two apples if you tell me where he is not?"

It is much the same with business ethics. One can hardly say where it is not. It is a discipline which addresses numerous issues, problems and dilemmas.

In this chapter on "Business Ethics: Conceptual Approach", the following aspects are covered:

1. Ethics.
2. Business ethics.
3. Nature of business ethics.
4. Ethical base of business.
5. A two-fold objective of business ethics.
6. Business ethics is now a management discipline.
7. Scope of business ethics.
8. The importance of ethics.

1. ETHICS

To begin with, let us understand, what is 'Ethics'? The word "Ethics" has origin in Greek word "Ethics" means character, norms, morals and ideals prevailing in a group, society.

Ethics may be referred to as some standardised form of conduct/behaviour of individuals understood and accepted in a particular field of activity, or

Ethics is a mass of moral principles or sets of values about what conduct ought to be. They give an idea what is right or wrong, true or false, fair or unfair, just or unjust, proper or improper, e.g. honesty, obedience, equality, fairness, etc. and respect and then doing the right thing.

Ethics is a fundamental, personal trait which one adopts and follows as a guiding principle or basic Dharma in one's life. It implies moral conduct and honourable behaviour on the part of an individual. Ethics in most cases runs parallel to law and shows due consideration of others' rights and interests in a civilized society. Compassion on the other hand may induce a person to give more than what ethics might demand.

Even while rendering a service for a *quid pro quo,* the individual is expected to ensure that his services do not mitigate against public good, are not morally indefensible or are not prohibited or punishable by law. Those placed in positions of trust and recognised for their knowledge and expertise shall perform their duty with integrity, independence, sincerity and honesty. That is the basic norm of professional ethics. A professional cannot justify his failure, negligence of compromise, with excuses and explanations.

Every rational human being practices ethics for his own and others' welfare and safety.

2. BUSINESS ETHICS

Different meaning is given to business ethics by various people. Business ethics are rules of business conduct, by which the propriety of business activities may be judged. Ethical principles are dictated by the society and underlie broad social policies. These principles when known, understood and accepted, determine generally the propriety or impropriety of business activities.

Business ethics also relates to the behaviour of manager. It can be defined as an attempt to ascertain the responsibilities and ethical obligations of business professionals. Here the focus is in people, how individuals should conduct themselves in fulfilling the ethical requirements of business?

One writer (Deepak Parekh, CMO HDFC in his J.R.D. Tata Corporate Leadership Award lecture in 27.2.1997) has given one line definition of ethics: "Do not do something that you would be ashamed of, if it becomes public." It is not too difficult to achieve this reality. There is no pillow as soft as a clear conscience.

Carter McNamara has defined: "Business ethics is generally coming to know what is right or wrong in the work place and doing what is right—this is in regard to effects of products/services and in relationships with stakeholders." "Attention to ethics in the work place sensitizes managers and staff to how they should act so that they retain a strong moral compass. Consequently, business ethics can be strong preventive medicine."

3. NATURE OF BUSINESS ETHICS

Ethical issues occur frequently in management and extend for beyond the commonly discussed problems of bribery, collusion and theft, reaching into area such as corporate acquisitions, marketing policies and capital investments. For example, after the merger of two firms, ethical question arises whether to demote or fire the employees those who have been serving honestly for so many years.

Ethics requires a manager to be honest with himself and society. The manager's performance and quality reflect in the success of a business. Sometimes ethical issues occur as managerial dilemmas because they represent a conflict between an organisation's economic performance (measured by revenues, costs and profits) and its social performance (stated in terms of obligation to persons both inside and outside the organisation).

4. ETHICAL BASE OF BUSINESS

Now, what is the relevance of ethics for business? A business, regardless of its organizational structure, is manned only by human beings. And so, business too cannot and shall not be immune to ethics. The *goal of business* is to provide goods and services to customers and clients and earn profits or income. If business has ethics, it will ensure that the goods and services are of reasonable quality and are offered at reasonable prices to earn reasonable profits, as distinguished from profiteering.

More importantly, the *interests of the stakeholders* shall receive care and consideration at the hands of business. The stakeholders include customers, suppliers, creditors, government employees, shareholders and the community. Business has to promote its growth with fairness and truth in its advertisements. This is broadly known as social responsibility of business. As an extension of this concept, business is also expected to share a part of its prosperity with the community in the midst of which it is located by offering amenities and services not otherwise available to the needy in that community.

The new concept of "Maximising shareholder value" is being shouted as the be all and end all of business in recent times. This concept assumes that the investors (promoters and large shareholders) are the most valuable constituents of business and all others are peripheral ones. If a company can enhance the value of its shares in the stock market, its market capitalization goes up. In many cases, speculative reports, creative accounting and other manipulative methods also achieve this even without proven fundamentals. Thus, this theory is not one without flaws. "Ethics is a matter of developing good habits, and it doesn't happen overnight. It happens through repetition and a long process of development." (P.T. Rangamani)

5. A TWO-FOLD OBJECTIVE OF BUSINESS ETHICS

According to Peter Pratley (The Essence of Business Ethics) business ethics has a two-fold objective: "it *evaluates human practices* by calling upon moral standards; also it may give *prescriptive advice* on how to act morally in a specific kind of situation.

(i) The first aim implies *analysis and evaluation*. It leads to an ethical diagnosis of past actions and events. The analysis consists of clarifying standards and lines of argument. Here ethics can be useful, as one is often unaware about most moral values and habits of thought. The basic assumptions behind our moral actions and judgements are mainly taken for granted.

Normative ethics sets itself a second and more curative purpose. Ethics develops rational methods for answering the present and future issues. In order to achieve this second objective one has to be well informed. *Balanced judgements* are based on the careful assessment of relevant information; also one has to be quite specific when deciding upon appropriate normative standards. If both these conditions are met, ethical thought may lead to valid prescriptions.

(ii) So, the second objective is to provide *therapeutic advice*. It suggests solutions and policies when facing the present dilemmas and future dangers, based on well-informed opinions. This especially requires an identification of relevant stakeholder and a clear understanding of the vital issues at stake.

6. BUSINESS ETHICS IS NOW A MANAGEMENT DISCIPLINE

McNamara further states that "Business ethics has come to be considered a management discipline, especially since the birth of the social responsibility of business." Business owes responsibility to work to improve society, e.g. environmental protection, equal rights, public health and improving education. Business operations have replaced the word "stockholder" with "stakeholder", meaning to include employees, customers, suppliers and the wider community.

According to Robert Kreitner in his book, "Management", "Highly publicized accounts of corporate misconduct in recent years have led widespread cynicism about business ethics. And when a 1992 Gallup Poll asked Americans to rate the ethical standards of various professions, only 18 per cent business executives scored either high or very high on honesty and ethical standards. Other professions rated as follows: druggists/pharmacists, 66 per cent; medical doctors, 52 per cent; police officers, 42 per cent; funeral directors, 35 per cent; journalists, 27 per cent; stock brokers, 13 per cent; members of Congress, 11 per cent; and car salespeople, 5 per cent." Fortunately, the subject of ethics is receiving serious attention in management circles these days.

7. SCOPE OF BUSINESS ETHICS

Ethical issues are there everywhere, at all levels of business activity. Business ethics concern the ground rules of individual company and societal behaviour.

(a) Societal Level

- Concern for poor and down-trodden.
- No discrimination against any particular section or group.
- Concern for clean environment.
- Preservation of scarce resources for posterity.
- Contributing to better quality of life.

(b) Stakeholder's Level

(i) Employees

- Security of job.
- Better working conditions.
- Better recommendation.
- Participative management.
- Welfare facilities.

(ii) Customers

- Better quality of goods.
- Goods and services at reasonably price.
- Not to corner stocks and create securities.

- Not to practice discriminatory pricing.
- Not to make false claims about products in advertisements.

(iii) Shareholders

- Ensure capital appreciation.
- Ensure steady and regular dividends.
- Disclose all relevant information.
- Protect minority shareholders' interests.
- Not to window dress balance sheets.
- Protect interests in times of mergers, amalgamations and takeovers.

(iv) Banks and other Lending Institutions

- Guarantee safety of borrowed funds.
- Prompt repayment of loans.

(v) Government

- Complying with rules and regulations.
- Honesty in paying taxes and other dues.
- Acting as partner in the progress of the country.

(c) Internal Policy Level

- Fair practices relating to recruitment, compensation, lay-offs, perks, promotion, etc.
- Transformational leadership to motivate employees to aim at better and higher things in life.
- Better communication at all levels.

(d) Personal Policy Level

- Not to misuse others for personal ends.
- Not to indulge in politics to gain power.
- Not to spoil promotional chances of others.
- Not to use office car, stationery and other facilities for personal use.
- Not to fall prey to shortcuts and easy money.
- Promise keeping.
- No violence, i.e. preventing or not causing physical harm to others.
- Mutual help.
- Respect for persons and property.

8. THE IMPORTANCE OF ETHICS

Patrica Hayes Andrews and Richard T. Herschel, 'Organisation Communication' (pp. 309-10) have excellently summarised the importance of ethics as under: "Unfortunately, in recent years an alarming number of "unethical" situations have arisen in American organizations. For example, the Ford Motor Company refused to alter the dangerous gas tank on its Pinto model because changing it would have cost the company $ 11 per car. In the end, the flaw cost Ford millions of dollars in lawsuits—and cost many people their lives. Equity Funding tried to hide 64,000 phony insurance claims but went bankrupt when the truth came out. Ivan Boesky engaged in "insider trading", an illegal practice for investment counsellors. A number of directors of savings and loan associations defrauded depositors, in many cases depriving people of their life savings. It is little wonder that a large majority of the public think executives are dishonest, overly profit-oriented, and willing to step on other people to get what they want (Andrews, 1989)."

In India also there are numerous cases of scams and cheating the small investors of their hard earned money. To name few—MS Shoes East Ltd. for misleading investing public, Manu Chabra Group for wrecking the fortunes of about half-a-dozen companies and facing investigations on FERA violations, the Harshad Mehta Epic Stock Scam, claims of the Sterling Group and a host of other engaged in teak plantations, ITC's violation of excise laws and the recent one UTI scam where they have left crores of investors high and dry. This is all to point how managements out of greed to make more money and achieve goals, take the various constituents of the company for a ride in the most unfair ways.

8.1 Why Ethical Behaviour is Important?

Whether or not everyone would agree that the behaviours described above are equally unethical, when considered together, they lead to a critical question: *Why ethical behaviour is important*? There are several compelling reasons.

First, *ethical behaviour is usually associated with important positive consequences*. Honesty in one's professional dealings promotes trust and establishes the foundation for relationship development and positive future interactions. Business in particular depends on the acceptance of rules and expectations, mutual trust and fairness. Thus, ethical business is good business. In contrast, unethical behaviour can cause serious damage affecting both the persons committing the behaviour and the people touched by it. In the cases described above, innocent people suffered serious financial losses, injury, or loss of life, and in some cases the perpetrators were sentenced to jail. But beyond that, the people and organisations that were involved lost credibility. Once an organisation's image is so tarnished that people are no longer willing to put their faith in it or its leaders, it is almost certain to fail. Nothing is more dangerous to business, than a tarnished public image—the fact is that a tarnished image has direct consequences, for sales, for profits, for morale, for the day-to-day running of the business. Distrust of a company can quickly drive it to bankruptcy.

Second, from a personal perspective, *ethical errors end careers more quickly* than any other mistakes in judgment and accounting. Lying, stealing, cheating, on contracts, and so on undermine the very foundation upon which the business and professional world is built. Ethical behaviour is especially important for organizational leaders because they influence the ethical climate for everyone else. Leaders are role models. When they make ethical blunders, they are held especially accountable. No one can excuse immorality. The US House of Representatives in July, 2002 expelled Democratic legislator James Traficant of Ohio, making the former sheriff turned convicted felon the second House member since the Civil War to be tossed out of Congress. On a vote of 420-1, law-makers booted the nine-term Traficant for ethics violations stemming from his April conviction on federal charges of bribery, kickbacks and tax evasion. Gene Green, a Texas Democrat, said, "If we can't remove a Congressman convicted of 10 felony counts . . . we risk losing the faith and trust of the American people." (*Reuters*)

Third, *ethical behaviour is empowering for all parties*. The manager who behaves ethically *establishes an organisational climate of supportiveness*, honesty, and trust. This climate in turn empowers employees to try out new ideas, take risks, express dissent, and generally assume enhanced responsibility.

Finally, *ethical behaviour is intrinsically valuable*. Those who know that they are honest, who behave humanely in their dealings with others, who are fair in their evaluations of others, and who are concerned for the welfare of the organization as a whole and the society it serves are rewarded with a peace of mind that carries no price tag.

Ultimately, managers who treat other people with unimpeachable integrity thereby *earn those people's trust and make them more willing to support the organization*. Conversely, managers who lack integrity promote mistrust among those with whom they deal and make their employees ashamed of their organization and the products and services they provide. Since workers feel their work is unworthy, they stop caring.

Andrew Sigler, "The Business Roundable", *New York Times*, February 1981 has highlighted that *"Ethics provides the broader framework within which business life must be understood,* there may be few people for whom business is all of life, for whom family and friendship are irrelevant. For them money means only more investment potential and has nothing to do with respect or status or enjoying the good life. But most successful executives understand that *business is part of life. Corporations are part of a society."*

"Executives are *most effective and successful* when they retain their "real life" view of themselves, their positions and the human world outside as well as inside the corporation. Business ethics, ultimately, is just business in its larger human context."

"A Corporation's responsibilities includes its impact of its actions on all, from shareholders, customers, employees and to the society at large. Its business activities must make business sense."

8.2 Ethics Plays Key Role in Business

Another writer Thomas Donaldson (Ethics in Business: A New Look) has observed that "There are three key reasons why business ethics is not a fad and why ethics plays a key role in business.

First, it is crucial that *ethics have a considerable influence* if we want an efficient, smoothly operating economy. Ethics helps the market to its best. For example, the economist, Alfred Marshall remarked in 1925, that a score of Tata's might well do more for India than any Government, British or local could accomplish—the emphasis is that history of Tata evolution is not just on any kind of capitalism but on ethically-based management.

Second, the *government, laws and lawyers cannot resolve certain key problems of business and protect the society: ethics can*. Ethics can only resolve futuristic issues such as technology races ahead much faster than the government. Regulations almost always lag behind. That companies social responsibility extends beyond what the law strictly requires.

Third, *ethical activity is valuable in itself*, for its own sake, because it *enhances the quality of lives* and the work we do—business has an ethical responsibility for fairness for humanity, e.g. employee."

8.3 To Sum Up—Importance of Business Ethics

Thomas Donaldson (Ethics in Business: A New Look) sums up that "There is a growing realisation all over the world that ethics is vitally important for any business and for the progress of any society. Ethics makes for an efficient economy; ethics alone, not government or laws, can protect society; ethics is good in itself; ethics and profits go together in the long-run. An ethically responsible company is one which has developed a culture of caring for people and for the environment; a culture which flows downwards from the top managers and leaders."

Reference

P.T. Rangamani, "Ethics, Business and Professions", *Chartered Secretary*, November 2003.

CHAPTER

2

Business Ethics: Emerging Issues

In this chapter on "Business Ethics: Emerging Issues" following aspects are discussed:

1. Meaning of business ethics.
2. Importance of business ethics.
3. Types of managerial ethics.
4. Contemporary ethical issues in organisations.
5. Three approaches having a similar focus in protecting various interests.

1. MEANING OF BUSINESS ETHICS

Ethics is a study of *moral behaviour.* It is the study of how the standards of moral conduct among individuals are established and expressed behaviourally. Terms such as business ethics, corporate ethics, medical ethics or legal ethics are used to indicate the particular area of application. But to have meaning, *the ethics involved in each area must still refer to the value-oriented decisions and behaviour of individuals.*

Business ethics refer to set of moral principles which play a very significant role in guiding the conduct of managers and employees in the operation of any enterprise. A code of ethics is concerned with what is right and what is wrong in human behaviour. It addresses the question of what ought to be. It refers both to the body of moral principles governing a particular society or group and to the personal moral precepts of an individual.

2. IMPORTANCE OF BUSINESS ETHICS

Business ethics has two-fold objective as it *evaluates* human practices by calling upon moral standards; also it may give *prescriptive advice* on how to act morally in a specific type of situation.

Ethical behaviour is *important* as it is *usually consequences.* Honesty in one's professional dealings promotes trust and establishes the foundation for relationship development and positive future interactions.

Second, from a personal perspective, *ethical errors end careers more quickly,* than any other mistakes in judgement and accounting.

Third, the manager who behaves ethically *establishes an organisation climate of supportiveness, honest and trust.* Business ethics promotes a strong public image.

Fourth, *ethical behaviour is transically valueable.* Those who know that they are honest, who behave humanely in their dealings with others, who are fair in their evaluations of others, and who are concerned for the welfare of the organisation as a whole and the society it serves, are rewarded with a peace of mind that carries no price tag.

Fifth, ethical behaviour is especially important for *organisation leader because they influence the ethical climate* for everyone else. Leaders are role models. They maintain a moral course in turbulent times.

Sixth, the *government, and laws cannot resolve certain key problems of business* and protect the society, ethics can, ethical companies extend beyond what the law strictly requires. Business has substantially improved society.

3. TYPES OF MANAGERIAL ETHICS

Managerial ethics are standards of conduct or moral judgement used by managers of organizations in carrying out their business. Archie B. Carroll notes that three major levels of moral or ethical judgement characterize managers: immoral management, amoral management, and moral management.

(a) Immoral Management

Immoral management not only lacks ethical principles but also is actively opposed to ethical behaviour. This perspective is characterized by principal or exclusive concern for company gains, undue emphasis on profits, company success at virtually any price, lack of concern about the desires of others to be treated fairly, views of laws as obstacles to be overcome, and a willingness to "cut corners".

(b) Amoral Management

The amoral management approach is neither immoral nor moral but, rather, ignores or is oblivious to ethical considerations. There are two types of amoral management:

Intentional

Amoral managers do not include ethical concerns in their decision-making, or behaviour, because they basically think that general ethical standards are more appropriate to other areas of life than to business.

Unintentional

Amoral managers also do not think about ethical issues in their business dealings, but the reason is different. These managers are basically inattentive or insensitive to the moral implications of their decision-making, actions, and behaviour. Overall, amoral managers pursue profitability as a goal and may be generally well meaning, but intentionally or unintentionally they pay little attention to the impacts of their behaviours on others.

(c) Moral Management

The Figure 1 shows the characteristics of Managerial Ethics.

FIGURE I

Characteristics of Managerial Ethics (Moral Management)

Organizational Characteristics	*Moral Management*
Ethical Norms	Management activity *conforms* to a standard of ethical, or right behaviour. Believes that not to do anything dishonourable which will harm his self-esteem. Conforms to accepted professional standards of conduct. Ethical leadership is commonplace on the part of management.
Motives	Good Management wants to succeed but only within the guidelines of ethical precepts (fairness, justice, due process).
Goals	Profitability *within the confines of legal obedience* and ethical standards.
Orientation toward Law	*Obedience* toward letter and spirit of the law. Law is a minimal ethical behaviour. Prefer to operate well above what law mandates.
Strategy	Live by sound ethical standards. Assume leadership position when ethical dilemmas arise. Enlightened self-interest.

3.1 Ethical Dilemmas

Dilemmas situations are where they are required to define right and wrong conduct. What constitutes good ethical behaviour has never been clearly defined. In recent years, the line differentiating right from wrong has become more blurred. Employees see people all around them engaging in unethical practices. When caught, they hear these people giving excuses like "everyone does it", or "I never thought I would get caught".

Managers and their organizations are responding to this problem from a number of directions. They are writing and distributing *codes of ethics* to guide employees through ethical dilemmas and they are creating protection mechanisms for employees who reveal internal unethical practices.

Today's manager needs to create an ethically healthy climate for his employees, where they can do their work sincerely, with high productivity and confront a minimal degree of ambiguity regarding what constitutes right and wrong behaviour.

3.2 Qualities for Ethical Decision-making

Making ethical decisions is part of each manager's job. It has been suggested by K.R. Andrews that ethical decision-making requires three qualities of individuals:

(a) *The competence to identify ethical issues* and evaluate the consequences alternative courses of action.
(b) The *self-confidence* to seek out different opinions about the issue and what is right in terms of a particular situation.
(c) *Tough-mindedness*—the willingness to make decisions when all that needs to be known cannot be known and when the ethical issue has no established unambiguous solution.

3.3 Values and Ethics

Sometimes, some people consider values and ethics synonymous and use them interchangeably. However, the two have different meanings. The major distinction between the two is that values are beliefs that affect an individual's judgemental ideas about what is good or bad. The ethics is the *way the values are acted out*. Ethical behaviour is acting in ways consisted with one's personal values and the commonly held values of the organization and society.

4. CONTEMPORARY ETHICAL ISSUES IN ORGANIZATIONS

In contemporary organizations, people face ethical and moral dilemmas in many diverse areas. The key areas are:

4.1 White-Collar Crime

Corporate criminal behaviours have resulted in big financial scandals. White-collar crime may occur in more subtle forms as well. Using work hours for conducting personal business, sending out personal mail using the company resources, inflating expenses, etc. are all practices some individuals would consider unethical. Whether the impact is large or small, white-collar crimes are important issues in organizations.

4.2 Employee's Right to Privacy

Safeguarding employee's right to privacy and at the same time restricting access to sensitive data only to those who need it requires that the manager judiciously balance competing interests.

4.3 Sexual Harassment

Sexual harassment is unwelcome sexual attention, whether verbal or physical, that affects an employee's job conditions or creates a hostile working environment. Sexual harassment costs the company in the form of absenteeism, turnover, and loss of productivity. Companies may be required to pay damages to victims of sexual harassment. Besides, the company may face negative publicity because of sexual harassment cases.

4.4 Romantic Involvements

Hugging, kissing, sexual innuendos, and repeated requests for dates may constitute sexual harassment for some, but they are prelude to romance for others. This situation carries with it a different set of ethical dilemmas for organizations. Conflicts occur within an organization when romantic involvements at work become disruptive. Moreover, employers are liable for acts of their employees and can thus be held liable for sexual harassment. Other employees might claim that the subordinate who is romantically involved with the supervisor gets preferential treatment.

Romantic involvements at work can create a conflict of interest. A comprehensive policy should require anyone who might be experiencing a conflict of interest to report it to his or her manager. The policy should also include an explanation of how unwelcome romantic advances can turn into sexual harassment.

4.5 Organizational Justice

Another area in which moral and ethical dilemmas may arise for people at work concerns organizational justice, both distributive and procedural.

(a) Distributive Justice

Concerns the fairness of outcomes meted out to individuals.

(b) Procedural Justice

Concerns the fairness of the process by which outcomes are allocated. The ethical questions here do not concern the just or unjust distribution of organizational resources. Rather, the ethical questions in *procedural justice concern the process.* Has the organization used the correct procedures in allocating resources? Have the right considerations such as competence and skill, been brought to bear in the decision process?

4.6 Whistle-blowing

Whistle-blowers are employees who inform authorities of wrongdoings of their companies or co-workers. Whistle-blowing is important because committed organizational members sometimes engage in unethical behaviour in an intense desire to succeed. Organizations can manage whistle-blowing by communicating the conditions that are appropriate for the disclosure of wrongdoing. Clearly delineating wrongful behaviour and the appropriate ways to respond are important organizational actions.

4.7 Social Responsibility

Corporate social responsibility is the obligation of an organization to behave in ethical ways in the social environment in which it operates. Socially responsible actions are expected of organizations. Current concerns include protecting the environment, promoting worker safety, supporting social issues, investing in the community, etc. Managers must encourage both individual ethical behaviour and organizational social responsibility.

5. THREE APPROACHES HAVING A SIMILAR FOCUS IN PROTECTING VARIOUS INTERESTS

(i) There are, at present, three approaches having a similar focus in protecting various interests, i.e. corporate social responsibility, business ethics and corporate governance. These subjects have, however, developed separately during different periods.

The first approach, CORPORATE SOCIAL RESPONSIBILITY has its origin in USA in

1930's. It is an obligation of decision-makers to take actions which *protect and improve the welfare of society* as a whole along with their own interests. Such *decisions may affect environment, consumers and community*. It was Peter Drucker who later emphatically argued that management should assume social responsibility. Management should consider the *impact of every business policy and action upon society*. It has to consider the actions that are likely to promote the public good and to advance the basic beliefs of society, and to contribute to its stability, strength and harmony. He laid emphasis on "Quality of product and customer service".

Later on Sandra Holmes emphasised that in addition to making profit, business should help *solve special problems* whether or not business creates these problems.

(ii) The second concept, BUSINESS ETHICS with its social values and social concerns came to focus in 1970's in USA, which forced companies to abstain their policies that violate consumer protection and environmental problems. Business ethics safeguards business practices relating to different stake-holders or constituencies (i.e. internal and external constituencies). *Business ethics are rules of business conduct by which propriety of business activities may be judged. Business ethics equally relates to the behaviour and responsibilities of managers and ethical obligations of business professionals. Here focus is on people, how individuals should conduct themselves in fulfilling the ethical requirements of business.* There is a growing realisation all over the world that ethics is vitally important for any business and for progress of any society. Ethical leadership can attain this by standing the test of environmental performance and development of corporate social performance (CSP) as recently highlighted by Clarkson. Ethics and profits go together in the long-run and it can protect the society. In fact, experience convincingly shows that good ethics is the foundation of good business.

Further business ethics highlights:

(a) *Ethical leadership*, commited to social values can change the organisation culture and behaviour of individuals. The moral environment of an organisation depends on the moral calibre and integrity of the leader.

(b) Management must assume responsibility of *disciplining wrong doers.*

(c) Company should provide mechanism for "whistle-blowing" to report unethical behaviour.

(d) Management should impart *training* programmes explaining their *code of ethics.*

(iii) The third approach is CORPORATE GOVERNANCE which advocates enhancing the accountability of the board of directors to shareholders, more transparent auditing and more responsibilities of independent directors, and a division of roles of chairman and chief executive, etc. The importance of good corporate governance can hardly be over-emphasised, specially after witnessing the shocking corporate failures like that of Enron recently, and many such crises caused earlier by inadequacies and malpractices in corporate governance.

CHAPTER

3

Why Business Ethics is Vital for Managers?

In this chapter on "Why Business Ethics is Vital for Managers?", the following aspects are covered"

1. Benefits for students.
2. Benefits of managing ethics in the organisation.
3. Essential principles of highly ethical organisation.
4. Three concepts with similar approach to protect various interests.
5. Social responsibility model.
6. Current issues in corporate ethics.

1. BENEFITS FOR STUDENTS

Apart from the hard skills, tools and management techniques like just-in-time, total quality management, business process re-engineering, etc., adequate attention must be paid to the relatively softer skills like business ethics and business practices. As a training ground of professional managers, the effort must first start in the management schools. In the west, a course on business ethics, cross-cultural variance with respect to values, corporate social responsibility, forms an integral part of the MBA curriculum.

Some benefits for the student young managers are:

(i) Young managers should understand and be aware of the reasons that underlie moral principles. These are helpful in fostering *ability to reason* when applying these principles. It is vital part of ensuring compliance by managers with company standards for conduct.

(ii) Knowledge of business ethics will help managers in *resolving ethical issues/dilemmas* as they arise.
(iii) Knowledge will help managers in setting highly *responsible tone for the organisation—* in individual judgements and decisions whether ethical or not.
(iv) The study of business ethics will *provide conscientious managers* with morally responsible approach to business. The need for responsible managers is acute as questions of business ethics cannot wholly be determined by law or government regulations, but must remain the concern of individual manager.
(v) It helps *managers to realise their social responsibility.* Many organisations find it wise to go beyond their primary mission and take into account needs of the community. Business ethics makes managers more accountable for social responsibility.
(vi) The study of business ethics *inculcates high level of integrity in managers.* Goal of ethics education is to share knowledge, build skills and develop minds. It helps to gain clarity and insight into business ethics and avoid business misconduct in organisations. The study of business ethics helps manager arrive at a decision that he feels to be "right and proper" 'just'. It facilitates individuals to understand their moral standards and ethical norms, beliefs and values so that they can decide when faced with business dilemma.
(vii) Business ethics *creates awareness of social and moral values* through education (value education) because erosion of essential values and increasing cynicism in society is leading to violence, superstition and fatalism.

In view of aforesaid benefits, majority of business management institutes in India have now introduced a separate course on business ethics for management students. Knowledge and awareness of the concepts and practices of business ethics is equally helpful to practicing managers in managerial conduct and decision-making. Business ethics improve the skills of reflective managers both in analyzing concrete moral issues and in deliberating and deciding upon strategies for solving moral dilemmas. The study of cases by students reminds them the importance of precise and accurate judgements that take into account the concrete facts and issues. Business ethics contributes by highlighting basic principles in a systematic manner.

In nutshell, business ethics provides a basic outlook to the training of a business manager. He would enter the bad word with fortified set of values and less of doubts.

Peter Pratley, in "The Essence of Business Ethics" cautions against one particular erroneous expectation: People with immoral habits will not change by reading a book on business ethics. He states that "Behaving with a sense of moral responsibility *require practice, it is reflective activity. Ethics can guide our reflection* on such matters, but cannot actually reorient and shape the qualities of our character, commitment and mind. This is a matter of education, giving the right example, and learning to practice moral behaviour in honest dialogue."

It has to be realised that business cannot do without ethics. Sound ethics pay-off in the long-run. Much neglect of ethics occurs out of incompetence, cowardice and myopia.

Azim Prem Ji, recently said that in his journey from tiny business of Rs. 5 crores to Wipro's net worth today touching some Rs. 3500 crores, everything in Wipro but *for values and integrity,* has undergone a drastic change. He cautioned the emerging breed of entrepreneurs and business managers to *desist from temptation of shortcuts and windfall gains.*

2. BENEFITS OF MANAGING ETHICS IN THE ORGANISATION

Carter McNamara describes various (ten) benefits from managing ethics in the work place as under:

(i) Attention to Business Ethics has Substantially Improved Society

A few decades ago, children in USA worked 16 hours a day. Workers' limbs were cut-off in accidents and disabled workers were condemned to poverty and often to starvation. Employees were terminated based on personalities. Then society reacted and demanded that businesses place high value on fairness and equal rights. Anti-trust laws were instituted. Government agencies were established. Unions were organised. Laws and regulations were established.

(ii) Ethics Programmes Help Maintain a Moral Course in Turbulent Times

Wallace and Pekel explain that attention to business ethics is critical during times of fundamental change—times much like those faced now by businesses. During times of change, there is often no clear moral compass to guide leaders through complex conflicts about what is right or wrong. Continuing attention to ethics in the work place sensitizes leaders and staff as to how they should act—consistently.

(iii) Ethics Programmes Cultivate Strong Teamwork and Productivity

Ethics programmes align employee behaviours with those top priority ethical values preferred by leaders of the organisation. Ongoing attention and dialogue regarding values in the work place builds openness, integrity and community—critical ingredients of strong teams in the work place. Employees feel strong alignment between their values and those of the organization. They react with strong motivation and performance.

(iv) Ethics Programmes Support Employee Growth and Meaning

Attention to ethics in the work place helps employees face reality, both good and bad—in the organization and themselves. Employees feel full confidence they can deal with whatever comes their way. Bennett explains that a consulting company tested a range of executives and managers. Their most striking finding: the more emotionally healthy executives, as measured on a battery of tests, the more likely they were to score high on ethics tests. *Ethics is necessary for human survival and existence.* In fact, one's own survival is linked with survival of others and this is ethics. The six main characteristics of ethics are—patience, tolerance, forgiveness, consideration, humility and compassion. These are *intertwined with the purpose of life.* Living a life of peace and happiness is the goal of everyone.

(v) Ethics Programmes are an Insurance Policy—They Help Ensure that Policies are Legal

Ethical principles are often state-of-the-art legal matters. These principles are often applied to current, major ethical issues to become legislation. Attention to ethics ensures highly ethical policies and procedures in the work place. It's far better to incur the cost of mechanisms to ensure ethical practices now than to incur costs of litigation later. A major intent of well-designed personnel policies is to ensure ethical treatment of employees, e.g., in matters of hiring, evaluating, disciplining, firing, etc.

(vi) Ethics Programmes Help Avoid Criminal Acts "Of Omission" and can Lower Fines

Ethics programmes tend to detect ethical issues and violations early on so they can be reported or addressed.

(vii) Ethics Programmes Help Manage Values Associated with Quality Management, Strategic Planning and Diversity Management—This Benefit Needs for More Attention

Ethics cannot be imbibed by laws alone, but by people and their systems. People have to understand ethical values. Ethics programmes *identify preferred values* and ensure organizational behaviours are aligned with those values. This effort includes recording the values, developing policies and procedures to align behaviours with preferred values, and then training all personnel about the policies and procedures. This overall effort is very useful for several other programmes in the work place that require *behaviours to be aligned with values*, including quality management, strategic planning and diversity management. Total Quality Management includes high priority on certain operating values, e.g., trust among stakeholders, performance, reliability, measurement, the feedback.

(viii) Ethics Programmes Promote a Strong Public Image

Attention to ethics is also strong public relations, frankly, the fact that an organization regularly gives attention to its ethics can portray a strong positive impression to the public. People see those organizations as valuing people more than profit, as striving to operate with the utmost of integrity and honour. Aligning behaviour with values is ethical to effective marketing and public relations programmes. Consider how Johnson and Johnson handled the Tylenol crisis *versus* how Exxon handled the oil spill in Alaska. "Ethical values, consistently applied, are the cornerstones in building a commercially successful and socially responsible business."

(ix) Overall Benefits of Ethics Programmes

Donaldson and Davis, in "Business Ethics? Yes, But What Can it Do for the Bottom Line?" (*Management Decision*, Vol. 28, No. 6, 1990) explain that managing ethical values in the work place legitimizes managerial actions, strengthens the coherence and balance of the organization's culture, improves trust in relationships between individuals and groups, supports greater consistency in standards and qualities of products, and cultivates greater sensitivity to the impact of the enterprise's values and messages.

(x) Last—and Most—Formal Attention to Ethics in the Work place is the Right Thing to do

(xi) Ethics Programmes to Uncover Values

In fact, ethics should a compulsory subject not just in B-schools, but in primary schools as well. These values need to be inculcated from childhood. But that alone will not help, "Parents need to set an example at home. Teachers too need to be active role models. Finally, the finishing touches should come from the employers themselves." Ethically-oriented managers are smarter, more alert with a stronger drive and they will take over the managers with the old school of thought. This will help in reducing the generation gap and should bring a revolutionary change in the way corporates are being run today.

The qualities we seek are already a part of us, not apart from us. We wouldn't yearn for them if they weren't already there. *Our risk is to uncover.*

(xii) Ethics is Important for Organisations for more than one Reason

(i) Ethics corresponds to basic human needs;
(ii) Ethics creates credibility with the public;
(iii) Ethical values bestow management with credibility before employees;
(iv) Ethics helps improve decision-making process; and
(v) No law can protect society but ethics can.

3. ESSENTIAL PRINCIPLES OF A HIGHLY ETHICAL ORGANIZATION

Mark Pastin, in the "Hard Problems of Management: Gaining the Ethics Edge (Jossey-Bass, 1986)", provides the following four principles for highly ethical organizations:

(i) They are at *ease interacting with diverse internal and external stakeholder groups*. The ground rules of these firms make the good of these stakeholder groups part of the organizations' own good.
(ii) They are *obsessed with fairness*. Their ground rules emphasize that the other persons' interests count as much as their own.
(iii) *Responsibility is individual* rather than collective, with individuals assuming personal responsibility for actions of the organization.
(iv) *They see their activities in terms of purpose*. This purpose is a way of operating that members of the organization highly value. And purpose ties the organization to its environment.

Doug Wallace asserts the following characteristics of a high integrity organization:

(a) There exists a *clear vision* and picture of *integrity* throughout the organization.
(b) The *vision is owned* and embodied by top management, over time.
(c) The *reward system is aligned with the vision* of integrity.
(d) *Policies and practices* of the organization are aligned with the vision, no mixed messages.
(e) It is understood that every significant management *decision has ethical value* dimensions.
(f) Everyone is expected to *work through conflicting-stakeholder value perspectives*.

4. THREE CONCEPTS WITH SIMILAR APPROACH TO PROTECT VARIOUS INTERESTS

(a) Corporate Social Responsibility,
(b) Business Ethics, and
(c) Corporate Governance.

Three major concepts which are almost similar in approach in protecting various interests. These are:

(a) *Corporate Social Responsibility*, which has its origin in USA and Government had passed Anti-Trust Act against monopolistic practices, so as to protect and improve the welfare of society.

(b) *Business Ethics,* which highlighted social values and society's concerns in the 1970s and forced corporates in the USA to abstain in their policies which violated consumer protection and environmental protection, etc.

(c) *Corporate Governance* commenced in the UK for improved accountability of directors to shareholders, emphasised for more transparent auditing and increased responsibilities of independent directors, division of rules of chairman and managing directors for safeguarding interests of shareholders.

5. SOCIAL RESPONSIBILITY MODEL

Here we present Carroll's four-part social responsibility model which clarifies distinction in various responsibilities, i.e. economic, legal, ethical and discretionary of business.

Economic Responsibilities	Legal Responsibilities	Ethical Responsibilities	Discretionary Responsibilities

Carroll's Four-Part Model

(i) The model suggests that business is basically an economic entity and primary responsibility is *economic,* i.e. produce goods and services that society wants and sell them at profit.

(ii) Legal responsibilities are also basic firms must *operate within laws* of the land.

(iii) Ethical responsibility refers to *behaviour by the firm* that is expected by the society—but not codified in a law. For example, until the passage of Foreign Corrupt Practices Act in 1977 it was not illegal in USA to bribe foreign officials. But there was public indignation to such practice.

(iv) Discretionary responsibility is *purely voluntary obligation* that an organisation assumes, e.g. providing philanthropic contributions to institutes, etc. Few people expect organisations to fulfil discretionary responsibilities, but all expect a firm to satisfy ethical obligations.

However, ethical and discretionary together constitute social responsibilities of business.

Discretionary responsibility of today may become the ethical responsibility of tomorrow, e.g. day care facilities for children is moving from discretionary to an ethical responsibility.

Carroll suggests that companys to undertake both activities voluntarily otherwise society will assert to make it legal.

6. CURRENT ISSUES IN CORPORATE ETHICS

These problems can be mentioned in 4 categories as under:

(i) Equity

Equity includes fairness apart from established legal human rights. For example, sometimes top directors' salary scales are inequitable—there is often controversy on such matters.

(ii) Rights

Rights are treatments to which a person has just claim—through legislation. The rights defend individual autonomy from encroachment. The rights keep a check on hire and fire, equal employment opportunity, etc.

(iii) Dignity

Dignity is sub-category of rights, e.g. employee privacy, protection from sexual harassment. There are lot of court decisions on these topics but no absolute formula is there to guide. Similarly, screening of employees for drug abuse to maintain safe work place is debatable issue.

(iv) Honesty

Honesty in corporate ethics relates to integrity and truthfulness of company policies, e.g. misleading advertising, gifts for foreign officials, fraud in government contracts are labelled as dishonest.

Which ethical Issues are now most important?

In addition to above, some current important issues which are ethical in nature are as under:

- Environmental issues.
- Product and work place safety.
- Security of company records.
- Employee health screening.
- Shareholder interests.

Organisations resort to different ways to enforce ethical behaviours on their employees. They draw elaborate codes of conduct and expect all employees to adhere to the guideline (Read Box 1 for a typical code of conduct).

Box I

Thomas Cook Frames Ethical Code for Staff

Thomas Cook India Ltd., the largest player in the travel trade, has become one of the first companies in India to enforce a formal code of business ethics and conduct for its employees and business associates.

A new hand book on business ethics and integrity, entitled 'Values That Work at Work', has been introduced and all employees have to give a written assurance that they will abide by the policies and guidelines laid down in it.

The *code of conduct* is divided into five main sections covering all the areas of interaction undertaken by TCIL employees. These include working with customers and suppliers, government business, fair competition, working in the TCIL community and personal integrity. To make all employees vigilant and alert against any possible violations, the booklet lists out ways in which personnel can get policy questions answered or report a possible violation. It also lists some of the things that may indicate a policy problem and the designated officers of the company to whom employees can report their concerns.

A corporate-level business ethics and integrity compliance review committee has been set-up comprising the CEO and managing director along with the executive director and heads of human resources, finance and internal audit.

For ensuring that the code is really enforced and does not remain merely a statement of objectives, any employee found flouting the code of conduct or failing to report a violation will face disciplinary action and even be dismissed.

TCIL will also terminate its contracts with all consultants, representatives, distributors and contractors who are unwilling or unable to represent it in a manner consistent with this policy.

CHAPTER

4

Understanding Ethics

"Talk is easy but doing the right thing for the *right reason* is not!"

In this chapter on "Understanding Ethics", the following aspects are covered:

1. Ethics is understanding about our values and norms.
2. Ethics is important for our well-being.
3. Ethics is doing the right thing.
4. Choosing an alternative of an ethical dilemma requires find purpose and reason.
5. Beware of pitfalls of letting science scope your moral problems.
6. Respect your values.

1. ETHICS IS UNDERSTANDING ABOUT OUR VALUES AND NORMS

Norms give meaning and purpose to life, but a life that has not been morally examined is not really worth living to be responsible moral adult. To be responsible moral adult being true to yourself really means norms are regular ways of doing things that every body agrees on. Unlike other conventions, ethical *norms regulate all aspects of our lives* in ways that are crucial for our existence of society. They are also a core part of who we are. Try to live by some ethical ideals; they give life a meaning.

2. ETHICS IS IMPORTANT FOR OUR WELL-BEING

Thinking about our values and norms rationally and impartially is key to solving moral dilemmas that we face in everyday life. Ethical issues arise in our everyday life.

3. ETHICS IS DOING THE RIGHT THING

You should not feel guilty for the choices you are making on a daily basis; just be aware of how filled with ethical issues your life is. Ethical helps to be self-aware such as how a habit or practice came to me and to rethink about that practice and to make a change. *Adopt the moral attitude* in your dealing with others. *Ethics aims at clarifying* the nature of right and wrong, good and bad. Besides clarifying the meaning and justification of ethical ideas, ethics tells us how we *ought to behave.*

4. CHOOSING AN ALTERNATIVE OF AN ETHICAL DILEMMA REQUIRES FIND PURPOSE AND REASON

- Ethical life is the life of imperfect mortal beings. Because your choices matter to you, you have to *give them purpose and meaning*. That involves making hard choices, and balancing conflicting duties, goals, and values.
- An ethical dilemma *forces us to choose* in a way that involves breaking some ethical norm or contradicting ethical value.
- Ethical dilemmas are hardly the sorts of things that happen once every blue moon. They happen all the time; every day, in fact, watch for them, sometimes they come in smaller packages.
- Not all ethical dilemmas involve choosing between two happy options. Sometimes ethical dilemma involves having to choose between two actions, both of which are undesirable options.
- Remember that what on first glance seems to be an ethical dilemma with no happy solution might not be. Always assume that there are more options than just two. Then try to think of all the factors that bear on the issue on hand. Make a list. Do the right thing.
- In thinking through ethical conflicts, remember that they typically have their source in the contradictory ethical demands placed upon us by our society. A value is standard—typically shared by others in a given community—for judging the goodness and badness of something or some action. Ethical values always *imply standards of worth.* They are the standards by which we measure the goodness of our lives.
- Although you should sometimes compromise with other on how best to act, *never compromise your values.* Compromising your values means lessening your concern for what is good and right. *Concern for what is good and right is the very stuff of ethical life.*

For example, the nineteenth century French poet Charles Baudelaire thought that basic values such as truth, moral goodness, and beauty sometimes clashed. Truth can be sometimes ugly; beauty can tempt us into vice; moral goodness can demand sacrifice and austerity.

5. BEWARE OF THE PITFALLS OF LETTING SCIENCE SOLVE YOUR PROBLEMS

In today's world, it often seems as if moral goodness is sacrificed for the sake of acquiring knowledge (science and technology) and sensuous pleasure (material consumption). Do we agree?

- Appealing to science as your sole moral guide is as risky as appealing to religion as your sole moral guide.
- Avoid both religious fanaticism and scientific extremism.
- *Appreciate how science, religion and ethics make different contributions to life.*
- Remember that science needs ethics as much as ethics need science.
- When you need technical advice, seek an expert for guidance. But when you need moral advice, seek out to trusted friend. After talking with your friend, you will be in a better position to take responsibility for your decision. There are no moral experts! *Let your informed conscience be your guide and do the right thing.*
- Beware of the pitfalls of letting science solve your moral problems.

Box

My students constantly ask me, "what is right thing to do in this (fill in your favourite moral dilemma) situation? Well, I got news for them. Philosophers like men who teach ethics do not have privileged access to the moral truth. Philosophy is not like science and moral knowledge is not like scientific knowledge. We philosophers are in the same boat as everyone else, except that we are a little more attuned to the complexities of moral questions and the difficulties involved in knowing how to answer them. For that reason, we are less likely to think that we know all the answers (as Socrates famously said, philosophical wisdom consists of knowing that you are ignorant).

6. RESPECT YOUR VALUES

- *Being ethical* is being true to your deepest beliefs, which means being true to yourself.
- *Ethical conflict* is the spice of life—do not avoid it. Take responsibility for your ethical life by examining your values.
- Be careful to *distinguish values from preferences.* For example, your parent tell you as a matter of etiquette, like holding the door open for somebody else—as if they were matter of moral principle; it is a matter of being considerate towards others. However, I tell them that this ritual is simply a matter of preference for me.
- *Being morally responsible* means you must think deeply about the meaning of your values and the norms you hold dear. Take control of your values, that otherwise would stay hidden. So dig them up and examine them.
- Thus, *moral dilemma are the spice of life,* but you need ethics to help resolve them.

Reference

David Bruce, Ingram and Jennifera Parks, "The complete idiot's guide to understanding ethics", Alpha Penguin Group (USA) Inc.

CHAPTER

5

Improving Ethical Decision-making

In this chapter on "Improving Ethical Decision-Making", the following aspects are covered:

1. Steps in decision-making must involve ethical considerations.
2. Four ethical decision-making criteria or principles of ethics.
3. Integrating ethical criteria of utility, rights, justice and caring.
4. Types of ethically questable managerial role-related acts.
5. Factors influencing ethical decision-making behaviour.
6. Factors that guide managers to make ethical decisions.
7. General recipes for guiding ethical decision-making.

STEPS IN DECISION-MAKING MUST INVOLVE ETHICAL CONSIDERATIONS

Every management school teaches its students, how they should take decisions such as:

(i) Identify the problem,
(ii) Generate alternative solutions,
(iii) Evaluate alternatives,
(iv) Selection of solution, and
(v) Implement the chosen solution.

However, the alternatives would be constrained by ethical considerations. As ethical considerations should be *important criteria* in organisation decision-making, there are three different ways to frame decisions and look at the factors that shape an individual's ethical decision-making behaviour.

2. FOUR ETHICAL DECISION-MAKING CRITERIA OR PRINCIPLES OF ETHICS

An individual may use different criteria in making ethical choices, but no single criteria is adequate to judge:

(i) Utilitarian Criterion

Decisions are made solely on the basis of their outcomes or consequences. The goal of utilitarian is to provide greatest good for the greatest number. This view tends to dominate business decision-making. For instance, by maximising profit, a business executive can argue he is securing the greatest good for greatest number—as he hands out termination notices to 10% of his employees. This promotes efficiency and productivity.

Raising prices, selling products with questionable effect on consumer health, closing down plants, laying-off large number of employees and similar decisions can be justified in utilitarian terms.

Decision-makers, tend to feel safe when they use utilitarianism. A lot of questionable actions can be justified as in best interests of "the organisation." But many argue that this perspective needs to change. Increased concern in society about individual rights and social justice suggests the need for managers to develop ethical standards based on non-utilitarian criteria.

(ii) Rights Criteria

Another ethical criteria is to focus on rights. This calls on individuals to make decisions consistent with fundamental liberties and privileges as laid in the constitution. It means decisions to respect and protect the basic rights of individuals, e.g. right to speech and due process.

For instance, use of this criteria would protect Whistle-Blowers when they report unethical or illegal practices by their organisation to press or government agencies on grounds of right to speech.

(iii) Focus on Justice Criteria

This requires individuals to impose and enforce rules fairly and impartially so there is equitable distribution of benefits and costs. It justifies paying the same wages for a given job and using seniority as the main determination in making retrenchment decision.

It looks at issues from the perspective of the other persons or affected parties. The questions to be asked are:

(i) Have you defined the problem accurately?
(ii) Would you define in the same way if you stood on the other side?
(iii) To whom and what is your loyalty as a person and as a member of the organisation.
(iv) Whom will the decision injure?
(v) Can you discuss with affected party?
(vi) Will the decision stand the test of time?

(iv) Ethics of Care

We mention fourth criteria advocated by Manuel G. Velasquez, i.e. Ethics of Care. This is based on the claim that individual cannot exist in isolation from *caring relationships with others*. I need others to feed and care for me when I am born, I need others to educate me and care for me as I grow. I need others as friends and lovers to care for me as I mature. Always I must live in a community on whose language, tradition, culture and other benefits I depend and that come to define me. *Relationships* are necessary for self to exist and should be maintained and nurtured.

Ethics of care means that we have an obligation to exercise special care toward those *particular persons* with whom we have *valuable close relationships,* particularly *relations of dependency*—A key concept in an "Ethic of Care." (advocated by feminist ethicists recently)—compassion, concern, love, friendship, and kindness are all sentiments or virtues that normally manifest this dimension of morality. The ethics of care emphasizes two moral demands:

(a) We exist in a web of relationships and should *preserve and nurture* those concrete relationships *with specific persons,* and
(b) We should *exercise special care* for those whom we are *concretely related* by *attending to their needs,* values, well-being by *responding* positively who are dependent on our care.

However, demands of caring are sometimes in conflict with demands of justice. For example, suppose one day a supervisor catches her friend stealing from company. Should she confront her friend as company policy requires from her. The demands of ethics of care would require that manager favour her friend. How conflicts of this sort be resolved.

Manager has certain role as duties of position. She has promised to protect the resources of the company and abide by company policy and uphold. We have to pay attention to impartial justice. If we want to favour friend then we relinquish, the institutional role—resign the job.

Then What is Alternative?

Increased concern in society about individual rights and social justice suggests the need for managers to develop ethical standards based on non-utilitarian criteria. This presents a challenge to managers to use criteria such as individual rights and social justice involves more ambiguities than using utilitarian criteria—such as effects on profits and efficiency. This helps to explain why managers are criticised for their actions.

But that may no longer be a single criteria by which good decisions should be judged.

3. INTEGRATING ETHICAL CRITERIA OF UTILITY, RIGHTS, JUSTICE AND CARING

Our morality contains four kinds of basic moral considerations—utilitarian standards, basic rights of individuals, standards of justice, standards of caring. But no one principle captures all the factors that must be taken into account in making moral judgements.

One simple strategy for ensuring that all four kinds are incorporated into one moral reasoning is as in Figure 1.

FIGURE I

Integrating Ethical Criteria

Moral Standards:	→	Factual Information:	→	Moral Judgement:
1. Maximise social utility 2. Respect moral rights 3. Distribute benefits and burdens justly 4. Exercise caring		Concerning the policy or deduction under consideration		On the rightness or wrongness of policy or decision

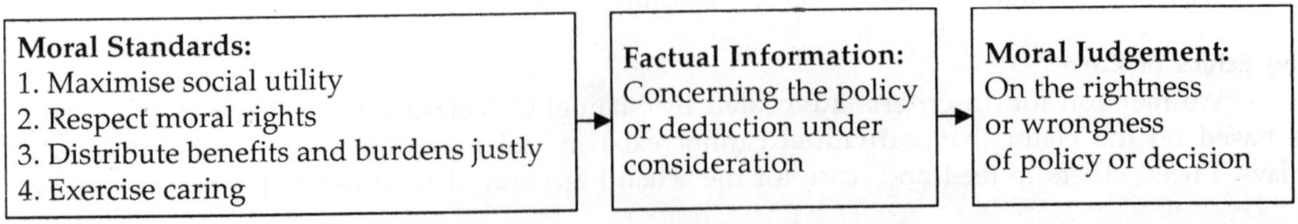

One might, ask a series of questions about an action that one is considering:

(a) Does the action, as far as possible, *maximise* social benefits and *minimise* social injuries?
(b) Is the action consistent with moral *rights* of those whom it will affect?
(c) Will the action lead to a *just* distribution of benefits and burdens?
(d) Does action exhibit *appropriate care* of those who are closely related or dependent on oneself?

In fact, we have no comprehensive moral theory capable of determining precisely when utilitarian considerations become sufficiently large to outweigh narrow infringements on a conflicting right, a standard of justice, or demands of caring. There is no universal rule.

Hence, these are rough criteria that can guide our thinking. However, these criteria remain rough and intuitive. This ethics can guide on moral reasoning.

4. TYPES OF ETHICALLY QUESTIONABLE MANAGERIAL ROLE-RELATED ACTS

These are given as under:

Type	*Direct effect*	*Examples*
1. Non-managerial role	The firm	• Expense account cheating • Embezzlement • Stealing supplies
2. Managerial role failure	-do-	• Superficial performance appraisal • Not confronting expense account cheating • Palming of poor performer to other department • Omission or commission of accounts
3. Managerial role distortion	For the firm advantage	• Bribery • Price fixing • Manipulation of suppliers
4. Managerial role—over-exertion	-do-	• Unauthorised high-risk investments • Continuing harmful environmental practices • Failure to cooperate with regulatory agencies.

Managers can unwittingly engage in wide range of types of role-related acts that are regarded as ethically questionable and need improvement in decision-making. 1st and 4th type acts are usually spotlighted and addressed. 2nd and 3rd type receive little attention as a form of proactive management control. Most of acts fall in these types. Senior management ignores/neglects/condones.

5. FACTORS INFLUENCING ETHICAL DECISION-MAKING BEHAVIOUR

What accounts for unethical behaviour in organisations? Is it immoral individuals or a work environment that promote unethical activity? The answer is both. Ethical or unethical actions are largely a function of both the *individual's characteristics* and *the environment* in which he works.

Following model explains ethical or unethical behaviour, i.e. factors affecting decision-making behaviour:

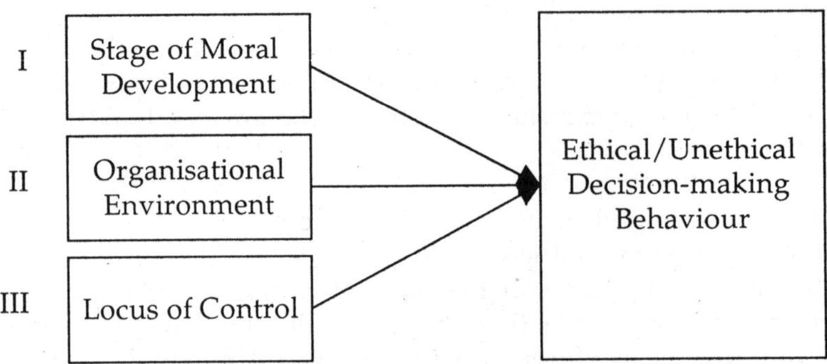

(i) Stage of Moral Development

It is an assessment of a person's capacity to judge what is morally right. The highest one's moral development, the less dependent he is on outside influences and hence more he will be ethically high. For instance, adults are at middle level of moral development—they are strongly influenced by peers and will follow an organisation's rules and procedures. Those individuals who have progressed to higher stages of moral development place increased value on the rights of others. Regardless of majority's opinion, they are likely to challenge organisation practices they believe are personally wrong.

(ii) Locus Control

It is a personality characteristic that taps the extent to which people believe they are responsible for the events in their lives.

People with external locus control (believe what happens to them in life is due to luck or chance) are less likely to take responsibility for their behaviour and are more likely to rely on external influences.

People with internal control are more likely to rely on their own internal standards of right or wrong to guide their behaviour.

(iii) Organisation Environment

It refers to an employee's perception of organisation expectations. Does the organisation encourage and support ethical behaviour by rewarding it or discourage unethical behaviour by punishing it?

Examples: Written codes of ethics, high moral behaviour by senior management, performance appraisal that evaluate means as well as ends, visible recognition and promotions for individuals who display high moral behaviour and visible punishment for those who act unethically are some examples of organisation environment that is likely to foster high ethical decision-making.

In summary, people who lack a *strong moral sense are much less likely* to make unethical decision if they are constrained by an organisational environment that frowns on such behaviour. Conversely, very *righteous individuals* can be corrupted by an organisational environment that permits or encourages unethical practices.

Thus, *managers at senior level can influence* the employee's work environment. Managers should overtly convey high ethical standards to employees through their actions. By what managers 'say', 'do', 'reward', 'punish' and 'overlook', they set the ethical tone for their employees. Managers can weed out ethically undesirable applicant at the time of recruitment in the selection process by learning about an individual's level of moral development and locus of control. Managers can identify individuals whose ethical standards might be in conflict with those of organisation or who are vulnerable to negative external influences.

6. FACTORS THAT GUIDE MANAGERS TO MAKE ETHICAL DECISIONS

Some factors are summarised below:

1. A man's *personal code of ethics*—i.e. what one considers moral. It is felt older a businessman becomes, the more ethical is his attitude.
2. The company's *formal policies* are values and culture.
3. The *ethical climate* in the industry.
4. Government regulations. It is morality that transcends conformity to law. Deep belief to *abide the laws.*
5. Behaviour of a *man's associates and superiors in the company*. People look their actions/ attitudes, and emulate them how honestly they prepare travelling bills, medical bills, sanction overtime to staff, etc.
6. *Professional managers* are more ethical. Ethical standards are deep-seated in them and they refuse to compromise.
7. As corporations become larger, their standards of *ethical conduct tend to rise* because of greater public exposure/image.

Box

General Recipes for Guideing Ethical Decision-making

We mention seven major strategies or approaches to solving ethical problems that arise in every-day life. These approaches include: (i) strategies that appeal to virtues and vices, (ii) divine commands, (iii) mutual benefits, (iv) absolute duties, (v) consequences for all, (vi) caring for and about others, and (vii) various combinations of the above.

(i) Being virtuous is a large part of living ethically

Thus, it is important that children model the virtuous behaviour of their elders. These virtues are generosity, courage, kindness, thoughtfulness, politeness, benevolence (doing good for others), honesty, loyalty. A character trait is a deeply ingrained feature of a person's personality. Some excellent traits of character are: honesty, generosity, integrity, kindness and courage.

Living virtuously is necessary for attaining true fulfilment in life. Virtues are the most important goods of all. A life without virtue is a life devoid of character and constantcy of purpose.

Integrity is a virtuous character trait that is closely connected to reliability, trust-worthiness, honesty and having principles. A person who has moral integrity can be counted on to behave in a way that is constant and harmonious. Persons who lack integrity are fickle because their wants and habits are constantly at war with one another.

(ii) Divine Commands

The moral law of nature is higher than human-made law. Natural law designates a law that is higher than human-made law just because it is based on nature itself, which is universal to all human society. For instance, since around the time of Locke, it has been used to justify the idea that some rights (so-called natural rights) are bestowed on each and everyone of us solely in virtue of our common humanity. Such natural rights designate basic demands for liberty and life's necessities. They impose absolute limits on what any governments can do to its citizens, and even entitle citizens to resist government when it oversteps its proper moral bounds.

(iii) Mutual Benefits or Modern Social Contract Theory

Remember that we are all dependent on one another for our well-being. So the least we can expect from any one (low ball ethics). The social contract theory fits our need for low-ball baseline ethics perfectly. We do come to lot of our moral obligations through promise-making and other voluntary agreements. Thomas Hobbes was the first philosopher to have really pushed this idea. The social contract theory shows why it is in everyone's best interest to thrust one another for purposes of mutually advantageous cooperation. We have to understand that the most important idea about social contract is fairness, not voluntary consent.

(iv) Absolute Duties

A moral theory that is deontological is one that focuses on your duties and to all. Kant's moral theory is this type because it takes duties to other people to be the core of ethics. You must do your duty whether you want to or not. It means that, no matter how you feel about it or what you want to do, you must do an act whether it is studying for school. *Duties are obligations that must be fulfilled.* Some basic duties are: always tell the truth, always keep your promises, never commit suicide. Thus, if you think everyone should follow the rules, then so should you.

(v) Consequences for All (Utilitarianism)

Think about the consequences of your actions. Do not be shortsighted when weighing out consequence: sometime you are better off doing something in the long-run that looks less appealing in the short-run. Consequentialism is an ethical theory that determines good or bad, right or wrong, based on outcomes. If you are struck up in ethical dilemma, then consequentialists tell you to choose the act that does the greatest good or the least amount of harm—for the greatest number or people.

Utilitarianism is a moral theory that treats pleasure or happiness as the only absolute moral good. According to utilitarian thinkers, the morality of your actions depends on their results. Acts that bring about an overall increase in happiness or pleasure are morally good.

- Remember: Not all pleasures are equal. Some are of higher quality than others. The quality of a pleasure is proportional to the degree to which it contributes to a person's overall intellectual, moral, and aesthetic development.
- There are no duties that cannot be compromised for the sake of furthering the greatest happiness for the greatest number.

(vi) Caring for and about others

When ethical dilemmas come up, think about the implications of your choices for people you love and care about. Further strive for equality and justice in your relationships, especially if they are care-giving relationships.

- Do not apply social contract theory to all areas of life; it just does not work for personal relationship of care.
- Men also take responsibility for care work, too.
- Care-giving has been mostly "women's work" throughout history; and even now it mostly falls on women to do care and maintain relationships. Feminist call it an "ethics of care".
- Duties of justice and happiness—promoting actions cannot replace our personal obligations as care-givers for dependent persons.

(vii) Various combinations of the above

- Remember, ethics is not a science and no ethical theory is perfect.
- Think about the proper 'fit' between ethical theories and your different areas of life/situations. Do not doggedly grade on to one theory and run with it. *Be aware of flaws with all ethical approaches.*
- Avoid moral absolutism and moral relativism. Both approaches can be traps.
- Despite their apparent incompatibilities, moral recipes complement one another and can be combined in useful ways.

Reference

Manuel G. Vecasquez, Business Ethics, Prentice Hall of India, New Delhi, 2003. Four Basic Principles in Business Ethics.

CHAPTER

6

Applied Ethics: Moral Problems

In this chapter on "Applied Ethics: Moral Problems", the following aspects are covered:

1. Environmental ethics.
2. Biomedical ethics.
3. Business ethics.
4. Ethics and animals.
5. The ethics of social justice.

General moral recipes can be applied to moral problems that occur. Some problems are such as: medicine and health care, business, the treatment of animals and environment.

1. ENVIRONMENTAL ETHICS

Our duties with respect to our environment *cannot all be decided on the basis* of cost-benefit analysis. Cost-benefit analysis involves placing rupee figures on the costs and benefits of doing variety of acts. The act that is determined morally correct, on this view, is the one that incurs the least amount of cost and that results in the greatest benefits.

Instead of writing-off militant environmental activities as mere *"extremists" think about their reasons for their actions,* such as repression, injustice or religious fanatism, etc.

2. BIOMEDICAL ETHICS

Decisions about life and death often boil down to the peculiarities of each individual case. Make sure you think about bio-ethical issues in a philosophical way; do not just respond from your gut.

- Just because we have the medical technology to do certain things does not mean we ought to do them.
- When discussing extremely controversial topics like abortion, you should not engage in the unhelpful and unphilosophical practice of attacking your opponents. To let yourself get side-tracked by emotional "gut" responses is to lose sight of the important moral questions and to close off debate. Be sure to see the connections between bioethical issues. Ethical issues in stem cell research and cloning are related to abortion.

3. BUSINESS ETHICS

- Putting profits before ethics is not profitable and it is wrong.
- Coveat emptor means "let the buyer beware". It basically requires that we be smart consumers. It puts responsibility on each of us as consumers to research our purchases with the consequences. *Thus, always research products you buy them.*
- Do not assume that advertisement must always tell the truth. Puffery (making exaggerated claims about their product) is common practice in advertising. There is nothing illegal about it. As long as the advertiser is not making false claims about the product, puffery is not against the law.
- If you have to decide whether to blow the whistle on someone in the workplace, make sure you do for ethical reasons, not as "payback". You can think about it from different perspectives such as consequentialist, feminist, social contract approach to determine what is morally right.
- Hold business to reasonable ethical standards: if they engage in unfair business practices or exploit their workers, do not buy their stuff.

4. ETHICS AND ANIMALS

- Even if you do not think animals have rights, you should think about the way *we treat them* and how that impacts our treatment of other human beings. This means we have a moral obligation to not treat animals in ways (cruel) that will likely lead to abuse of human beings.
- Remember that animals are sentient, too. We must have really good reasons for inflicting pain upon them.
- When determining whether animal experimentation is morally justified, consider the human need that is being served.
- Avoid challenging others on their vegetarianism. It is not a judgement of your moral choices, but an expression of their own values and beliefs about animals.

5. THE ETHICS OF SOCIAL JUSTICE

The ethics of social justice shows why personal morality requires political engagement in making social, economic, and *political institutions more fair* than they are now. We address problems of social justice and welfare, economic and political justice, and race and gender justice.

(i) Social and Economic Justice

Yes, society does owe us something.

- Governments of the world should ensure that everyone has their basic subsistence needs met.
- Wealthy countries ought to forgive the third world debt.

(ii) Political Justice

- Democracy is more than a political system; it is way of life.
- Democracy only flourishes among people who respect one another as free and equal, and who are in fact free and equal.
- Democratic tyranny can be avoided only if all vulnerable groups are represented.
- Justice may well require implementing democracy in the workplace and in global structures of governance.

(iii) Gender Justice

Patriarchy (system within which men dominate women or in the sexual domination of women by men) is the root of many practices that harm and degrade women. When considering issues like prostitution, pronography, and equal pay for equal work, remember that these problems are connected by this system of patriarchy.

- Be committed to women's equal treatment in the workplace. Making inappropriate comments and hanging up posters of 'pin-up-girls' make the work environment hostile for women. It creates hostile or offensive work environment.

(iv) Multi-racism and Multi-culturalism

Anti-racism and multi-culturalism promote justice through racial integration and respect for cultural differences. Bringing about racial justice will require far-ranging solutions to poverty and educational inequality. Affirmative action (leveling the play field) is fair in theory, but perhaps less fair in practice.

It is really important to finish this chapter on a positive note. The ethical life is about good things. The Greeks thought that ethical life was the best life lived, and the utilitarians think ethics is about bringing as much happiness into the world as possible.

It is important to remember this point: even though people may not have completely eliminated the moral evils that occur in the world, people have certainly been moving in the right direction. Over the course of centuries, people have made progress with issues like slavery, women's rights, animal rights, environment protection, democracy, and social welfare.

It is hoped, you will be on your way to leading a thoughtful, reflective, moral life. This is not to say we were not always a good, ethical person. We can be fully responsible or responsive by thinking deeper reasons underlying our actions and institutions.

One can express ethical life, for example, by joining a service-oriented club that helps people in your community, one can get involved in a charity, give a hand at animal shelters, or participate in grass roots political organisations that lobby on behalf of the environment, etc.

PART II

MANAGING ETHICAL ORGANISATION

CHAPTER

7

Elements of Building Ethical Organisation

In this chapter on "Elements of Building Ethical Organisation", the following aspects are covered:

1. Commitment of top management.
2. Assignment of responsibility for implementation.
3. Clarifying the company's ethical standards.
4. Building systems that support ethical behaviour.
5. Constructive steps to be taken by the management.
6. Ethics training.
7. Encourage fundamental values among employees.

Various measures for building commitment to ethics in the organisation are as under:

1. COMMITMENT OF TOP MANAGEMENT

- Top management to ensure adequate resources are invested in programmes for building commitment to ethics.
- Ethical behaviour is truly supported by the top management.
- Top management to provide leadership through example.
- Top management to ensure ethics is folded into every aspect of corporate life—including strategic planning process. One CEO personally saw to programmes and its integration in company, planning and management procedures, e.g. (i) strategic management, (ii) HRM, (iii) participative management, (iv) quality management, and (v) ethical decision-making.

- The chairman of the company must fully support ethics programme and also announce it and ensure its implementation.
- An ethics committee at board of director's level, if established, will oversee development and operation of ethics programme.

2. ASSIGNMENT OF RESPONSIBILITY FOR IMPLEMENTATION OF ETHICS PROGRAMME

Some top level manager is to be responsible for development, coordination and implementation of programme. He is to be assisted by full time manager to implement and is a business ethics specialist. He can function as ombuds person. He can also have ethics management committee of senior officers for administering policies and procedures. The most important aspect is the process of reflection and dialogue while preparing codes, policies and procedures, etc. The Ethics Management Committee becomes decisions in groups, which should be cross functional teams. These code of ethics can avoid the occurrence of ethical dilemmas.

3. CLARIFYING THE COMPANY'S ETHICAL STANDARDS

In written statement or ethical code or credos, "code of ethics", this includes:

(i) Company's mission, purpose or beliefs.
(ii) Main stockholders, employees, suppliers, consumers, community, etc. are stakeholders to whom company is obliged. Specific obligations to above groups or behaviours required or permitted are to be laid.
(iii) Penalties for violation of obligations of the management.
(iv) An organisational code of ethics is to be firmly supported by top management and equitably enforced through the reward and punishment system. Selective or uneven enforcement is the quickest way to kill the effectiveness of an ethical code according to Robert Kreitner.

4. BUILDING SYSTEMS THAT SUPPORT ETHICAL BEHAVIOUR

(a) Ensuring that systems are established, e.g. audit is done to monitor and enforce the ethical behaviour.
    - *New employees are being informed of ethical standards.*
    - Annual performance appraisal includes observance of standards and deviations noted in files. Corrective actions that managers have taken to remedy deviations.
    - GTE Corporation of USA states in ethical guidelines that "personal integrity and moral fibre are as important to advancement as technical competence."

(b) *Communicating the company's values,* to all employees plays a vital role.
    - Employees should alert the company about any unethical behaviour that is—"Internal whistle-blowing" made higher management aware of violations in time.

5. CONSTRUCTIVE STEPS TO BE TAKEN BY THE MANAGEMENT

The challenge for today's management is to create an organisational climate in which the need to blow the whistle is reduced. Constructive steps include the following:

- Encourage the free expression of controversial and dissenting viewpoints.
- Streamline the organisation's grievance procedure so that problems receive a prompt and fair hearing.
- Find out what employees think about the organisation's social responsibility policies and make appropriate changes.
- Let employees know that management respects and is sensitive to their individual consciences.
- Recognise that the harsh treatment of a whistle-blower will probably lead to adverse public opinion.
- Company to provide advisory service in case doubts/clarification.

6. ETHICS TRAINING

To arrange workshops for employees regularly and to make aware of company commitment to ethics. Such 1/2 day workshops are lead by the line managers. Thus concerted and systematic attention to ethics will reduce and eliminate such risks. Carefully designed and administered ethics training programmes can make a positive contribution. According to Robert Kreitner key features of effective ethics training programmes include the following:

- Top management support.
- Open discussion in resolving of realistic cases/dilemmas.
- A clear focus on ethical themes in all training.
- A mechanism for anonymously reporting ethical violations.
- An organisation climate that rewards ethical conduct.
- Supplying all staff a copy of code of ethics/code of conduct. Also explain all employees how these work and what is their role in it.

7. ENCOURAGE FUNDAMENTAL VALUES AMONG EMPLOYEES

In the final analysis, individual behaviour makes organisations ethical or unethical. The organisational forces can help bring out the best in people by clearly identifying and rewarding ethical conduct. Personal values play a pivotal role in decision-making and ethics. Such issues are basic, i.e. trust, honesty, respect, dignity, commitment, integrity and accountability.

Box I

I. Roles and Responsibilities in Managing Ethics at Workplace

Certain roles can prove useful in managing ethics in the workplace. Following responsibilities that should be included somewhere in the organisation are:

(a) The organisation's chief executive must fully support the programme

The chief executive should announce the programme, and champion its development and implementation. Most important, the chief executive should consistently aspire to lead in an ethical manner. If a mistake is made, admit it.

(b) Consider establishing an ethics committee at the board level

The committee would be charged to oversee development and operation of the ethics management programme.

(c) Consider establishing an ethics management committee

It would be charged with implementing and administrating an ethics management programme including administrating and training about policies and procedures, and resolving ethical dilemmas. The committee should be comprised of senior officers.

(d) Consider assigning/developing an ethics officer

This role is becoming more common, particularly in larger and more progressive organizations. The ethics officer is usually trained about matters of ethics in the workplace, particularly about resolving ethical dilemma.

(e) Consider establishing an ombudsperson

The ombudsperson is responsible to help coordinate development of the policies and procedures to institutionalize moral values in the workplace. This position usually is directly responsible for resolving ethical dilemmas by interpreting policies and procedures.

2. Managing Ethics

Following guidelines can ensure the ethics management:

(i) The best way to handle ethical dilemmas is to avoid their occurrence in the first place

That's why practices such as developing codes of ethics and codes of conduct are so important. Their development sensitizes employees to ethical considerations and minimizes the chances of unethical behaviour occurring in the first place.

(ii) Make ethics decisions in groups, and make decisions public, as appropriate

This usually produces better quality decisions by including diverse interests and perspectives, and increases the credibility of the decision process and outcome by reducing suspicion of unfair bias.

(iii) Integrate ethics management with other strategic management practices

When developing the values statement during strategic planning, include ethical values preferred in the workplace.

(iv) Use cross-functional teams when developing and implementing the ethics management programme

It's vital that the organization's employees feel a sense of participation and ownership in the programme if they are to adhere to its ethical values. Therefore, include employees in developing and operating the programme.

(v) Trying to operate ethically and making a few mistakes is better than not trying at all

It's the trying that counts and brings peace of mind—not achieving a heroic status in society.

CHAPTER

8

Manager's Role in Influencing Ethical Climate

In this chapter on "Manager's Role in Influencing Ethical Climate", the following aspects are covered:

1. Communicating ethical values.
2. Promoting ethical climate *versus* opposing unethical practices.
3. Great people leave something behind.
4. Managerial competencies. (Box I)
5. Evaluating ethical behaviour in performance review. (Box II)
6. Convince me that I am wrong. (Box III)

1. COMMUNICATING ETHICAL VALUES

As organisation's attempt to grapple with ethics, they increasingly seek varied routes for communicating their values. For instance, they may *develop corporate mission statements* to tell employees what the organisation is about and where it is going. These statements may serve to separate an organisation from its competitors and provide it with a sense of identity, legitimacy and direction.

The mission statement may be accompanied by a *code of ethics* (a general code, as well as one that is technology-focussed), which speaks to activities that cannot be closely supervised by management, like honesty in dealing with clients or mutual respect among employees.

Now adopted by more than 200 of the **Fortune 500** companies, ethical codes contribute to long-term organisational success only to the extent that they are upheld by both employers and employees; that is, they depend upon voluntary cooperation.

Finally, and most important, management behaviours remain the real key to developing organisational ethics.

Managers can influence their organisation's ethical climate in several ways:

(i) They may, for instance, emphasize and discuss ethics continually. A code of ethics becomes real only when a manager talks about it by *encouraging subordinates* to *raise ethics-related issues*, doubts or concerns; by referring to it when answering questions or making decisions; and by keeping others' attention focussed on it.

(ii) Managers must also develop and *articulate realistic goals*.

(iii) Employees who are confronted with goals they *cannot achieve are tempted* to cut corners, sacrificing ethics for achievement.

(iv) By *identifying areas that are vulnerable to unethical* practices, managers may also avoid ethical problems by discussing with employees the sorts of temptations that might arise.

(v) Finally, by encouraging *reporting of unethical activities*, managers let all employees know that each of them has an important role in enforcing ethical standards; at the same time, they indicate their serious intent to ensure ethical behaviour (Dolcheck, 1989).

(vi) Ultimately, values cannot be taught; they must be lived. *People emulate what they see*, not what they are told. If they see that unethical behaviours are practiced or tolerated, they will pay little attention to written codes of ethics or mission statements. Richard Zimmerman, Chairman and CEO of Hershey Foods Corporation, refers to his company's value system as an "anchor" for the organisation and asserts, "Each *manager must have a grip on those clearly defined values* and be able to demonstrate them through their own behaviour to employee groups" (Blank, 1986, p. 33).

(vii) Andrews (1989) argued that *ethical decision-making* is the key to effective management, maintaining that ethical decisions require three qualities of those making them:

   (a) Competence to recognise ethical issues and to think through the consequences of alternative resolutions.

   (b) *Self-confidence* to seek out different points of view and then to decide what is right at a given time and place in a particular set of relationships and circumstances.

   (c) *Tough-mindedness* or the willingness to make decisions when all that needs to be known cannot be known and when the questions that press for answers have no established and incontrovertible solutions.

(viii) *Role of Top Management is Critical*: Maya Reddi in her article on "Ethical Organisation: Role of Top Management" states that the role of top management becomes critical to the setting of standards of business behaviour. Senior management is often perceived to have double standards, at least that's the general perception, which is: one rule for themselves and another for the rest of the corporation. And, invariably when one goes around talking to people, they always say, "Yah, all that is fine, it is all accepted but what is the real story among the top management? Do you really pay your taxes; do you really produce vouchers for payments you claim; do you really follow the rules when travelling or do you get additional perks?" These are the kinds of questions one has to answer which really imply people's belief that there is one rule for the top management and another rule for the rest of the employees.

(ix) *Integration of Ethics in Personal Life and Business Life*: Business ethics has to be preached, practised and shouted from the roof tops, in both, one's personal and one's official life. Before setting business standards, *ethics and morality have to be internalized*, so that

> they become a part of the blood stream. This is rather a strong statement; but there really is this sort of *integration between personal life and business life,* so that it is not done one thing to slip a transistor through customs just as it is not right to evade customs duty when one has a large system being imported. What one does when one goes up to the customs officer as an individual and later when one is talking inside the organisation, these are both one and the same thing; they are not two different stories.

When this happens, values will permeate the organisation and get translated into business standards and practices. *Top management must stand out like a light and be able to pass the test of intense scrutiny.* And, the penalty for not conforming to accepted ethical behaviour must be severe, whoever may be involved.

2. PROMOTING ETHICAL CLIMATE *VERSUS* OPPOSING UNETHICAL PRACTICES

Some writers make a distinction between doing things to encourage and promote ethical practices and doing things to oppose unethical activities or decisions (e.g., Nielsen, 1989). Examples of each approach are shown in Figure 1. The two approaches are not mutually exclusive, and both can be used at the same time.

Leaders can do many things to promote ethical practices in organizations. The leader's own actions provide an example of ethical behaviour to be imitated by people.

FIGURE I

Two Aspects of Ethical Leadership Behaviour

Promoting an Ethical Climate

- Set *an example* of ethical behaviour in your own actions.
- Facilitate the development and dissemination of a *code of ethical* conduct.
- *Initiate discussions* with followers or colleagues about ethics and integrity.
- Recognize and *reward ethical behaviour* by others.
- Take personal risks to *advocate moral solutions* to problems.
- *Help others* find fair and ethical solutions to conflicts.
- Initiate support services (e.g., ethics hotline, online advisory group).

Opposing Unethical Practices

- *Refuse to share* in the benefits provided by unethical activities.
- *Refuse to accept* assignments that involve unethical activities.
- Try to *discourage unethical* actions by others.
- *Speak out publicly* against unethical or unfair policies in the organization.
- Oppose *unethical decisions* and seek to get them reversed.
- *Inform proper authorities* about dangerous products or harmful practices.
- *Provide assistance* to others who oppose unethical decisions or practices.

Source: Gary Yukl, *Leadership in Organisations*, Pearson Education, Singapore, p. 248.

3. GREAT PEOPLE LEAVE SOMETHING BEHIND

Winners leave a legacy

Socrates taught Plato,
Plato taught Aristotle,
Aristotle taught Alexander the Great.
Knowledge, had it not been passed along, would have died.

Our greatest responsibility is to pass on a legacy of ethical values that the coming generations can be proud of.

Box I

Leadership (Managerial) Competencies

Globalisation has altered all aspects of business and to compete successfully in this environment, a different set of competencies are needed.

The leadership as a source of competitiveness is shifting and knowledge is emerging as the leading source of competitive advantage.

Indian Leadership (Managers) Competencies
10 Top Most Important Competencies

In Old Economy	*Digital Economy*
1. Vision	1. Vision/integrity
2. *Integrity*	2. Customer-orientation
3. Initiative	3. Technology adoption and its management
4. Negotiation	4. Speed in decision-making
5. Problem-solving	5. Innovation and creativity
6. Influencing others	6. External awareness
7. Customer-orientation	7. Team-building and team work
8. Team-building and team working	8. Ability and willingness to learn
9. Inter-personal skills	9. Ability to take risks
10. Communication skills	10. Flexibility

Competencies where importance has changed most:

- Technology adoption and management.
- External awareness.
- Speed of decision-making.
- Teaching.
- Ability and willingness to learn.
- Innovation and creative thinking.
- Customer-orientation.
- Human resource management.
- Flexibility.
- Ability to take risks.

Source: A survey of Indian leaders by Ajay Gaur, Department of Business Policy, National University, Singapore, as appear in IIMB, *Management Review*, June 2006, Bangalore.

Box II

Evaluating Ethical Behaviour

Some phrases for performance reviews

Outstanding

- Exceptionally scrupulous and *honest in all activities.*
- Does what is right regardless of consequences.
- Always demonstrates *integrity and honesty.*
- Is exceptionally conscientious in potential conflict of interest situations.
- Has received high praise for swift and generous remedies for product defects.
- Has retained or gained new customers due to honesty.

Exceed Expectations

- Never lies or bends the truth.
- Argues vigorously for fair dealing.
- Created a clear value statement for staff about ethics.
- Knows and follows applicable laws.
- Customer have been happily surprised by honesty.

Meets Expectations

- Deal with customers fairly.
- Will not exploit loopholes in-laws for benefit.
- Staff understand and follow ethical guidelines.
- Is noted for honesty and fairness.

Needs Improvement

- Sometimes sees ethics as an inconvenience.
- Has been known to stretch the law for gain.
- Has behaved unethically in dealing with clients.
- Complaints have been lodged about his tactics.

Unacceptable

- Does not behave ethically.
- Has lied to others in department.
- Violates ethical guidelines.
- Legal action has been initiated against him.
- Actions have resulted in customer refusing to do business with us.

Box III

Convince Me that I am Wrong

- You have to think through moral problems with others in a way that is both logical and impartial. Make sure you have reasons supporting your beliefs and actions. *Give your reasons if you believe that way.*
- Ancient philosophers thought that having moral role models was crucial to leading and learning to lead on ethical good life. *Have moral role models, but still think for yourself.*
- Do not be manipulated by others into their beliefs.
- Be impartial, unless you have a good reason for treating people different.
- Take a skeptical attitude to ethical claims.

CHAPTER

9

Codes of Ethics

In this chapter on "Codes of Ethics", the following aspects are mentioned:

1. Developing codes in ethics.
2. Conditions for making codes effective.
3. Difficulties in implementing codes of ethics.
4. Code of conduct or ethics for professional groups.

1. DEVELOPING CODES IN ETHICS

Ethical codes are statements of the norms and beliefs of an organisation. These norms and beliefs are generally proposed, discussed, and defined by senior executives in the firm and then published and distributed to all the members. A code of ethics specifies the ethical rules of operation.

Most important thing is *developing and continuing dialogue* around codes and values. Occasionally, employees react to codes with suspicion, believing code and values are window dressing. But Carter McNamara points out "that when managing a complex issue, especially in a crisis, having code is critical." He further highlights that "continued dialogue and reflection around ethical values produces ethical sensitivity and consensus."

Also *update the code periodically*—all ethical values are attractive to include in a code; however, we should include those that provoke behaviours needed in the organisation.

2. CONDITIONS FOR MAKING CODES EFFECTIVE

In a recent Dutch study Kaptein and Klamer (1991) list six conditions for effective codes of ethics:

(i) *A valid motivation for its introduction*: It should insist on important benefit for adopting and complying with the code. An 'us too' attitude is not enough.

(ii) *Broad acceptance within the company*: Involve representatives from all departments in the process of elaborating the code. The code should be discussed, checked and redefined before it is finally laid down.

(iii) *Continuous feedback*: Difficulties occur during the implementation of the code, and also norms on how to act in specific situations change. This calls for feedback. Living up to a code is not simply a matter of blindly applying rules, it is part of a process.

(iv) *Verification and control*: Any inconsistencies between rules and practice should be disclosed. One method of achieving this is peer discussions. New guidelines should be drawn up if the rules prove inadequate in any way.

(v) *Integration into a broad company philosophy on corporate services and responsibilities*: The set of rules should be part of a wider ethical mission statement. This may involve staff training programmes, a company ethical committee or discussions with external stakeholders.

(vi) *Sanctions and control*: Compliance with codes needs enforcement— both positive and negative. In order to become effective, some system of sanctions must exist. Free-wheeling permissiveness would only lead to lip service. Many companies do now have severe sanctions against, for example, bribery.

3. DIFFICULTIES IN IMPLEMENTING CODES OF ETHICS

However, the basic difficulty with codes of ethics is that they do not establish priority between norms and beliefs. The priorities are true values of a firm, and they are not included:

(a) As an example, one division in a firm is faced with declining sales and profits; the question is whether to reduce employment and cut overhead costs (the classic downsizing decision), but code of ethics says in one section that we respect our employees and in another section that we expect "fair" profits. How do we decide? The code of ethics does not tell us.

(b) Another example, whether direct distribution from factory "to retailer would be economical" when our code of ethics says "we will work closely with distributors, for they too deserve a profit." But we can reduce our prices to our customers and gain a competitive advantage for ourselves, if we eliminate the wholesalers and ship directly. The code does not tell us to choose.

(c) Are ethical codes—effective at ensuring that the moral standards of senior executives are known and followed throughout the organisation. If yes, then some events can be just anomalies such as—for years, GE has been regarded in USA as one of the examplarly companies, a breed ground for managerial excellence, a good corporate citizen. But unfortunately GE was convicted 3 times of crimes, i.e. price fixing, bribery and fraud. GE pleaded guilty of charges of defrauding the government on missile-warhead contracts.

In such a case we have to examine causes of unethical actions in individual cases. In this connection an example of code of ethics of Johnson & Johnson, Inc. helped managers in time of crisis. Johnson & Johnson spent over $ 100 million removing Tylenol from shelves of every store after non-prescription drug was found to have been deliberately poisoned in Chicago area during 1982, causing death of 4 individuals. James Burke, Chairman of Johnson & Johnson, credits that code with guiding the actions of his company. "This document of code of ethics spells out our responsibilities to all our constituencies: consumers, employees, community, stock-holders. It served to guide all of us during the crisis, when hard decision had to be made. All our employees world-wide were able to watch the process of Tylenol, withdrawal and subsequent reintroduction in temper-resistant packaging." "There was a great sense of shared pride in the knowledge that the credo was being tested and it worked." "I think we can agree that the employees of J & J should be proud of the response of the firm which put consumer safety ahead of company profits."

4. CODE OF CONDUCT OR ETHICS FOR PROFESSIONAL GROUPS

Professional Associations lay down code of ethics for their members—behaviour required or expected of its members, Doctors, Personnel Managers, etc.

These codes give clue to what type of response is expected in given situation. It comprises of norms and standards of discipline, honesty and integrity and professional ethics to be followed and enforced by association.

As an illustration extracts from some codes of conduct of professional bodies are mentioned.

A. Codes of the Medical Council of India

The codes cover 33 principles:

(i) General principles.
(ii) Duties to patients.
(iii) Duties to profession.
(iv) Doctor to doctor relationship.

Example: They should educate public on correct and ethical use of drugs.

List of misconduct as well given, e.g. refusing to perform a sterilisation operation on religious grounds.

B. Ethics for Chartered Accountants in Chartered Accountant's Act

Some misconducts are:

(i) If he allows any person to practise as C.A. if he is not one.
(ii) If he advertises or solicits work.
(iii) If he accepts a position held by another C.A. without communicating with him.
(iv) If he discloses confidential information about his client.
(v) He certifies a statement without adequate scrutiny.

C. The Engineer's Code

The National Society of Professional Engineers has a code, which requires professionals to:

1. Dissociate themselves from organisations that are of a questionable character.
2. Further the cause of public good.
3. Avoid engineeringly unsafe ventures.
4. Maintain confidentiality.
5. Advise clarity, the consequences, if a technical opinion is overruled by a non-technical person.

D. Code for Marketing Managers

A code of ethics for marketing managers is issued by the American Marketing Association. It includes:

1. *Basic guidelines*: Not doing harm knowingly, accurate representation of their education and training, following the laws in letter and spirit.
2. *Honesty and fairness*: Serving customers, clients, employees, distributors and public, avoid conflict of interest, employ equitable fee schedules of payments or receipt.
3. *Follow the well-understood principles of rights and duties in the process of exchange*: Products should be safe, communications not deceptive in good faith, adequate processes for redressal of grievances.
4. *Product development*: Safety standards, any component substitution to be advised to the customer, extra cost and added features.
5. *Promotion*: Avoid false, misleading, high pressure and manipulative tactics.
6. *Distribution*: No coercion, ensuring free channels, etc.
7. *Pricing*: Neither predatory nor rigged.
8. *Market research*: Prohibit selling under the guise of market research, research integrity, confidentiality and privacy of respondents.
9. *Organisational*: Avoid adverse organisational behaviour.

E. Code of Ethics of Public Relations Practitioners

1. The core philosophy of the code is to uphold the Universal Declaration of Human Rights of the UNO.
2. It upholds the free flow of information.
3. It requires behaviour, in a manner, as to develop the confidence of those, with whom they come in contact, whether clients or employers.
4. The practitioners must avoid ambiguous language and maintain loyalty to the clients and employers.
5. They must protect the interests of the organisation they serve and the general public.
6. They must never compromise on the truth due to other requirements.
7. They must never manipulate to create sub-conscious motivations.
8. They must never impair human dignity and integrity.

F. Code of Ethics of the Association for Computer Machinery (ACM)

The ACM has five canons. An ACM member should:

1. Act with integrity at all times.
2. Strive to increase his own competence and the competence and prestige of the profession.
3. Accept responsibility for his work.
4. Act with professional responsibility.
5. Use his knowledge and skills for the advancement of human welfare.

G. Code of Advertisers issued by the Advertisement Council of India

1. Moral and religious sentiment should not be offended.
2. Advertisements should not directly and adversely compare products with those of the competitors.
3. Rhetoric like offering to refund money, if the product is not good should be avoided.

H. The ICSI Code of Conduct

In order to evoke the necessary interest and awareness among the members company secretaries and to create the necessary climate for laying down the right type of conduct which should govern the profession; the ICSI organised in February 1976 a National Convention primarily to evolve the necessary framework for a code of conduct. After the conclusion of that Convention, the Council of the Institute appointed a Code of Conduct Committee with the task of formulating a model code of conduct. The Council of the Institute accepted the recommendations of the Code of Conduct Committee which *inter alia* prescribed:

(a) rules applicable to all members; and
(b) rules applicable to members in service or practice.

In formulating the code of conduct, the Committee and the Council adopted a certain normative approach or value judgement. The codes evolved were rooted in the principles of Dharma stating positively what the profession stands for, what it expects from the members and what it cherishes as valued ideals of the society. The code also negatively laid down what may or may not constitute a breach of the code in any given situation and the penal consequences for any violation or misconduct.

The ICSI code of conduct acquired statutory status with the conversion of the Institute into a statutory body under the Company Secretaries Act, 1980, with effect from 1st January, 1981. The First and the Second Schedules to the Act enumerate in detail, various instances of professional misconduct on the part of the members of the Institute in practice as well as in service.

In view of the development of the profession during the last decade, the ICSI has brought out revised edition of the Guidance Note on Code of Conduct to focus the attention of the members in general and those in practice in particular, to the various provisions of the code of conduct to enable them to uphold the professional values.

I. Code of Ethics of Automotive Service Association (ASA)

Code of Ethics

The owners and managers of automotive service businesses that belong to the Automotive Service Association (ASA) agree to adhere to a Code of Ethics. ASA's Code of Ethics is the automotive service industry's standard for professional business practices—

- To perform high quality repair service at a fair and just price.
- To use only proven merchandise of high quality distributed by reputable firms.
- To employ the best skilled technicians obtainable.

- To furnish an itemized invoice for fairly priced parts and services that clearly identifies any used or remanufactured parts.
- Replaced parts may be inspected upon request.
- To have a sense of personal obligation to each customer.
- To promote goodwill between the motorist and members of the association.
- To recommend corrective and maintenance services, explaining to the customer which of these are required to correct existing problems and which are for preventive maintenance.
- To offer the customer a price estimate for work to be performed.
- To furnish or post copies of any warranties covering parts or services.
- To obtain prior authorization for all work done, in writing, or by other means satisfactory to the customer.
- To notify the customer if appointments or completion promises cannot be kept.
- To maintain customer service records for one year or more.
- To exercise reasonable care for the customer's property while in our possession.
- To maintain a system for fair settlement of customer's complaints.
- To cooperate with established consumer complaint mediation activities.
- To uphold the high standards of our profession and always seek to correct any and all abuses within the automotive industry.
- To uphold the integrity of all members of the Automotive Service Association.

CHAPTER

10

Codes of Conduct

In this chapter on "Codes of Conduct", the following aspects are covered:

1. Meaning of codes of conduct.
2. Guidelines for developing codes of conduct.
3. Illustration of ethical value of 'integrity'.
4. Conduct, discipline and appeal rule.

1. MEANING OF CODES OF CONDUCT

"*Codes of conduct* specify actions in the work place and *codes of ethics* are general guides to decisions about those actions", explains Graig Nordlund, of Hewlett Packard. He suggests that codes of conduct contain examples of appropriate behaviour to be meaningful. Codes of conduct are focussed at lower levels in companies.

2. GUIDELINES FOR DEVELOPING CODES OF CONDUCT

While developing a code of conduct Carter McNamara lays following guidelines:

"1. *Identify key behaviours* needed to adhere to the ethical values proclaimed in your code of ethics."

"2. *Include wording* that indicates all employees are expected to conform to behaviours specified in the code of conduct."

"3. *Obtain review* from key members of the organisation and not confined to legal or human resource department. Such reviews to ensure these policies are in accordance with laws and regulations."

Some topics covered in codes of conduct are: e.g. following instructions of superiors, maintaining confidentiality, not accepting costly gifts from stakeholders as a result of company role, complying with laws and regulations, not using company's property for personal use, etc.

3. ILLUSTRATION OF ETHICAL VALUE OF 'INTEGRITY'

We would like to elaborate first point, i.e. identify *key behaviours needed to adhere to the ethical values* mentioned in code of ethics. We quote views of Karen Trisko in her paper titled, "Power of Integrity" (*Executive Excellence*, July 2001). Many organisations include "integrity" in their values and in their marketing communications to prospects and customers. Naturally, most people want to do business with people and organisations with integrity. So, explicitly claiming your organization has integrity seems useful for attracting customers, employees and suppliers.

Declaring integrity has many impacts, mostly positive. The positive impacts include setting expectations for behaviour and communicating a desirable image. Yet, it is difficult to remain in a state of integrity because of the many people and processes involved. Every breach of integrity—and there are many each day—hurts the level of trust and the self-esteem among employees, not to mention damaging relationships with customers and suppliers.

Integrity has many meanings: living one's word, delivering on promises, alignment of beliefs and actions, wholeness, honesty, sincerity and authenticity. There are hundreds of opportunities in anyone's workday where a break in integrity can occur. For example, the company misses a delivery commitment to a customer or supplier; someone arrives late to a meeting; a salesperson exaggerates the company's experience; a sales proposal includes incorrect data; managers don't conduct performance reviews; a worker explains a mistake in a way that makes him or her appear blameless.

Some might argue that some of these examples are not breaches of integrity, but the results of mistakes. They all represent broken commitments or promises. Eliminating these breaks yields a higher level of integrity.

Breaks in integrity by leaders have very high negative impact. People develop trust in others based on their actions more than their words. Furthermore, employees tend to emulate their leaders' behaviour or that of people who appear to be valued. Breaks in integrity that go unacknowledged also cause damage because they breed more mistrust. Companies that publicly acknowledge product safety problems and take positive actions to correct them fare better in regaining market share after the incidents than companies that try to cover up problems.

If you say your organisation has integrity or you are people of integrity, you must live up to your word with extraordinary effort—or the loss of trust will be even greater than if you never claimed integrity at all. Leaders who value integrity and publicly declare it must understand the meaning of integrity; recognise integrity breakdowns when they occur; admit when they break integrity; apologize for the impact on others; provide processes and training that assure promises to customers, employees, and suppliers can be met; continually reinforce the value of integrity; and reward behaviour that shows integrity.

Don't assume everyone understands the meaning of integrity. Your interpretation of integrity, aligned with your values and mission, needs to be made explicit.

Karen Trisko once worked for a CEO who said he would help or make time to talk with anyone who asked. He kept his word almost perfectly over seven years. What a wonderful role model he was, and what a refreshing culture his behavoiur created because employees emulated him.

Apology is a powerful way to repair breaks in integrity and regain trust—if it is not overused. A colleague of mine was chronically late to meetings. He apologized almost every time, but ultimatley his apologies were received with cynicism.

In a high-trust environment, employees, customers and suppliers genuinely want to be part of the organization and eagerly refer others as potential employees and customers. Warren Bennis notes: "Integrity is the basis of trust, which is not as much an ingredient of leadership as it is a product. It is the one quality that cannot be acquired, but must be earned. It is given by co-workers and followers; without it, the leader can't function."

The intentional pursuit of integrity satisfies a basic human need for trust in relationships and breeds higher employee and customer loyalty, which lead to improved profitability.

4. CONDUCT, DISCIPLINE AND APPEAL RULES

Majority of corporations both in the private and public sector in India have laid down elaborate rules often termed as "Conduct, Discipline and Appeal Rules." These lay down do's and don'ts for codes of behaviour.

4.1 Features of Conduct, Discipline and Appeal Rules

Salient Features of such rules are:

- Employees to maintain absolute integrity, devotion to duty and do nothing unbecoming of in employee.
- Acts and omissions constituting misconduct.
    - Such acts are mentioned as illustrative in nature.
- Certain Do's and Don'ts:
    - Unauthorised communication of information.
    - Employment of relatives of employees in firms enjoying company's patronage.
    - Private trade or employment.
    - Bigamous marriage.
    - Inventions.
    - Movable, immovable and valuable property.
    - Gifts acceptance.
- Suspension rules.
- Penalties and procedure for imposing penalties.
- Special procedure in certain cases:
    - Conviction on criminal charge.
    - Cases where it is not practicable to hold an inquiry.
    - In the interest of security of company, not expedient to hold an enquiry.
- Appeals.
- Review.

CHAPTER

11

Ethical Leadership

Under the topic of "Ethical Leadership", we have elaborated following aspects:

1. Importance of ethical leadership.
2. Criteria of ethical leadership.
3. Corporate leaders focus on three aspects of ethics.
4. Three dimensions of ethical leadership.
5. Steps for becoming an ethical leader.
6. Managers/leaders can influence their organisation's ethical climate.
7. Promoting ethical climate and opposing unethical practices.
8. Criteria for evaluating ethical leadership.
9. Great people leave something behind.

1. IMPORTANCE OF ETHICAL LEADERSHIP

True leadership assesses the *follower's needs* and expectations and inspires them to realise *a vision* which best serves the followers and the organisation. Leader communicates the beliefs and values which influence and shape organisation's culture and behaviour norms. Since leadership influences on the lives of followers. This is one important reason, so many people are interested in the ethical aspects of leadership.

It is the *leader's moral principles and integrity* which impart legitimacy and creditability to the vision and sustain it. *Without ethical leadership* the organisation is *soulless* structure. Ethical leadership exists in the organisation when *moral intent* and *principles* infuse and guide the leader's actions in achieving.

For example, we see reports of widespread bribery in government officials, extensive environmental pollution, corporate scams and other instances of morally questionable conduct in our organisations. People have become increasingly cynical about the motives, competence and integrity of business and political leaders.

Such observations lead to realisation today that organisational leaders need to be more sensitive to their moral obligations to larger society, which includes all their stakeholders, i.e. consumers, employees, suppliers, government, local communities and protection of environment.

As such there is an absolute need for moral leadership in organisations and in society, if we truly want to achieve the common good of human welfare at the personal, organisational and society levels.

2. CRITERIA OF ETHICAL LEADERSHIP

Several criteria are relevant for judging individual leaders, including the person's values, stage of *moral development*, conscious *intentions*, *freedom of choice*, use of ethical and unethical behaviour, and types of influence.

James McGregor Burns has stated that a primary leadership role or function is to increase awareness about ethical issues and help people resolve conflicting values. Leaders and followers raise one another to higher levels of morality and motivation—these leaders seek to raise the *consciousness of followers* by appealing to ideals and *moral values such as liberty, justice, equality, peace and humanitarianism,* not to baser emotions such as fear, greed, jealousy, or hatred. *Transforming* leadership involves not only the moral elevation of individual followers, but also collective efforts to accomplish social reforms for organisations, community, and nation. (Gary Yukl)

3. CORPORATE LEADERS FOCUS ON THREE ASPECTS OF ORGANISATIONAL ETHICS

An organisation's *code of ethics* establishes ethical principles that should govern the *leader's decision and behaviours* in order that the leader can fulfil the mission of uplifting the moral climate of the organisation. For this purpose leader must *develop morally as a person* and also *assist in the moral development of his followers.* This is possible, when corporate leaders focus their attention on three aspects of organisational ethics:

(i) The leader's development as a *moral person,* i.e. ethical qualities and no compromise on moral values.

(ii) The development of *moral environment,* i.e. moral calibre of employees.

(iii) The promotion and *encouragement of activities that serve economic and ethical* performance. It is marriage between profit and social responsibility of business. (Figure 1)

4. THREE DIMENSIONS OF ETHICAL LEADERSHIP

The ethical leadership manifests itself on three dimensions:

(i) Leader *intention/motive* to serve the interest of the institution. Leader's identification and commitment to organisation's objectives and interests.

(ii) Leader's *influence strategy,* i.e. transformation. Under this, leader is to use empowerment (rather than control) strategies to bring about change in their followers' core beliefs and values as they move the organisation towards its future goals. It is to transform followers' beliefs and values that are consistent with the vision. Transformational mode enhances followers' self-growth and self-worth to function as autonomous persons.

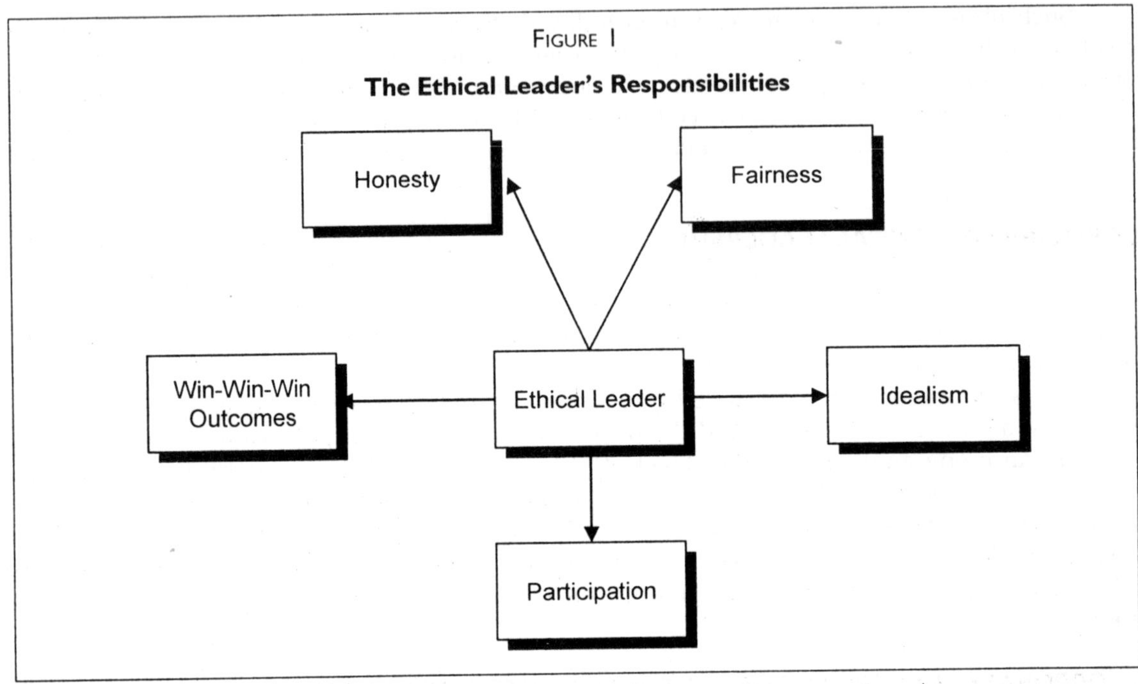

FIGURE I

The Ethical Leader's Responsibilities

(iii) Leader's *character* through efforts to incorporate store universal standard moral principles in their beliefs, values and behaviour.

This will lead to development of both the leader and the followers which will serve organisational and societal interests (for example: contribution to social welfare, community needs in areas of health, education, environmental pollution control, arts and culture and lobbying for public interest legislation.

The leader's moral development is an aspect of *character formation* through the practice of virtue in private as well as public lite. This is facilitated by the leader through the use of morally appropriate influence strategies and tactics which are motivated and guided by moral intent.

5. STEPS FOR BECOMING AN ETHICAL LEADER

(i) What *motivates* a leader to be ethical? It *comes from within—the basic motivation* comes from one's decision to live a certain way, and to conduct yourself in that way, i.e. an ethical way. *Personal integrity* is an attribute that contributes to ethical leadership and it is an essential requirement for effectiveness. A leader who is at higher stage of moral development is usually regarded more ethical than one on lower stage of moral development, the primary motivation is to fulfil internalised values and moral principles.

(ii) After you have to established some things that you believe in to be consistent and strong you have to be *guided by your basic beliefs*.

Then you take your beliefs and mold them into a way of being effective, a style of leading, a way of showing that "here's what I believe in" and "here's why" and "here's how we can make progress by living this way."

(iii) Then I think that you need to *work closely with the people* around you, persuade them, lead them. That's what leaders are for—to have ideas and to sell those ideas, to listen, and to get people to move with you.

So, first you have to believe, then you have to find a way to be effective, and then you have to work with people to cause them to join with you in doing what you're doing. I think what you do is *lead by example*. You have to *do the right things*. You *live within the rules*. You're open about what you're doing. You're willing to declare what you're doing.

6. MANAGERS/LEADERS CAN INFLUENCE THEIR ORGANISATION'S ETHICAL CLIMATE

Some ways managers influence their organisation's ethical climate are:

(i) They may, for instance, emphasize and discuss ethics continually. A *code of ethics* becomes real only when a manager talks about it by *encouraging subordinates* to *raise ethics-related* issues, doubts or concerns; by referring to it when answering questions or making decisions; and by keeping others' attention focussed on it.

(ii) Managers must also *develop and articulate realistic* goals.

(iii) Employees who are confronted with *goals they cannot achieve* are tempted to cut corners, sacrificing ethics for achievement.

(iv) By *identifying areas* that are vulnerable to unethical practices, managers may also avoid ethical problems by discussing with employees the *sorts of temptations* that might arise.

(v) By encouraging *reporting of unethical activities*, managers let all employees know that each of them has an important role in enforcing ethical standards; at the same time, they indicate their serious intent to ensure ethical behaviour (Dolcheck, 1989).

(vi) Ultimately, values cannot be taught; they must be lived. People emulate what they see, not what they are told. If they see that *unethical behaviours are practiced or tolerated*, they will pay little attention to written codes of ethics or mission statements. Richard Zimmerman, Chairman and CEO of Hershey Foods Corporation, refers to his company's value system as an "anchor" for the organisation and asserts, "Each manager must have a grip on those clearly defined values and be able to demonstrate them through their own behaviour to employee groups."

(vii) Andrews (1989) argued that *ethical decision-making* is the key to effective management maintaining that ethical decisions require three qualities of those making them:

   (a) Competence to *recognise ethical issues* and to think through the consequences of alternative resolutions.

   (b) Self-confidence to seek out different points of view and then to *decide what is right* at a given time and place in a particular set of relationships and circumstances.

   (c) *Tough-mindedness* or the willingness to make decisions when all that needs to be known cannot be known and when the questions that press for answers have no established and incontrovertible solutions.

(viii) *Role of Top Management is Critical*: Maya Reddi states that the role of top management becomes critical to the setting of standards of business behaviour. Senior management is often perceived to have double standards. There should not be one rule for the top management and another rule for the rest of the employees.

(ix) *Integration of ethics in personal life and business life*: Business ethics has to be preached, practised and shouted from the roof tops, in both, one's personal and one's official life. Before setting business standards, *ethics and morality have to be internalized*, so that they become a part of the blood stream.

When this happens, values will permeate the organisation and get translated into business standards and practices. Top management must stand out like a light and be able to pass the test of intense scrutiny. And, the penalty for not conforming to accepted ethical behaviour must be severe, whoever may be involved.

7. PROMOTING ETHICAL CLIMATE AND OPPOSING UNETHICAL PRACTICES

Some writers make a distinction between doing things to encourage and promote ethical practices and doing things to oppose unethical activities or decisions (e.g., Nielsen, 1989). Examples of each approach are shown in Figure 2. The two approaches are not mutually exclusive, and both can be used at the same time.

Leaders can do many things to promote ethical practices in organizations. The leader's own actions provide an example of ethical behaviour to be imitated by people.

FIGURE 2

Two Aspects of Ethical Leadership Behaviour

Promoting an Ethical Climate

- Set *an example* of ethical behaviour in your own actions.
- Facilitate the development and dissemination of a *code of ethical* conduct.
- *Initiate discussions* with followers or colleagues about ethics and integrity.
- Recognize and *reward ethical behaviour* by others.
- Take personal risks to *advocate moral solutions* to problems.
- *Help others* find fair and ethical solutions to conflicts.
- Initiate support services (e.g., ethics hotline, online advisory group).

Opposing Unethical Practices

- *Refuse to share* in the benefits provided by unethical activities.
- *Refuse to accept* assignments that involve unethical activities.
- Try to *discourage unethical* actions by others.
- *Speak out publicly* against unethical or unfair policies in the organization.
- Oppose *unethical decisions* and seek to get them reversed.
- *Inform proper authorities* about dangerous products or harmful practices.
- *Provide assistance* to others who oppose unethical decisions or practices.

Source: Gary Yukl, *Leadership in Organisations*, Pearson Education, Singapore, p. 248.

8. CRITERIA FOR EVALUATING ETHICAL LEADERSHIP

Various authors have come up with the criteria for evaluating ethical leadership. The objective is determine when leadership influence is proper. This is explained in Figure 3 and analyse with respect to Indian leader in mind.

FIGURE 3

Criteria for Evaluating Ethical Leadership

Criterion	*Ethical Leadership*	*Unethical Leadership*
Use of leader power and influence.	To serve followers and the organization.	To satisfy personal needs and career objectives.
Handling the diverse interests of the multiple stakeholders.	Attempts to balance and integrate them whenever feasible.	Favours coalition partners who offer the most personal gain.
Development of a vision for the organization.	Develops a vision that builds on follower input about their needs, values, and ideas.	Attempts to sell a personal vision as the only way for the organization to succeed.
Integrity of leader behaviour.	Acts in a way that is consistent with espoused values.	Does what is expedient for attaining personal objectives.
Risk-taking in leader decisions and actions.	Is willing to take personal risks and actions to accomplish the mission or achieve the vision.	Avoids necessary decisions or actions that involve personal risk to the leader.
Communication of relevant information about operations.	Makes a complete and timely disclosure of relevant information about events, problems, and actions.	Uses deception and distortion to bias follower perceptions about problems and progress.
Response to criticism and dissent by followers.	Encourages critical evaluation to find better solutions to problems.	Discourages and suppresses any criticism or dissent.
Development of follower skills and self-confidence.	Makes extensive use of coaching, mentoring, and training to develop followers.	De-emphasizes development to keep followers weak and dependent on the leader.

Source: Gary Yukl, *Leadership in Organisations*, Pearson Education, Singapore, p. 426.

The evaluation must take into account the extent to which a leader balances and integrates the interests of different stakeholders within the constraints imposed by legal and contractual obligations. An integrative orientation appears to be more ethical for leaders than supporting the faction that will provide the highest personal gain for the leader, playing stakeholders off against each other.

9. GREAT PEOPLE LEAVE SOMETHING BEHIND

Winners leave a legacy

Socrates taught Plato,
Plato taught Aristotle,
Aristotle taught Alexander the Great.

Knowledge, had it not been passed along, would have died.

Our greatest responsibility is to pass on a legacy of ethical values that the coming generations can be proud of.

CHAPTER

12

Ethical Organisation

In this chapter on "Ethical Organisation", the following aspects are covered:

1. What is ethics?
2. Ethical behaviour of the corporation.
   2.1 Ethical behaviour.
   2.2 Unethical behaviour.
3. How do we improve ethics in a corporation?
4. 'Enron', USA and the creation of an unethical culture. (Box 1)
5. Creating an ethical organisational culture, Johnson and Johnson. (Box 2)

We reproduce here the excerpts from speech of N.R. Narayana Murthy, Infosys Technologies conveying his views.

1. WHAT IS ETHICS?

Ethics is not definable, is not implementable, because it is not conscious; it involves not *only our thinking, but also our feeling* said Valdemar W. Setzer.

Ethics is in origin the art of recommending to others the sacrifices required for *cooperation with oneself*—Bertrand Russell.

Ethical behaviour is doing what is best in *enhancing the trust and confidence* between two entities so that both the entities feel energised and enthused to work towards the betterment of the common good.

Dr. Stephen Covey who has a book on ethics in organisations says that *interdependence is a higher value* than independence. These entities that can potentially work together could be individuals, institutions, states or even nations. Generally, what is ethical in one society may be legal in another.

As a society becomes more developed, more and more norms of behaviour move from ethical to legal. For instance, before Sebi was established, insider trading norms were merely ethical issues in India while they were already legal issues in the US. Similarly, what I consider *ethical now may become legal* later on.

Thus, ethics go beyond the domain of legality. It is about *decent behaviour*. It is about desirable behaviour. It is about putting the interest of the community ahead of oneself.

There are no policemen who can arrest us nor are there any courts that will try you for not being ethical. We will be judged only in the court of the Lord.

The need of the day is to remove poverty. This requires that we *place the interest of the community above one's own*. It is also about making sacrifices to ensure that the next-generation is better-off.

If India is what it is today, it because of the *low ethical behaviour* of our corporate leaders, politicians and bureaucrats. Unless we can change this, there is no hope.

2. ETHICAL BEHAVIOUR OF THE CORPORATION

2.1 Ethical Behaviour

The framework for ethical behaviour of a corporation is predicted on *the ethical behaviour of its owners, managers, employees* and directors towards its stakeholders—customers, investors, employees, vendor-partners, government of the land and the society.

To me, ethical behaviour is *putting the interest of the company above that of one's own personal interest* in all transactions.

- It is about fairness to all stakeholders.
- It is about transparency.
- It is about raising the trust and confidence of stakeholders in the way the company is run.
- It is about understanding and discharging societal responsibilities.
- It is about long-term thinking.
- It is about overcoming greed, insecurity and lack of self-confidence.
- It is about following every law of the land even when the law-enforcers may not be able to detect your violation.

The measure of a man's real character is what he would do if he knew he would never be found out, said Lord T.B. Macaulay.

While most people believe that Corporate Governance (CG) principles provide the legal and procedural framework for ensuring proper conduct of a corporation. I believe that it is an *issue of ethical behaviour* of the owner-managers of the corporation. Let me give you some examples of unethical behaviour.

2.2 Unethical Behaviour

Here are some examples of unethical behaviour.

The Chairman, CEO and CFO of a well known corporation sell shares with $ 150 million knowing that their corporation is shaky and then tell employees whose savings are in the company stock that all is well.

Nearer home, I have seen directors of several family-owned companies calling their homes, and staying in guesthouses, and booking all their expenses to the company.

There are sick companies but no sick industrialists!

A computer company ships a lower capacity machine to an uniformed customer and charges the price for a higher capacity machine.

A female sales employee of a company agrees to sleep with the prospective customer if he purchases her company's products.

A boss transfers his subordinate because she went over him to the senior level manager on an issue.

A senior manager tricks his boss into hiding information about his indiscretion.

3. HOW DO WE IMPROVE ETHICS IN A CORPORATION?

(a) The most powerful lessons about ethics and morality *come from family life* where people treat one another with respect, consideration and love.

Thus, I believe good behaviour is a result of your culture, your upbringing and the company you keep. It is a matter of the heart and not the mind. The solution is to develop such a culture.

(b) The behaviour of a corporation is generally shaped by the behaviour of its *CEO and other leaders*. This is particularly so in a feudal society like India.

Leadership is a potent combination of strategy and character. But if you must be without one, be without the strategy.

We need CEOs who are men and women of integrity—people who will walk the talk in demonstrating their commitment to a value system. As Nobel laureate Jane Addams has said: Action indeed is the sole medium of expression for ethics. Without this, no corporate governance will ever work. For example, at Infosys our value system can be summed up as: The softest pillow is a clear conscience.

The CEO should realise that the best index of success of a corporation is its longevity. The long-term success of a corporation is predicted on maintaining harmonious relations with employees, customers, vendor-partners, the government and the society. This is predicted on trust and confidence.

(c) I believe in *simple rules*. They are easy to understand, easy to follow, and easy to communicate. Above all, you cannot cheat with simple rules. CEOs should concentrate on simple business rules. If they want to implement complex rules, they should first understand them and translate them to a set of simple rules.

(d) Building *trust and confidence* requires an environment where there is premium on transparency, openness, lack of fear, fairness and justice. CEOs should encourage this. At Infosys, our philosophy is: When in doubt, How do we improve ethics in a corporation?

(e) We have to create a *climate of opinion* which says respect is more important than wealth. We can create this climate by instituting awards for good corporate behaviour and giving these awardees better exposure at international fora.

(f) Everybody in the company should *accept meritocracy* for, meritocracy forces ethical behaviour.

Respect for elders and God generally helps in practicing ethical behaviour.

Only morality in our actions can give beauty and dignity to life.—Albert Einstein.

Finally, pride is one-self, one's company, and one's nation is likely to inspire ethical behaviour.

Box I

Enron and the Creation of an Unethical Culture

Enron Corp., which in December 2001 became the largest-ever U.S. bankruptcy, didn't fail solely because of improper accounting practices, although that was certainly a major contributor. It also failed because it had a culture that pushed executives into unethical behaviour.

During Enron's heyday in the late 1990s, the press regularly praised use company for its entrepreneurial culture smart, sassy, creative, and risk-taking a post-mortem analysis reveals a different culture—an unrelenting emphasis on earnings growth and individual initiative. Instead of rewarding new ideas, the company encouraged unethical cutting. How? First, it pressured executives to make their numbers. Second, it instilled lax controls over how those numbers were created. Third, it bred a "yes-man" culture among executives. People were afraid to speak out on questionable practices for fear that it would adversely affect their performance evaluations and the size of their bonuses. Fourth, bonuses and money became the Almighty God. The company sought out and rewarded people who placed a high value on money, Jeff Skilling the CEO who created Enron's in your face culture, is quoted as saying, "all that matters is money. You can buy loyalty with money." Fifth, although managers were supposed to be graded on teamwork, the culture was heavily built around star players, with little value attached to team-building. The organization rewarded highly competitive people who were less likely to share power, authority, or information. Finally, the company continually set itself wildly optimistic expectations for growth and then drove executives, to find ways to meet them. "You've got someone at the top saying the stock price is the most important thing, which is driven by earnings," said one insider. Whoever could provide earnings quickly would be promoted."

One former Enron employee summed up the Enron culture this way: if your boss was [fudging], and you have never worked anywhere else, you just assume that everybody fudges earnings. Once you get there and you realized how it was, do you stand up and lose your job? It was scary. It was easy to get into 'Well, everybody else is doing it, so maybe it isn't so bad."

Source: Based on W. Zelliner, "Jeff Skilling: Enron's Missing Man", *Business Week*, February 1, 2002, pp. 38-40; and J.A. Byrne, "The environment was Ripe for Abuse", *Business Week*, February 25, 2002, pp. 118-20.

Box 2

Creating an Ethical Organisational Culture, Johnson and Johnson

The content and strength of a culture influences an organization's ethical climate and the ethical behaviour of its members.

An organizational culture most likely to shape high ethical standards is one that's high in risk tolerance, low to moderate in aggressiveness, and focuses on means as well as outcomes. Managers in such a culture are supported for taking risks and innovating, are discouraged from engaging in unbridled competition, and will pay attention to how goals are achieved as well as to what goals are achieved.

A strong organizational culture will exert more influence on employees than a weak one. If the culture is strong and supports high ethical standards, it should have a very powerful and positive influence on employee behaviour. Johnson & Johnson, for example, has a strong culture that has long stressed corporate obligations to customers, employees, the community, and shareholders, in that order. When poisoned Tylenol (a Johnson & Johnson product) was found on store shelves, employees at Johnson & Johnson across the United States independently pulled the product from these stores before management had even issued a statement concerning the tamperings. No one had to tell these individuals what was morally right; they knew what Johnson & Johnson would expect them to do.

What can management do to create a more ethical culture? We suggest a combination of the following practices:

Be a visible role model

Employees will look to top-management behaviour as a benchmark for defining appropriate behaviour. When senior management is seen as taking the ethical high-road, it provides a positive message for all employees. Communicate ethical expectations. Ethical ambiguities can be minimized by creating and disseminating an organizational code of ethics. It should state the organization's primary values and the ethical rules that employees are expected to follow.

Communicate ethical expectation

Ethical ambiguities can be minimized by creating and disseminationg an organisational code of ethics. It should state the organisation's primary values and the ethical rules that employees are expected to follow.

Provide ethical training

Set-up seminars, workshops, and similar ethical training programs. Use these training sessions to reinforce the organization's standards of conduct; to clarify what practices are and are not permissible, and to address possible ethical dilemmas.

Visibly reward ethical acts and punish unethical ones

Performance appraisals of managers should include a point-by-point evaluation of how his or her decisions measure up against the organization's code of ethics. Appraisals must include the means taken to achieve goals as well as the ends themselves. People who act ethically should be visibly rewarded for their behaviour. Just as importantly, unethical acts should be conspicuously punished.

Provide protective mechanisms

The organization needs to provide formal mechanisms so that employees can discuss ethical dilemmas and report unethical behaviour without fear of reprimand. This might include creation of ethical counselors, ombudsmen, or ethical officers.

Reference

N.R. Narayana Murthy, Chairman and chief mentor of Infosys Technologies. These are the excerpts from his presentation at the first Raman Kant Munjal Memorial Lecture in New Delhi.

PART III

VALUES AND CULTURE

CHAPTER

13

Values

We will deal with the topic of values under following broad heads:

(i) Values, definition, characteristics, importance, types of values,

(ii) Personal values,

(iii) Formulation of values,

(iv) Managerial values,

(v) Corporate values,

(vi) Business values, and

(vii) Managing by values.

(I) VALUES MEANING

People at work have many *opinions and preconceived notions in the form of values* and attitudes. They often influence our behaviour. We have values about work, equality, authority, self-respect, freedom, honesty, obedience and other matters. These values provide the basic foundation for understanding a person's personality, perceptions and attitudes.

Values shape → Beliefs → Perceptions → Attitudes → Behaviour, Interests, Personality.

Edward Spranger defines the values "as the constellation of likes, dislikes, viewpoints, inner inclinations, rational and irrational judgments, prejudices, and association patterns that *determine a person's view of the world.*"

In other words, values represent basic convictions or enduring belief that "a specific mode of conduct or end-state of existence is personally or socially preferable to an opposite or converse mode of conduct or end-state of existence."

1. Features of Values

(i) Values are at the core of personality and are a *powerful force affecting behaviour.*
(ii) Values contain a *judgmental element* in that they carry an individual's ideas as to what is right, or desirable.
(iii) Values have both *content and intensity* attributes. The content attribute indicates that a mode of conduct or end-state of existence is important. The intensity attribute specifies how important it is.
(iv) Values are not fixed, but they *change over time.*
(v) Many values are relatively stable and enduring. This is because of the way in which they are originally learned.
(vi) All of us have a *hierarchy of values* that forms our value system. But everyone does not hold the same values.

2. Importance of Values

The study of values is fundamental to the *understanding of managing* and *organizational behaviour*. The value orientations of managers underlie managerial behaviour. Values are pervasive because they involve in the selection of missions, goals and objectives. The job of planning, organizing and controlling the behaviour of individuals should also be compatible with managers' values. Values lay the foundation for the understanding of attitudes, motivation and perceptions.

Fred E. Fiedler's theory of leadership effectiveness argues that managers cannot be expected to adopt a particular leadership style if it is contrary to their "need-structures" or value orientations. Moreover, managers' values are reflected in the evaluation of subordinates. Interpersonal activities of managers are based on different and contradictory values. Similarly, various managerial strategies and behavioural patterns are characterised by particular value orientations. Organisational conflicts can be solved by accommodating different values between managers and workers.

3. Types of Values

According to M. Rokeach (*The Nature of Human Values*, New York, Free Press, 1973) there are two types of values:

(i) *Instrumental values* are those values concerning the *way we approach* end states. These relate to *means* for achieving desired results. That is, do we believe in ambition, cleanliness, honesty or obedience, courage, etc. What factors guide our everyday behaviour?
(ii) *Terminal values* are those *end-state goals* that we praise such as comfortable life, a sense of accomplishment, equality among all people, self-respect, family security.

Both sets of values have significant influence on daily behaviour at work.

People are influenced by a wide variety of personal values. In fact, it has been argued that values represent a major influence on how we process information, how we feel about issues, and how we behave. Below are listed two sets of statements of personal values. The first list presents several instrumental values, while the second list presents several terminal values.

Instrumental Values

- Assertiveness; standing up for yourself
- Being helpful or caring toward others
- Dependability; being counted upon by others
- Education and intellectual pursuits
- Hard work and achievement
- Obedience; following the wishes of others
- Open-mindedness; receptivity to new ideas
- Self-sufficiency; independence
- Truthfulness; honesty
- Being well-mannered and courteous toward others

Terminal Values

- Happiness; satisfaction in life
- Knowledge and wisdom
- Peace and harmony in the world
- Pride in accomplishment
- Prosperity; wealth
- Lasting friendships
- Recognition from peers
- Salvation; finding eternal life
- Security; freedom from threat

According to Jones, E.E. and Gerard (1967) anything "for which the individual strives, or approaches extols, embraces, voluntarily consumes, incurs expense to acquire is a positive value. Anything that the individual avoids, escapes from, deplores, rejects, or attacks is a negative value."

(II) PERSONAL VALUES

Business leaders are surprised at the accusations of unethical behaviour of today's companies. Such as stock market manipulations, disregard of environmental hazards, bribes and kick-backs, adulteration. To understand this we must understand role of values and personal ethics.

Personal Values Serve Five Purposes in Organisations

1. Values Serve as Standards of Behaviour

Values serve as standards of behaviour for determining a correct course of action. Values place limits on our behaviour—ethical behaviour. Employees have to make decisions concerning what to them is right or wrong, proper or improper.

For example—Would you conceal information about a hazardous product made by your company, or would you feel obliged to tell someone? How would you respond to petty theft on the part of your supervisor? As individual, often determine for themselves what is proper and what is not, this is particularly true when people find themselves in "grey zone", where ethical standards are unclear. People have to determine their own standards of behaviour.

To some extent, ethical behaviour is influenced by societal values. Societal norms tell us it is wrong to engage in certain behaviour.

2. Guidelines for Decision-making and Conflict Resolution

Managers who value personal integrity are less likely to make decisions they know to be injurious to someone else. An interesting development in area of values and decision-making involves integrity or honesty tests.

3. Values Effect our Thoughts and Action

If the values are gracious, it consequently reflects in actions of the person—excellence brings forth excellent rewards. If values are not healthy, the quality of thoughts will be negative which only create sorrow and disaster.

4. Values Serve as an Influence on Employee Motivation and Influence Perceptions

Values affect employee motivation by determining what rewards are sought. Whether I prefer overtime work money or free time with family.

5. Values Generally Influence Attitude and Behaviour

For example, suppose you enter an organisation with view that allocating pay on the basis of performance is right, whereas allocating pay on the basis of seniority is wrong. How are you going to react if organisation rewards on seniority. You are likely to be disappointed and it can lead to job-dissatisfaction and you may not put high level effort. An employees performance and satisfaction are likely to be higher if his values fit well with organisation.

(III) FORMULATION OF OUR VALUES

1. A significant portion is *genetically* determined say about 40 per cent.

2. *Environmental factors*. The rest is due to factors like culture, parental dictates, teachers, friends and similar environmental influences. In every culture certain values have developed over time such as in USA—achievement, equity and democracy, etc. as societal values. They change very slowly.

3. Values we hold are *established in our early years*—from parents, teachers and friends, etc.—on topics as education, sex and politics. For instance, we are taught that lying and stealing is always unacceptable. So values secure them firmly in our belief system.

As you grow old, *values may undergo change*. For example, in high school, if you join social club who believe that "every person should carry a gun", you change your values to align with club members. Even if it meant rejecting your parent's value that "only gang members carry guns and they are bad."

Figure 1 on next page shows that a person's ethics are formulated through the operation of five key forces in the individual's environment: (i) family influences; (ii) peer influences; (iii) experiences; (iv) values and morals; and (v) situational factors (Griffin, 1990, pp. 809-10).

FIGURE I

Determinants of Individual Ethics

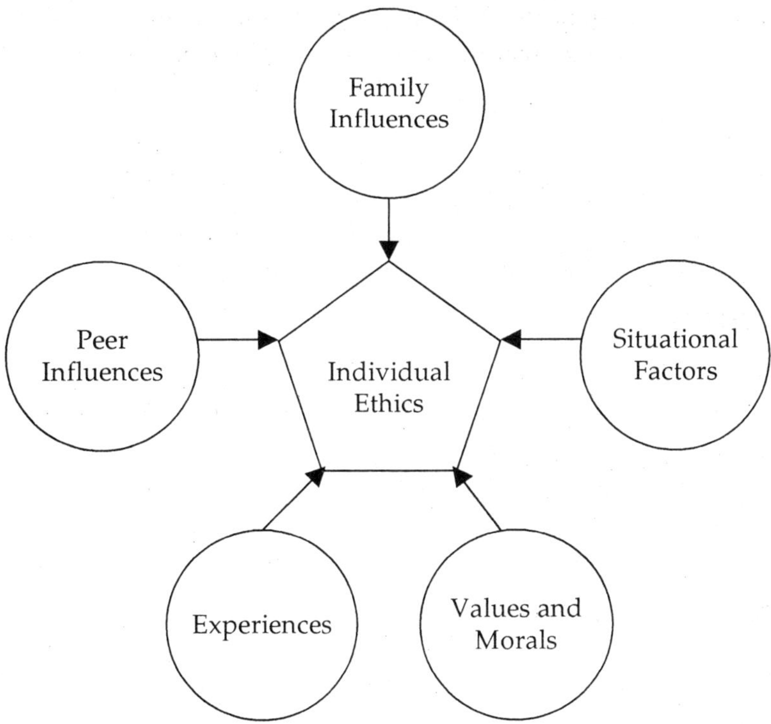

(i) Family Influences

The formulation of ethics begins when the individual is a small child. Thus, the family environment has significant influence in determining what the child learns about good and bad, right and wrong. Typically, when parents demonstrate high ethical standards, rewarding good behaviour and punishing bad behaviour, the child will adopt similar ethical standards.

(ii) Peer Influences

As the child develops contacts outside the home through school, play, and work, peers exert considerable influence on the individual's ethical beliefs. If the child makes friends that conduct themselves within high ethical standards, he or she will come to adopt those same standards. On the other hand, if the child makes friends with peers who steal and use drugs, the child will probably accept those behaviours as being ethical.

(iii) Experiences

As a person matures and develops as a human being, he or she will be exposed to many critical experiences that will affect his or her ethical standards. If a person is punished or not appropriately rewarded for "good" behaviour, while others are seen as rewarded for "bad" behaviour, the person will probably alter both ethical standards and behavioural patterns.

(iv) Values and Morals

One's ethical standards are also greatly influenced by values and morals. People who place a high value on money and material possessions may not have strong ethical standards regarding behaviours that facilitate the accumulation of that wealth. People who value the quality of life enjoyed by all living creatures will probably have strong ethics with respect to the proper treatment of others.

(v) Situational Factors

People often change their ethics in response to unforeseen situational factors. An employee, who is threatened with losing a job that has been held for years, may commit unethical acts in order to save the job. A father with a sick child might use the threat of physical violence to secure treatment for the child at an understaffed clinic.

VALUES OF WORKFORCE

(a) Old Values of Work Life

Hard work, conservative, loyalty to the employer organisation.

(b) Present Values of Workforce

Job satisfaction, leisure time, loyalty to relationships, flexibility, success and achievement, ambition, loyalty to career.

They consider the ethical implications of their actions on others around them.

(c) Negative and Positive Personal Values

Personal values denote a sense of right or wrong, good or bad and other judgemental criteria based on our strong sense of what the ideal ought to be.

(i) Negative Values

- Anger
- Meanness
- Arrogance
- Crookedness
- Greed
- Lust

They generate negative thoughts.

(ii) Positive Values

- Integrity, honesty
- Truthfulness
- Kind heartedness, humility
- Friendliness
- Faith
- Self-respect
- Open mindedness
- Creativity

- Civil sense
- Simplicity
- Forgiveness
- Poise
- Detachment, etc.

They generate positive thoughts.

(IV) MANAGERIAL VALUES

1. Leaders to Conduct themselves Ideally

Managerial leadership values are people's enduring beliefs regarding how they wish the leaders of their organisations *to conduct themselves ideally*. A core component of a managerial leadership philosophy consists of the values the organisation wishes its leaders at all levels to live out. Major organisations like Hewlett-Packard have defined clear codes of values that serve as a selection criteria and a foundation of the training and development. Their leaders receive, and provide guides to their behaviour.

2. Preferred Leadership Values

We share here the findings of a study regarding "Preferred Leadership Values" in a Wisconsin's (USA) organisation done in March, 2000. This study covered 518 respondents. The questionnaire contained 20 value statements for which rankings of values was to be given by executives from all functional areas of the organisation. A copy of questionnaire administered is attached which gives us idea of the managerial values.

The managerial values which emerged as most preferred are given in table below:

(a) Values that Emerged as Most Preferred

Ranking	*Value*	*Average*
1	Honest (trustworthy, truthful, reliable)	5.50
2	Competent (capable, qualified, skillful, effective)	5.41
3	Fair-minded (just, objective, unbiased)	4.70
4	Broad-minded (open, flexible, receptive)	4.67
5	Dependable (reliable, conscientious)	4.60
6	Supportive (helpful, championing, comforting)	4.42
7	Forward-looking (visionary, future-oriented)	4.37

(b) Do these Value Preferences go together? Yes.

Values	*Rank*	*Label*
Dependable + Honest	1	Good citizen
Fair-minded + Straight-forward	2	Open-minded
Supportive + Caring + Cooperative	3	Socially supportive
Broad-minded + Forward-looking + Imaginative + Inspiring	4	Visionary
Competent + Intelligent + Mature + Self-controlled	5	Emotionally stable
Ambitious + Dedicated	6	Career-minded

(c) The following, although all important, were rated as Least Preferred

Ranking	*Values*	*Average*
20	Courageous (brave, bold, daring)	2.38
19	Independent (self-reliant, autonomous, original)	2.75
18	Ambitious (aspiring, eager, venturesome)	2.77
17	Mature (seasoned, experienced, wise)	3.22
16	Loyal (faithful, constant, steadfast)	3.51
15	Self-controlled (emotionally even, self-disciplined)	3.53
14	Imaginative (creative, innovative, inventive)	3.69

This study thus provide the managerial leadership values as general guides to appropriate leadership behaviour in dealing with their various stakeholders.

3. Changing Managerial Values

The organization must be a dynamic entity as it operates in changing environments. As the needs of its members change, managerial philosophies and values must change. Table 1 below summarizes the major trends that are occurring in managerial values.

TABLE I

The Transition of Managerial Values

Away from . . .	*Towards . . .*
1. A view of people as essentially bad.	A view of people as basically good.
2. Avoidance or negative evolution of individuals.	Confirming individuals as human beings.
3. A view of individuals as fixed.	Seeing individuals as being in process.
4. Resisting and fearing individual differences.	Accepting and utilizing individual differences.
5. Utilizing an individual primarily with reference to the job description.	Viewing an individual as a whole person.
6. Walling off the expression of feelings.	Making possible both appropriate expression and effective use of feelings.
7. Maskmanship and game playing.	Authentic behaviour.
8. Use of status for maintaining power and personal prestige.	Use of status for organizationally relevant purposes.
9. Distrusting people.	Trusting people.
10. Avoiding facing others with relevant data.	Making appropriate confrontation.
11. Avoidance of risk-taking.	Willingness to risk-taking.
12. A view of process work as being unproductive effort.	Seeing process work as essential to effective task accomplishment.
13. A primary emphasis on competition.	A much greater emphasis on collaboration.

(V) CORPORATE VALUES

Many management theorists stress that companies must operate according to values that *guide the thinking and behaviour of people in an organisation*. But what should those values be? Rom Lebow, former director of marketing communications at Microsoft, and William L. Simon offer an important set of values for successful organisation.

They introduce ten fundamental shared values. The ten shared values are:

Truth:	Treat others with uncompromising truth
Trust:	Lavish trust on your associates
Mentoring:	Mentor unselfishly
Openness:	Be receptive to new ideas
Giving Credit:	Give credit where it is due
Risk-taking:	Take personal risks for the good of the organisation
Honesty:	Be honest in all dealings, do not touch dishonest money
Caring:	Put the interests of others before your own Social conscience.

Responsibility and accountability

These are the people values that guide employee behaviour, specifically how they deal with each other. They represent the first step in creating a positive and productive work environment. In addition to adopting people values, a company must also develop its *business values*. These values guide what people do every day to be successful in the market place. Unlike people values, business values change from organisation to organisation. But they should all share certain characteristics. They should be aspirational, quantifiable, and controllable. They must affect everything in the organisation, not just part of it.

(VI) BUSINESS VALUES

Business in India is passing through turbulent times as there is lot of concern for business survival and growth due to various factors such as global and domestic competition of MNCs, ecological and environmental degradation, need for balancing multiple stakeholders' expectations, etc.

In view of the above circumstances, it is appropriate to mention the business values enunciated by a management thinker of international repute. Dr. M.B. Athreya, Advisor, Indian Industry and former professor at the London, Scotish Business School and IMM, Calcutta (article, "Business Values for the 21st Century"):

"(i) *Righteousness (Dharma)*: It is important for business to follow 'Dharma' in the creation and sharing of wealth; maintaining the highest standards of ethics and integrity in every action we take.

(ii) *Public Good (Loka Sangraha)*: Another important value is that individuals and organisations should work not just for private gain, but also for well-being of community/public good including external and internal stakeholders.

(iii) *Efficacy (Kauslam)*: It is critical that all businesses persue efficiency, productivity resource optimisation and conserve rsources so as to internalise the value of efficacy in the best interest of preserving mother earth for future generations.

(iv) *Innovation (Vivdata)*: Business has to be engine of innovation, constantly seeking more effective solutions to meet economic and social expectations.

(v) *Learning (Jigasa)*: Business will be the key instrument to solve the problems of growth, employment, eduction, consumption, information, entertainment and quality of life.

Business will have to keep learning from the feedback. Loop from society and also through internal process of question, challenge, search, debates, sharing, training, monitoring, etc. The viability and health of nations and global society will depend on the skills of learning and utilisation of such learning by business. To put it in Senge's words the "Concept of Learning Organisation."

(vi) Learned Prof. M.B. Athreya adds other Business Values as *"respect for individual and human dignity*. These will increase creativity and team play."

(vii) *Dharmayudh*. We expect business to be aggressive, competitive, with lot of initiative, creating wealth, and, therefore, our philosophy talks about Dharmayudh. Yudh is necessary, but it has to be Dharmayudh. Translated into business that would mean that to the *marketing and sales*. Your role is not lose your market share, but to increase market share. And for that whatever needs to be done you can do. But we can learn to be sure if that is not done ethically, in the long-run, it is going to erode business.

(VII) MANAGING BY VALUES

In a book that Ken Blanchard has co-authored with Michael O'Connor entitled, "Managing by Values", has highlighted that where *there is alignment between core values and common practices, profitably will directly follow*. We reproduce Ken Blanchard's "Three Precepts" (*Executive Excellence*, July 2001).

"To define, communicate, and align your values with your practices. Unless values are prioritized, you have nothing but situational ethics where anything goes."

(a) Identifying Core Values

Many companies claim that have a set of core values, but what they mean is a list of business beliefs that everyone would agree with, such as having integrity, making a profit, and responding to customers. Such values have meaning only when they are further defined in terms of how people actually behave and are rank-ordered to reveal priority.

For example, Disney's four core values are: safety, courtesy, the show (performing your particular role well), and efficiency. If these values aren't carefully ordered, people are left to their own devices. For example, a bottom line-oriented manager might overemphasize efficiency and thus jeopardize the three higher-ranking values.

Fortunate 500 companies first emphasize the beliefs, attitudes, and feelings that top management have about employees, customers, quality, ethics, integrity, social responsibility, growth, stability, innovation, and flexibility. Organizations today must know what they stand for and on what principles they operate. Value-based behaviour is a requisite for survival. Once you have a clear picture of your mission and values, you have a basis for evaluating your management practices and bringing them into alignment.

Ethics means doing the right thing by being honest, acting in a legally and socially responsible manner, being fair in our treatment of others, and acting in ways that result in feeling good about ourselves and our company.

(b) Communicating Core Values

Make sure that your values are evident to all stakeholders—employees, customers, suppliers, stock-holders, and the community. Involve employees in decisions that affect them—or better yet—whenever possible let them make the decisions.

(c) Aligning Values and Practices

Once your values have been broadly communicated, you need to assess how well these values are practiced. To be effective, values and strategies need to unite the energies of all people, especially those dealing with the company's various publics. Without some way of identifying gaps between values and behaviour, a set of core values is nothing more than a wish list.

In Fortunate 500 companies, the behaviour of the leaders is aligned with corporate values. Management "walks its talk." For example, if executives indicate that they value innovation and flexibility but then have an authoritarian-based bureaucracy, there is an alignment problem.

Or, if executives say that they value the full development of people's potential but then have a performance review system that forces managers to rate people on a normal distribution curve, again there is an alignment problem. Misalignment between values and practices creates an energy drain that sabotages productive behaviour. Alignment liberates energy and empowers people to act congruently. That makes for loyal customers and employees and a productive environment.

Annexure

QUESTIONNAIRE

Preferred Leadership Values

First, find the one value that you believe is most important and place its number under the column 7 below.

Next, find one value that you believe is least important and place its number under the column 1 below.

Proceed to column 6 and place in it the number of the two values that you believe are the next most important.

Go then to column 2 and select the two that you believe are the next least important.

Proceed in this fashion until you have accounted for all the 20 values.

1. Ambitious (aspiring, eager, venturous)
2. Broad-minded (open, flexible, receptive)
3. Caring (appreciative, compassionate, concerned)
4. Competent (capable, qualified, skillful, effective)
5. Cooperative (helping, hospitable, companionable)
6. Courageous (brave, bold, daring)
7. Dependable (reliable, conscientious)
8. Dedicated (devoted, resolute, persistent)
9. Fair-minded (just, objective, unbiased)
10. Forward-looking (visionary, future-oriented)
11. Honest (trustworthy, truthful, reliable)
12. Imaginative (creative, innovative, inventive)
13. Independent (self-reliant, autonomous, original)
14. Inspiring (enthusiastic, influential)
15. Intelligent (sharp, keen, acute, clever, ingenious)
16. Loyal (faithful, constant, steadfast)
17. Mature (seasoned, experienced, wise)
18. Self-controlled (emotionally even, self-disciplined)
19. Straight-forward (direct, candid, forthright)
20. Supportive (helpful, championing, comforting)

1 (least important)						7 (most important)

CHAPTER

14

Developing Managerial Values

In this chapter on "Developing Managerial Values", the following aspects are covered:

1. Importance of managerial values.
2. Purposes of managerial values.
3. What are preferred managerial values?
4. Essential principles of managerial values.
5. Factors for developing managerial values.
   (i) Leader's moral motives development.
   (ii) Leader's influence strategy for followers.
   (iii) Leader's moral character formation.

1. IMPORTANCE OF MANAGERIAL VALUES

Managerial values are most important aspect of manager's behaviour. It *gives a positive direction and brings out the best* in him. It has tremendous *influence on his performance*. It is the manager's *moral principles and integrity* which impart legitimacy and creditability to the vision and sustain it. Without right managerial values, the organisation is soulless structure. These managerial values guide the leader in *achieving common good of human welfare* at the personal, organisational and society levels.

Manager's values and his effectiveness is interlinked what we refer as value driven management. Effectiveness of managers and employees is a function of values as explained below:

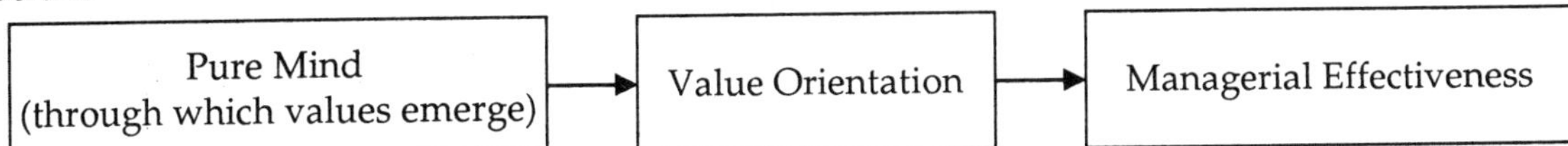

As such knowledge and awareness of managerial values is very important and vital for all professionals (technical or non-technical) in performance of their roles effectively. Such values can help and ensure professionals to *desist from mistakes, temptations of short-cuts* and windfall gains.

Fred E. Fiedler's theory of leadership effectiveness argues that managers cannot be expected to adopt a particular leadership style if it is contrary to their "need-structures" or value orientations. Moreover, managers' values are reflected in the evaluation of subordinates. Interpersonal activities of managers are based on different and contradictory values. Similarly, various managerial strategies and behavioural patterns are characterised by particular value orientations. Organisational conflicts can be solved by accommodating different values between managers and workers.

2. PURPOSES OF MANAGERIAL VALUES

Managers are surprised at the accusations of unethical behaviour of today's companies, such as stock market manipulations, disregard of environmental hazards, bribes and kick-backs, adulteration. To understand this we must understand role of manager's values and personal ethics.

Managerial Values Serve Four Major Purposes in Organisations

(i) *Values serve as standards of behaviour* for determining a correct course of action. Values place limits on our behaviour—ethical behaviour. Employees have to make decisions concerning what to them is right or wrong, proper or improper.

(ii) *Guidelines for decision-making and conflict resolution* managers who value personal integrity are less likely to make decisions they know to be injurious to someone else.

(iii) *Managerial values effect our thoughts and action.* If the values are gracious, it consequently reflects in actions of the person—excellence brings forth excellent rewards. If values are not healthy, the quality of thoughts will be negative which only create sorrow and disaster.

(iv) Values serve as an influence on employee motivation and influence perceptions.

3. WHAT ARE PREFERRED MANAGERIAL VALUES?

Preferred managerial leadership values. We share here the findings of a study regarding "Preferred Leadership Values" in a Wisconsin's (USA) organisation done in March 2000. This study covered 518 respondents. The questionnaire contained 20 value statements for which rankings of values was to be given by executives from all functional areas of the organisation. A copy of questionnaire administered is attached which gives us idea of the managerial values. (Annexure 1, Chapter 13). The managerial values which emerged as most preferred are given in Table 1.

This study thus provides the managerial values as general guides to appropriate leadership behaviour in dealing with their various stake-holders.

TABLE I

Managerial Values: Values that Emerged as Most Preferred

Ranking	*Values*	*Average*
1	Honest (trustworthy, truthful, reliable)	5.50
2	Competent (capable, qualified, skillful, effective)	5.41
3	Fair-minded (just, objective, unbiased)	4.70
4	Broad-minded (open, flexible, receptive)	4.67
5	Dependable (reliable, conscientious)	4.60
6	Supportive (helpful, championing, comforting)	4.42
7	Forward-looking (visionary, future-oriented)	4.37

4. ESSENTIAL PRINCIPLES OF MANAGERIAL VALUES

Following are five principles of managerial values in ethical organisations:

1. They are at *ease interacting with diverse internal and external conflicting stakeholder groups.* The ground rules of these managers is to make the good of these stakeholder groups part of the organizations' own good.
2. They are *obsessed with fairness.* Their ground rules emphasize that the other persons' interests count as much as their own. It is understood by managers that every decision has value-based perspective. Right thing to do.
3. *Responsibility is individual* rather than collective, with individuals assuming personal responsibility for actions of the organization.
4. *They see their activities in terms of purpose.* This purpose is a way of operating that members of the organisation highly value. And purpose ties the organisation to its environment. There exists a *clear shared vision* and picture of *integrity* throughout the organization.
5. The *reward system is aligned with the vision* of integrity.

5. FACTORS FOR DEVELOPING MANAGERIAL VALUES

Manager's decision and behaviours can fulfil the mission of uplifting the moral climate of the organisation. For this purpose *leader must develop morally as a person* and also *assist in the moral development of his followers.* This is possible, when corporate leaders focus their attention on three aspects of their moral values:

(i) The leader's development as a *moral person,* i.e. ethical qualities and no compromise on moral values or motives.

(ii) The development of a *moral environment,* i.e. moral caliber of employees by influence strategy.

(iii) The leader's *moral character* formation.

We shall discuss these three aspects in some details as also explained in Figure 2.

FIGURE 2

Ethical Leadership in Three Dimensions

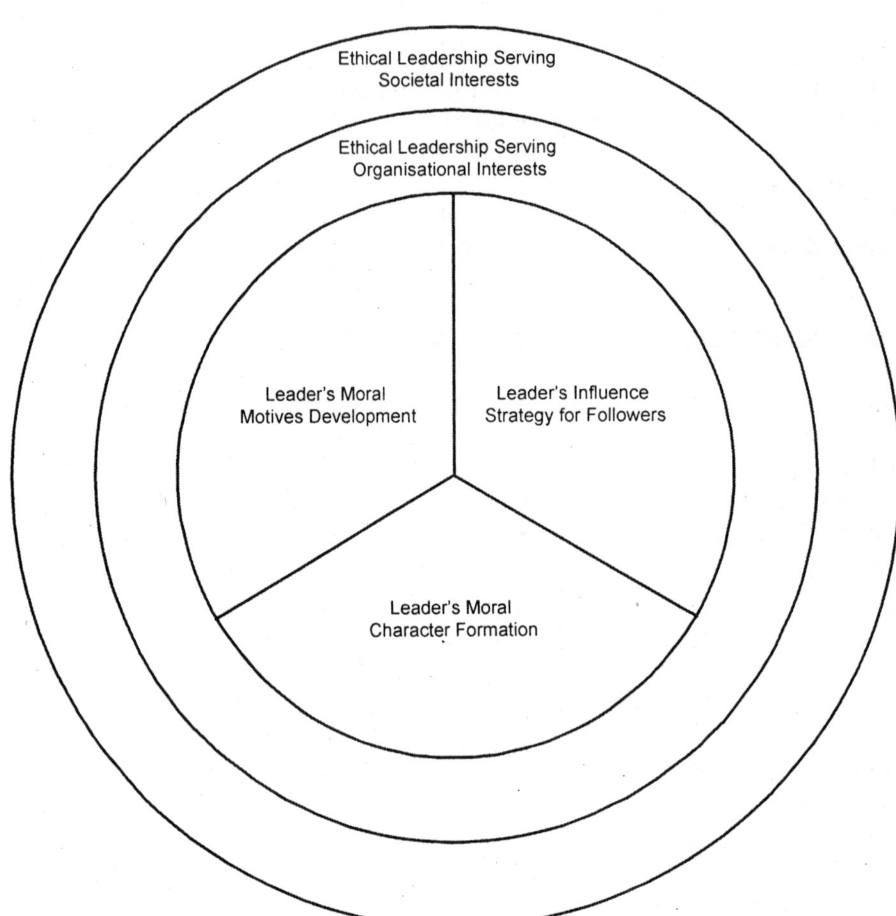

(i) Leader's Moral Motives Development

The manager's moral development is an aspect of character formation through the practice of virtue in private as well as public life. This is facilitated by the leader through the use of morally appropriate influence strategies and tactics which are motivated and guided by *moral intent*. The manager's *intentions and motives for action* are as under:

(a) Leaders are truly motivated by a *concern for others* (as against benefit to self), i.e. others are organisation members and society at large.

(b) Leaders have high need for *affiliation motive*. They regard warm and friendly relationships with their followers and are sensitive to their feelings and wishes. This suggests concern for others.

(c) The leader is not motivated by power motive to personal power (self-interest) but by power to serve the interest of the institution.
(d) Achievement motive of leader brings satisfaction from achieving goals of the organisation and assuming high degree of responsibility for them.

(ii) Leader's Influence Strategy for Followers (i.e. Transformational)

Under this, leader is to use empowerment (rather than control) strategies to bring about change in their followers' core beliefs and values as they move the organisation towards its future goals.

Leaders use their *personal expertise and good example* to transform their followers' beliefs and values that are consistent with the vision (not overt compliance behaviour).

The *empowerment strategy* achieves two objectives. First, followers internalise the beliefs and values. Second, empowerment changes followers' self-efficacy beliefs and they feel more competent to handle tasks required for realisation of the vision. Followers become more ethical and their effectiveness is high and enduring.

(iii) Leader's Moral Character Formation

Leaders must make efforts to incorporate moral principles in their beliefs, values and behaviour. Ethical leaders recognise that self-transformation ought to begin with one's self. For this leader should follow practical principles:

(a) He should have higher *purpose and priorities* for organisation vision.
(b) Practice *prudence and justice* to assess situations and take a decision. This strengthens leader's moral character and also enhances the followers' perceptions of the leader's trust worthiness.
(c) Leader to have high *self-esteem* and healthy pride of his accomplishments as well as esteem of his followers.
(d) Leader to exercise *patience* towards the realisation of vision. It takes time and effort to overcome obstacles. Hence, need for patience. He should not resort to unethical practices when things do not proceed as planned.
(e) *Persistence* as of Winston Churchill's perseverance. Never! Never! Give up!
(f) Acquiring a *sense of perspective* that what is really important in a given situation through observing, inner silence that allow him to reflect on the higher purpose.

The above suggestions which managers can adopt in their effort to develop their inner strength they need to function as ethical, moral persons.

A periodic examination of behaviour in the light of higher purpose can prevent one from, or at least alert one, that one might be treading the slippery slope of unethical behaviour.

To conclude, leader can set examples of personal commitment and loyalty and make efforts to maintain integrity of the organisation. Thus, leader's altruistic behaviour in three dimensions contribute to the development of both manager and the followers.

References

Bhatia, S.K., *Business Ethics and Managerial Values*, Deep & Deep Publications Pvt. Ltd., New Delhi, 2003.
Joseph H. Boyett and Jimmie T. Boyett, *The Guru Guide to the Knowledge Economy*, 2001.

CHAPTER

15

Emerging Values of Corporates

In this chapter on "Emerging Values of Corporates", the following aspects are covered:

1. Emerging values of corporates today.
2. Changing managerial values.

1. EMERGING VALUES OF CORPORATES TODAY

Some of the emerging values of corporates are given below:

(i) A clear, simple and shared vision for the future.
(ii) Developing a culture of strategic thinking (aligned to organisation objectives) to overhauling the organisation, if called for.
(iii) Define core values around which organisation will operate.
(iv) Seek *excellence* in all we do.
(v) Belief in quality *excellence* and customer satisfaction, which is foremost.
(vi) Contribution to a *clean environment, quality of life,* and *worklife balance.*
(vii) Mutual *loyalty* and *prosperity* for *vendors and suppliers.*
(viii) Ethos of *discipline* and *commitment* to achieve objectives.
(ix) *Integrity* (honesty), *fairness* and *equity* in business dealings, set high standards of ethics.
(x) Contribute to *benefit of society—Social responsibility of business.*
(xi) Generate competitive ability and take advantage of change—*Learning organisation.*
(xii) Gaurding against *global warming.*
(xiii) Global and positive mindset for managing cultural diversity and subsidaries to be treated as partners.

Human-oriented values

(xiv) Charisimatic leadership.

(xv) *Employees,* being the most important resource, to be *treated with respect* and dignity. Focus on effective management of human resources to broaden individual perspective and identification with goals of the organisation.
(xvi) Everyone can be source of useful ideas.
(xvii) Learning flows up and down the hierarchy—team learning.
(xviii) Promotion of team ownership and empowerment.
(xix) Openness to new ideas. Positive encouragement to foster creativity and innovation.
(xx) Mistakes are viewed as learning opportunities.
(xxi) Proactive approach.
(xxii) Calculated risk-taking.
(xxiii) Resolving conflicts through the use of collaboration.
(xxiv) *Avoid all discriminations.*

2. CHANGING MANAGERIAL VALUES

Values are not fixed, but they *change over time*. The organization must be a dynamic entity as it operates in changing environments. As the needs of its members change, managerial philosophies and values must change. Figure 1 summarizes the major trends that are occurring in managerial values.

FIGURE I

The Transition of Managerial Values

Away from . . .	*Towards . . .*
1. A view of people as essentially bad.	A view of people as basically good.
2. Avoidance or negative evolution of individuals.	Confirming individuals as human beings.
3. A view of individuals as fixed.	Seeing individuals as being in process.
4. Resisting and fearing individual differences.	Accepting and utilizing individual differences.
5. Utilizing an individual primarily with reference to the job description.	Viewing an individual as a whole person.
6. Walling-off the expression of feelings.	Making possible both appropriate expression and effective use of feelings.
7. Maskmanship and game playing.	Authentic behaviour.
8. Use of status for maintaining power and personal prestige.	Use of status for organisationally relevant purposes.
9. Distrusting people.	Trusting people.
10. Avoiding facing others with relevant data.	Making appropriate confrontation.
11. Avoidance of risk-taking.	Willingness to risk-taking.
12. A view of process work as being unproductive effort.	Seeing process work as essential to effective task accomplishment.
13. A primary emphasis on competition.	A much greater emphasis on collaboration.

CHAPTER

16

Hierarchism as an Organisation Value

In this chapter on "Hierarchism as an Organisation Value", the following aspects are covered:

1. Meaning of hierarchism.
2. Some examples of hierarchism in organisations.
3. Purposes it serves.

1. MEANING OF HIERARCHISM

Hierarchy is a *system of ranking* and organising things or people.

A *hierarchical organisation* is an organisation structured in a way that every entity is subordinate to a single other entity. Most corporations, governments and religions are hierarchical organisations.

For example hierarchy starts with a single supreme *ruler* at the top who passes the authority down the line. Single ruler also retains the power. Hierarchy has a genuine organisational value. This pattern is also in religions. For example, Pope is the head of Christians, head of Hindus is Math's Shankracharya.

2. SOME EXAMPLES OF HIERARCHISM IN ORGANISATIONS

(a) In *modern states,* head of state is President or King. Same is true in *business organisations.* Business owner is at the top as Chairman of the company and then Board of Directors followed by Managing Director. Structuring in this way *improves communication* flow to the followers.

(b) Hierarchy is also observed in *Indian Culture* and *Indian Legal System.* India has been hierarchical *society*, people are ranked according to various qualities, castes system is in all religions.

(c) In every organisation, the superior gets the work done through his subordinate levels. Hierarchism is an important *tool for organising activities* and maintaining discipline in organisations. Thus, *hierarchy is a tool of discipline.* Hierarchism ensures discipline in the organisation. Age factor can also be used as a tool of ensuring a disciplined environment, i.e. to avoid abusive talks/language, etc. in the offices.

(d) Hierarchy can serve a convenient way of *conflict resolution*. Even in *family* disputes, head of the family takes decisions. Similarly in organisations also hierarchy can play a vital role where in case of differences on a subject is decided by the senior boss.

(e) Hierarchism *imposes a psychic effect on superiors to strive for very high standards of conduct.* Forgiveness of mistakes of juniors is an important way by elders. It makes occasional reprimand more acceptable. The superior or the elder in the family or the organisation stands as the symbol of character and morality. Obedience then follows from lower levels. Hierarchism is symbolic, as in joint family it passes to generations. Role of Karta is for guidance and protection in times of need.

(f) In some organisations hierarchical structure fosters tight supervision with narrow spans of control, which has its own advantages and disadvantages.

3. PURPOSES IT SERVES

It will be observed that system of hierarchy has large benefits such as *organising* activities, for effective *communication* up and downwards, for maintaining *discipline*, for *resolving* differences, for forgetting *mature guidance* and *protection* of sick in families and organisations.

CHAPTER

17

Personal Values of Children

One of the greatest gifts we can give our children is a strong sense of personal values. Helping our children develop values such as honesty, self-reliance, and dependability is as an important part of the education as teaching them to read or how to cross the road, etc.

The values we teach our children are their best protection from the influence of peer pressure and the temptation.

Why?

Living by certain tried-and-proven *standards* is the best route to personal happiness as well as to a stable and productive society.

When?

Values should be taught to children of all ages—
with differing agendas and changing emphasis as children mature.

Where?

Values are best taught in the home.

Who?

Parents are the crucial examplars and instructors.

What?

Each parent must decide which values to teach.

How?

There are some methods especially well suited to teaching values to pre-schoolers. Other methods work best for elementary ages, and still others are effective for adolescents.

VALUES TO IMBIBE

Some important values to imbibe children are as under:

(i) **Honesty** . . . with other individuals, with institutions, with society, with self . . . the *inner strength and confidence* that is bred by exacting truthfulness, trustworthiness, and integrity.

(ii) **Courage** . . . daring to *attempt difficult things that are good* . . . strength *not* to follow the crowd, to say *no* and mean it and influence others by it . . . being true to convictions and following good impulses, even when they are unpopular or inconvenient. . . boldness to be outgoing and friendly.

(iii) **Peaceability, calmness, peacefulness, serenity**. . . *the tendency to try to accommodate* rather than argue . . . the understanding that differences are seldom resolved through conflict and that meanness in others is an indication of *their* problem or insecurity and thus of their need for your understanding. . . the ability to understand how others feel rather than simply reacting to them . . . *control of temper.*

(iv) **Self-Reliance and Potential individuality**. . . awareness and development of uniqueness . . . taking responsibility for own actions . . . overcoming the tendency to blame others for difficulties . . . *commitment to personal excellence.*

(v) **Self-Discipline and Moderation, physical, mental, financial self-discipline** . . . moderation in speaking, in eating, in exercising. . . the controlling of one's own appetites . . . understanding the limits of body and mind. . . avoiding the dangers of extreme, unbalanced viewpoints . . . *the ability to balance self-discipline* with spontaneity.

(vi) **Fidelity and Chasity** . . . the value and security of fidelity within marriage and of restraint and limits before marriage . . . the commitments that go with marriage and that should go with sex. . . a grasp of the long-range (and widespread) consequences that can result from sexual amorality and infidelity.

VALUES OF GIVING

(vii) **Loyalty and Dependability** . . . to family, to employers, to country, church/temple, schools, and other organizations and institutions to which commitments are made. . . provide support, service, contribution . . . *reliability and consistency in doing* what you say you will do.

(viii) **Respect** . . . for life, for property, for parents, for elders, for nature, and for the beliefs and rights of others . . . *courtesy, politeness, and manners* . . . self-respect and the avoidance of self-criticism.

(ix) **Love** . . . individual and personal caring that goes both beneath and beyond loyalty and respect . . . love for friends, neighbours, even adversaries . . . and a prioritized, lifelong commitment of *love for family.*

(x) **Unselfishness and Sensitivity** . . . becoming more extra-centered and less self-centered. . . learning to feel with and for others. . . empathy, tolerance, brotherhood, *sensitivity to needs in people and situations.*

(xi) **Kindness and Friendliness** . . . awareness that being kind and considerate is more admirable than being tough or strong . . . the tendency to understand rather than confront. . . gentleness, particularly toward those who are younger or weaker. . . the *ability to make and keep friends* . . . helpfulness, cheerfulness.

(xii) **Justice and Mercy** . . . obedience to law, fairness in work and play. . . an understanding of natural consequences and the law of the harvest. . . a grasp of mercy and forgiveness and an understanding of the futility (and bitter poison) of carrying a grudge.

Reference

This is an extract from Linda and Richard Eyre, "Teaching Your Children Values", Fireside, New York-10020.

CHAPTER

18

Values of Indian Culture

INDIA: A MULTI-CULTURE NATION

India is said to be country of multi-cultures. It is because of long history of thousands of years. At different times different rulers ruled over the country. Further, at the same time there had been different rulers in different parts of India. The different rulers had different systems of governance and social practices. All these factors left a deep imprint on culture. As in olden days means of transport and communication were very poor; large number of languages, systems, habits, values developed which continue even today. These facts of history made India a multi-culture nation but as will be evident from later discussion the core values are same throughout the country. Thus, *there is unity in diversity*. But the diversity gave birth to ever increasing number of states. At present, there are 29 states and six union territories, each having its own culture and in some states there are more than one sub-culture.

In this chapter we have attempted to share some characteristics and traditions of Indian culture. It has both positive aspects and non-work elements. We have covered this under following headings:

(1) Values of Indian culture.

(2) Norms of behaviour in Indian culture.

(3) Factors influencing development of different cultures in India.

(4) Common core values in Indian culture.

(5) Cultural integration in India.

(6) Differences between Indian culture and western culture.

(7) Functionality and dysfunctionality of some characteristics of Indian culture.

(1) VALUES OF INDIAN CULTURE

Indians believe in *freedom of thoughts*, beliefs and experiences which has given birth to democracy, freedom of press, free communication, independent judiciary, freedom of choice of products as per one's preferences and freedom to enterprise to develop products, new technologies but not to exploit consumers who have been given freedom to complaint for deficiency in product or service. Indians believe in *spiritualism, faith and luck*. Values of Indian culture are given in Figure 1.

FIGURE 1

Values of Indian Culture

Values rooted in the deep in the Indian culture and society in Indian management context are as under. These are on the basis of Vedanta, Yogic psychology, Puranic literature and Buddhist literature. This is a compact profile of human values.

1. The individual must be aspected because of fevine in him.
2. Cooperation and trust.
3. Jealousy is harmful for mental health.
4. Purification of mind with noble thoughts of compassion, humility, gratitude and friendliness leads to accurate perceptions of human relationships and their contributing to sounder decisions.
5. Belief in top quality product/service which is due to quality of the mind or consciousness of the doer.
6. Work is worship. It can stimulate work ethic in a healthiest way.
7. Containment of greed because it cause stress and robs individual of wisdom.
8. Ethico-moral soundness gives peace of mind and promotes mental health.
9. Self-discipline and self-restraint because they conserve energy, strength, will power, confer dignity and create trust.
10. Customer satisfaction as he is divine in human garb.
11. Creativity to be cultivated through mind-stilling.
12. Inspiration to give because giving is fulfiling. It adds meaning to lives in society.
13. Renunciation and detachment from egoistic demands in the workplace, selfish results and rewards.

(i) These basic values must be relived by each generation and this is no child's play.

(ii) Four great Indians spanning the last ninety years from 1860 to 1950 are Tagore, Vivekananda, Gandhi and Aurobindo and are reliable and authentic guides to the true nature of Indian society and ethos.

(2) NORMS OF BEHAVIOUR IN INDIAN CULTURE

The norms of public behaviour is another important aspect of culture which relates to *public appearance*. For instance, in the west there is full freedom of dress specially at beaches, swimming pools, hotels, but too much exposure in India in dress is considered obscene and nudity in public or even in private is not permissible. In India, there is *respect for elders*. Disrespect of elderly persons is considered bad behaviour in India. Children specially sons are expected to look after their parents in old-age.

Another norm is *respect to women* in Indian culture and religion. No Pooja is complete without wife. But they enjoy lesser freedom of jobs and movement. But now gradually in urban areas women are taking to jobs making them more independent economically.

(3) FACTORS INFLUENCING DIFFERENT CULTURES IN INDIA

The various factors influencing different cultures are:

(i) Geographical Factors in Indian Sub-continent

India, being a country of many states and union territories, exhibits diverse cultures. Each state and in some cases different regions in single state have different culture. For instance, in U.P. even after division of the state there are different cultures in Bundelkhand, Ruhelkhand, East U.P. and West U.P. In Madhya Pradesh, Vidharbha has lot of cultural differences compared to rest of M.P. Rajasthan is one state but culture of Jaipur, Jodhpur, Udaipur, Bikaner, Jaisalmer, etc. have different distinct features. Culture of Assam, Bengal, Gujarat, Goa, Karnataka, Kashmir, Punjab, Haryana, Pondicherry, Mizoram, Nagaland, etc. differs widely from each other. Therefore, consumer preferences also differ and same policy cannot succeed every where.

(ii) Language

India is a multi-language country. There are 18 languages officially recognised in the constitution which are spoken or used in different parts of the country.

Besides 18 languages, English is official language in most private offices and for interstate correspondence, teaching of technical courses. There are also wide variations of languages from district to district in spoken language and if they are used by marketer in communication in person, and on radio they have greater impact on consumers and population at large.

(iii) Religion

Religion has great impact on culture and buying behaviour of consumers. In India, there are following major religions as per 2000 census. Religions: Hindus, Muslims, Sikhs, Christians, Jains, Buddhas. Every religion has its own values, faith, beliefs and greatly affect consumer behaviour.

(iv) Races and Ethnic Groups

India has large number of races like Dravidians, Aryans, Mangols and through immigration many ethnic groups have settled in India during British Rule; Anglo-Indian communities are found largely in Kolkata. There are Chinese who have settled in shoe business in Kolkata. Within Hindus there are large number of ethnic groups like Jats, Rajputs, Gujjars, Tyagi, Brahmins, Yadavs and so on. In Jains there are Agarwals, Oswals, etc. These groups have more affinities with the group and culturally they are near to each other and there are certain distinct features in their behaviour and customs. Then there are tribes and each tribe has its own customs and preferences. Customs of Sindhis are different than that of Parsis or others and each one of them has to be approached differently.

(v) Education

The level of education has great impact on the extent of development, knowledge, level of income. It also affects values, faiths and beliefs. A poor educated country has greater faith in superstitions and traditions and greater belief in luck, fate and god.

(4) COMMON CORE VALUES IN INDIA

Though there are wide variations in various cultural variables in the country, there are some core values which are common to all the cultures of India. These widely held beliefs, interests, feelings, relationships has brought similarity in diversity (variations) and unified the country. These core values should be properly understood for business.

(a) Tolerance

Tolerance is very fabric of all Indian cultures and our society is based on this principle. The co-existence of various religions, cultures, languages has been possible due to tolerance.

(b) Liberty and Equality

The principle of equality of sex, castes, religions, voting right and employment have been provided in various articles of the Indian constitution.

(c) Respect to Religious Leaders

The religious leaders are given great respect by followers of their religion. They are respected by every one irrespective of his economic and/or political powers. Many wealthy persons build places of worship, education and charitable institutions on their advise and interaction. All the big industrialists and politicians seek blessings of religious leaders and *sadhus*.

(d) Importance of Cross Culture

Indian society whether urban or rural feel that foreign goods, goods made by MNCs or with their collaboration by and large are better than other Indian product, hence, there is big market for smuggled products and services, they often have premium over Indian goods and are sought after. For the same reasons foreign brand names like Gillete, Surf, Palmolive, Colgate, Tide, Honda, Sony, LG, etc. are preferred.

(e) Faith in Superstitions

Indians by and large irrespective of level of education and income have great faith in superstitions. People normally do not buy goods made of iron on Tuesdays and Saturdays. They would prefer to make any big investment in Navratras and would not purchase during Pitra Paksha which is considered unauspicious. No new clothes, consumer durables, house and so on will be bought during this period. Therefore, for fifteen days sales come down and so the price of certain products. There are many symbols and numbers which are considered lucky or unlucky.

(f) Care of Tomorrow

Indians think more for tomorrow, they save good percentage of their income for future (around 22% in 2000-01) for their children education, marriage and life insurance, providend funds, bank deposits and like. Because of sense of insecurity people do not enjoy life and care more for their children than for themselves.

(g) Value of Time

In America, UK, Japan, etc. people are punctual and activities are held on schedule. But in India and many other countries it is a fashion to be late in social functions and marriages but Americans are irritated if one misses appointment or arrives late; the same applies to delivery. In USA or Japan the delivery must be strictly as per schedule otherwise food or service will not be accepted because it disturbs all their planning, same is the culture in many other countries. But there are many African and Asian countries for whom time is less valuable and they do not keep to the time.

(h) Persistance in Efforts

Effort is rewarded, competition is encouraged and achievement is paramount. Entrepreneurship is result of these values. They have optimism much more than in some other countries and spirit of competition much more than in east and in the socialist countries, but in some countries it is not every thing, someone will win and some one will loose. This spirit encourages to continue to make efforts and achieve one's mission.

In conclusion, it may be stated that basic core values are narrowing down in various countries through cultural interaction which has been made easy by revolution in transport, communication and information technology but still there are lot of cultural differences for which markets will have to be segregated.

(5) CULTURAL INTEGRATION IN INDIA

In a country like India, there are large *number of sub-cultures* like Bengali culture, Punjabi culture, Marathi culture, Gujarati culture, Malyali culture, Bihari culture and so on. These sub-cultures are due to various factors explained earlier, among which language, race, history, religion, region are some of the most important factors. But the greater interaction of people of various cultures, long period of stay in metros atleast children learn local languages, they develop taste for local food, dress and participate in festivals of the region though they continue to have affection with people of their culture. *English language* in India has influenced many sub-cultures and have brought them nearer to each other. When students of different sub-cultures study in same *school*, they learn other cultures and gradually two or more sub-cultures merge into each other.

The *art of communication* has also helped to bring various sub-cultures nearer to each other. In this respect Hindi films have played a very significant role which are viewed in all parts of the country. They have helped people of South India, Bengal, Gujarat or Assam, etc. to understand culture of North and it has helped to propagate Hindi language in all parts of the country and so the culture of North. However, with the settlement of people from Southern region in North, East and West and travel of people from these regions to South has made Bada, Dosha and Idli popular in all parts of India from Srinagar to Kolkata, Mumbai and even Assam. Similarly, *lassi* of Punjab or sweets of Bengal have become popular in other parts of the country. Chinese food shops have been established in vast numbers and people of various regions have developed taste for them. Chinese food has become delicacy. Italian pizzas and French fries have also become popular.

Print media, TV, internet and other such devices have also helped to bring various sub-cultures closer to each other and sub-cultural differences are narrowing down, but social and religious differences are keeping various cultures and sub-cultures away from each other whether it is India, USA, Arabs, European or Africans. Everyone feels himself to be superior and right because of which even now there are disputes and long political or military struggles. In India, more states have been divided on culture factors and demand is still going on for more states. Ethnic differences are quite strong in India.

(6) DIFFERENCES BETWEEN INDIAN CULTURE AND WESTERN CULTURE

Basis	*Indian Culture*	*Western Culture*
❑ Belief in faith and luck	Strong believers.	Do not believe in faith and luck. Rather believe that everything is possible through hard work and efforts.
❑ Belief in spiritualism	Indians believe in spiritualism.	Westerners believe in materialism.
❑ Public appearance	Exposure of body in dress strongly objected to and considered obscene.	Fashionable clothes even exposing they may be are 'in thing' in west.
❑ Care of old people	Sons are expected to take care of their parents.	Old parents are not cared for. They have to look for old persons' homes.
❑ Respect for women	No religious ceremony is complete without wife. Woman is given respect in traditional sense.	Women are looked as an object of pleasure.
❑ Freedom to women	Lesser freedom of doing jobs and movement.	Women are very free in every aspect.

(7) FUNCTIONALITY AND DYSFUNCTIONALITY OF SOME CHARACTERISTICS OF INDIAN CULTURE

India has old cultures, which have functional (pro-democratic or pro-equity or positive aspects) as well as dysfunctional (non-work, non-equity) characteristics. We here quote learned Prof. Udai Pareek about the elements of Indian culture. He has stressed that "culture of an organisation can give it competitive advantage, provided it is rooted in the functional aspects of the country's culture. This should be accompanied by the development of new functional values to keep the organisation pro-active, as well as to empower individuals and teams to achieve results." Functionality and dysfunctionality of some characteristics of Indian culture are mentioned in Table 1.

TABLE I

Functionality and Dysfunctionality of Some Characteristics of Indian Culture

Aspects of Culture	*Functionality (Positive aspects)*	*Dysfunctionality (Non-work aspects)*
1. Fatalism	(i) High realism. (ii) Awareness of constraints.	(i) Individuals and groups become passive, reactive and tolerant of dysfunctionalities. (ii) High level of superstition. (iii) Lower self-confidence. (iv) Low urge for change.
2. Ambiguity tolerance	(i) Development of role flexibility.	(i) Low respect for structure and time.
3. Contextuation	(i) Better insight into social complexities. (ii) Empathy for deviation/deviants. (iii) Sensitivity to others (including groups). (iv) Quicker understanding of contexts.	(i) Delay in developing common norms and procedures. (ii) Confusion in interpretation of some facts.
4. Present-orientation	(i) High involvement in current activity. (ii) 'Here and now' focuses on current problems.	(i) Lower long-term perspective. (ii) Poor in long-term planning. (iii) Low commitment to future goals.
5. Collectivism	(i) Maintenance of good relations. (ii) High potential for collaboration. (iii) More frequent consensus. (iv) Shared work and reward. (v) Strong sense of belonging.	(i) Lack of initiative by individuals. (ii) Slow development of identity.
6. Particularism	(i) High identification with group.	(i) Low objectivity. (ii) Favouritism (iii) Clique formation

Source: Udai Pareek, Cultures as Competitive Advantage.

References

http://www.globalsources.com

Peer J. Dowling, Denice E. Welch and Randal S. Schuler, "International Human Resource Management", South Western College Publishing, Cincinanati.

Udai Pareek, "Cultures as Competitive Advantage", in *Designing and Developing Organisation for Tomorrow*, edited by Anup R. Singh, Rajan K. Gupta and Abad Ahmad, Response Books, New Delhi.

CHAPTER

19

Concept of Culture and Types of Corporate Culture

In this chapter on "Concept of Culture and Types of Corporate Culture", the following aspects are covered:

(i) Role of culture.
(ii) Meaning of culture.
(iii) Components of culture.
(iv) Characteristics of culture.
(v) Precursors of culture.
(vi) Effects of culture on individuals and organisations.
(vii) Types of corporate culture.
(viii) Effectiveness of organisation culture.

(I) ROLE OF CULTURE

IRCON International Ltd., a leading public sector company—Indian Railway Project Construction Corporation adopts a policy of appointing only top personnel from India and other staff from host country in case of foreign assignments. Why is it so? Anil Jain, a senior executive gives the reason as—greater understanding of the country by the local personnel. This understanding relates to the understanding of the people, their customs, norms and systems of the country. But here comes one more problem—the top management personnel from the home country have to supervise the host country staff. This is a major problem because the living and working patterns of both the countries are different. The only solution to this problem according to Anil Jain is making the Indian personnel at the top aware of the culture of the host country. This is because of it that is the culture of the country has bearing on the conduct of business in every functional area.

Internationalisation of businesses has posed new challenges for the organisations. The major challenge that is faced by any global business house today is that of handling diversity in the cultures. At the root of this diversity are the cultural aspects of the nations.

(II) MEANING OF CULTURE

Culture, today, is being defined as an intellectual or moral discipline and training, a state of intellectual and artistic development or a historically transmitted pattern of meanings. Culture has also been described as a set of rules, values and beliefs—good or bad—which community adopts as its norm.

(III) COMPONENTS OF CULTURE

1. Communication

Some cultures are polite and gracious, others are demanding. Japanese are more non-verbal and we have to understand their total communication.

2. Language

Language can become a confusion or convey clear meaning.

3. Dress and Appearance

Dress and appearance identify culture. Arabs wear particular type of dress.

4. Food Habits

Food habits typify a culture, for example, Pizza is cherished in Italy, Dosa in India.

5. Time

Time consciousness from punctuality of Japanese or Americans to flexible attitude towards time of Arabs and Indians.

6. Rewards and Recognition

Rewards and recognition differ from country to country, for example, giving 15% of fare tip to taxi driver in USA is customary, in India it is optional.

7. Values and Norms

Values and norms, e.g. attitude towards corruption vary in Germany and Italy.

(IV) CHARACTERISTICS OF CULTURE

The culture is associated with following characteristics:

1. Culture is Learnt

Culture is acquired through experience and learning. People learn culture of a group when they become members. Children are born into a family and are taught the values and norms of that family and society.

2. Culture is Shared

People who are members of particular groups, organisations, and societies share a particular culture; it is not specific to a single individual. These groups include family groups, occupational groups, regional groups and national groups.

3. Culture is Transgenerational

Culture is passed on in the cumulative process from one generation to the next, from parents to children, from teachers to pupils and similarly in organisations. This process is called socialisation.

4. Culture is Symbolic

Culture depends upon individual's capacity to symbolize or to use one thing to represent another.

5. Culture is Patterned

Culture processes structure and is integrated. Change in one aspect of culture causes changes in another.

6. Culture is Adaptive

Culture depends on human capacity to adapt to change.

7. Culture is Descriptive

Culture defines the boundaries of different groups. These boundaries act as demarcations for characterising those groups.

8. Culture has Historical Dimension

A particular nation's *culture develops over-time* due to history, economic development, etc. A warm climate, for example, limits inhabitants to a completely different life style than a cold climate. The *societal norms* that develop over-time lead to the development of institutions such as family patterns, religious, political and legal systems which reflect these shared ways of acting and thinking. For example, social inequality is more generally accepted in France than in Netherland.

9. Finally, Culture has Different Layers

Hofstede (1991) mentions four levels of culture:

(a) First level consist of *symbols*, e.g. words, gestures and objects that carry a particular meaning for the members of a society such as country's flag, its national anthem.

(b) *Heroes* constitute the *second level* of culture. This refers to persons that are highly prized in society and who may serve as role models.

(c) *The third level* of culture consists of *rituals*. These are social norms that need to be followed. For example, how we greet friends, etc. which may differ from one nation to other nation.

(d) *The deepest level* of culture distinguished by Hofstede consists of *shared values* which represent collective beliefs and feelings what is good, rational and valuable. We normally take values for granted. We become aware of own values when we meet people from other cultures with different set of values. We normally consider our values as most appropriate. In international collaboration such a belief increases the potential for conflict.

(V) PRECURSORS OF CULTURE

The constituents or rather the precursors of culture are the interrelated concepts of beliefs, values, attitudes and behaviour.

Here, one factor leads to another in sequence but the feedback loop is multifaceted, indicating that consequences of a given behaviour will have implications for each of the precursors, which in turn define culture. Each of these factors can be understood as under:

1. Beliefs

One's beliefs are the result of direct observations as well as from inferences that are drawn from previously learnt relationships. One's belief system is the cognitive representation of one's relevant environment, complete with right-or-wrong, good-or-bad, and cause-and-effect relationships. The Principle of Belief Congruence holds that we tend to value a given belief or a belief system in direct proportion to the degree of congruence with our own belief system, and we tend to value individuals with respect to the degree to which they exhibit beliefs and belief systems congruent with our own.

2. Values

A value is "an enduring belief that a specific mode of conduct or end-state of existence is personally or socially preferable to an opposite or converse mode of conduct or end-state of existence." A value system is "an enduring organisation of beliefs concerning preferable modes of conduct or end-states of existence along a continuum of relative importance." Thus, a value is comprised of one or more *centrally-important* and *enduring beliefs*.

Values have a considerable influence on the *identity and role* of individual rights and duties as opposed to collective ones. For example, in most Western European countries and North America children are raised to be self-sufficient as adults. Children are taught to take their own decisions and solve their own problems. This *reflects individualism*. In contrast, in other societies children are taught that they belong to extended family and they owe their loyalty. Similarly, property in western society belongs to individuals while in others it is shared with other members of the group.

3. Attitudes

An attitude is "a learned predisposition to respond in a consistently favourable or unfavourable manner with respect to a given object." Attitudes are based on central belief and value systems.

4. Behaviour

Beliefs lead to values that, in turn, are predispositions to behave in a certain prescribed manners. Therefore, belief and value systems are maintained by the consistency of behaviour that is predisposed by the person's strongest values. If the behaviour results in positive consequences, that feedback will reinforce and strengthen the person's related beliefs, values, and attitudes; and the person will acquire even greater predisposition to behave in that manner again. If, however, the behaviour results in negative consequences, the person's related beliefs, values and attitudes will be weakened; and the person will be less disposed to behave in that manner again.

Hence, the combined relationship between beliefs, values, attitudes and behaviour may be seen as components of culture.

(VI) CULTURE: ITS EFFECTS ON ORGANISATIONS

The culture of the society comprises the shared values, understanding, assumptions, and goals that are learned from earlier generations, imposed by present members of the society, and passed on to succeeding generations. This shared outlook results, in the large part, in common attitudes, codes of conduct, and expectations that sub-consciously guide and control certain norms of behaviour. One is born into a given culture and then gradually internalizes its subtle effects through the socialisation process. Culture results in the basis for living grounded in shared communication, standards, codes of conduct, and expectations. These differences result from societal, or socio-cultural variables of culture, such as religion and language, in addition to prevailing national variables, such as economic, legal, and political factors.

Cultural Diversity and the Work Organisation

Initially, national culture shapes the organisation through values, attitudes which leaders bring into the organisation. They will shape organisation according to dominant preferences, norms and values of that environment. For example, a society characterised by distinct inequalities of the son-parent, pupil-teacher, it is anticipated the work organisations will also reflect this tendency. In most Asian countries, it is common to accept the authority of one's elders. So superior-subordinate relationship in the organisation are also characterised by a larger power distance and by centralisation of authority.

In a second way, national culture shapes the organisation through institutions in that country, such as democratic or dictatorship. For example, participative legislation which grants employees a say in organisational decision-making may be reflection of shaping of power and influence in that country which is democratic.

(VII) TYPES OF CORPORATE CULTURE

Corporate culture can be of various types, as it has common characteristics:

(a) Bureaucratic Culture

An organisation that values formality, rules, standard operating procedures and hierarchical coordination has a bureaucratic culture. Tasks, responsibilities and authority for employees are clearly defined. The organisation's rules and processes are spelled out in manuals and employees believe their duty is to follow them.

(b) Clan Culture

Tradition, loyalty, personal commitment, extensive socialisation, teamwork, self-management and social influence are attributes of a clan culture. Loyalty is rewarded by security. Because the individuals believe that organisation will treat them fairly in all respects and aspects. Long-time clan members serve as mentors and role models for the newer members. This type of a culture, members share a sense of identification and recognise the interdependence.

(c) Entrepreneurial Culture

High levels of risk taking, dynamism and creativity characterise an entrepreneurial culture. There is a commitment to experimentation, innovation and being on the leading edge. Individual initiative, flexibility and freedom foster growth and are encouraged and well rewarded.

(d) Market Culture

The achievement of measurable and demanding goals, especially those which are financial and market-based (eg., sales growth, profitability and market share) characterize a market culture. Hard-driving competitiveness and profit-orientation prevail throughout the organisation. Market culture is often tied to monthly, quarterly and annual performance goals based on profits.

(VIII) EFFECTIVENESS OF ORGANISATION CULTURE

Organisational culture has the potential to enhance *organizational effectiveness, individual satisfaction*, the *sense of certainty* about how problems need to be handled and so on.

A strong organisational culture facilitates *goal alignment*. The idea is that because all employees share the same basic assumptions, they can agree what is to be achieved. A strong culture leads to high levels of employees' motivation. A strong culture is better able to learn from its past.

The rationale of attempting to change the culture is to create a more effective organisation.

References

Helen Deresky, International Management: Managing Across Borders.
Manab Thakur, Concepts of International Management.

CHAPTER

20

Building and Maintaining Organisation Culture

In this chapter on "Building and Maintaining Organisation Culture", we have attempted to share some vital aspects of the organisation culture:

1. Meaning of organisation cultue.
2. Advantages of organisation culture.
3. Organisation culture as a technique in OD.
4. Characteristics of organisation culture.
5. Elements of organisation culture transmitted to employees.
6. How organisation culture starts in an organisation.
7. Socialisation process—familiarisation with organisation culture.
8. Maintaining organisation's culture.
9. Can organisation culture be altered or realigned?
10. Is corporate culture now in crisis?
11. Steps for rebuilding organisation culture in highly turbulent competitive environment.
12. Shaping organisational culture. (Box 1)

1. MEANING OF ORGANISATION CULTUE

(i) Organisation culture is a *common perception* held by the organisation's members. Organisation culture is the shared understandings of norms, values, attitudes and beliefs—of an organisation, which can foster or impede change. It is a system of shared meaning. An understanding to employees of "the way things are done here." Organisation culture conveys the ways in which "people work and think."

"An organisation's culture consists of the shared values and common assumptions held by the people within the organisation." In dynamic organisations, these values and assumptions drive behaviours that create value for the organisation's major stakeholders, be it customers, employees or other groups such as suppliers, etc.

(ii) Organisation culture may be referred to pattern of beliefs, values and learned ways of coping within an organisation. These are visible in structures and processes of the organisation and the ways its employees behave.

The strong, widely recognised corporate culture is frequently cited as a reason for the success of such companies as IBM and Procter and Gamble. A company's predominant culture may change quite rapidly or be forced by competition into change. Vijay Sathe has shown that culture's durability and efficiency represent both an asset and a liability for an organisation, and a smart manager must learn when to stop perpetuating a culture that is unresponsive to the needs of business. In such circumstances Chief Executive may institute a change in overall organisational culture, which involves not merely structural and technological change, but also change in shared symbols, rituals and beliefs.

2. ADVANTAGES OF ORGANISATION CULTURE

It has came to be realised that corporate culture is important to corporate growth, success, excellence and survival. It has motivating effect on employees. Culture influences an organisation's competitiveness over time. It can make organisation more effective. If developed to be a strategy for organisation effectiveness, which OD aims at. It has various advantages for the organisation such as:

(i) Organisation culture is necessary to adapt for changes arising due to competition.
(ii) Values and beliefs provide a sense to common direction, energy and guidelines for day-to-day behaviour. Common bond promotes emotional and social cohesion and establishes sense of identity. Values provide a spirit and drive for achievement. Values also provide guidelines for employees for taking decisions.
(iii) It influences every one's perceptions of business and accepted ways of behaving.
(iv) Strong and positive culture give many benefits to companies. It leads to high morale, sense of commitment and organisation pride. Strong cultures are core values (shared by majority) are intensely held and widely shared.
(v) Variations in cultural values has significant impact on employee turnover and job performance.

Any organisation that wants a lead over its competitors, therefore, needs to have a clearly defined, *commonly shared set of values* which guide the stakeholders in all their actions and decisions. If these are not in place, the decentralised organisation may well become the disintegrated organisation.

3. IMPORTANCE OF ORGANISATION CULTURE AS A TECHNIQUE IN OD

1. Background

In USA, during 1980s, CEOs were successful in taking over a firm that had problems, by cutting the work force and rebuild organisation to be effective. However, during 1990s, much different approach has followed for survival a growth of an organisation:

(a) Create pride and enthusiasm in *the firm;*
(b) CEOs worked as *role models* to direct and work long hours to attain goals;
(c) Encouraging *positive way* how things can be done efficiently and differently;
(d) CEOs *shared* in meeting with managers to turn out best programme; and
(e) To *look after the best people* and place them best suited jobs, so as to encourage team work and creative ideas, etc.

Thus, various aspects which influenced culture were initiatve, trust, support and innovation. *One culture is usually typified* by quality of excellence, high quality, openness in communication, participation in decision-making, high standard of safety, good corporate citizen, emphasis on new technology, modern management trends.

The other extreme type culture can be devoid of initiative and flexibility, lack of discipline, *chalta hai* mentality, mere conformity to rules rather than ends.

4. CHARACTERISTICS OF ORGANISATION CULTURE

Stephen P. Robbins has stated that the following seven primary characteristics, capture the essence of an organisation culture:

(i) The degree to which employees are encouraged to be *innovative and risk-taking.*
(ii) Degree of expected *precision and attention to detail.*
(iii) Degree to which management focuses on *result orientation* rather than techniques and processes.
(iv) Degree to which management has *people orientation*—its decisions effect of outcomes on employees.
(v) Degree to which activities are organised on *team work* rather than individuals.
(vi) Degree to which people are *competitive and aggressive* rather than people are easy going.
(vii) Degree to which organisation activities emphasise *on stability* (maintaining *status quo*) in contrast to growth.

These characteristics exists on a continuum from low to high. How things are done in organisation and the way members are supposed to behave.

FIGURE I

How Organisation Culture Effects Performance and Satisfaction

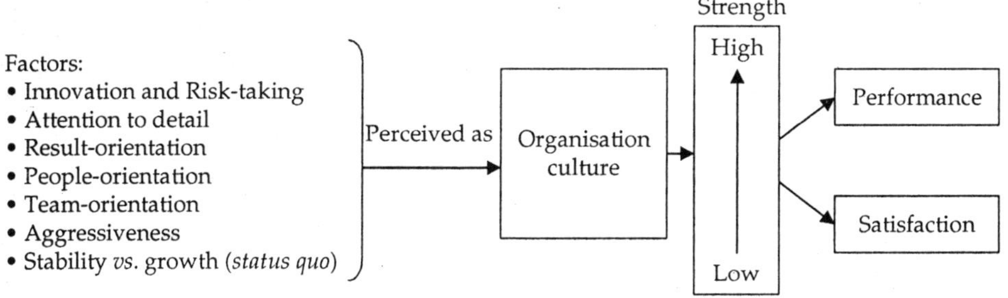

How organisation culture effects the performance and satisfaction of employees? We have observed that seven characteristics highlighted by Stephen P. Robbins (Organisation Behaviour) are the essence of organisation culture. These characteristics exists on a continuum from low to high. If those characteristics are appraised as high by the employees then they perceive the organisation's culture as favourable. Their common perceptions then affect employee's performance and satisfaction as high. This is depicted in Figure 1 on previous page.

5. ELEMENTS OF ORGANISATION CULTURE TRANSMITTED TO EMPLOYEES

Employees learn organisation culture in number of forms, the most potent being values, rites and rituals, stories, heroes, etc.

(a) Values

Values are core of the culture. Both values and beliefs provide guidelines for employees to follow in their work. Values provide sense of direction and shape behaviour. They indicate what matters are to be attended carefully.

Few examples of Credo's in organisations are: Cater Pillar (USA) committed to customers "in 24 hours parts service anywhere in the world." Larson and Tubro (India)—"People are prime movers." Bill Gates (USA)—"Computer on every desk and every house." TERI (India)—"Faith in youth and tap the youth."

(b) Heroes

Heroes personify these values. Manager's provide as role-models for employees. They set the standards of performance and dress norms as formal codes of behaviour.

(c) Rites and Rituals

If culture and values are to thrive (and not die) these must be ritualised and celebrated repeatedly. These rituals may be of different types such as social rituals, work rituals, management rituals, recognition rituals, etc. For example, some companies celebrate their annual day function on regular basis and publically recognise outstanding performers at these functions which serves as motivator.

(d) Setting-up of Cultural Network for Communication

These are story tellers, priests, gossips. This network reinforces the values of the organisation. Some jargon and jokes are only understood by insiders. These elements are manifestations of organisation culture and new people have to learn them. When employees interpret the meanings of these, their beliefs, perceptions, experiences constitute culture. During the days of Henry Ford II when he was Chairman of the Ford Motors Company, it was famous story reminding his executives. When one got too arrogant with the chairman, he would point that "It is my name that is on the building." The message was clear: Henry Ford ran the company!

6. HOW ORGANISATION CULTURE STARTS IN AN ORGANISATION?

Some steps commonly adopted by organisations in starting and maintaining their culture are indicated in Figure 2.

FIGURE 2

Starting, Formation and Maintaining of Organisation Culture

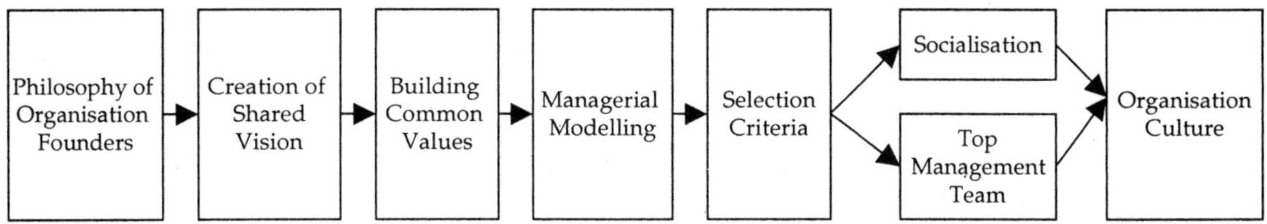

These steps are elaborated as under:

(i) Schein has emphasised the role of the founder in creating organisation value (culture) in his book *Organisation Dynamics*, 1983. Founder has an idea for new enterprise. Leadership behaviour sets the culture tone. *They formulate a statement of organisational philosophy* and communicate to employees. A particularly deep intervention is E.H. Schein's *"cultural analysis."* It probes deeply into the organisation:
   (a) Artifacts (such as symbols, modes of dress, office layout),
   (b) Values behind artifacts, and
   (c) Cultural assumptions in group meetings.

   Some contemporary examples of founders who had an immeasurable impact on their organisational culture would include Bill Gates at Microsoft, Akio Moritra at Sony, David Packard at Hewlett Packard, Naraina Murty at Infosys and Azim Premji at WIPRO.

(ii) *Creation of a Vision*: Transformation leadership *creates a vision*. He provides *mission* and *mobilises commitment* and support.

(iii) Takes key people and creates a core group that *share a common vision*, mission, values, goals and strategies so that it is institutionalised and become reality.

(iv) Founding group *acts in concert* to create an organisation culture. They *adhere* faithfully to the values.

(v) Involving of others' employees and common values begin to be *built and solidify*. Organisation's values are in various areas such as—relationships to customers, social responsibility, managerial style are focused.

(vi) *Managerial modelling behaviour* strongly influences the employees.

7. SOCIALISATION PROCESS—FAMILIARISATION WITH ORGANISATION CULTURE

New employees are unfamiliar with the organisation culture. The new employees are thus potential who may disturb the beliefs and customs of a new place. The organisations, therefore, want to help new employees to *adapt to its culture*. This adaptation process is called *socialisation*.

The most critical socialisation stage is at the time of entry into the organisation. This is when organisation seeks to mold the outsider into an employee, i.e. its standards and norms. Socialisation can be conceptualised as a process made of 3 stages—*pre-arrival, encounter, metamorphosis*. (Maanen and Schein) (See Figure 3).

FIGURE 3

A Socialisation Model

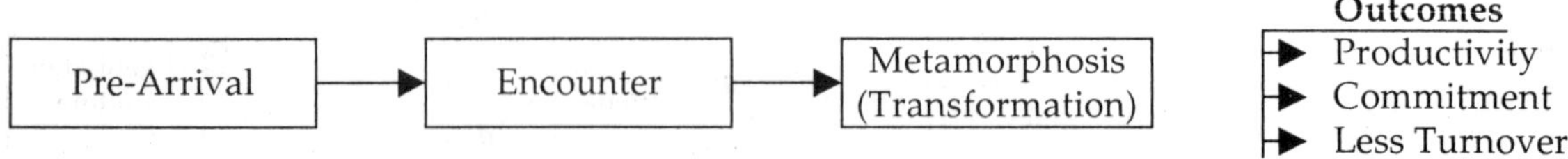

(i) Pre-Arrival Stage

It is process that occurs before new employee joins the organisation. The success depends on the degree *new candidate* has correctly *anticipated* the expectations and desires of selection members. Those type of people should be selected, who will fit into organisation culture.

One major purpose of a business school is to socialise business students to the attitudes and behaviours that business firms want. Management students should value the will to work, loyalty, desire to achieve and willingness to accept directions from superiors, then firms can hire executive from business schools, who have been pre-moulded in this pattern.

(ii) Encounter Stage

This is a stage in socialisation process in which new employee sees what the organisation is really like and *detatch his previous assumptions* and replace them with another set that the organisation deems desirable.

(iii) Metamorphosis Stage

This is a process in which a new employee *adjusts* to his work group values and norms. He has become comfortable with the organisation and his job. He is now committed to the organisation and productivity increase.

8. MAINTAINING ORGANISATION'S CULTURE

Once organisation culture is build, various steps of socialisation are given below. These steps are also explained in Figure 4.

(a) *Selection Criteria*: *Selection of entry-level personnel.* Using standardised procedures and seeking specific traits that lead to effective performance and candidate will fit into the organisation's team-oriented culture.

(b) *Socialisation—the process that adapts employees to the organisation's culture: Placement on the Job itself.* Exposure to different experiences whose purpose is to cause them to question the organization's norms and values and to decide whether or not they can accept them.

(c) *Job Mastery*: Once the initial "cultural shock" is over, the next step is mastery of one's job. This is done via extensive and carefully reinforced field experience.

(d) Measuring and rewarding indvidual performance and matching employee's values to those of the organisation. The actions of top management have a major impact on the organisation culture as to what actions will pay-off in terms of pay raises, promotions and other rewards.

FIGURE 4

Steps in Maintaining of Organisation Culture

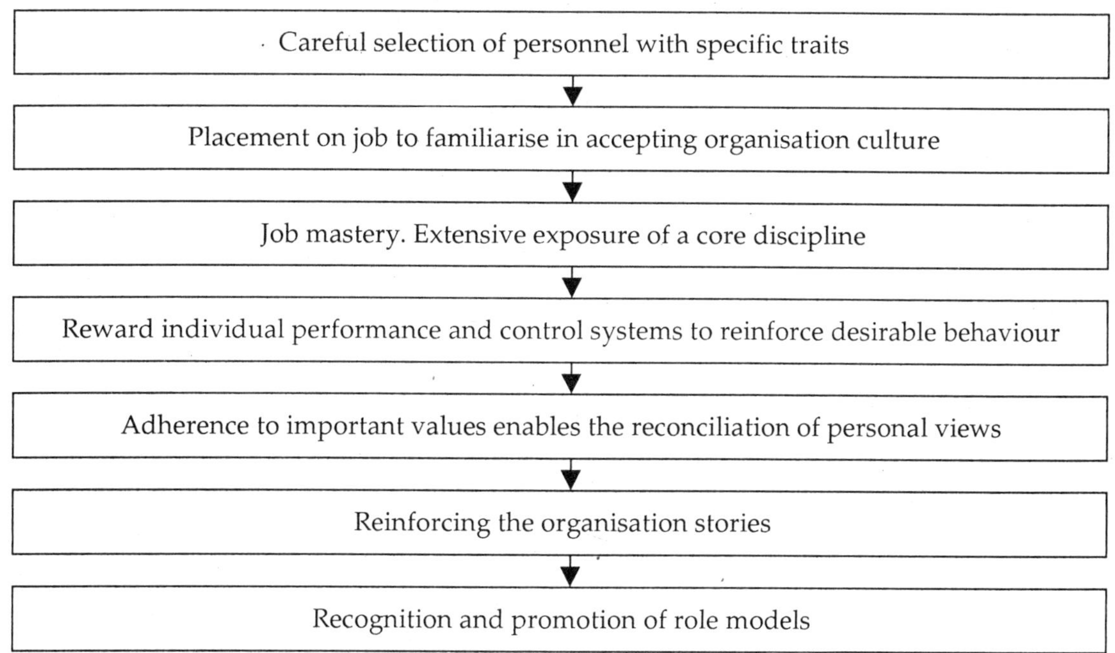

9. CAN ORGANISATION CULTURE BE ALTERED OR REALIGNED?

Organisation culture can be altered. It can be managed and realigned to the strategic direction an organisation wishes to take. Bate (1995) argues that, within organisations, culture is a *dynamic, continuously developing phenomenon.* If managers can manage organisations' cultures they can change culture and also prevent its change as well as abandon or destroy it (Ogbonna, 1993). We explore possible frameworks for managing both gradual or developmental change and more radical or transformational change to a new culture.

Frameworks for Managing the Change

Lewis (1996) reviews a range of frameworks for managing cultural change. One of the most widely quoted of these is Lewin's (1952) three steps of unfreezing, moving and refreezing. Lewin's framework emphasises that before an organisation can be transformed to a completely new culture, the embedded culture must be unfrozen and made more susceptible to change. Subsequent to the change his framework highlights the importance of stabilising and institutionalising the new culture, in Lewin's words refreezing.

Cultural change can occur from within an existing organisational culture or be influenced by wider societal and national cultures. Strategies for cultural change can be either top-down or bottom-up approach.

10. IS CORPORATE CULTURE NOW IN CRISIS?

Even in the beginning of new millennium the "corporate culture" had become widely accepted term in business.

Commonly shared values and assumptions are important, but are of no use, if they are just a set of phrases and sayings that are written down, but not actually practised, by each and every person in the organisation. In fact, when an organisation pays only lip service to its values, the management of organisation loses credibility and faith not only within, but also outside the organisation.

Terrence E. Deal and Alian A. Kennedy have now focussed that the *corporate culture landscape has shifted*. In some corporations traditional cultural pattern have seriously eroded, e.g. GM, GE, Kodak, IBM, Woolworth. It is not easy to maintain a cohesive culture in the face of external flux and economic ups and downs. It is *difficult to balance* the conflicting demands of customers, shareholders and employees. So managers are bereft of ideas for where to turn.

(a) Factors Causing Crisis in Corporate Culture

According to them the corporate cultures are in crisis—due to following factors:

(i) *Shareholder's value* movement and the impact it has had on corporate decision-making.
(ii) Focus on *downsizing*, which has cut the soul of many corporations.
(iii) *Outsourcing* has emerged as new tool of cost-cutting when conventional cost-reduction approaches have begun to run out of steam.
(iv) How *corporate merger-mania* has forced the most—unlikely combinations on the work-forces which are still dealing from waves of cost-cutting of early 1990s.
(v) How *computerisation* (potentially a tool for relieving employees from drudgery), has instead violated employees from one another and made them *servants to machines*.
(vi) How *narrowing boundaries* of the world have thrown peoples together in *global work place*.

Combination of these factors have thrown traditional corporate cultures, replacing joy, commitment and loyalty with fear, alienation and self-interest.

(b) Need for Building New Corporate Culture

So they have stressed the need for rebuilding new corporate culture. So task is to rebuild cohesive cultures:

(i) *Importance of leadership*. In an effort to rebuild the cultural cohesion of business leadership role is vital. They can add momentum to a culture re-building.
(ii) It is essential to rebuild the *social context of work*, if *people are to be motivated* to give their best efforts to their employers. This is the challenge of decade.
   - Manager can begin the process of *redefining the work place* as a meaningful *human environment* with high potential for top productivity.
   - They can help to make work an attractive place to be.
   - Managers can recapture the spirit of employees and channel this energy into furthering the goals of the business. But they can do so only if they recognise the *mutual dependencies* of employees and employers and need to create a cultural milieu that benefits all. Managers who accept this challenge will become the business leaders of tomorrow.

II. STEPS FOR REBUILDING ORGANISATION CULTURE IN HIGHLY TURBULENT COMPETITIVE ENVIRONMENT

Terrence and Kennedy have suggested following steps:

(i) Making people *want to go to work*, by providing good *favourable compensation* and remove pay as demotivating factor.

(ii) Reasonable level of *job security*. Employers have created the problem of rampant job insecurity by their own actions. Although the promise of a job security for two years is hardly enough to allow workers to feel secure, even such a limited guarantee can make a much difference. All it takes on the part an employer is a little foresight and a willingness to be *fair to employees*.

(iii) Focus on *job content and job satisfacton*. Decentralisation of work can help in this aspect.

(iv) A *socially rewarding environment*:

- the first crucial element is *respect* for employee and feeling that *he is valued*,
- building *happy and productive* employees through fun and adventure (full of challenge) at work, and
- *fellowship at work*. Teamwork with similar values.

(v) Physically comfortable work environment:

- cleanliness, and
- *informal place for interaction* and socially friendly working environment.

(vi) Preparing to *live in globalised world*, such as *cross-cultural differences* and preparing to learn from others:

- Develop potential synergies to be gained from *understanding and using other's values, knowledge and experience*.
- Not to undermine foreign cultures and team members to work together.

(vii) Building a *learning environment at work*, e.g.:

- creating a knowledge-based environment,
- steps for individual learning and organisation learning, and
- knowledge people as the basis of future business.

Terrence and Kennedy have concluded with the observations that *business inevitably moves in cycles*. Americans are optimistic enough to balance and shake-off some of the recent excesses. The rebalance of business interests is needed to help restore some semblance of sanity to the work place. The ability to judiciously manage and balance the competing interests (of the stakeholders) is of vital importance. The need of any one particular stakeholder is best met by serving the needs of all the stakeholders. Also refer Box 1.

Box I

Shaping Organizational Culture

An organizational cultural reshapes in response to two major challenges that confront every organization. These are:

(i) External Adaptation and Survival

It has to do with how the organization will find a niche in and cope with its constantly changing external environment. It involves addressing the following issues:

(a) Mission and strategy: Identifying the primary propose of the organization selecting strategies to pursue this mission.
(b) Goals: Setting specific targets to achieve.
(c) Means Determining: How to pursue goals, including selecting an organizational structure and reward systems.
(d) Measurement: Establishing criteria to determine how well individuals and teams are accomplishing their goals.

(ii) Internal Integration

It has to do with the establishment and maintenance of effective working relationships among the members of the organizations. Internal integration involves addressing the following issues:

(a) Language and concepts: Identifying methods of communication and developing a shared meaning for important concepts.
(b) Group and team boundaries: Establishing criteria for membership in groups and teams.
(c) Power and status: Determining rules for acquiring, maintaining and losing power and status.
(d) Reward and punishments : Developing systems for encouraging desirable behaviours and discouraging undesirable ones.

An organizational culture emerges when members share knowledge and assumptions as they discover or develop ways of coping with issues of external adaptation in internal integration.

The national culture, customs and societal norms of the country also shape the culture of the organisations operation it.

CHAPTER

21

Ethical Theories

In this chapter on "Ethical Theories", the following aspects are covered:

1. Evolution of ethical theories.
2. Various theories.
   2.1 Greek ethics.
   2.2 Medieval ethics.
   2.3 Modern ethics.
   2.4 Teleological ethics theories.
   2.5 Virtue ethics theories.
   2.6 System development ethics theories.
3. Summary of beliefs and problems in five major ethical systems.
4. The nature of ethics—some challenges. (Box 1)

1. EVOLUTION OF ETHICAL THEORIES

According to Jack Griffin in his article on "Development of Ethics and Ethical Theory" he has mentioned that "there are three periods in history of ethics such as Greek period (500 BC-AD 500), the medieval period (AD 500-AD 1500), and modern period (AD 1500 onwards).

2. VARIOUS THEORIES

2.1 Greek Ethics

In this period the man who performed his *duties* as a citizen was regarded as good man. When an individual realizes that his conscience shows to him the rightness of same action, which other people regard as wrong, his reflection is likely to lead him to the fundamental problem of ethics. What is in an action that makes it right or wrong or what standard or test by which we discriminate good or bad actions. According to Greeks, *"Man is the measure of all things."* He decides for himself what is right and what is wrong and there is no other standard.

Socrates, Plato and Aristotle emphasised the need and importance of understanding the nature of goodness. The Stoics emphasised that *goodness is natural to man,* for the laws of morality are the laws of nature, perfectly rational and so comprehensible to human reason.

2.2 Medieval Ethics

More attention was given to the *inner aspect of morality* because of the spread of Christianity in Europe. It had changed the previous view of Greeks that ethics is a part of politics, but on the other hand, it encouraged to increase inner aspect of morality. But middle age did not encourage moral speculation and consequent development of ethical theory. The standard of right and wrong was according to *God's law in the Bible* and it was against any doubts.

2.3 Modern Ethics

Individualism crept over priest's preaching and church's principle. Human freedom and human accomplishment were given more importance than Christian revelation. According to some thinkers, the difference between right and wrong was merely subjective, depending upon the *attitude of the individual* making moral judgement.

There are different ethical theories or ethical frameworks in this period with which to approach ethical decisions.

(i) Relativistic Ethics

This states that moral stand varies with different circumstances. According to Joseph H. Boyett and Jimmie T. Boyett (The Guru Guide to Knowledge Economy) "the proponents of relativism hold that we cannot decide on matters of right and wrong, or good and evil. Things are rarely black or white—there are so many shades of grey. Relativism proposes that ethics are *'relative' to the personal, social and cultural circumstances in which one finds oneself.* Relativists are torn by ethical dilemmas, since they do not believe that truth can be discovered by soul searching. Professor teach relativism so that students guard against it.

Relativism holds that *every person has his own standard that enables him to make choices.* No one can make a moral judgement about another person's behaviour. So many variables affect behaviour that an outsider cannot possibly be privy to all the elements that went into making a decision. For example, role relativism distinguishes between own private selves and our public roles. The public roles call for a 'special' morality, which we separate from individual making the choices. The president of a fishing company may personally dislike the incidental killing of dolphins in his company's tuna nets, but as an executive, he must not let his feelings interfere with the best interests of the company."

(ii) Absolute Ethics

According to this, there is one universal and eternal moral code, changing circumstances of different opinions make no difference.

(iii) Deontological Theory

This theory states that the rightness and wrongness of an action depends on the action itself and not on the consequences it produces. They maintain that fulfilling obligations, following proper procedure "Doing the Right Thing" and adhering to moral standards determine the ethical values of actions. It maintains that *actions are morally right independent of their consequences.* It also covers that an action is right, if it conforms to terms agreed upon (Social Contract Theory).

Managers who follow internal process model of management stress dutiful compliance with standards of efficiency and make decisions by the book regardless consequences.

2.4 Teleological Ethics Theories

This holds the view that *rightness and wrongness of an action depends on its consequences or results.* Pleasantness or unpleasantness it causes. They maintain that good ends and/or results determine the ethical values of actions. It can be ethical egoism, i.e. that an action is good if it produces results that maximise a particular person self-interest. It can be *utilitarism,* i.e. an action is good if it produces greatest amount of satisfaction for greatest number of affected by the action. *Example*—Manager prepares vacation schedule after obtaining preferences from all employees. He maximises the pleasure of employees.

Example—If manager enforces health and safety standards at work, he is ensuring natural components of happiness.

Rational goal theory managers support teleological ethics. "All is well that ends well", regardless of means used to produce results.

2.5 Virtue Ethics Theories

Virtue ethics theories maintain that habitual development of *sound character traits* determines the ethical values of persons.

Persons with strong character have cultivated intellectual, moral, emotional and social virtues to achieve the self-discipline to do the right thing. Character provides moral foundation for one's actions.

Virtue ethics maintains that sound, balanced character, motivation and intention is more important than actual conduct and its consequences.

Three major types of virtue ethics theories focus on individual, work and professional character:

(a) *Individual Character Ethics* maintains development of human traits of nobility—such as courage, moderation, justice, gratitude, sense of humour, self-discipline, reliability, benevolence, caring, sincerity, understanding and wisdom—determine value of human ethical interactions.

(b) *Work Character Ethics* maintains development of traits of work such as:
Competence, creativity, honesty, fairness, trust-worthiness, appreciation, task completion, loyalty, resourcefulness, shared work pride, level-headedness, dependability, empathy, cooperativeness, supportiveness, tolerance.
These determine ethical quality of work life. As more and more occupations, including management, undergo process of "professionalisation", standards of work character ethics increase.

(c) *Professional Character Ethics* maintains the credentialed expertise, licensed monopoly, self-regulation, trust, truthfulness, impartiality, independence of judgement and public service of individual in associated community. There is *loyalty to a professional code of ethics.*

Adhere to your conscience. The human relations theory of management stresses interpersonal development and team-building skills as the criteria of flexible work communities. Managers who endorse this approach demonstrate virtue ethics.

This approach emphasises supporting character, development, facilitating, participative decision-making, foster win-win dispute resolutions and recognising employees contributions. Such managers endorse the dictum "Character counts" and avoid pressurising people to use means or achieve ends that violate their conscience.

2.6 System Development Ethics Theories

System development ethics theories maintain that the nature of *supportive framework* for continuous improvement of ethical conduct determines the ethical value of actions. Managers implement ethics development systems that will sustain integrity building environments. Managers who do not implement recognition process for exemplary moral conduct by employees or refrain from taking swift action against wrongdoers at work are guilty of both moral and managerial malfeasance.

The *open system theory* of management stresses innovative adaptability and acquisition of external resources as the criteria of effectiveness. And managers who support this approach exhibit system development ethics. In concrete terms for managers, this approach emphasises creative change management, resourcefulness, respectful negotiation and collaborative networking with diverse global interests. Managers who adopt this perspective encourage organisational flexibility to make organisation moral progress and manage ethically.

3. SUMMARY OF BELIEFS AND PROBLEMS IN FIVE MAJOR ETHICAL SYSTEMS

Jack Griffin (article on *Development of Ethics and Ethical Theory*) has given summary of beliefs and problems in the five major ethical systems in tabular form. (Figure 1)

FIGURE 1

Summary of Beliefs and Problems in the Five Major Ethical Systems

	Nature of the Ethical Belief	*Problems in the Ethical System*
Eternal Law	Moral standards are given in an Eternal law, which is revealed in Scripture or apparent in nature and then interpreted by religious leaders or humanist philosophers; the belief is that everyone should act in accordance with the interpretation.	There are multiple interpretations of the Law, but no method to choose among them beyond human rationality needs an absolute principle or value at the basis for choice.
Utilitarian Theory	Moral standards are applied to the outcome of an action or decision; the principle is that everyone should act to generate the greatest benefits for the largest number of people.	Immoral acts can be justified if they provide substantial benefits of the majority, even at an unbearable cost or harm to the minority; an additional principle or value is needed or balance the benefit-cost equation.
Universalist Theory	Moral standards are applied to the intent of an action or decision; the principle is that everyone should act to ensure that similar decisions would be reached by others, given similar circumstances.	Immoral acts can be justified by persons who are prone to self-deception or self-importance, and there is no scale to judge between "wills", an additional principle or value is needed to refine the Categorical Imperative concept.

Distributive Justice	Moral standards are based upon the primacy of a single value, which is justice. Everyone should act to ensure a more equitable distribution of benefit, for this promotes individual self-respect, which is essential for social cooperation.	The primacy of the value of justice is dependent upon acceptance of the proposition that an equitable distribution of benefits ensures social co-operation.
Personal Liberty	Moral standards are based upon the primacy of a single value, which is liberty. Everyone should act to ensure greater freedom of choice, for this promotes market exchange, which is essential for social productivity.	The primacy of the value of liberty is dependent upon acceptance of the proposition that a market system of exchange ensures social productivity.

Box I

The Nature of Ethics—Some Challenges

The nature of ethics (what does it mean) raises *tough challenges to ethics:* (i) Chief among them is the fact that almost everything we do seems to be driven by self-interest. (ii) Another is the ideas that selfishness (putting yourself first) is itself a duty, according to the prevailing wisdom of our competitive age. (iii) Finally, there is the problem that people disagree about what is right and wrong in ways that mirror deep religious and cultural differences. Together, these challenges to ethics encourages profound cynicism about ethics.

- Ethically speaking, there is big difference between acting out of *self-interest and acting selfishly*, and you should not mix them. A person can act out of self-interest and not selfish. For example, if I go to the dentist to fill a throbing cavity, it is in my self-interest (no more pain), but you cannot say it is a selfish thing to do.
- *Ethical egoism* says that we should only look out for ourselves. But where we would be if everyone did that. Children, elderly and other dependent people need others to look out for their interests. And guess what—we all have been (or will become) those dependent people. Question theories of human nature that suggest we are inherently self-interested. Do not assign greater weight to your own interests than the interests of other people.
- *Feel good* about doing morally good acts for other people. It is just one of the benefits of leading an ethical life.
- Remember that at one time or another, each and everyone of us will benefit from *other's charity* altruism.
- You should be self-interested; you should *not be selfish.*
- *Ethical subjectivity* is not a moral theory that tells us what is right or wrong, good or bad. It is a claim about the nature of moral judgements: that moral judgements are nothing more than *expressions of personal opinion*. That's all. *Do not accept* ethical subjectivity. Just because you believe something does not mean it is right. Ethical subjectivism makes you a moral expert on all issues. Because, according to this view, if you believe something right then it is right for you, and that is the end of story. The next person may believe something different, and that would be true for him. So there are no disagreements possible according to ethical subjectivists.

- *Moral objectivism* is the belief that morality is universal, eternal, and unchanging. For example, murder is always wrong, for all times and places.
- *Cultural relativism* (also called 'moral relativism') is the belief that morality is relative to each individual culture, and that we cannot make universal moral claims like "murder is always wrong". Be respectful of cultural differences, but be willing to criticize different cultural practices that do harm to people.
- *Do not accept the "majority rules"* approach to ethics: that what the majority thinks is right must be right. This cuts out the possibility of dissent and abandons individuals to their societies. Besides, sometimes the majority is wrong about things. So avoid "majority rules" approach to ethics as some times the majority is just plain wrong.

PART IV

INDIAN ETHOS IN MANAGEMENT

CHAPTER

22

Indian Ancient Ethos in Management

In this chapter on "Indian Ancient Ethos in Management", the following aspects are covered:

1. Ancient approaches relevant for managers.
2. Ethical standards (moral) drawn from philosophy and religions through ages.

I. ANCIENT APPROACHES RELEVANT FOR MANAGERS

Some Indian ancient vedantic approaches (vedantic) relevant for managers are as under. These are basic requirements for successful management:

1. *Holistic approach* to man. This is based on spiritual principle that entire humanity is one, and there is respect for all human beings. Managers to follow whole man approach of combining values and physical aspects of life (wordly life). Spiritual and wordly life are recognised. Higher consciousness will adopt holistic attitude.
2. Each person is a potential *divine human*. The divine means perfection in knowledge, wisdom and power. Therefore, a human being has immense potential power or energy for self-development. The goal of life is to manifest the divinity within through work or worship, meditation.
3. *Selfless work (Karmayoga)* as a basis for human action. Work is worship. Do your duty without ego and without calculation of fruits of action. Do your duty better and better. Work is important for personal growth and good of society.
4. Indian ethos give greater *emphasis on values*. It is value-based approach to management and doing right things.

Human and ethical value-based management is essential to combine subjective aspect (money, as well human skills), objective phenomena (inner resources of human beings, i.e. wisdom and work ethics). So development of inner potential, i.e. vision, insight, values are important for wisdom and character.

5. *Cooperation and team work* important for business success.
6. Excellence at work through self-motivation and self-development are best means of total quality management (TQM), i.e. perfection.
7. *Awaken and empower your people* to shoulder higher responsibility.
8. *Leader's love and inspiration* are important for dedicated effort by your people.
9. *Leader to entrust right job* for right man after knowing capabilities of his men.
10. Manager to *develop complete vision* (Jnanam) of entire organisation and its relations.
11. Manager to acquire *ability (Budhi) to understand problems* in imparting (sharing) vision to his men.
12. Leader must have extreme *patience* (Dhriti) to win his men and achieve the goal.
13. Meditation means *concentration* to withdraw mind into inner intelligence and then contemplating for highest goals.
14. *Self-control* is channeling our energies towards a purposeful end to achieve higher goals in life.
15. *Man-making education* can make a man of firm character, i.e. by strengthening his mind and he is not swayed by others. He is focusing on *character education* to developing morality, integrity and values for societal wellness.

The Bhagwad Gita is the repository of highest knowledge and is book of life in everyday living. The above are basic requirements in successful management.

(II) ETHICAL STANDARDS (MORAL) DRAWN FROM PHILOSOPHY AND RELIGIONS THROUGH AGES

Meaning of Ethics

Ethics is a set of standards, or a code, or value system worked out from human reason and experience, by which free human actions are determined as ultimately right or wrong, good or evil. If an action agrees with these standards, it is ethical, otherwise, it is unethical.

Ethical standards are set in attempt to reach an ultimate goal. As human goals change by human experience over time, ethical standards are changed or refined. Historically this has happened. For example, 'equality of men' and 'right to freedom are relatively new human goals'.

Some ethical standards through ages are as under:

1. Treat all men with fairness and justice.
2. Do to others as you would have them do to you.
3. Treat individuals with respect and dignity.
4. Love your neighbour as you love yourself.
5. Always ask whether my action, "will it hurt anyone"?

6. Know thyself—be always honest with yourself and with others.
7. Evaluate the morality of an action by examining into intention behind it.
8. Long range utility standard. So act that your act will produce maximum happiness in terms of consequences.
9. The law of general standard, i.e. your act could be made a general law for all towards the greatest good of the greatest number, i.e. utalitarian.
10. Where all alternative actions appear unethical (and action is unavoidable), then act which action is lesser evil.

CHAPTER

23

Core Values in Indian Culture

Though there are wide variations in various cultural variables in the vast country, there are some core values which are common to all the cultures of India which are as under:

1. Tolerance

The co-existence of various religions, cultures and languages has been possible due to tolerance of people.

2. Liberty and Equality

Principle of equality of sex, castes, religions, voting right and employment have been now provided in the various articles of the Constitution of India.

3. Respect for Religious Leaders

Even all big industrialists and politicians seek blessings of religious leaders, *sadhus* and priests.

4. Faith in Superstitions Irrespective of Education

Some examples are: There are many *symbols and numbers* which are considered lucky or unlucky. People believe in Vastu. People do not *buy goods* made of iron on Tuesday and on Saturday. Make investment in Navratras. No purchases during Pitra Paksha which is considered unauspicious.

5. Care for Tomorrow

Indian save good percentage of earnings for their children education, marriage, etc. They do not enjoy life because of sense of insecurity.

6. Value of Time is Less

It is fashion to be late in social functions, whereas in west people are punctual and activities are held on schedule.

7. Persistence in Efforts and Achieve one's Mission

We have belief that sincere effort is rewarded and achievement is paramount.

8. Belief in Faith and *Luck* is Strong.
9. Belief in *spiritualism* rather that Western Materialism.
10. Care of old people by family members.
11. *Respect for women.* No ceremony is complete without wife in a family.
12. *Less freedom for women* as compared to males children.
13. *Tolerance of ambiguity, lack of respect for time and structure.*
14. *Delay in developing common norms and procedures.*
15. Though believe in collectivism (good relations) but slow in development of *identity of group.*
16. Lack of *performance-based* culture.
17. There is *cultural integration* based on tolerance. Unity in diversity. India is land where there are sub-cultures as Marathi, Gujrati, Punjabi, etc. There are different races, e.g. Dravidian, Aryan, Parsies, etc. There are differences in religions, languages.

CHAPTER

24

Karma Yoga and Nishkam Karma

In this chapter on "Karma Yoga and Nishkam Karma", the following aspects are covered:

1. Meaning of karma yoga.
2. Features of karma yoga.
3. Detached involvement/nishkam karma and sakam karma.
4. Shivam satyam sundram.

1. MEANING OF KARAMA YOGA

Karma Yoga simply means, do your *duty without ego and without calculation of gain* or loss. Pour your heart and soul in the *performance* of your assigned duty. Work offers double benefit, personal benefit (self-purification, salvation personal growth and development) and social benefits (that is to society). Work is a form of sacrifice, a selfless work. *Focus on action,* not fruit. The fruit is nothing but the proper culmination of one's actions. Focus on the job alone.

Yoga means *excellence* at work, seek to perform your assigned duty or work in an excellent manner. It is perfection in work and quality of output. This leads to Total Quality Management. Ethics is based on most important element of activity. In Gita the call is to "Act in the living Present" that is Karma Yoga. Karma means action, duty or work done not with selfish motive but with the objective of serving humanity. A man's primary duty is to perform the job allocated to him with devotion and perfection, only then we can achieve salvation.

Thus, Gita gives new dignity to work. Work is not unpleasant activity or some sort of punishment, but a way of life, ordained by the Lord.

Work is something inherit in the nature of people. McGregor says the same thing that work is something inherent. Gita practices the *mantra* of Karma Yoga. It preaches devotion to duty, regardless of its consequences. Work is not only necessary to keep the body and mind occupied, it is necessary for perfection.

2. FEATURES OF KARMA YOGA

(a) No living being can live without performing actions.

(b) Karma Yoga prescribes to place action above ego as against the usual ego—centric action. Egoness is the root cause of our problems and sufferings. But the moment the ego is detached from action, it becomes spiritual action in objective reality. The Gita prescribes to *overlook the outcome of action,* but not the action.

(c) Karma Yoga is the *path of right action* and leads to harmony and solution to problems.

(d) The much talked doctrine of Karma Yoga is difficult to practise as it includes *controlling of senses* and overcoming desires.

(e) Karma Yoga is essentially wisdom in practice in daily life.

(f) The inner mind and inner aspect of man are important. Work must be done in right spirit and with *right attitude* and in perfect way. These are also the views of Divine Mother of Pondicherry.

(g) Action requires *determination.* Those who are of unstable mind and are attached to fruits of action are not determined. They cannot be good performers. Duty should be done without attachment and irrespective of consequences of action.

(h) Excellence can be achieved through Karma Yoga only. This would free you from anxiety and will attain you supreme bliss.

(i) Nishkama Karma Yoga (Self-Motivation) is the best route for self-development of all. Self-motivation can assure you self-development. In this process you grow and also other's grow. When everyone does duty towards others, everyone's rights are automatically assured. Work is performed without hatred, without arrogance and desire. Karma Yoga should also engage in welfare of the society.

(j) A person or society sensitive to its *obligations* is progressive and prosperous.

3. DETACHED INVOLVEMENT/NISHKAM KARMA AND SAKAM KARMA

(i) Nishkam Karma

The theory of Nishkam Karma is explained in Bhagwat Gita. It speaks about duty to act, but not the right to claim fruits from it. Trees, sun, rivers are the live examples of performance of full swadharma and not expecting anything in return. It helps in inner purification and realization of self. It is a bliss which external, relative and competitive reward can never bring.

(ii) Sakam Karma

Vedas have talked about Sakam Karma. Most of our lives in today's world are based on Sakam Karma. When we talk about eradicating malaria or small pox from planet, we all are talking about Sakam Karma.

In Gita, Sakam Sadhana is a spiritual practice done with the *expectations of worldly* achievements like a good job, a house, promotion at work, fame, wealth, etc. and Nishkam Sadhana is a spiritual practice done with the *sole aim of spiritual growth.* Thus, in this mode of spiritual practice, the spiritual seekers will continue with their spiritual practice. They ignore their current worldly state of being.

(iii) Nishkam Karma brings Spiritual Growth of Continued Bliss

In the energy that we invest in doing *nishkam spiritual* practice bear fruit, since it is utilized solely for spiritual growth. In the *nishkam mode*, the person's spiritual as well as material/worldly aspirations are fulfilled.

People experience worldly happiness by doing sakam spiritual practice, while they experience bliss by doing nishkam spiritual practice.

(iv) Sakam Spiritual Practice cannot give Permanance Peace

For example, suppose the person does spiritual practice to acquire a lot of wealth. Once he gets wealthy, he asks for good health, then, maybe, a good spouse, then he continues to do spiritual practice to have a child, and so on. Such a quest can never end, as there is always something yet to be fulfilled. Thus, one can never experience complete satisfaction from this *nishkam mode* of spiritual practice. However, in the mode of spiritual practice, once your sole aim of *spiritual progress is achieved, you realize your true self,* or become Self-Realized (God-Realized), and get permanent experience of continued Bliss.

(v) Sakam spiritual practice is about experiencing all creation or *created objects*, whereas nishkam spiritual practice is about *experiencing the Creator.*

(vi) In *nishkam karma*, the objectives are perfection, inner autonomy, work commitment, work is worship for excellence, and mind enrichment.

(vii) Whereas objectives of *sakam karma* are success, *reward*-based commitment, to earn praise, competitive rivalary for excellence work, and job-enrichment.

4. SHIVAM SATYAM SUNDRAM

These three words mean as under:

- Shivam is the life giver. It means consciousness. Life is one of the manifestations of consciousness in our mind, intellectual or the body.
- Satyam is truth, i.e. that which ever exists. It is imperishable and unchanging.
- Sundram is beautiful.

References

M.N. Kundu, *Hindustan Times*, New Delhi, 20.10.2003.

S.A. Sherlekar, *Ethics in Management*, Himalaya Publishing House, Mumbai.

CHAPTER

25

Concepts of Mahatma Gandhi

Mahatma Gandhi, the great karma yogi (action leader) of the 20th century, pride of India, was a motivator, leader, and general manager of the Independence India campaign. He writes, his mission—I have nothing new to teach the word, *Truth and Non-violence* are as old as hills. Gandhi's life was a straight line of work and prayer. He acknowledges his lifelong pursuit of truth. His name was among the ten top leaders of 20th century in the world.

Mahatma Gandhi still continues to be a role model to a countless many. Albery Einstein said: 'Generations to come will wonder that such a man as this ever walked upon this earth.' Jim Collins, author of famous book 'Built to last', says "one key concept in the context of Mahatma Gandhi is level 5 leadership." Level 5 leaders are a study in polarity in being both modest yet determined, humble yet bold. C.K. Prahalad adjudged world's greatest management thinker in 2007 says, "Mahatma Gandhi broke tradition. He understood that you cannot fight the English with force. So he decided to change the game in a fundamentally different way. He unleashed the power of ordinary people, inspired women and men in the country to fight under a unifying goal. Resource constraint did not bother him. He aimed at a common agenda : Poorna Swaraj."

HIS PRINCIPLES/CONCEPTS

Some of his favourite principles are as under:

(i) Non-Violence

Which is non-cooperation rather than using violent means in freedom struggle. The word "Non-Violence" is a translation of Sanskrit word "Ahimsa", which comes from Hindu scripture, Bhagwad Gita.

(ii) Trusteeship Theory

A new meaning to business, which says that all business belongs to the society and the owner is only a trustee of the business. The end of business must be happiness and welfare of the people. This is what corporate social responsibility is all about. In this, he got the support of the Birla's and the Bajaj's to fund the freedom movement.

(iii) Swadeshi

His political thoughts were connected to business. His call for Swadeshi was based on self-reliance and self-sufficiency. He wanted an enlightened interest of the country. Take the famous example of the textile mills, which were using Indian cotton and churning out cloth in England and selling it expensively to Indians.

(iv) Tolerance

It means participation and openness to divergence of ideas. You need to be a really good listener and hear all that comes your way. This is what networking is all about. Still, he had the capability to carry people with him. He delivered the results also. Gandhi gave us the concept of religious tolerance. He believed violence can never resolve any conflict.

(v) Managing Social Reforms

Gandhi was good at managing social reforms. If we see carefully, the process for freedom started only in 1930 and we were free by 1947, which is the fastest Independence in the World, 17 years. A short time if we compare to that of South Africa. He had lofty visions but manageable targets—dealing with untouchability, child marriage, etc.

(vi) Satyagraha

Gandhi said, "We must become the change we wish to see in the World". He discussed economic and political problems from a higher moral and humanistic point of view and started satyagraha movements. He galvanized the whole nation to gain independence. Whatever he did made an impact. Satyagraha or non-violent approach to conflict resolution and beauty of compromise : Here, the aim is not to hurt the opponent, but through love, persuasion, dialogue, meditation and self-suffering, to resist the wrong and uphold what one perceives to be truth and justice. Gandhi's satyagraha means satya and 'agrha'—firmness, openness, honesty, darkness, 'ahimsa' and 'tapasya'.

(vii) Ethics and Value

Truth and ahimsa (non-violence) are core principles of Gandhian ethics. He said: "For me, Truth is the sovereign principle, which includes numerous other principles. This truth is not truthfulness in word, but in thought." God is truth.

(viii) Collaboration

The Mahatma played the role of a collaborator, getting everyone to join forces and ideas. He played the role of getting people together at the leadership level and also with the masses. The Dandi March was of his collaboration skills, of getting people together as an example grass-root level. He had great net-working skills.

To conclude

We mention his seven social sins:

In 1947, a year before he was assassinated, M.K. Gandhi wrote what he called the seven blunders of the world:

(i) Wealth without work.

(ii) Pleasure without conscience.

(iii) Commerce without morality.

(iv) Politics without principles.

(v) Knowledge without character.

(vi) Science without humanity.

(vii) Worship without sacrifice.

CHAPTER

26

Sri Aurobindo on Ethics

Some important views on ethics by Sri Aurobindo are as under:

(i) *True ethical being* remains always same, i.e. having *character, self-discipline, self-mastry*. These are the first conditions of *human-perfection*. Ethics field is confined to character and action.

(ii) *Utilitarian ethics* leads to reduction of ethical action. *Good* (not utility) must be the principle. There is only one *safe rule* for ethical man, *to stick* to his *good conduct*.

(iii) In fact, ethics is not in its essence a calculation of good and evil in the action, it is an attempt to *grow into the divine nature*.

(iv) Our *greed breaks the harmony* of our life. We lose the true standard of values. Virtue comes to the natural man by a struggle with his pleasure seeking nature.

(v) *Moral side* represents control of desire. *Spiritual side* represents sympathy.

(vi) Man's *character and life of purpose* is life of the moral world.

CHAPTER

27

Indian Ethos on Leadership

In this chapter on "Indian Ethos on Leadership", the following aspects are covered:

1. Leadership qualities.
2. Teamwork.
3. Individual's characteristics.
4. Conclusion.

The Bhagwad Gita is the repository of highest knowledge and is book of life in everyday living, i.e. dynamic living. Here we give some ancient Indian approaches on leadership, team-working and human characteristics.

1. LEADERSHIP QUALITIES

Some roles and qualities required of leaders are as under:

(i) Janam (Vision)

Leader must develop *complete vision* (Janam) of the entire organisation, its aims and objectives, its place in the country and also in relation to other nations. Head of organisation must see unity in all functional divisions. The relationship between the parts and the whole must be understood very well.

(ii) Buddhi (Ability)

Discriminating and discretion. The chief should be capable of imparting his vision to all his workers at their own level of understanding and field of work. This *ability is Buddhi*. While translating this vision into reality there will arise many problems, difficulties and obstacles that may be objective or man-made as well. At such moments what is required is *Buddhi—the ability to understand the very cause of such problems* and to remove it effectively. *Buddhi* is required to manage two kinds of people: those who have difficulties and those who are difficult people. In order to do all this the Executive must have a good knowledge of the human mind.

(iii) Dhriti (Patience)

Dhriti means patience and fortitude. The ability to consistently hold on to your goal is called *Dhriti*. It is a well known fact that no goal is achieved easily and quickly. We meet with many obstacles which try our patience. Similar is the case when all workers are not able to see the vision and they act strangely enough as to frustrate even an effective leader. On all such occasions the leader must have *extreme patience to win them over and achieve the goal*. This ability is called *Dhriti*.

(iv) Right Person for Right Job

Another important point to be considered is that the success of a project depends on the *appointment of right persons for various jobs*. There will be diversity in jobs and functions but there should be unity in purpose and total dedication to it. The greater the goal and higher the inspiration, the more spectacular success will be. The way Lord Krishna managed the crisis at time of war, teaching Arjuna and then leading the Pandavas to victory, is proof of this fact.

The great Chanakya has said it well; a person should be engaged only in a job that he is capable of doing efficiently.

(v) Brain Stilling (Decision-making by leader in meditative silence)

Western management resorts to brain storming, i.e. loud thinking for decisions to solve problems. Indian insights advocates a better alternative in the form of brain stilling, i.e. silent mind is more effective medium to get sound solution to problems.

(vi) Combination of Value and Skills

A leader with proper combination of values and skills can assume harmony and progress of the organisation as well as of society. This is unique contribution of Indian ethos.

(vii) Listen, Listen, Listen more

Arjuna starts weakening. Arjuna starts mentally manufacturing cowardly thoughts of retreat from post of duty where destiny has called upon him to act. Fighting is Arjuna's *karma*.

Krishna listens to Arjuna and is silent as a statue. Arjuna does not want to start the battle. Krishna listens. Krishna is silent. Arjuna goes on and on with his long-drawn limping arguments.

Let us draw an inspiration from this famous battle. In our day-to-day life at the office and at home, whenever we see difficulties ahead we come up with several mental scenes. We find excuses. We get into our cocoon, our shell, our box! The worm mentality!! Don't bully! Listen, Try, Act. You will be on the path of a Karmayogi. You will start thinking outside your box.

(viii) Leader's Good Relationships

Leader's good relationships with people are more valuable than money, because he cannot buy good relationships. Networking is a higher form of *karma*. Do good to people, keep your visiting cards folder up-to-date. And don't keep a ledger—even a mental ledger—of debits and credits. Do it for the sake of giving, for the love of giving. You will become bigger than Ford, Billgates and Rockfeller, Tata and Ambani. Not in the eyes of the world around you may be—but in your own eyes. And that is good *karma*.

(ix) Awaken and Empower your People, the Way Master HRD Specialist Lord Krishna did

The whole of Lord Krishna is striking example of developing and empowering the people. Look at him in the roles of a counselor, trainer, philosopher, guide and motivator leading by example. He distinctly earmarked Arjuna's role to achieve success. He even chose to become Arjuna's Sarathi (driver) and impress upon him to pick up his bow and arrow to fulfil his duties and obligations. Lord Krishna gave Arjuna not only the sermon but also enthused him morally to fight his battle.

(x) Leader's Love and Inspiration are Important to Develop Human Resources

The element of love in leaders enables them to collect and harness fortitudes of ardent and dedicated effort. Nothing significant can be achieved by official authority, post or position. The Ramayana brings out this point fully.

Lord Rama and Ravana were both great, but with a vast difference in their greatness. Ravana tried to become big and great by making other people small. He thought that when others became small his own greatness would shine ! On the other hand, Lord Rama's greatness was in that He made every person also great and equal to Himself. He even elevated the restless monkeys to the status of divinity. He achieved "monkey resource development"! It is through the mobilization of the monkey forces that He gained victory over the invincible and well equipped Ravana. This is one of the most fascinating aspects of the Ramayana. The secret of Lord Rama's success was His pure love for all.

(xi) Respect the Authority of Others and do not give Orders Directly

Another interesting aspect of Lord Rama's character was that He did not exercise any kind of authority over others. Sugreeva, the monkey king, offered his services along with his army to Lord Rama and awaited His orders. Rama, however, declined to give orders and gave Sugreeva the freedom of planning the search for Sita Devi. We are aware of the problems of authority in management. If the boss gives orders directly to the workers then the departmental head resents it and feels that his or her authority has been undermined or by-passed. Lord Rama understood this fact, and so He respected the authority of others' love and regard for others can do wonders.

(xii) Leader's Inspiration is Vital

The Mahabharata too contains many fine examples. We know that the Kauravas had a much larger army than the Pandavas, yet, the Pandavas won the war, Why? It was because of Lord Shri Krishna. He was their leader and inspiration. He mobilized them well. The Kauravas had no such inspiration on their side. Moreover, the Pandavas were convinced of their righteous cause and were totally devoted to Lord Krishna. This too was lacking in the Kauravas.

(xiii) Leader Surrenders Individual for Higher Goals

Lord Krishna saw to it that a person must rise above individual importance for the sake of the totality. Without this sacrifice or higher goal great things cannot be achieved.

(xiv) Leaders to Impart Man-making Education

To his followers, which can make them men of firm character. This means strengthening their mind and they are not swayed by others. Leader focuses on character building education by developing morality, integrity and values for societal wellness.

(xv) Leader Exercises Self-Control

So as channelising his energies to a purposeful end and to achieve higher goals in life.

(xvi) Finally Leaders Adopt Holistic Approach in Management

This is based on *spiritual* principle that *entire humanity is one,* and there is respect for all human beings. Leaders to follow *whole man* approach of combining *values* and *physical aspects* of life (worldly life). Spiritual and worldly life are recognised. Leader's higher *consciousness* will adopt holistic attitude.

2. TEAMWORK

Indian ethos say, that for human beings the royal road is 'cooperation' as a powerful instrument for teamwork. The Gita says, "by cooperation mutual help all shall achieve the highest human welfare."

It is generally considered healthy competition is a powerful motivator for excellence and success in business. However, cooperation and collaboration have now become instrument for teamwork and success of any domestic or global enterprise.

3. INDIVIDUAL'S CHARACTERISTICS

Indian ethos highlight some individual's qualities as under:

(a) Each person is a potential divine human

The *divine* means *perfection* in knowledge, wisdom and power. Therefore, a human being has immense potential power or energy for *self-development*. The goal of life is to manifest the *divinity* within through work or worship and meditation.

(b) Selfless work (Karmayoga) as a basic for human action

Work is worship. Do your duty without ego and without calculation of fruits of action. Do your *duty better and better*. Work is important for *personal growth* and good of the society.

Work brings *inner joy* out of selfless service. Dignity of work is valuable. It is possible to harness the potential through work. Excellence at work comes through self-motivation and self-development.

(c) Indian ethos give greater emphasis on values (value-based approach to management and doing right things)

Human ethical value-based management is essential to combine *subjective* (money, as well as human skills) and *objective phenomena* (inner resources of human beings, i.e. wisdom and work ethics). So, development of inner potential—*vision, insight, values are important for wisdom and character.*

4. CONCLUSION

To conclude, Lord Krishna's message pulls Arjuna out of a despondent state and enables him to gain victory and glory. This message is directed how leaders can help people from inactivity. Gita is a marvellous book of guidance for achieving one's objectives.

Further, management with proper combination of *values* and *skills* can assume the harmony, progress of organisations and society. *Spiritual* aspects is necessary to achieve worldly goals. This is the unique contribution of Indian ethos.

PART V

BUSINESS ETHICS IN PROFESSIONS

CHAPTER

28

How to Humanise Management?

In this chapter on "How to Humanise Management?", we have mentioned following aspects:

1. Steps to humanise management.
2. Personal values in transition.

1. STEPS TO HUMANISE MANAGEMENT

Our ancient scriptures provide solution to humanise management as given in Figure 1.

FIGURE 1

Steps to Humanise Management

Step 1: Individual Self-realisation.
Step 2: Mission.
Step 3: Allocation of Duties.
Step 4: Team Spirit.
Step 5: Excellence.
Step 6: Integrated Development.
Step 7: Empowerment.

Step 1: *Self-realisation* of one's potential. Earn money to make life comfortable. Besides *physical needs,* there are also intellectual and spiritual needs to meet by adopting the righteous process of 'Dharma'. Only through Dharma can one realise one's potential.

Step 2: *Mission* is organisation's continuing purpose to guide individuals, groups and managers to determining goals of the organisation. Missions serves as a source of inspiration from which flows the life of the organisation.

Step 3: *Proper placement of subordinates* by knowing each one's nature, knowledge, skills and experience.

Step 4: *Team spirit*. Employees have to work in harmony (in team) to produce results. Without opportunity to work and serve, human beings will be unhappy.

Step 5: *Achieve excellence* through continuous innovation, at all levels, group, division, factory, region, etc. Each of us have *hidden potential* and if we tap it, company's profits will increase manifold as well as our development .

Step 6: Close synchronisation between employees, managers, society and global world. All are interdependent and interconnected. There is need to *unify and integrate* these for advancement of society in global village.

Step 7: *Empowering employees* to take decisions and freedom to experiment with new techniques and practices. This will motivate team to *excel* and give stellar performance.

Thus there is need to rekindle old principles and ethical values, which are ignored at present, to achieve quicker profits and wealth.

In practice, we need *humanistic ideas in dealing* with human beings. *Bhagwat Gita* has laid the rights and obligations of each one of us.

Similarly, *Arthasasthra* lays duty of manager to keep *complete accounts*, which should be subject to *audit*. These should give clarity and truth. *Scriptures* also propound that everyone is endowed with infinite *faculties and talents* to achieve highest goals in life, and translate our aspirations.

2. PERSONAL VALUES IN TRANSITION

(a) Various fast changes are occurring which in the long-run affect organisational values. Some changes are as under:

From	*To*
Contentment	Greed
Selflessness	Selfishness
Duties	Rights
Giving	Grabbing
Patience	Haste
Humility	Arrogance
Self-restraint (morality)	Promiscuity in the name of individual liberty/sexual freedom
Discipline	Indulgence
Sacred	Secular

(b) India at present a land of many contrasts and extremes. We have resigned to live with them. Some contrasts and extremes are as under:

- Abject poverty and abundant wealth,
- Moral depravity and spiritual richness,
- Ancient culture and modern ambitions,
- Donate huge sums to charity but cheat in their business,

- Struggle with backwardness and we claim as world power house,
- Indulging in corruption of public funds but some are who do not take a pencil from office,
- Continuing disparities while leaders assure glorious tomorrow?
- Practicing of violence (terrorism) and non-violence,
- Burn their daughter-in-law yet love their daughters,
- Preach morality, but have habits without morality, and
- Talk of ancient heritage and values but society without morality.

With the above few examples of contrast and other extremes existing, it is pertinant to mention that:

(i) Is it then possible to achieve that glorious future? India is waiting for dawn. A new vision and new hope.

(ii) Greatness of our country will be determined not by economic prosperity alone, but also by inherent moral values and ethical standards.

CHAPTER

29

Ethical Concerns in Human Resource Management (HRM)

1. UNETHICAL PRACTICES IN VIOLATION OF THE CONSTITUTION OF INDIA AND LABOUR LAWS

Unethical practices may emerge because of lack of ensuring certain guarantees provided to the employees, both in *labour legislation* as well as the *Constitution of India*.

Some of the articles in the *Constitution, directly related to HRM practices* are as under:

(i) *Article 16* of the Constitution of India stipulates *equal opportunity* in matters of public employment, no discrimination should be on grounds only of religion, race, caste, sex, place of birth, residence. It requires employers to hire employees on basis of merit, irrespective of other considerations. However, we see advertisements suggesting bias, e.g. women need not apply.

(ii) *Article 39* of the Constitution requires that there should be *equal pay for equal work* for both men and women.

(iii) *Article 42* of the Constitution stipulates that state shall make provisions for securing just and humane *conditions of work and for maternity relief*. Thus, the Factories Act, 1948 stipulates minimum conditions of work, health, hygiene and safety.

(iv) *Article 43* of the Constitution stipulates that state shall endeavour to secure by legislation *a living wage*, conditions of work, ensuring a *decent standard of life*. However, it is hardly put in practice.

2. ETHICS AND HRM

2.1 Expectations of ethical behaviour

Expectations of ethical behaviour are communicated to employees through vision and mission statement, code of conduct, policies, training and the role model behaviour of the top management.

2.2 HR management should be starting point for any ethical programme

If fairness, justice and parity are important to achieve *HR function can play a key role* in fostering fairness in the organisation. Any failure to foster fairness in the HR policies can undermine the organisation's attempts to encourage ethical behaviour. *Fairness* suggests that employees are valued and organisation respects them. Fairness also indicates to people that they are respected as an end and not as a means to achieve ends.

Further, HRM activities are more *susceptible to violation* of the code of ethics because most of its activities are based on *judgement* and discretionary aspects are involved. Further, there are large number of rules, policies are involved. To ensure fairness, *some HR functions covered* in Figure 1 are discussed as under:

FIGURE I

Areas of Ethical Misconduct in HRM

- Lack of ensuring guarantees under laws.
- Failure in fairness.
- Recruitment and selection.
- Performance appraisal.
- Training and development.
- Reward system.
- Restructuring and down-sizing
- Health and safety.
- Employee privacy.
- Other concern.

2.3 Recruitment and selection

The selection process that values ethical behaviour can contribute to work place. Selection process should focus on attracting and selecting employees who *share the organisation* values. From selection process, potential employees from *first ideas* of the organisation's ethical-orientation. HR staff must ensure that their first impression is positive. If employees get negative impression, then they may assume that ethical behaviour is not important in the organisation. Similarly, *quick interview* may give the impression that selection decisions are already made and interview process is a facade. Avoiding discrimination on religion, caste, sex basis in recruitment, promotion and discharge programme is to be ensured.

2.4 Training and development

Training is best way to foster ethical programmes of organisations which focus on culture of the organisation, its values and expectations. Content of the programme highlight values cherished by the organisation.

2.5 Performance appraisal

Appraisal process should incorporate *values/ethics as criteria* of evaluation in conduct of appraisal. Performance must support overall ethical goals of the organisation.

Appraisal becomes the key to conveying information *about fairness*. It should be free from bias and should be *communicated* honestly to employees. Employees should be given explanations, in case of negative results. *Criteria* of evaluation must be clear to employees. Those involved in appraisals are to be properly trained. Ethics has to be cornerstone of performance evaluation and performance reviews and should be able to provide an honest assessment.

2.6 Reward system

Rewarding ethical behaviour and punishing unethical conduct reinforces ethical expectations from employees, reward for ethical conduct might best presented in the long-term with promotion, recognition, etc.

One of the most sensitive areas are in connection with fairness in salary such as employees feeling they are underpaid for their work, or unequality in sexes.

For HR, executive perquisites make unethical issues. For example, a story relates to a Bangalore-based, loss-making public sector, whose CEO spent 50 lakhs to get a swimming pool build at his residence.

2.7 Restructuring and Down-sizing

Restructuring and down-sizing without the knowledge of employees particularly due to poor management. If down-sizing is conducted, in an atmosphere of fairness, and equity and with the dignity of affected in mind, the action is ethical.

2.8 Health and Safety

Accidents, injuries, and illness are likely to occur due to industrial hazardous work. Work pressure may cause stress and disorders such as through repetitive motion or terminal display.

Issues involved in health and safety is regarding assessment of risk can be by judgement of amount of compensation only. Bhopal gas leakage tragedy, 1981 is an instance.

2.9 Protection of Privacy

Privacy refers to protecting a person's private life, i.e. religious, social beliefs as well as personal lifestyle, etc. from intrusive actions. Such intrusive actions include five areas which pose *ethical dilemmas* to employers. (Figure 2)

FIGURE 2

Ethical Issues in Employee's Privacy

(a) Information technology
(b) Aids testing
(c) Whistle blowing
(d) Drug testing
(e) Genetic testing

(a) Information technology

First relates to *information technology*. Employees are *viewed on close-circuit TV*, phones are tapped, computer files are read. Thus, respect for person is denied.

(b) Aids

Aids has become a major public health problem. For HR manager the disease raises two issues. Whether a new hire be subject to aids test? What treatment should be meted out to an employee who is affected with the disease? USA has a legislation that bar job discrimination against people with aids.

(c) Whistle blowing

Another area of ethical concern is *whistle blowing*. L.G. India, Xerox USA, etc. Dubey of High Way Transport Authority of India. In some countries like USA, England, Australia, etc. whistle blowers are protected. In India, law for protection of whistle blowers is in process. Whistle blowing is an attempt by a member of or ex-member of an organisation to disclose wrong doing in or by the organisation (illegal/immoral conduct/against public interest). Employee may feel it obligatory to blow the whistle without following sequence of actions laid down by the company. Employee makes organisational misconduct. For example, cases of Enron, World.com., Kellog India.

(d) Drug Testing

It may assume an ethical dimension. If the information obtained from drug testing is *relevant to the job*, subjecting an employee to such a test assumes legitimacy. Where information obtained from drug testing is irrelevant to the job, it amounts to invading an employee's personal life. Such information may also be held against the employee concerned.

(e) Genetic Testing

Another dilemma is genetic testing which links between one's inherited characteristics and certain illnesses. Genetic testing may be of two forms. Genetic screening is used to identify persons who are susceptible to certain genetically-based illness. The goal of screening is to single out individual who have certain genetic traits. *Genetic monitoring* is to single out (not people) but harmful substances. Genetic make sense for business as detecting disabled employees means reduction in costs due to illness, absenteeism, health insurance and compensation, etc. Genetic testing can be held against job-seekers or discriminate against some employees. In addition, it gives way to social stigma to people with genetic defects.

2.10 Other Ethical Concerns

Other challenges commonly faced by employers are such as: (i) pressure to hire relative or a friend of a highly placed executives, (ii) faked credentials submitted by a job applicant while discovery of this kind of fabrication usually leads to termination of employment. This choice becomes difficult if employee has done well and has a race blend of skills and a proven track record with his previous employers.

CHAPTER

30

Ethical Issues in Marketing and Advertising

1. MEANING OF ETHICS

Ethics is a choice between good or bad, between right and wrong. Ethics is governed by a set of principles of morality at a given time and at a given place. Ethics is related to group behaviour in ultimate analysis, thus, setting norms for an individual to follow in accordance with the group norms.

2. MARKETING ETHICS

It refers to ethics especially in the area of interaction of an enterprise with the customers. Ethics in marketing is more important because it determines whether the customer will stay with the organisation. Unethical organisations lose their customers soon.

- *Market professionals* are often faced with decisions regarding the appropriateness of their actions which are *based on ethical considerations* rather than what is within the law or industry guidelines.
- *Customer's expectations from marketing* and corporates.
- Marketing have to be responsive and accountable to customers and public in following aspects:
    - Better *quality* of goods,
    - Goods and services at reasonable *price,* timeliness and courtesy,
    - Not to *cornerstocks* and create scarcities,
    - Not to practice *discriminatory pricing,*
    - Not to make false claims about producers in advertisements,

- Respect right of public information on activities and transactions of the organisation,
- *Certain factors,* for example, higher level of education of consumers, competition and availability of variety of products, legislation leading to consumer protection, consumer associations, aggressive state role, forums for protection of grievances of consumers, *lok adalats* being set-up by some corporates, i.e. MTNL, DESU, etc. have made *consumers more aware of their rights and are demanding.* Marketers have to accept obligation to recognise consumer's right of speedy redressal of grievances, and
- *Corporate image* has gained importance in competitive markets, so winning and maintaining customer relationship is vital. In addition, to fulfil social responsibility is important. So marketing has to be sensitive to needs of society. In global economy marketing is a sensitive area.

3. ADVERTISING

Advertising is a highly visible business activity and any lapse in ethical standards can often be risky for the company in order to be consumer-oriented, an advertisement will have to be truthful and ethical.

3.1 What can be Ethical Advertising?

(a) Which contains truth.
(b) Which is right in its approach and claims.
(c) Which keeps social morality.
(d) Which observes the relevant laws/norms/codes framed to keep the scene ethical.

3.2 What Exactly is Unethical Advertising?

(i) Advertising which will *degrade rival* products. War between Pepsi and Coke led to bringing negative publicity of competitors.
(ii) Which give *misleading information,* such as a medicine will increase the memory, whiten your black colour, etc.
(iii) Advertisements which give *false information* such as guarantee or warranty promising with no intention to perform.
(iv) Which *conceal important* information that vitally affect human life such as giving testimonials, discrimination on quality and service among buyers, tie up sales, etc.
(v) Which makes *exaggerated or tall claims.* For example, advertisement offering products/ medicines promising colour fairness, loss of weight, growth in height, increase in sexual energy, improvement in strength, hair growth for baldness, etc.
(vi) Which is *obscene or immoral* creating erotic or sensuous adds, sex projections in CDs.
(vii) Which is *against the national and public interest.*

In fact, many unethical ways are being practised towards building relationships. However, a customer can be retained permanently only by means of quality products, services and developing brand image.

Box

Unethical Marketing Behaviour

Some unethical marketing practices are given here under different headings:

1. Product

Unsafe, shoddy goods (cannot withstand wear and tear), inadequate warranties, environmental pollution (plastic product), mislabelled products (for example, flavoured sugar water sold as apple juice), development (to secure agency approval by bribery), manufacturing (unauthorised brand), counterfeit brand goods as originals.

2. Price

- *Excessive mark-up* prices to connote quality.
- *Price differentiation* in Air tickets on day-to-day.
- *Price discrimination* for preferred ethnic groups.
- *Unfair pricing*—to *drive competitors* by low prices.
- *Deceptive pricing*—buy one saree take another free or low price mentioned outside to lure customers into store and then influence them to buy of higher price.

3. Promotion/Advertising

- *Exaggerated* claims such as smoothest razor which another company challenges.
- *Tasteless* advertising—sexual indecency.
- Inappropriate targeting.
- Deceptive advertising.
- *Persuasive role models* for inappropriate products, e.g. a celebrity say an actor speaks for liquor or cigarette ads targeted to youth.
- *Naive audiences,* e.g. bill boards for alcohol in urban areas.
- *Tele-marketing,* e.g. prizes offers for credit card purchases of touted goods.
- *Captive audience,* e.g. TV commercial shown to students in schools.

4. Distributors

- Fraudulent sales.
- Direct marketing—misleading claims of product performance.

5. Packing

- Deceptive quantities, e.g. decreases product quantity while maintaining same package and price.

CHAPTER

31

Marketing Ethics

The *laws* and *regulations* are desinged to protect the consumer from unethical practices by business. However, some unethical practices are just *one step* short of being unlawful and are overlooked by the regulatory agencies.

Ultimately each marketer must rely on his own *value system* to determine what is and is not ethical. This value system should recognise consumer rights to *safety*, to full *information* and to provide value for the price paid.

American Marketing Association (AMA) has established *codes of ethics* to provide guidelines for ethical conduct. Marketer shall uphold the integrity, honour and dignity of the marketing profession, by being honest in serving consumers, clients, employees, suppliers, distributors and the public. The code also outlines responsibilities for each component of the marketing mix.

ASPECTS OF MARKETING MIX AS PER AMA CODE

1. Product and Services

Marketer has responsibility to ensure *product safety* to disclose all *product risks*, and to identify any factor that might change product performance. For example, General Motors failed to fulfil the responsibilities by providing faulty brakes for 1.1 million X body cars. Maruti replaced the faulty steering of a certain model of car few years ago. Similarly, Nokia advertised recently to replace batteries of cellular phones of certain numbers

2. Advertising

Marketers to avoid deceptive and misleading communications and sales tactics. Marketers must avoid manupulating consumers to buy. For example, Warner Lambert failed to fulfil the responsibilities when advertised listerine as praventing of colds.

3. Distribution

Suppliers should not coerce their intermediaries into taking unwanted products. They should not create false shortages to drive up prices of their products. For example, Chrisler (USA) in 1960 forced dealers to take unwanted cars during economic downtown.

4. Pricing

Marketers must not engage in price fixing low but also disclose all prices associated with purchase including service, installation and delivery. In 1960 GE's (USA) several executives were indicted for price fixing.

5. Insurance

Regarding insurance of consumer rights, AMA code states that marketers should hear customer complaints and settle equitably.

Areas not covered by law or AMA code in such issues must bear on level of integrity of individual marketer.

Reasons for Unethical Practices

(i) Pressure of competition
(ii) Loss in profits
(iii) Prevailing practices in firm or industry
(iv) The values of the manager
(v) Failure of the firm itself to provide ethical standards and control system

Reasons for Behaving Ethically by Marketers

(a) Because it is *morally correct* and simple concept.
(b) To *protect the image* of organisation by being highly ethical.
(c) Marketers wield great deal of *social power to influence markets*. This power has to be used in acceptable manner.
(d) To avoid *damage to reputation* and public confidence in marketing.
(e) To avoid increases in *government regulations* and loose economic freedoms.

CHAPTER

32

Ethics in Finance Profession

Finance would be impossible without ethics. We are placing our assets in the hands of others, which requires immense trust. These persons may include stock broker, insurance agent, attorney, financial planners, tax advisers and other financial professionals.

Though the law governs much financial activity, strong emphasis has to be palced on the *integrity of the finance professionals* and on *ethical leadership* in our financial institutions.

Some major areas of finance involved in unethical issues are:

(i) Financial Services

Three objectionable practices in selling financial products to clients are:

(a) *Deception* (deceiving and not revealing, e.g. telling to client, it is tax free when it is only tax deferred).

(b) *Churning* means inappropriate trading for clients account by a broker to generate his commission rather than benefit the client. Churning is breach of confidence held as a trust.

(c) *Transacting in unsuitable* type of securities.

(ii) Inside Trading

Inside trading is illegal. Famous examples are Enron, USA case. The person who trades on insider information in effect 'steals' this information and gains unfair advantage over general public.

Similarly lawyer, accountant or corporate executive may benefit personally from use of information acquired in confidence from client is breach of fiduciary duty.

(iii) Financial Statements

The ethical issues relating to accounting practices can be as under:

(a) Under reporting income,
(b) Falsifying documents,
(c) Taking questable deductions, and
(d) Illegally evading income taxes or engaging in fraud. However, to prevent such cases chartered accountants' codes of professional conduct are laid.

CHAPTER

33

Ethics in Computer Profession

Information technology is functional specialisation in which considerable attention is given to ethical issues. Computer science, information *processing and communication* technologies are accelerating changes in our working life and of the entire society. Society will ultimately hold the technology, its developers and its implementers to account for problems such as:

(a) Software piracy is a global problem

One such ethical issue is software theft (software piracy). Research shows about 90% software is illegally copied in all advanced countries like Japan, Germany, Italy, Spain, etc.

(b) Other ethical problems which managers confront with computerisation are:

(i) Invasion of Privacy such as:

- Company snooping on employees' data;
- Employees using company data for their own purposes; and
- Employees peeking into each other's correspondence (through insecure filing system).

(ii) Misappropriation of Company Assets and Misuse of Data

Some examples are such as employees diverting corporate computing power for personal use. Writing personal letters, playing games. It tantamounts to cheating the company and its time. IBM, USA has well published policy on the computer at work for personal business of employees. Policy forbids, leaking out trade secrets, copyrights. Code of ethics do help create essential values for employees to adhere.

(iii) Special Implications of Artifical Intelligence

Computer display behaviours, which would be considered intelligent if displayed by a person. It means liberate computers from being dependent on our control. Some fears are:

- Computers will take over my job,
- Some one will find out everything about me,
- Computers will tap phone calls,
- Computers might cause world wars,
- Autonomous machines will start robot riots,
- Robots may do jobs not meant for people,
- Computer crimes, i.e. computer can be used as a tool for executing the crimes such as destruction of software data, alternation of software/data, embezzlement of funds, etc.,
- Spread of computer viruses by someone who writes in most programmes, and
- Violation of intellectual property rights for software.

(iv) Computer Health Risks

Such as occupational diseases due to repetitive stress, vision syndrome—headaches, irritated eyes, screen radiation diseases such as birth defects in pregnant women.

CHAPTER

34

Business Ethics in Media

1. PRESS FREEDOM IS MIXED BLESSINGS

In business world, *press freedom is mixed blessing*. Too often journalists get stories *wrong*, either in fact or interpretation and cause damage to corporate reputation. The blessing aspect is that without freedom of investigation and reporting, many episodes of scandalous behaviour would not have been highlighted by media and many people continue to be cheated and robbed by the unscrupulous persons.

2. PRINT NEWS MEDIA AND ELECTRONIC MEDIA IN BUSINESS ETHICS

Obligations of media are as under:

(a) Many professional organisations/NGOs supply to media/press releases and give briefing. Some people are only too ready in furthering their own interests and even attempt manipulation, distortion of the news.

This does not in any way reduce the *media obligation* to seek accuracy, fairness and balance in their reporting. Media (e.g. radio, TV, print, etc.) *cannot escape responsibility* for misinforming the public. Recently one TV channel had intentionally implicated a lady teacher in school innefarious acts.

(b) *Journalism can help* business and economy, politics and society by adhering to following six appeals:

To continue:

(i) Continue to investigate *wrong doings* fairly and with balance.

(ii) To *challenge industry* to achieve higher standards of public responsibility.

(iii) To seek out and to report correct and good news.

To Cease

(iv) Cease to *bias or exaggerate* stories in order to create sensational headlines.

(v) Cease to seek personal stature by *belitting or destroying* the reputation and careers of others.

(vi) Cease to *confuse forceful interviewing* with an urge to belittle or to discredit the person.

(c) The Society of Professional Journalists (SPJ) USA, in its code of conduct includes four main sections as under:

- seek truth and report it,
- minimise harm,
- act independently, and
- be accountable.

Media has to realise, if society gives freedom to its press, it has every right to demand total integrity in return. In addition to the code of conduct, there are other conditions imposed by government and other statutory regulatory bodies.

CHAPTER

35

Ethics in Production Management

A number of workers are killed and seriously injured as a result of job accidents. The right of employees to a safe and healthy workplace is necessary. Similarly, corresponding obligations of employers to *provide working conditions* free from recognised hazards is vital.

1. UNETHICAL ISSUES

There are numerous unethical issues where exploitation of employees is involved inspite of various labour laws. Some of these are:

(i) Unsafe workplace, bad working conditions, long working hours.
(ii) Employment of women and children for long hours prohibited by laws.
(iii) Unfair labour practices, e.g. retrenchment and closing of factories without following of proper procedure in the laws.
(iv) Denying compensation for accident injuries and death at works.
(v) Hardly any procedure for redressal of grievances by employees, etc.

2. MAJOR LAWS

Major labour laws for protection of employees women, children relating to working conditions are:

(i) The Factories Act, 1948. (Box 1)
(ii) The Shops and Establishment Act, 1951.
(iii) The Mines Act, 1952.
(iv) The Plantation Labour Act, 1951.
(v) The Contract Labour (Regulation & Abolition) Act, 1970.
(vi) The Workmen's Compensation Act, 1923.
(vii) The Employee's State Insurance Act, 1948.

Besides, there are state government regulations under these laws.

3. Health, safety and welfare matters relating to *hazardous processes* and substances are also given in these acts, particularly The Factories Act, 1948.

4. Further victims of racial or sexual discrimination or sexual harassment also suffer violation of their rights.

Box I

Health, Safety and Welfare Measures Required under the Factories Act, 1948

1. Occupier to provide for *health measures* as under:
   - (a) On cleanliness,
   - (b) Disposal of wastes and affluents,
   - (c) Proper ventilation and temperatures,
   - (d) Protection against dust and fumes,
   - (e) Avoidance of over-crowding,
   - (f) Protection from glare. Provision of sufficient natural light and artificial lights, drinking cool water at suitable points, and
   - (g) Separate latrines and urinals for male and female workers to be provided in sufficient number and kept clean.
2. Undertake *safety measures*:
   - (i) Dangerous parts of machinery to be securely fenced,
   - (ii) Keep floors and stairs free from obstruction,
   - (iii) Prohibition of young persons and women at certain places,
   - (iv) Periodical examination of hoists, lifts, cranes and chains, etc.,
   - (v) Provision of safety appliances, e.g. goggles, gloves, hats and equipment for fire fighting, and
   - (vi) Appoint safety officer if 1000 or more workers in the factory.
3. Provide *welfare measures*:
   - (i) Washing facilities, storing of clothes not work during working hours,
   - (ii) First aid boxes at least 1 for 150 employees under the charge of one person,
   - (iii) A canteen when—250 or more workers in the factory and lunch room—if 150 workers or more are there,
   - (iv) Creches, when 30 women and more workers are employed,
   - (v) Ambulance room when 500 or more workers are employed in the factory,
   - (vi) Working hours, and
   - (vii) Welfare officer for 500 or more workers are in the factory.
4. Observing working hours/holidays and over time:
   - (a) Restrictions on employment of women, children and adolescents—
     - Women not to be employed between 7 p.m. and 6 a.m.
     - No child below age of 14 years to be employed.
     - No dual employment if he has worked in any other factory.
   - (b) Working hours:
     - Working hours of an adult worker not to exceed 48 hours in a week and 9 hours a day.

       Rest interval of ½ hour before 5 hours at a stretch.

       Spread over not more than 10½ hours in a day.

(c) No overlapping of shifts in the factory.
(d) Weekly holiday to worker in a week. Compensatory holiday is given if worker is required to work on a weekly holiday within the same month or within two months.
(e) Overtime:
  - A worker working more than 9 hours on any day, or for more than 48 hours in any week shall be entitled to overtime wages, in respect of such overtime work at twice "The Ordinary Rate of Wages".
  - Total working hours in a week including overtime hours should not exceed 60, and the total overtime hours in a quarter should not exceed 50.
(f) Notice of periods of work:
  - The manager is required to display on notice board periods of work.
  - Periods of work can be changed only after obtaining approval of the inspector.

CHAPTER

36

Professional Ethics in Civil Engineering

PREAMBLE

- The purpose of Civil Engineering is to *improve living conditions* for mankind, always safeguarding life, health and property.
- A Civil Engineer is a servant of society and a *promoter of culture and quality of life.*
- A Civil Engineer must survey and analyse the demands of the present and *anticipate future developments.*
- A Civil Engineer should treat this Code actively as a set of *dynamic principles.*

1. The society

An Engineer:

(a) will act with *integrity* and have full regard to the *public interest;*
(b) will have due regard for the *health and safety of the public* and other colleagues and employees;
(c) will endeavour to *improve public knowledge* of the benefits of Civil Engineering;
(d) will express professional opinion only when founded on *adequate knowledge;*
(e) will *reject bribery* in all forms; and
(f) will seek opportunities to be of constructive service in civic affairs.

2. The environment

An Engineer:

(a) will understand the *effect of his/her work on society* and the natural environment;
(b) will further the aims of *sustainable development* and change;

(c) will be committed to *improving the environment* and enhancing the *quality of life* wherever possible;
(d) will recognise the *interdependence of the planet's ecosystems* and their capacity to assimilate change due to Civil Engineering activity;
(e) will ensure the *minimal adverse effects* on the environment;
(f) will promote the use of *renewable and recycle* materials; and
(g) will strive to accomplish his/her work with the lowest possible use of natural resources.

3. The profession

An Engineer:

(a) will uphold the *standard of his profession* and will co-operate in extending the effectiveness of the profession;
(b) will *avoid all conduct* likely to discredit or injure the dignity and honour of the profession;
(c) will endeavour to *protect the profession* from misrepresentation; and
(d) will *report the facts* to the appropriate authority if another engineer is guilty or unethical or illegal practice.

Reference

This is an extract from Code of Professional Conduct of Civil Engineers (European Council of Civil Engineers (ECCE) England and Wales). Courtesy Sandeepa Fanda, YMCA.

CHAPTER

37

Business Ethics (Tata's Group)

J.R.D. TATA

India has several outstanding entrepreneurs but there had been one towering personality whose outstanding achievement was his regard for *ethical standards*—a staunch supporter of business ethics and social audit in business.

Within organisation, *values are imparted* by the founder-entrepreneur or a dominant chief executive and they remain in some form, a long time after that person is not there. J.R.D. Tata, the previous Chairman of the Tata group, when asked to define the House of Tatas and what links the different Tata companies together said: "I would call it a group of individually managed companies united by two factors. First, a feeling that they are part of a larger group which carrers the name and prestige of Tatas, and *public recognition of honesty and reliability—trustworthiness*. The other reason is more metaphysical. There is an innate loyalty, a sharing of certain beliefs. We all feel a certain pride that we are somewhat different from others" (Lala, 1981).

In the year 2001, Tata Group present Chairman Ratan Tata bagged the Government of India award for Corporate Governance. Here is a brief profile of this *towering personality J.R.D. Tata*: J.R.D. Tata became the Chairman of Tata Sons on the eve of World War II. There was a lesser known shade to his personality that few knew about his deep passion for flying. He piloted a flight from Karachi to Bombay at the age of 24 and repeated the feat in his 'eighties. As a business strategist, he diversified Tata's interests in chemicals in 1938-39 into Tata Engineering and Locomotives in collaboration with Mercedez-Benz and went on to become the leading manufacturer of Tata Trucks. He went on to purchase tea plantations from James. Finally, set-up Tata Airways, which later came to be known as Air India. In J.R.D. Tata's time, Air India was ranked as a leading international carrier and remained so till 1977-78. The Taj chain of hotels was also enlarged during JRD's time both in India and abroad. However, what is still regarded as one of his most outstanding achievement was his regard for *ethical standards*—a staunch supporter of business ethics, social audit and population control. Till his end, he rendered the high leadership and entrepreneurial dynamism wedded to high quality standards, research and development as he went on to set-up Tata Administrative Services in pursuit of global excellence. He formulated the Bombay Plan in 1944-45 to double India's GDP with seven other industrialists and won many international awards. In my opinion, he was uncompromising in the ideals he held and lived quite modestly.

Role of a Citizen

JRD Tata took the *role of a citizen* very seriously and never failed to be of service to the nation. His nation-building activity began soon after he was appointed a trustee of the Sir Dorabji Tata Trust in 1932. The concept of establishing Asia's first *cancer hospital* in Bombay was implemented under his guidance in 1941. Citizen Tata's greatest gift to the scientific establishment came in 1945 when he gave the founding grant to Homi Bhabha to set-up the *Tata Institute of Fundamental Research*. This institute has proved to be, in Bhabha's words, "the cradle of our *atomic energy programme*."

JRD Tata was among the first Indians to be drawn to the cause of *population in control* when he realised the drag unchecked population growth could have on the country's developmental efforts. In 1951, when he came across statistics revealing that India had crossed the 350-million population mark, JRD sounded out Jawaharlal Nehru (the country's first prime minister) on the issue. Nehru ignored the issue. But JRD didn't wait for the government to act. He part-funded Avabai Wadia's efforts to start the Family Planning Association of India.

JRD firmly believed in *employee welfare* and espoused the principles of an eight-hour working day, free medical aid, workers' provident fund scheme, workmen's accident compensation schemes, which were later adopted as statutory requirements in the country.

These measures were introduced at Tata Steel, Jamshedpur, and many more were added during JRD Tata's regime. In 1956, he initiated a programme of closer "employee association with management" to give workers a stronger voice in the affairs of the company. He also introduced a scheme of 'ex-gratia payment for road accident while coming to or returning from duty'.

In 1970, he started the *Family Planning Foundation* jointly with the Ford Foundation, and was instrumental in conditioning the thinking of an entire generation, treating the issue as one of essential transformation of society. For his crusading endeavours in the field, JRD Tata was bestowed with the United Nations Population Award in 1992.

For these endeavours, JRD Tata was awarded the country's highest civilian honour, the Bharat Ratna, in 1992—one of the rare instances when the award was granted during a person's lifetime.

Other awards won by him include commander of the Legion of Honour by France, Knight Commander of the order of St. Gregory of the Great, Knight Commander's cross of the order of merit of the Federal Republic of Germany, Hon. Air Vice Marshal of the Indian Air Force and has been named international Management Man.

He passed away on November 29, 1993. On his death, the Indian Parliament was adjourned in his memory—an honour not usually given to private citizens. His home state of Maharashtra too declared three days of mourning. Though Mr. J.R.D. Tata is no more, the *values, traditions and business ethics* which he lived by will continue to be the driving force of the Group. Mr Tata made his mark on India during his lifetime, and his legend lives on after him.

After death of Mr. J.R.D. Tata, Mr. Ratan Tata took reins of Tata Group and has maintained ethical traditions of his ancestors. Egon Zehnder (A Global Consultant's Company) has selected Mr. Ratan Tata on the corporate governance board. Reasons given by them are: We needed somebody who is truly an international personality and I think Mr. Tata fits into that mould. Secondly, we needed to raise the level of debate on corporate governance in India. And at least one company that is doing something about corporate governance here are the Tatas.

References

P.N. Agarwala, A noted author, htc careers @ hindustan times.com
Azhar Kazmi, Chairman, Deptt. of Business Administration, Aligarh Muslim University.

CHAPTER

38

Work Ethics

In this chapter on "Work Ethics", the following aspects are covered:

1. Meaning of work ethics.
2. Definition of work ethics.
3. Four P's of work ethics and individual attitude to work.
4. Benefits of ethics at work place.
5. Improving work ethics.
6. Functions of work—why is work important?
7. Different views on work.

1. MEANING OF WORK ETHICS

"Ethics" means a set of *moral principles*—A code of conduct. In any social set-up, the members of a group tend to adopt a set of *rules of behaviour for the establishment of good order.*

Such rules may be or may not be codified, but so long as they have the acceptance of the members of the group, they tend to be observed.

Work ethics refers to certain accepted *norms of behaviour* governing the conduct of a group of persons involved in work-situation to achieve certain desired objectives.

In some business organisations, such rules are codified and represent the "Do's and Don'ts", meant to be observed by the staff. For example:

Do's—Requiring members to do things that are morally good or right, e.g. punctuality, courtesy, efficiency, hard-work, sincerity, devotion to duty, regularity, discipline, promptness, enterprise, initiative, etc.

Don'ts—Seek to restrain the employees from doing things that are morally bad or wrong, e.g. insubordination, lethargy and indolence, corruption, dishonety, etc.

Work ethics is thus a part of moral philosophy.

In sum, work ethics means "the characteristic spirit or attitudes of a community, people, or system." Work ethic is a characteristic attitude of a group toward what constitutes the morality of work.

To do "good work" is a good thing. But when the work ethic benefits only the owner and not the workers, it's not such a wonderful concept.

2. DEFINITION OF WORK ETHICS

A work ethics can be defined at different levels:

(i) At the *basic level* it is about discipline, namely, coming to work on time, behaving with respect and dignity in relation to subordinates, colleagues and superiors, staying at work place during working hours, not wasting time by roaming and chattering, etc. There is strong *work orientation*.

(ii) At the *highest level*, work ethics is about commitment and *accountability*. Does manager feel responsible for the task assigned to him and does he complete in time and in satisfactory way.

(iii) *Another aspect* of work ethics is *protecting the interests* of the organisation by employees. Avoiding negative comments in public.

(iv) To *perform one's job* with devotion and perfection (Gita).

(v) Simply put, work ethics refers to the *strength of one's commitment and dedication to hard work*. It is employee's attitude. Americans work hard. Japanese work harder or too hard.

A professional manager describes work ethics as under:

"Work ethics embraces work responsibility, work conscience, ethical work conduct. If one has the satisfaction that he is *contributing* his very best to his organisation and is not just earning the bread, then this would be the true feeling of work ethics. Work ethics demands that one works for attaining organisational objectives in its fullest measure.

3. FOUR P's OF WORK ETHICS AND INDIVIDUAL ATTITUDE TO WORK

To explain it more explicitly, a person joining any work organisation does so under a "Contract"—that he will be entitled to receive or take from organisation, a package of compensation against what he gives to the organisation by way of physical and mental efforts leading to concrete tangible results.

Compliance with this *Contractual obligation* and *fulfilling this commitment* which he has made to his employer—organisation by entering into "work contract" is the crux of work ethics, that must honour.

In order to fulfil his obligations and commitment, he has to exhibit certain attitudes, apply certain skills to the desired levels of excellence. He has to translate certain desirable habits, such as, regularity, punctuality, discipline, promptness, initiative and so on. All these together, contribute an ethical value system, which every employee must follow.

However, organisational atmosphere presents a picture of anti-work ethics or absence of work ethics.

People seem to be obsessed with only 3 P's, viz. *Pay*, *Prospects*, and *Promotion* and forgetting the 4th viz. *Performance*—which is so fundamental to the concept of work ethics.

Thus, Central to Theme of Work Ethics is the Individual and his Attitude to Work

We give examples of poor work ethics. *Few Illustrations*: We are faced with numerous problems like—sub-standard performance, wasteful and restrictive practices by trade unions, apathy towards punctuality, quality of work, passing the buck, etc.

A Japanese visitor to India was impressed by widespread use of wrist watches by our people and remarked to his Indian friend that while every one here sported a watch, but no one is punctual and watch appears to be status symbol than useful instrument of punctuality.

We have aped western life style and habits. One common being calling our seniors by their first names. Fostering so intimate relationship with Boss has affected our work ethics adversely. Employees refuse to accomplish task and take advantage of intimacy. They show undisciplined behaviour, arrogance and irregular habits. All leading to bad work ethics. This does not happen in western culture calling first name is quite natural in their society.

4. BENEFITS OF ETHICS AT WORK PLACE

Managing ethics at work place has various benefits as under:

(i) Ethics at work place brings *discipline and order*. It improves and strengthens relationships amongst superiors, peers and subordinates. It enhances commitment and accountability of the top managers and ensures safety of interest of its various stakeholders.

(ii) Ethics programmes *support employee growth* and also the more emotionally healthy executives are higher on ethics work.

(iii) Work ethics *promotes team work and productivity* as employees feel strong alignment between their values and those of the organisation.

(iv) Ethics programmes help *avoid criminal acts of omission* and lower penalties.

(v) Ethics at work place helps *manage values* associated with quality management, strategic planning and diversity management. TQM includes high priority on certain operating values, e.g. trust among employees, customers, performance reliability, measurement and feedback.

(vi) Ethics programmes help ensure that *legal course of action* is adopted in procedures. Personnel policies to ensure ethical treatment of employees.

(vii) Ethics programmes *promote a strong public image* as employees operate with integrity and self-respect. Ethical values build socially responsible business and commercially successful.

(viii) Ethics at work place helps employees to *maintain a moral course* in turbulent times as they continuously pay attention to ethics consistently.

(ix) To sum up with the views of Donaldson and Davis that managing ethical values in the work place *legitimize managerial actions*, strengthens the organisation's culture, improves trust in relationships between individuals and groups, supports greater consistency in standards and qualities of products, and cultivates greater sensitivity to the enterprise's values and messages.

5. IMPROVING WORK ETHICS

(i) *Imparting Man-making Education*. Solution to the problem of work ethics does not lie merely in spelling out in impressive codes of conduct. Let us not forget Swami Vivekananda's warning that man cannot be made moral by an act of parliament. The only way to change a man for the better character is through *imparting man-making education*, i.e. education by which *character is formed, strength of mind is increased* and by which one can *stand on one's own feet* and not merely collect some degrees.

(ii) Other *Indian approaches* for improving work ethics are:

(a) Employer should love his employees. Loving does not mean refraining from punishing the guilty, inefficient and corrupt employees.

(b) To cultivate the attitude of sport or "Lila" towards work.

(c) Inculcating among employees shifting mindset from "taking" to "giving modes." We always look at what I am getting benefits from the organisation. We forget what we have to contribute. Change our attitude from "Begger's mode" to "Achiever's mode."

(d) "To work like a master and not like a slave." Swami Vivekananda further emphasises that 99% of us work like slave and this results in misery. It is all selfish work. We should work through freedom, work through love. To view work as an act of love and freedom, which can bring about a revolution in one's attitude towards work ethic. It is a case of tiger cubs believing themselves as to be lambs. How we can contribute as leader in work if we degenerate as slaves.

(e) Renunciation and service are twin ideals rest will take care of itself (Gita).

(iii) Organisations can *create strong work culture* through appropriate systems, as well as rewards and penalties. For example, in same building there are offices of private companies, government offices and public sector undertaking. Government work culture is highly undisciplined—people come to work at will, stay away from work. Productivity is poor. Parks around building are full with employees playing cards. On the other hand, if same person joins private employer, he puts in greater effort. It is ethos of government that is at fault. Number of holidays in government offices are numerous.

If work discipline in terms of *time and staying at work place* becomes mandatory and subject of penalties for non-compliance, we will quickly change culture. Top persons in organisations have to set examples.

(iv) Further, *commitment, accountability and taking responsibility* can be inculcated through various practices such as role clarity, performance evaluations to be objective, etc. for creating organisation discipline.

(v) *Protecting the organisation from loose talk comes as a result of pride in the organisation*. This pride can be inculcated through good internal communications, such as to fully inform employees about company programmes. Work ethics can be created and nurtured among employees. Managerial action is required to achieve it.

(vi) *Involvement of employees* so that work is kept challenging, more satisfying and rewarding for individuals. It is productive.

(vii) *Developing an Attitude in Work*. It is relevant here to quote S.K. Chakraborty ("Human Values in Organisations—an Attitudinal Exploration of Values", in *Human Values for Managers*, Wheeler Publishing) that broadly, it is possible to *develop an attitude in work* situations on the following lines:

- I am blessed in this situation because, compared to millions of unemployed and underemployed, I have the *opportunity of working* in this position and enjoying relatively greater benefits and a better working environment.
- For whatever the organization has given me and done for me, I am grateful, and whatever *I do in return can never adequately compensate for them.*
- While it is my *duty to help my subordinates and peers* in enabling them to do their best for the overall welfare of the organization, it is not my business to sit in judgement over their actions, nor to take on the responsibility of reforming them to conform to what I think is right.
- The *Law of Karma* ensures a perfect balance between what I give to others and what I receive from them, no matter whether it is a mere thought/action/attitude, favourable or unfavourable, material or non-material. So, there is no reason for me either to feel depressed when PTE do not respond favourably to what I have done, or feel elated when my expectations come true.
- All those who work with me are essentially *different forms of my own true Self* and, therefore, I cannot injure others without in effect injuring my own Self, nor can I help them without in effect helping myself.
- If another person shows a negative attitude towards me, the real cause for that lies in myself and not in that person. It is infinitely more fruitful to *undergo introspection* to find and root out the negative attitude in my conduct.
- If I *discharge my duties properly, my rights will automatically be fulfilled,* sooner or later. It is the divine law. It is the law of Karma. It is the time-tested and confirmed theory of retribution and reward.

6. FUNCTIONS OF WORK, WHY IS WORK IMPORTANT TO INDIVIDUALS?

Some advantages from work and various functions it serves are:

(i) First, work serves *economic function* in exchange for work we receive income to support self and family. It provides economic self-sufficiency.

(ii) Second, work serves several *social functions*. The work place provides opportunities for meeting new people and develop friends and source of social interchange.

(iii) Third, work provides a source of *social status* in community. One's occupation gives importance to an individual in society. It serves as a source of social differentiation and also a source of social integration.

(iv) Fourth, work is an important *source of identify and self-esteem* and it is a means for self-actualisation. It provides a *sense of purpose* and clarify their contribution to society. Work shows employees mastery or competence in their job. It also reassures that they are of value to others.

(v) *Without work,* individual's experience *meaninglessness and powerlessness.*

(vi) It will be relevant to quote Sorab Sadri (*Business Ethics,* McGraw Hill) what he calls as new work ethics:
  - "Man is the *author* of his work.
  - It is through work that man elect to *identify* and nurture his talents.

- Work can *neither* be goalless nor motiveless.
- It is the integrity and honesty with which a man *executes a role* that distinguishes him from others.
- In work, the mind of man should merge knowledge, faith, contemplation and action.
- Fundamentally, *work is the manifestation of man* himself.
- It is the nature of man to work, as it is the nature of the sun to radiate.
- To deny man of work unjustly, therefore, is *to deny him of the opportunity to manifest himself.*
- Ultimately, when work ethics are redefined, it is really man who is being redefined; for both work and ethics relate to man."

7. DIFFERENT VIEWS ON WORK

- Max-Weber's—Protestant ethics, i.e. hard work, conservative, loyalty to organisation.
- Argyris, McGregor and Brown feel that work is basically a pleasant activity—it is driving force which gives direction and meaning to one's life.
- Another view is that work is an escape from hunger, boredom and illness.
- Like the Greeks, the Hebrews too regard work as drudgery.
- According to Freud, "work is an unpleasant activity."
- Bhagwat Gita advocates an entirely new philosophy to work. While *Vedas* preached the ethics of desires.

The Upanishads advocated an ethics based on pure knowledge, but Gita based itself not only on the elements of "desires" and "knowledge" in human nature, but also on third element in it, "activity."

Here the call is to act, "Act in the living present"—*Karma Yoga*. *Karma* means action, duty or work done not with selfish motive, but with the object of serving humanity. A man's primary duty is to perform the job allocated to him with devotion and perfection. Only then he can hope to achieve salvation.

Thus, Gita gives new dignity to work. Work is not unpleasant activity or some sort of punishment, but a way of life ordained by the Lord.

Work is something inherent in the nature of people. McGregor says the same thing. The Gita preaches the *mantra* of *Karma Yogi*. It preaches devotion to duty, to one's calling regardless of it's consequences.

Work is not only necessary to keep the body and mind occupied, it is necessary for perfection.

No work is inferior. All men who work have to be treated with dignity. Work is an end in itself according to Gita. Work is worship.

Human relations is a passion with Gita. The Lord sets a unique example in human relations by acting as the charioteer of Arjuna. He wanted to emphasize that no job was low or high. Besides he wanted to establish that a leader has to serve the masses. A leader is not the master but the servant of the people.

PART VI

CORPORATE GOVERNANCE

CHAPTER

39

Corporate Governance—Basic Ingredients

In this chapter on "Corporate Governance—Basic Ingredients", following aspects are mentioned:

1. Introduction.
2. Meaning of corporate governance.
3. Objectives of corporate governance.
4. Basic ingredients for good governance.
5. Corporate governance framework.
6. Reasons for recent interest in corporate governance.
7. Importance of corporate governance.
8. Philosophy on corporate governance of some companies. (Box 1)

1. INTRODUCTION

Suddenly the entire corporate world is talking about a subject which was not in the vocabulary a few years ago—corporate governance.

Governance implies a degree of control to be exercised by key stakeholders' representatives. Governance is about governing. It is not merely about ownership. Even an owner has to learn to govern. Good governance implies that the institution is run for the optimal benefit of the stakeholders in it.

The recognition of issues relating to corporate governance is timely as it is appalling that we come across so many instances of well regarded corporates looting their shareholders for personal gains of managers or the owners.

The list of companies that usually indulge in unethical business practices perhaps exceeds the list of good companies. A few companies which have attained the dubious distinction of appearing in press are—NEPC Group, MS Shoes East Limited (arrest of P. Sachdeva), Manu Chhabria Group, Orkay Mills, Harshad Mehta epic stock scam, Stern Group, JVJ, UTI 64 Scam, and host of engaged in teak plantations.

Immediately after liberalisation of Indian economy. in 1991-92 there were spate of public issues for capital (see Table 1) and hard earned money of small shareholder has been looted by the companies promoting public issues. Even their addresses are not available with the SEBI.

TABLE I

Public Issues for Capital

Year	*No. of Issues*	*Money Raised (Rupees in Crores)*
1989-90	186	2522
1990-91	140	1450
1991-92	195	1400
1992-93	526	5651
1993-94	765	10824
1994-95	1343	13302
1995-96	1423	8882
1996-97	740	4671
1997-98	58	1132
1998-99	22	504
1999-2000	56	2975
2000-June	56	701
	5510	54024

These companies have *betrayed the trust and confidence* by not fulfilling tall promises made to investors at the time of public issues.

This led to immediate economic depression in Indian economy and stock market was on downward trend on account of fraud, cheating, and breach of trust by corporate sector.

2. MEANING OF CORPORATE GOVERNANCE

Corporate governance is a *system by which companies are directed and controlled.* Thus, placing board of directors of a company in centre.

A corporate governance is "a conscious, deliberate and sustained efforts on the part of corporate entity to strike a *judicious balance between its own* interest and the interest of various constituents on the environment in which it is operating."

Simply stated corporate governance is a *formal system of accountability* of senior management to corporate stakeholders. It attempts to maintain balance between company's economic goals and social goals. Corporate governance includes company's accountability to shareholders and other shareholders such as employees, suppliers, customers and local community.

It ensures that corporate managers run their businesses successfully and in doing so *take care of long-term interests of all its stakeholders.* It improves capital efficiency of companies and deploys its wealth in more productive areas of the economy.

3. OBJECTIVES OF CORPORATE GOVERNANCE

Corporate governance has the following objectives:

(i) *To align* corporate goals with the goals of its stakeholders (society, shareholders, etc.).
(ii) To strengthen corporate functioning and *discourage its mismanagement*.
(iii) To achieve corporate goals by making investment in *best possible investment* corporates.
(iv) To *specify responsibility* of the Board of Directors and Managers in order to ensure good corporate performance.

The underlying philosophy in these efforts is to enhance the accountability of board members to shareholders. Good governance implies that institution is run for optimal benefit of stakeholders in it.

Even in a competitive environment, the expectations all around are of fair play and effort to excel by ethical means. Indeed ethical conduct promotes corporate success. It motivates the employees. Good corporate governance and ethical conduct is good policy for achieving success.

4. BASIC INGREDIENTS FOR GOOD GOVERNANCE

(a) *Accountability* of Board of Directors and their constituent responsibilities to the ultimate owners-shareholders.
(b) A key element of good governance is *transparency* and is perceived as such. It is shared way of corporate functioning and not a set of rules. Transparency in turn requires the right to information, timeliness and integrity of the information produced.
(c) System of *checks and balances* and greater simplicity in process of governance.
(d) *Clarity of responsibility* to enhance accountability.
(e) *Adherence to the rules*. Corporate action need to conform to letter and spirit to codes.
(f) Good governance involves *adequate reporting* to the shareholders and other stakeholders, for example, publish periodical reports in newspapers.

5. CORPORATE GOVERNANCE FRAMEWORK

Corporate governance refers to their structure, systems and processes in a corporation, that are considered most appropriate to enhance its wealth generating capacity. Codes of corporate governance are necessary as business organisation has to match upto both societal expectations and stakeholders' aspirations. The National Award for Excellence in Corporate Governance, 2006 went to ITC for IT Strong Corporate Governance Model and its visionary Leadership.

(a) As for example in ITC, decision-making within company has been broadly divided among 3 levels:

(i) *The Board of Directors* at the apex, as trustee of shareholders. Board bears responsibility of strategic supervision of company apart from fulfilling statutory obligations. Board bears the principal responsibility of fashioning a governance code.
Board's composition is a balanced mix of executive and non-executive directors, with non-executive directors constituting a fair majority.

(ii) Major responsibilities of board are on recommendations of *various sub-committees*:
  (a) Nominations committee,
  (b) Audit, legal committee, and
  (c) Remuneration committee concerned with senior management succession and appointment to board-related remuneration, compensation.

  Membership of sub-committees is confined to non-executive directors as a measure of transparency.

(iii) *Strategic management is delegated to corporate management committee* (comprising of whole time directors and senior management) for reviewing strategic business plans.

Through this 3-tired inter-linked governance process, a balance has been created for need for executive freedom and need for supervision, control and checks and balances.

The *formalised governance code prescribes* the highest ethical standards in the conduct of company business. Chairman of ITC sets personal example so that governance code is internalised within the organisation and becomes part of its culture.

6. REASONS FOR RECENT INTEREST IN CORPORATE GOVERNANCE

Some reasons for recent awareness for corporate governance are:

(i) Directors must realise that their job is to represent the shareholders and other stakeholders, and not offer themselves as the rubber stamp of the managing director.

(ii) There is rise of financial institutional investors and to safeguard their interest.

(iii) In the wake of globalisation, there are numerous takeover moves in corporate world. Significant foreign institutional investment is taking place in India. These investors expect companies to adopt globally acceptable practices of corporate governance and well-developed capital market.

(iv) Advent of investigating reporting in business journalism.

(v) Activism of regulatory bodies such as SEBI.

(vi) Corporate governance has to do with power and accountability.

(vii) Economy today is globalised. Economy demands that Indian firms should conform to the standards of international rules. Corporate governance helps in doing this.

Numerous companies have now laid elaborate systems, structures and processes as part of corporate governance. Companies are highlighting their practices of corporate governance in their annual reports.

7. IMPORTANCE OF CORPORATE GOVERNANCE

Corporate governance is important for the following reasons:

(a) It shapes the growth and future of capital markets of an economy.

(b) It helps firms in raising adequate finance from capital markets.

(c) It links company's management system with its financial reporting system.

(d) It enables management to take innovative decisions for effective functioning of an enterprise within the legal framework of accountability.

(e) It provides support to investors by making corporate accounting practices transparent to them. Corporate enterprises have to resort to disclosure of financial reporting structures.

(f) It provides for adequate and timely disclosure, reporting requirements, code of conduct etc. It avoids insider trading.

(g) It adds to international image of the corporate sector and enables home company to raise global capital.

Box I

Sixty-first Annual Report, 2005-06

TATA MOTORS LIMITED

Report on Corporate Governance

Company's Philosophy on Corporate Governance

As part of the Tata group, the Company's philosophy on Corporate Governance is founded upon a rich legacy of fair, ethical and transparent governance practices, many of which were in place even before they were mandated by adopting the highest standards of professionalism, honesty, integrity and ethical behaviour. Board, being elected by the shareholders is their representative and a bridge between them and the executive management. Since shareholders are residual claimants, the value creation and sustainability of all the stakeholders viz. customers, creditors, employees, vendors, community and the State are of paramount significance to the Company and its shareholders. The Board would therefore have a fiduciary relationship and a corresponding duty to all its stakeholders to ensure that their rights are protected. Through the Governance mechanism in the Company, the Board alongwith its Committees endeavours to strike the right balance with its various stakeholders. The Corporate Governance philosophy has been further strengthened with the implementation, a few years ago, by the Company of the Tata Business Excellence Model and the Tata Code of Conduct applicable to the Company, its directors and employees. The Company is in full compliance with the requirements of Corporate Governance under the revised Clause 49 of the Listing Agreement with the Indian Stock Exchanges. With the listing of the Company's Depositary Programme on the New York Stock Exchange, the Company is also compliant with US regulations, as applicable to Foreign Private Issuers (non-US listed companies) which cast upon the Board of Directors and the Audit Committee, onerous responsibilities to improve the operating efficiencies. Risk management and internal control functions are being geared up to meet the progressive governance standards.

BHARAT HEAVY ELECTRICALS LTD.

Report on Corporate Governance (Annual Report, 2005-06)

Philosophy on Corporate Governance

BHEL's Vision is to build a world class Engineering Enterprise committed to enhancing Stakeholder Value and its Mission is to be an Indian Multinational Engineering Enterprise providing total business solutions through quality products, systems and services in the fields of energy, industry, transportation, infrastructure and other potential areas.

However, all these are to be achieved within the parameters determined by our values—those which we have set and stood for, and those which we have imbibed from our international experience with reputed institutions world wide. Though our business environment will change, our commitment to ethical and moral standards of business conduct will remain constant.

BHEL believes that proper Corporate Governance facilitates effective realization of goals; simultaneously ensuring high level of business ethics. Therefore, emphasis is on fulfilling the true spirit of Corporate Governance and not just the letter of law. BHEL's Corporate Governance policy is based on the following principles:

(i) Independence and versatility of the Board;
(ii) Integrity and ethical behaviour of all personnel;
(iii) Recognition of obligations towards all stakeholders—customers, employees and shareholders;
(iv) High degree of disclosure and transparency levels;
(v) Total compliance with laws in all environments in which the company operates; and
(vi) Achievement of above goals with compassion for people and environment.

To conclude, the company believes that conducting business in a manner that complies with the Corporate Governance procedures and Code of Conduct, exemplifies each of our core values, positions us to deliver long-term returns for our shareholders, favourable outcomes for our customers and attractive opportunities for our employees.

CHAPTER

40

Company Management

In this chapter we shall briefly discuss the following aspects relating to managing companies:

(1) Government machinery for administration of The Companies Act, 1956.
(2) Functions of the board of directors.
(3) The Chairman of the board.
(4) The Committees of the board.
(5) Duties of Directors.
(6) Role of Company Secretary.

(1) GOVERNMENT MACHINERY FOR ADMINISTRATION OF THE COMPANIES ACT, 1956

Central Government is to administer and enforce this Act through *Department of Company Affairs* under Ministry of Finance.

1.1 The Company Law Board

For day-to-day administration of the Act, the Company Law Board is set-up. Its powers have enlarged from 1991.

(i) It is a quasi-judicial body. It exercises powers of the court or hitherto with government.
(ii) Members of Company Law Board not to exceed 9 and are to be appointed by the Government and one of them to be the Chairman. Tenure of members is upto 3 years.
(iii) Members form separate benches and will enjoy powers of civil court to enforce inspection of documents/evidence.
(iv) Members have powers for execution of its orders.
(v) Appeal against the orders of the Company Law Board lies before High Court and is final.

1.2 Registrar of Companies (RoC)

He is for most of routine functions of Company Law Board, such as for filing documents and returns. RoC is basically a registry and an office of record. It has four regional offices at Mumbai, Kolkata, Madras and Kanpur.

Advisory Committee: It is to advise Company Law Board and the government as may be referred by either of them.

1.3 Jurisdiction of Courts

Respective High Courts have power for their jurisdiction. Central government may empower any district court to exercise powers of High Court except for:

(i) Investigation into company's affairs,
(ii) Power to sanction compromise with creditors, and
(iii) Sanction amalgamation.

Civil Courts under general law can exercise power for personal rights, i.e. matters such as breach of trust, compensation by company to shareholders.

(2) FUNCTIONS OF THE BOARD OF DIRECTORS

Good governance is the primary duty of the board. It is responsible for setting standards and ensurance that company achieves them. The Chairman will have a major impact. Board is considered as agent or trustees. They are liable for negligence, breach of trust under the Companies Law.

(a) Board is the representative of the shareholders to ensure the company has clear goals and to measure progress against these goals.
(b) The board will agree the strategy and resources needed to achieve it.
(c) The chief executive is appointed by the board who monitors his performance.
(d) Board must annually review succession and management development plans.
(e) Board will set and monitor the operating climate in the company through statement of values (policies, etc.).
(f) Limiting senior executive's compensation.
(g) Environmental protection.
(h) Avoidance of fraud within company.
(i) Hiring and firing key executives.
(j) Caring for employee's interest.
(k) Ensuring active participation in local community welfare schemes.
(l) Acquisition and disposal of assets of the company or its subsidiaries.
(m) Investments, capital projects, authority levels, treasury (banking policies and risk management policies).
(n) Director to act in good faith and act honestly.

(3) THE CHAIRMAN OF THE BOARD

It is proper to separate role of Chairman from Chief Executive in the interest or providing checks and balances.

- Chairman is leader of the Board.
- Chairman must set standards for Board of Directors.
- Chairman is a link between Board and shareholders.
- Chairman must be satisfied with corporate reporting to shareholders such as interim and annual results, annual general meeting, etc.

(4) THE COMMITTEES OF THE BOARD

There are three major committees of the Board. Their role is explained:

(i) Audit Committee

(a) Most important committee for providing checks and balances and for internal control.
(b) Review the interim and final accounts.
(c) Keep board informed of financial reporting and areas of disagreements with the auditors.
(d) To decide impartially disputes between management and external auditors.
(e) Audit fee is appropriate and auditor work plan is adequate.
(f) Meet atleast twice a year.
(g) It comprises of minimum three directors who are non-executives.

(ii) Remuneration Committee

(a) To keep lid on executive remuneration.
(b) To have a reward policy that can attract, retain and motivate directors to achieve goals of the company.
(c) Acts independently with access to its own external advice.
(d) Performance packages decided are linked with shareholder interest.
(e) Annual Report presents clear view of policies of the company.

(iii) Nomination Committee

It is chaired by the Chairman and non-ex-Directors are brought in for selection.

(5) DUTIES OF DIRECTORS

1. To attend board meetings and devote attention and care to the affairs of the company.
2. Not allow other Directors to commit liable acts.
3. Not to exceed his powers.
4. Act in best interests of company and stakeholders and customers, also creditors (not to defraud them).
5. Maintain confidentiality.
6. Not to make secret profits.

7. Not to misapply company assets.
8. Not to compete in business with the company.

Directors to "act in good faith and genuinually otherwise liable in the court under Secs. 201 and 633 of the Companies Act, 1956. Court to be satisfied that director had acted honestly and reasonably.

(6) ROLE OF COMPANY SECRETARY

The Company Secretary finds his or her rightful place as a professional by virtue of being a member of a recognized professional body, which exercises supervisory jurisdiction over its members. The Institute of the Company Secretaries of India highlights that in every corporate, there is a strong back-bone—the company secretary. By virtue of integrated knowledge of multiple disciplines of law, management, finance and corporate goverance, a Company Secretary is the vital link between the company, its board of directors, shareholders, government and other agencies.

The Company Secretary is:

- An expert in corporate laws, securities laws and capital market and corporate governance.
- Chief advisor to the board of directors on best practices in corporate governance.
- Responsible for all regulatory compliances of company.
- Corporate planner and strategic manager.
- Continuing professional development.
- Pre-membership Training (16 Months).
- Final Examination (9 Papers).
- Intermediate Examination (8 Papers).
- Foundation Examination (5 Papers).

CS Course: Eligibility

- For Intermediate Course: Graduation.
- For Foundation Course: 10+2.
- Students of any discipline in Arts, Commerce and Science excluding Fine Arts can pursue this course.

Under the Company Secretaries Act, 1980

When the ICSI became a statutory body under the Company Secretaries Act, 1980, the code of conduct envisioned in the First and the Second Schedules to the Act became a statutory prescription. These schedules describe certain items of conduct, which are prohibited and they are considered as "Professional Misconduct." The Company Secretaries are required not to indulge in such practices. The professional misconducts are broadly described in the said schedules as under:

First Schedule

Part I: Professional misconduct applicable to the members of the Institute in *Practice*—(12 Clauses).

Part II: Professional misconduct in relation to the members of the Institute in *Service*—(3 Clauses).

Part III: Professional misconduct in relation to members of the Institute *generally*—(4 Clauses).

Second Schedule

Part I: Professional misconduct in relation to the members of the Institute in *Practice* requiring action by a High Court—(10 Clauses).

Part II: Professional misconduct in relation to the members of the Institute *generally* requiring action by a High Court—(2 Clauses).

With the Companies (Amendment) Act of 1988, the practising side of the Company Secretaries Profession came into being. This aspect has been growing very fast during the last few years, as can be seen from the certification works mentioned below:

(a) With the increase in the threshold limit to Rs. 2 crores, for appointment of whole-time secretary, secretarial compliance report has been introduced in the case of companies having a paid up share capital of ten lakhs of rupees or more, as to whether the company has complied with all the provisions of the Companies Act, 1956 and such a Certificate of Compliance issued by a Secretary in whole-time practice should be attached to the Board's report.

(b) Certification of Annual Return by a Secretary in whole time practice in the case of listed companies.

(c) Certification of certain forms and returns filed with the ROC.

(d) Secretarial Audit Report introduced by SEBI regarding reconciliation of total admitted capital with both the depositories and the total issued and listed capital.

(e) Certification of Compliance of Corporate Governance.

(f) Various recognitions and certification work secured by the Institute.

The Companies (Amendment) Bill, 2003 proposes to enlarge further the scope of practice by a Company Secretary, as under:

(i) The Central Government may at any time, direct Secretarial Compliance audit of a Company, if that Government is of the opinion that the affairs of the Company are not being conducted in accordance with the provisions of the Companies Act, 1956 and such an audit should be conducted by a Company Secretary—Section 383B of the Bill.

(ii) All documents, returns, and forms required to be filed with the Registrar or any statutory authority should be pre-certified by a Company Secretary in whole-time practice [Section 383C of the Bill].

Need for Evolving New Norms of Professional Ethics and Etiquette

What the Company Secretaries Act, 1980 describes as professional misconduct are minimum expectations. There is no limit for maximising and enhancing these values and norms.

Any effective system of code of conduct or misconduct cannot be legislated to meet all situations. There is a limit to legislative effort. At the same time, any code of conduct, however pervasive it may be, cannot remain static, as the value system keeps changing from time to time.

The professional misconducts described in the Company Secretaries Act are prohibitive in nature, as they are worded negatively. However, the professional ethics and etiquette must make positive assertions of uncompromising honesty, integrity, professional competence, high quality of service, maintenance of confidentiality of clients' information and a high degree of ethical behaviour and morality. These are sterling qualities of head and heart and needs to be cultivated consciously.

Observance of Code of Conduct and Professional Ethics

It is clear from the above that the Company Secretary, be it in employment or practice renders a host of services to the corporate sector and other clients. The practising side of the Profession is fast expanding and the Company Secretary is being called upon to shoulder higher responsibilities. This calls for extensive training and an ability to distinguish between righteous conduct from those deviant and unedifying.

P.T. Rangamani states that Professionals are key figures in corporate management. They are change agents with the capability to clean up the organisation and put in place proper legal and ethical strategies as part of the day-to-day management. A professional worth the name should have faith and commitment to the basic ethics of his calling.

References

S. Krishnamoorthy, Professional Ethics and Social Commitment, *Chartered Secretary*, November 2003.

D.K. Prahlada Rao, Code of Conduct and Professional Ethics, *Chartered Secretary*, November 2003.

Code of Conduct for Company Secretaries, issued by ICSI.

P.T. Rangamani, Ethics, Business and Professions, *Chartered Secretary*, November 2003.

www.icsi.edu

CHAPTER

41

Factors for Success of Corporate Governance

In this chapter on "Factors for Success of Corporate Governance", (C.G.) the following aspects are covered:

(i) C.G. subject not in vacabulary a decade ago.
(ii) Meaning and basic ingredients of good governance.
(iii) Corporate governance followed by companies.
(iv) Factors for success of C.G.
(v) Factors influencing quality of governance.
(iv) To conclude.

(I) C.G. SUBJECT NOT IN VOCABULARY A DECADE AGO

C.G. has an important role to play as an instrument of *investor's protection*. It is a tool to judge and evaluate the standards and ethics of corporate management.

C.G. Code *is a guide* to govern the operations and affairs of the company in a manner which will *enhance the long-term* value of the company for all those who are associated with it, viz. shareholders, creditors, customers, government, employees and society at large.

The importance of C.G. lies in its contribution both to *business prosperity* and to accountability to shareholders. C.G. has its origin in U.K. Issues involving C.G. are taking a high profile and have *come to the fore* recently *in India*.

Awareness of C.G. in India is timely as it is appalling that we come across many instances of *corporates looting their shareholders* for personal gains of owners.

IMF study shows that after liberalisation between *1992 to 1998* large number of *public issues* for capital collected large amounts:

Period	*No. of Issues*	*Money Raised (Rs. in crores)*
1991-92	195	1400
1992-98	4855	44462
1998-99	22	504

- IMF study states Indians deposited hundred billion dollars in *foreign banks.*
- USA research study during 1994 and 1995, showed India's capital *flight to USA* was to tune of four to eleven billion dollars.

To mention some scams in India—Harshad Mehta, Ketan Parekh, UTI, RIL, etc. Corporate accounting scandals have created a crises of investor's confidence.

USA also facing scams—Worldcom, ENRON, TYCO, VIVEDI, MARCONI, QUEST, MERC, XEROX, etc. in 2001. Greed and dishonesty has lead to dismal ethical standards in business. USA is passing through trying time.

Pressures of competition have raised *fresh concern about legal, ethical and moral* dimensions of enterprise, such as invoking codes of conduct and benchmark best system and practices as a part of good corporate responsibility.

(II) MEANING AND BASIC INGREDIENTS OF GOOD GOVERNANCE

Meaning

In practice, C.G. means *role of the board of directors* of the company, and *its* ***auditors,*** towards protecting the shareholders' (in fact all stakeholders) interest in every business decisions. The board of directors have *to set proper* organisation structure, systems, norms and processes for *direction, supervision* and *accountability* of their corporation.

Basic ingredients of CG are:

(i) *Accountability* of board of directors to ultimate owners, shareholders and their satisfaction programme. Promoting a social and economic order.

(ii) *Transparency in timely disclosures* of right information with integrity.

(iii) *Clarity in responsibilities* of directors, chairman and managing director through empowerment to enhance accountability.

(iv) *Quality and competence of directors* and their track record. Popular participation in decision-making, implementation and responsiveness.

(v) *Checks and balances* in governance. Conforming to, laws, rules and spirit of codes.

- Thus good C.G. is adaptation of *best practices* by ensuring higher level of *transparency* and *accountability, fairness* in operations, *full disclosure,* and *integrity* and compliance to laws.

(III) CORPORATE GOVERNANCE FOLLOWED BY COMPANIES

Now companies are explaining in their annual reports about the compliance of C.G. I.T.C. Ltd. highlighted C.G. (in August 1998) compliance set-up in their corporation.

Every year the prestigious "Golden Peacock award for excellence in Corporate Governance and Corporate Social Responsibility" is given. Last year it was won by TISCO.

(IV) FACTORS FOR SUCCESS OF C.G.

1. Structural-Dimension

Norms of conduct for board of directors are laid in *Indian Companies Act*. Activism of *regulatory bodies (SEBI)* is essential. Lot more tightening of regulations is needed.

Legislation alone cannot ensure ethical conduct. The spirit invoked by *voluntary codes* is also important. *Chairman has to set* personal example so that governance code is internalised within the organisation. Emphasis on this is a positive trend, but still more to go.

2. Cultural-Dimension

Society—their values, morals and awakening, their *responses to corrupt practices* are crucial to be highlighted by investigative business journalism. Role of internal *"whistle blowers"* is vital to bring to light wrong practices.

In final analysis, success of corporation depends on the professional ethics of managers/ directors and they should not offer themselves as rubber stamp of M.D./owner. They have to create a *value-based* organisation culture by following ethical standards. The chairman has to set personal example to interalise code of corporate governance.

3. Commitment to Ethical Values

Corporations have to recognise the importance of *commitment to values and servicing the interest of the stakeholders*, which alone can ensure survival and growth in the long-run. Good C.G. can be created *consciously adhering* to entrepreneurship and pursuit of excellence. Corporation to ensure that highest *standards of ethics* and responsible conduct *are met* throughout the organisation.

It is now established that a high sense of professional morality must comprise one of the core-values of corporate governance, for long-term as well as short-term success of the industry. Ethical values are now-a-days not looked upon, any more, as costs imposed on the industry, or a check on efficiency and profit maximization, but are considered imperatives for sustainable corporate growth. Prof. Amartya Sen asserts that ethics can be good economics and, thus a valid pursuit of corporate governance.

A high-developed sense of integrity and ethics enables corporate governance to build a trusting, long-term relationship with customers and consumers. Ethics, thus surely makes a lot of economic sense.

(V) FACTORS INFLUENCING QUALITY OF GOVERNANCE

Quality of governance is influenced by integrity of the management, ability of the board, adequacy of the processes, commitment level of individual board members, and quality of corporate reporting and participation of stakeholders in the management. [Sanjiv Agarwal]

Quality of governance depends on the following factors:

(i) *Integrity of Management*: A Board of directors with a low level of integrity is tempted to misuse the trust reposed by shareholders and other stakeholders to take decisions that benefit a few at the cost of others.

(ii) *Ability of the Board*: The collective ability, in terms of knowledge and skill, determines the effectiveness of the Board.

(iii) *Adequacy of the process*: Board of Directors cannot effectively supervise the executive management if the process fails to provide sufficient and timely information to the Board, necessary for reviewing plans and the performance of the enterprise.

(iv) *Commitment level of individual board members*: The quality of a board depends on the commitment of individual members to tasks, which they are expected to perform as board members.

(v) *Financial Reporting*: Accuracy and transparency in financial statements and disclosure, internal controls and independence of auditors.

(vi) *Participation of stakeholders in the management*: The level of participation of stakeholders determines the number of new ideas being generated in optimum utilization of resources and for improving the administrative structure and the process.

(vii) *Quality of Corporate Reporting*: The quality of corporate reporting depends on the transparency and timeliness of corporate communication with shareholders. This helps the shareholders in making economic decisions and in correctly evaluating the management in its stewardship.

Best practices of corporate governance will broadly include—a definition of practices that define good governance; a code of best practices covering the constitution of the board, its various Committees, defining their goals and responsibilities, exploring preferred internal systems and disclosure requirements. Qualitative improvement in the corporate governance in our country based on a code of good corporate practices and meaningful disclosure of information to shareholders hold the key to corporate success.

This is necessary in the context of changing profile of corporate ownership, with the increasing flow of foreign investment, preferential allotment of shares to the promoters of companies and the new role being given to mutual funds. This means better governance and management of corporate bodies, prompt compliance of legal and financial obligations and adherence to ecological and environmental standards. The benefit of such governance must accrue to the investors, customers, and lenders of finance and to the society at large.

Objective of Good Governance

It is felt that objective of corporate governance, i.e. the overall objective of wealth generation and competitiveness for the benefit of all can best be achieved through the twin components of:

- An "inclusive approach to *director's duties* which requires directors to have regard to all the relationship on which the company depends and to the long, as well as the short-term implications of their actions, with a view to achieving company success for the benefit of shareholders as a whole; and
- Wider *public accountability*: this is to be achieved principally through improved company reporting.

(VI) TO CONCLUDE

Corporate governance is a *process or a set of systems and processes* to ensure that company is managed to suit the best interest of all stakeholders. The stakeholders may be internal (promoters, members, workmen and executives) and external (shareholders, customers, lenders, dealers, vendors, bankers, community, government and regulators, etc.). It is interplay between companys, shareholders, creditors, capital markets, financial sectors, institutions and law. Corporate governance is concerned with the *establishment of a system* whereby the directors are entrusted with responsibilities and duties in relation to the directions of corporate affairs. Maximization of shareholder's wealth is the cornerstone of good governance.

The concept of corporate governance hinges on total transparency, integrity and accountability of the management, which includes non-executive directors. The importance of corporate governance lies in its contribution both to business prosperity and to accountability.

C.G. has attained international importance. More than profits, it is the quality of governance which will ensure corporate survival and growth and reinforce the faith of different stakeholders in a company. This will help in retaining customer's loyalty in the knowledge millennium. Leadership's ethical values can infuse new work culture throughout the organisation.

Reference

Sanjiv Agarwal, Corporate Excellence—A Product of Good Corporate Governance, *Vistar*, New Delhi.

CHAPTER

42

Codes of Corporate Governance

In this chapter on "Codes of Corporate Governance", the following aspects are covered:

1. Work on corporate governance in India.
2. Committees on corporate governance: Global perspective.
3. Need for audit committees.
4. Recommendations of Naresh Chandra Committee.

In view of many scandals and frauds in accounting, it is felt that corporate governance should extend beyond corporate law. There should be greater *transparency* and maximising *shareholder's value,* so there should be good corporate code containing corporate practices.

Many developed countries have documented corporate codes to meet the need.

I. WORK ON CORPORATE GOVERNANCE IN INDIA

India has formulated codes of corporate governance through various committees, more important ones being:

(i) CII (Rahul Bajaj) Committee, 1996 Recommendations

On Board of Directors

(i) Simple structure of Board and should meet 6 times a year and 1/2 days' discussion.
(ii) Listed companies in excess of Rs. 200 crores and above to have non-executive directors atleast 30%. They were to pay an important role in the interest of shareholders.
(iii) Director not to be on the board of 10 companies.
(iv) Director who does not attend 50% or more meetings not to be considered for re-appointment.

(v) Audit committee to be appointed to assist the Board.
(vi) All key information to be placed before the Board of Directors.

Rules for Governance of Companies

(i) Members of the Board to have clearly defined responsibilities.
(ii) Board should not be bull dozed by the nominees of the management.
(iii) Financial institutions to divest their stake if less than 10% stake in company.
(iv) Company should not accept further deposits, if they have defaulted on fixed deposits.
(v) Key information e.g., annual operating plans and budgets, quarterly results, internal audit reports to be reported to the Board.

(ii) Kumar Mangalam Birla Committee on Corporate Governance (2000) Recommended that:

- Board to set-up qualified and independent audit committee to enhance the credibility of financial disclosures and to promote transparency.
- Companies to provide consolidated statements in respect of all its subsidiaries in which they hold 51% or more of the share capital.
- Shareholders to show greater degree of interest and involvement in the appointment of directors and auditors.
- SEBI norms to be laid.

(iii) Naresh Chandra Committee on Corporate Audit and Governance (2002) Recommended that:

- Audit firm's rotation is not required.
- Every five years, audit partner should rotate.
- Audit committee to be set-up of all independent directors.
- Companies to have atleast 50 percent independent directors.
- Certain professional assignments should not be undertaken by auditors.

(iv) Recommendations of Narayana Murthy Committee

SEBI constituted a Committee on Corporate Governance with the Chairmanship of Shri N.R. Narayana Murthy. The Committee included representatives from the stock exchanges, chambers, commerce and industry, investor associations and professionals, and debated on key issues and made recommendations as under. Some mandatory recommendations of the Committee are:

(a) Audit Committees of Publicly Listed Companies should required to review the following information mandatorily

(i) Financial statements and draft audit report including quarterly, half yearly financial information.
(ii) Management discussion and analysis of financial condition results of operations.
(iii) Reports relating to compliance with laws.
(iv) Management letter/letters of internal control weaknesses issues by statutory/internal auditors.
(v) Records of related party transactions.

(b) Disclosure of Accounting Treatment

In case a company has followed a treatment different from the prescribed in an accounting standard, companies should be give reasonable period of time within which to cure the qualifications SEBI/Stock Exchanges. Mere explanations from companies is not be sufficient.

(c) Risk Management—Board Disclosure

Procedures should be in place to inform Board members about the risk assessment and minimization procedures.

(d) Training of Board Members

Companies should be encouraged to train their Board members on the business model of the company as well as the risk profile of the business parameters of the company, their responsibilities as directors and the best ways to discharge them.

(e) Written Code of Conduct for Executive Management

It should be obligatory for the Board of a company to lay down the code of conduct for all Board members and senior management of a company. The code of conduct shall be posted on the website of the company.

All Board members and senior management personnel shall affirm compliance with the code on an annual basis. The annual report of be company shall contain a declaration to this effect signed-off by the CEO and COO.

(f) Nominee Directors—Exclusion of Nominee Directors from the Definition of Independent Directors

The committee recommends that there shall be no nominee directors where an institution wishes to appoint a director on the board, such appointment should be made by the shareholders. An institutional director so appointed shall be subject to the same abilities as any other director. Similarly, nominee of the Government on public sector companies shall be similarly elected and shall be subject to the same responsibilities and liabilities as other directors.

(g) Non-executive Directors' Compensation—Limits on Compensation paid to Independent Directors

All compensation paid non-executive directors may be fixed by the Board of Directors and should be approved by the shareholders in general meetings. Limits should be set for the maximum number of stock options that can be granted to non-executive directors in any financial year and in aggregate. The stock options granted to the non-executive directors shall vest after a period of at least one year from the date such non-executive directors have retired from the Board of the company.

(h) Internal Policy on Access to Audit Committees

Personnel who observe an unethical or improper practice (not necessarily a violation of law) should be able to approach the audit committee without necessarily informing their supervisors. Companies should take measures to ensure that this right of access is communicated to all employees through means of internal circulars, etc.

(i) Whistle Blower Policy

Companies should annually affirm that they have not denied any personnel access to the audit committee of the company and that they have provided protection to 'whistle blower' from unfair termination and other unfair or prejudicial employment practices.

The appointment, removal and terms of remunerations of the chief internal auditor must be subject to review by the audit committee. Such affirmation shall form part of the Board's Report on corporate governance that is required to be prepared and submitted together with the annual report.

2. COMMITTEES ON CORPORATE GOVERNANCE: GLOBAL PERSPECTIVE

A number of Committees were set-up to look into the various aspects of corporate governance. These include:

(i) Sir Adrian Cadbury Committee on Financial Aspects of Corporate Governance (1992).
(ii) Mervyn E. King's Committee on Corporate Governance (1994).
(iii) Greenbury Committee on directors' remuneration (1995).
(iv) Calpers global corporate governance principles (1996).
(v) Business Round Table (BRT) Statement on Corporate Governance (1997).
(vi) Hampel Committee on Corporate Governance (1998).
(vii) Blue Ribbon Committee on Improving the Effectiveness of Corporate Audit Committees (1999).
(viii) Combined Code of best practices (LSE), 1998.
(ix) OECD Principles of Corporate Governance (1999).
(x) CACG principles for Corporate Governance in Commonwealth (1999).

These committees/codes recommended the following in relation to accounts, reporting audit.

(i) Cadbury Committee on Financial Aspects of Corporate Governance (1992)

- Audit committee to have minimum three members, written terms of reference and authority to investigate.
- Listed companies to publish full financial statements annually and half yearly reports interim.

Code of Best Practice to Incorporate

(i) Board to present assessment of company's position.
(ii) Directors to report on effectiveness of internal control systems.
(iii) Aspects to be included by audit committee.

(ii) King's Committee on Corporate Governance (1994)

- Effective internal Audit function.
- Establishment of Audit Committee.
- Observance of highest level of business and professional ethics.
- Accounting standards in line with international standards.

(iii) Blue Ribbon Committee on improving the Effectiveness of Corporate Audit Committees (1999)

- Members of Audit Committee to be independent.
- Audit Committee to consist of independent directors only.
- Audit Committee to have minimum of three directors—each to be financially literate.
- Audit committee to have formal written charter, approved by the full board, specifying.
  - o responsibilities, and
  - o structure, process and membership.
- Charter to specify outside auditor's responsibility towards board and Committee.
- Companies to attach with Annual Report a letter from Audit Committee as to whether or not:
  - o management reviewed the audited financial statements with the committee;
  - o outside auditors discussed with the committee, their judgements; and
  - o committee believes that company's financial statements are fairly presented in conformity with generally accepted accounting practices (GAAP).

(iv) CACG Guidelines—Principles for Corporate Governance in the Commonwealth (1999)

- ensure that the corporation complies with all relevant laws, regulations and codes of best business practice;
- ensure that the corporation communicates with shareholders and other stakeholders effectively;
- serve the legitimate interests of the shareholders of the corporation and account to them fully;
- Regularly review processes and procedures to ensure the effectiveness of its internal systems and control, so that the decision- making capability and the accuracy of its reporting and financial results are maintained at a high level at times; and
- Ensure annually that the corporation will continue as a going concern for its next fiscal year.

Companies and auditors should apply the following principles:

- *Financial reporting*—The Board should present a balanced and understandable assessment of the company's position and prospects.
- *Internal control*—The Board should maintain a sound system of internal control to safeguard shareholder's investments and repay assets.
- *Relationship with auditors*—The Board should establish forms and transparent arrangements for maintaining and appropriate relationships with the company's auditors. Audit committee should be established and be responsible to board. It should review the scope and result of the audit, its cost effectiveness and the independence and objectivity of auditors.
- *External Auditors*—The external auditors should independently report to shareholder in accordance with statutory and professional requirements and independently assure

the board on the discharge of its responsibilities (financial reporting, internal control) in accordance with professional guidance.
- *The auditors have dual responsibility*—The public report to shareholders on the statutory financial statements and on other matters and additional private reporting to directors on operational matters.

Ronnie Hampel's final findings are as follows:

- Each company should establish an audit committee of at least three non-executive directors, at least two of them independent. It does not favour a general relaxation for smaller companies, but recommend shareholder to show flexibility in considering cases of difficulty on their merits.
- It does not recommend any additional requirements on auditors to report on governance issues, nor the removal of any existing prescribed requirements.
- It suggests that the bodies concerned should consider reducing from 10 percent the limit on the proportion of total income which an audit firm may earn from one audit client.
- It suggests that the audit committee should keep under review the overall financial relationship between the company and its auditors to ensure a balance between the maintenance of objectivity and value for money.
- It recommends that the directors should report on the company's system of internal control. It also recommends that the auditors should report on internal control privately to the directors, which allows for an effective dialogue to take place and for best practice to evolve.
- Directors should maintain and review controls relating to all relevant control objectives, and not merely financial controls.
- Companies which do not already have a separate internal audit function should from time to time review the need for one.
- The requirement on directors to include a "going concern" statement in annual report should be retained.
- Auditors are inhibited from going beyond their present functions by concerns about the law on liability. Account should be taken of these concerns by those responsible for professional standards and in taking decisions on changes in the law.

Similar principles have been incorporated by combined code of good corporate governance and code of best practices as adopted by London Stock Exchange.

3. NEED FOR AUDIT COMMITTEES

(a) The corporate accounting malaise is spreading world over. The reasons for accounting failures could be varied, but are certainly worrisome. The examples of Enron Corporation's financial scandal, Worldcom's accounting absurdity and myriad of complex financial interrelationships between widely dispersed subsidiaries, Xerox's overstating revenues, Merck, Quest Communications, etc. These suggest the clue that audit committee function can come to rescue to solve this problem. In India too, there are reasons that demand necessity for strengthening of accounting and audit function—siphoning of funds, capital erosion, non-repayment of deposits and debentures, etc.—all have something to do with financial reporting. It is now seen everywhere that it is the *accounting issues that are becoming major issues of corporate governance.*

(b) An effective audit committee should not function as a policing agent, to assess risk or to guess or judge audit performance. A good *audit committee should satisfy themselves* that auditors are to watch the interests of stakeholders if something foul and fishy is observed. Audit committee should instill confidence and trust amongst readers and uses of financial statements. Infact, more valuable than the qualified report one gets from the auditors, might be an assurance from the audit committee that the figures and reporting ought to be correct and reliable.

(c) Corporate scandals are the good reasons for having effective audit committee.

(d) Recently, KPMG in UK has launched a UK Audit Committee Institute (ACI) to help members of audit committee meet their increasing governance demands placed upon them.

(e) Audit Committee as a Committee of Board

The Audit Committee should ideally comprise of at least 3-4 non-executive directors (wholetime directors to be invitees). The Audit Committee is established to give additional assurance regarding the quality and reliability of the financial information used by the board and financial information issued by the company. Its activities would normally include reviewing financial statements and inspection reports, ensuring the sound functioning and compliance with various relevant statutes; monitoring: (a) control of corporate risks, (b) establishment of an appropriate internal control framework, (c) activities of the internal audit department; and liaison with external auditors. The Audit Committee should ensure that adequate mechanism for prevention and detection of frauds, is in place. The Audit Committee should confirm to the board once a year that the internal controls of the company are adequate. The Committee should meet at least four times a year.

(f) Audit Function under Sarbanes—Oxley Act

The Sarbanes—Oxley Act, 2002, a recent enactment in US which deals with corporate governance and corporate social responsibilities has also emphasized on the audit function and financial disclosures. It strengthens the power, importance and *independence of audit committee.* It provides for constitution of Public Company Accounting Oversight Board to oversee the audit of public companies that are subject to securities laws, establish audit report standards and rules and inspect, investigate and enforce compliance on the part of registered public accounting firms, their associates and accountants. It also lays emphasis on audit independence and prohibits an auditor from performing specified non-audit services alongwith an audit. Audit firms will be appointed by and will report directly to the audit committee and subjected to rotation of partner and firm.

In India, the office of Comptroller and Audition General (CAG) functions as an oversight audit body for audit of public sector companies.

(g) Audit Committee: Statutory Provisions in India

Section 292A of the Companies Act, 1956 (inserted w.e.f. 13.12.2000) contains a provision relating to establishment of audit committee by every public company having paid up capital of Rs. five crores or more.

Clause 49 of the uniform listing agreement prescribed by the Securities and Exchange Board of India is applicable to all listed companies. Clause 49 of listing agreement deals with corporate governance and prescribes for setting up of a qualified and independent audit committee.

(h) As per section 292A of Companies Act, 1956, audit committee should have discussions with the auditors periodically about internal control systems, scope of audit including the observations of auditors and review of the half yearly and annual financial statements before submission to the board and also ensure compliance of internal control systems. It shall have authority to investigate into any matter in relation to such matters and shall have full access to information contained in records of the company.

(i) As per clause 49 of the listing agreement, audit committee is empowered to investigate any activity within terms of reference, seek information from any employee and recommend appointment and removal of external auditor, fixation of audit fees, approval for payment for other services, review with the management the annual financial statements before submission to board, review adequacy of internal control system, oversight of company's financial reporting process and disclosure of its financial information to ensure that financial statements are correct, sufficient and credible, reviewing adequacy of internal audit function, reviewing company's financial and risk management policies, etc.

4. RECOMMENDATIONS OF NARESH CHANDRA COMMITTEE

Naresh Chandra Committee on corporate audit and governance has suggested that the audit committees should consist entirely of independent directors. An audit committee charter would have to be prepared which would lay down the role and functions of the audit committee. It has suggested that audit committee of listed companies and unlisted public company with paid up share capital and free reserves of Rs. 10 crore or more or turnover of Rs. 50 crore or more should be made up entirely of independent directors.

Naresh Chandra Committee on Corporate audit and governance which submitted its report in last week of December 2002, has also not recommended statutory rotation of audit firms but favoured compulsory audit partner rotation on the lines of recently enacted US Sarbanes Oxley Act. Going by global practices and the fact that there is no conclusive proof of the gains before deciding the audit firm rotation, it has observed that rotation of audit firms would not result in any better governance. Rotation of auditors is likely to cause a major dislocation when a new auditor firm is appointed. It takes time to understand the complexities of a business and more mistakes tend to happen in the first two years.

It has suggested that the partners and atleast fifty percent of the engagement team (excluding article clerks and trainees) responsible for the audit of either a listed company or companies whose paid up capital and free reserves exceed Rs. 10 crore or companies whose turnover exceed Rs. 50 crore should be rotated every five years. It has also held that persons who are compulsorily rotated could, need be, allowed to return after a break of three years, as prevail in European Union and IFAC. It has, however, recommended setting up of Corporate Serious Fraud Office/Quality Review Boards for punishing erring professionals.

Reference

Sanjiv Agarwal, Corporate Governance and Audit Committee, *Chartered Secretary*, October 2003.

CHAPTER

43

Evaluation of Corporate Governance

In this chapter on "Evaluation of Corporate Governance", the following aspects are covered:

1. Evaluation process of corporate governance.
2. Conducting board's performance evaluation.
3. Role of the chairman of the board.

I. EVALUATION PROCESS OF CORPORATE GOVERNANCE

Evaluation is a process of judging performance and efficiency of boards. Whether boards are executing its role and responsibility effectively.

It is like *introspection* and a part of board planning process. It helps in continuous feedback as termed by Zandera.

Feedback Cycle in a Board

(1) Board's Goals and Plan of Action → (2) Action by Board → (3) Effect on Board, Organisation or Environment

↓

(4) Information Gathered on Board's Output and its Effects → (5) Board to Compare Board's Goals and Actual Performance Introspection → (6) Steps to Reduce Discrepancy by Changing Board's Actions

2. CONDUCTING BOARD'S PERFORMANCE EVALUATION

Demb and Neubauer has suggested evaluation as under:

(a) The Directors Themselves

Their *intent* e.g. of CEO/Chairman; loyalty to company and stakeholders, choosing directors with skill, balance, their numbers, identify departures.

(b) The Role of Board

Agreeing on board's mission; allocation of responsibilities (fortfolio); setting priorities, decide delegations to management to avoid undue power compliance of legal requirements; level of board's involvement.

(c) Board's Working Style

Setting committees; enough meetings for monitoring; ensuring adequate information to board for decision.

(d) Assessing Individual Directors by the Chairman

Directors preparedness for meetings, whether they do their home work, ask probing questions, exhibits ideas and enthusiasm, make suggestions on innovations and planning. Board to adopt rule of retirement age or director's term, etc.

(e) The Chairman

Board as a whole to decide appraisal of the chairman. Directors may air dissatisfaction on various areas.

(f) The CEO

He has service contract. Comparing performance against set task standards, e.g. financial ratios, comparing with other similar companies. Conduct evaluation of CEO in his absence and other executive directors.

With increasing responsibilities and accountability being placed on the board of directors, performance evaluation may emerge as an essential tool for in-house introspection and continuous improvement.

3. ROLE OF THE CHAIRMAN OF THE BOARD

We present here extracts from the book titled "Chairman of the Board" by Brian Lechem, John Wiley & Sons, appeared in *Hindustan Times*, New Delhi.

Chairman of the Board provides practical guidance on this critical role. The title Chairman of the Board conveys a number of meanings. The word 'Chairman' is said to be gender neutral as a person chosen to preside over a meeting of a corporate body. The terms he, she, his or her—are frequently used in this context to signify that both men and women can occupy this position.

With globalisation, the role of the Chairman has assumed greater significance. In fact, today the Chairman should ensure that the company's Board comprises efficient team members who can pave the way for strategic and successful leadership.

The role of the Chairman is subject to change with time. The person occupying the position is responsible for ensuring that the board fulfils its obligations and commitments. She should see that the board is committed to work towards its goals.

(i) Duties of the Chairman

The following lines suggest *some of the duties* that a Chairman must fulfil order to ensure smooth functioning of the company:

- The Chairman must provide a style. While autocracy or consensus styles are tolerated, democratic views are more welcomed by the Board members.
- The Chairman must also structuring the agenda. This does not mean imposing one's will upon the Board.
- The Chairman must maintain a balance while discussing matters. Spontaneous participation tends to militate against constructive and pragmatic dialogue.
- The Chairman must ensure prompt implementation of all action plans taken during Board meetings.
- Efforts should be made by the Chairman to ensure that the Board meetings are properly conducted.
- Many corporate commentators have suggested that the corporate failure in the recent times had efficient boards. And that it was quality of decision-making that deteriorated leading to the collapse of the company.

(ii) Leadership

The Chairman must *show leadership capabilities* apart from maintaing relationship with the top management. Traditionally, the Chairman acts as the spokesperson of the company. To fulfil this role, he must be briefed well. The Chairman must also cultivate appropriate temperament, personality and public speaking skills.

(iii) Selecting the Chairman

Often the Chairman's selection does not occur as prescribed in books. In theory shareholders elect the Directors at the AGM. In private and closely held companies, this theory may be followed to an extent. In theory, however, the Directors are supposed to be elected in the annual meetings. But in reality, the company owners select them and rest is a formality. Shareholder's participation is rarely witnessed. However, larger companies form nominating committees that operate independently though recent surveys suggest that personal acquaintance is disproportionately important in the selection process of a Director.

(iv) Training

A growing need has been felt for training the Directors before they assume responsibilities. Induction and orientation are two different components of a Director-training programme. Many companies have initiated the process of providing newly appointed Directors with a briefing kit comprising past board minutes, current and previous financial statements, organisation charts, and the key decisions taken by the company

(v) Balance of Roles

Usually the Chairman is often considered as the CEO of the company. It's therefore extremely crucial to maintain the balance between the two roles. Clearly, the CEO holds a great deal of power. She controls the agenda and the flow of information to the Board, has massive knowledge of the affairs of the company makes recommendations regarding senior appointments, handles capitals spending initiatives, etc.

A Board must maintain the checks and balances on management. The crucial point is that the role of the Chairman is essentially different from that of the CEO. Not every one who makes a good CEO is a successful Chairman. The following are few of the touch-stones that should be remembered while executing the roles of both the Chairman as well as the CEO:

- There should be a clearly accepted division between the Heads of a company to ensure a balance of power and authority.
- The Board should include non-executive Directors of sufficient calibre to carry significant weight in the Board's decision.
- The Board should have a schedule of matter specifically reserved to ensure that the decision and control of the company is firmly in its hands.

(vi) Succession Plan

The most important role of the Board is to safeguard the succession of the CEO. The first thing that the Board should do in evaluating the CEO performance is to detect a period of relative mediocrity as early as possible rather than being complacent and wait until the situation demands more urgent action.

(vii) Board in Action

The purpose of the Board meeting is to deal with an agenda. In other words, the meeting must be planned and not left to informal unstructured discussion.

(viii) Collective Responsibillty

The term 'principle of collective responsibility' is very powerful. Even if the Director votes against or abstains from the motion he is bound by the decision of the majority and, by law, is equally liable for the implications of the decision.

(ix) Developing Corporate Strategy

Until recently the Board used to be the only approving-body in the process of strategy development. The management took care of the complete process. The fundamental in developing a corporate strategy consists of determination of precise objectives according to a specified time frame. It gives a clear idea of what we are trying to achieve and how long should it take us to get there. Strategy development consists of SWOT analysis that helps in identifying the strengths, weaknesses, opportunities; and threats to the organisation. Strategy development involves preparation of a set of clear-cut objectives that shows the changes necessary in marketing, production and use capital, management, human resources.

(x) Legal Liabilities—Interpretation of the Situation

Many Directors have expressed concern that in this age of technological change, it is impossible, or perhaps not practical to know everything that's going on in the company or the extent of potential legal liability. Unfortunately, the law does not easily distinguish between the different types of Directors. They are all considered equal and are equally exposed legally. If

Box I

World Leaders in Graft/Corruption

(30 Countries Survey World Economic Forum's)

(Executive Opinion Survey, Oct. 2006)

They Give and Take Bribe

The Worst	*The Least*
1. India	1. Switzerland
2. China	2. Sweden
3. Russia	3. Australia
4. Turkey	4. Austria
5. Taiwan	5. Canada
6. Malaysia	6. UK
7. S. Africa	7. Germany
8. Brazil	8. Netherland
9. Saudi Arabia	9. Belgium
10. South Korea	10. USA

the Directors individually or collectively make discerning inquiries or independent judgements, then they will perhaps have a better chance to prove that they've acted diligently.

Reference

Extracted from 'Chairman of the Board' by Brian Lechem (John Wiley & Sons). (*Courtesy*: K.B.S. Kumar, Trainee Analyst, ICFAI Press), *Hindustan Times*, New Delhi, gratefully acknowledged.

CHAPTER

44

Whistle Blowing

In this chapter following pros and cons of 'Whistle Blowing' are discussed:

1. Meaning of whistle blowing.
2. Consequences of retaliation to whistle blowers.
3. Some drawbacks of whistle blowing.
4. Company's whistle blowing policy.
5. Law on protection of whistle blowers.

1. MEANING OF WHISTLE BLOWING

When an employee thinks that his/her firm is resorting to some act that is unethical or harmful to public, he "blows the whistle" by reporting alleged organisational misconduct to the public or to top executives. Whistle blowing refrains the firm from indulging in unethical and harmful practices.

Some cases of whistle blowing are given as an illustration given in Figure 1.

Whistle blowing is, in fact, an attempt by a member or ex-member of an organisation to disclose wrong doing in or by the organisation (illegal/immoral conduct against public interest).

These are not Whistle Blowing

- When a witness of a crime notifies the police and testifies in court.
- For a reporter who uncovers some illegal practice in a corporation to expose it in print.

FIGURE I

Cases of Whistle Blowing

Name of the organisation	*Whistle blower*	*Consequences*
(i) Enron	Sherron Watkins	Liquidation of the company
(ii) Kellogg India	Senior Executive	Sacking of two senior managers who were promoted for excellent performance a few months ago
(iii) Directorate of FBI, US	Coleen Rowley	Attack on the World Trade Centre, US
(iv) world.com	Cynthia	Company Gone Bust
(v) Heinz India (vi) Johnson and Johnson (vii) Bayer India	Installed Whistle Blowing Systems	No incident reported
(viii) LG India	10-12 cases reported to head office, South Korea	Not known

In these cases, both witness and reporter are not under any obligation that prevents them from making it public.

2. CONSEQUENCES OF RETALIATION TO WHISTLE BLOWERS

Retaliation to whistle blowing has many forms. Often whistle blowers have to pay a high price for their acts of dissent such as:

(i) They are victimised with poor performance evaluation and punishment demotion to outright dismissal.
(ii) Black listing of whistle blowers, so that they cannot obtain jobs in the same industry.
(iii) They may suffer career disruption and financial hardship in pursuing legal expenses.
(iv) It involves severe emotional strain on whistle blowers their families as co-workers, friends turn against them.
(v) Losing life as it happened in case of Dubey, an engineer with Highway Transport Authority of India sent a letter to Prime Minister highlighting an alleged irregularity by petrol pump dealer in U.P.
(vi) Whistle blowing also jeoparadises the well-being of the firm, even closure as has happened to Enron.

3. SOME DRAWBACKS OF ALLOWING WHISTLE BLOWING

(a) Companies might prefer to ignore wrong doing. They may continue to make profits and then take corrective action only when the problems become public.

(b) It may encouraging employees to report on each other and intimidation an environment of mistrust and intimidation due to false accusations.

4. COMPANY'S WHISTLE BLOWING POLICY

No company is immune from wrong doing and an effective policy on whistle blowing enables a company to deal with misconduct internally, thereby preventing embarrassing public disclosure. An effective policy should assure employees that their reports will be taken seriously by proper investigation and appropriate action taken. Further employees also to be assured that they will not suffer retaliation.

Whistle blowing policies benefit employees by providing them with a channel of communication. Some methods provided by companies to know deviant behaviour of employees are as under:

(i) Ethics Committees

Many companies have ethics committees to advise on ethical issues. Such a committee can be a high-level one comprising the board of directors, chaired by the CEO of the company.

The committees seek questions from employees, which help the company in establishing policies in new or uncertain areas. Ethics committees also advise the board of directors on ethical issues, and oversee the enforcement of the code of ethics.

(ii) Ethics Hot Lines

In some companies, when employees are troubled about some ethical issue but may be reluctant to raise it with their immediate supervisor, they can call on the company's 'ethics hot line'. A member of the ethics committee receives the confidential call and then quickly investigates the situation. Elaborate steps are taken to protect the identity of the caller, so as to encourage more employees to report any such deviant behaviour. This technique is advantageous in as much as the matter is settled internally, which is better for a company than to have a situation where disgruntled employees take their ethical complaints to the media.

5. LAW ON PROTECTION OF WHISTLE BLOWERS

The whistle blowers can also play a very important role in providing information about corruption and maladministration. Public servants working in the same department know better as to who is corrupt in their department. But unfortunately, they are not bold enough to convey the said information to their high authorities for fear of reprisals by those against whom complaints are made. If adequate legal protection is granted, the government will be able to get rid of maladministration. Such provisions exist in various countries such as England (Public Interest Disclosure Act, 1998), in USA (Whistle Blower's Protection Act, 1989), Australia (Public Interest Disclosure Act, 1994), New Zealand (Protected Disclosure Act, 2000). In India, Law Commission in 2001 had recommended necessity of Whistle Blowing. Government of India is still in the process of getting through Public Interest Disclosure (Protection of Information) Bill, 2002, approved by the Parliament.

PART VII

CORPORATE SOCIAL RESPONSIBILITY

Social Responsibility towards Interest Groups—Stakeholders

In this chapter we have attempted to present social responsibilities of business for various interest groups. These can be divided under two broad categories:

1. Internal interest groups.
2. External interest groups.

Various interest groups which have stake in the business are explained in the Figure 1.

INTERNAL INTEREST GROUPS

1. Responsibilities towards Owners

It is to be ensured that owners, share-holders, partners get fair dividend or a fair return on the capital invested. Fair return has to be more than bank rate and it should be reasonable.

Further share-holders expect security of investment and share in capital appreciation as bonus shares.

2. Responsibility towards Employees

The traditional concept of "master-servant relationship" has to change to the concept of "partnership" between labour and management.

The major areas of relationship are:

(a) *Wages*—These should be need-based and productivity-related.

FIGURE I

Business and its Interest Groups

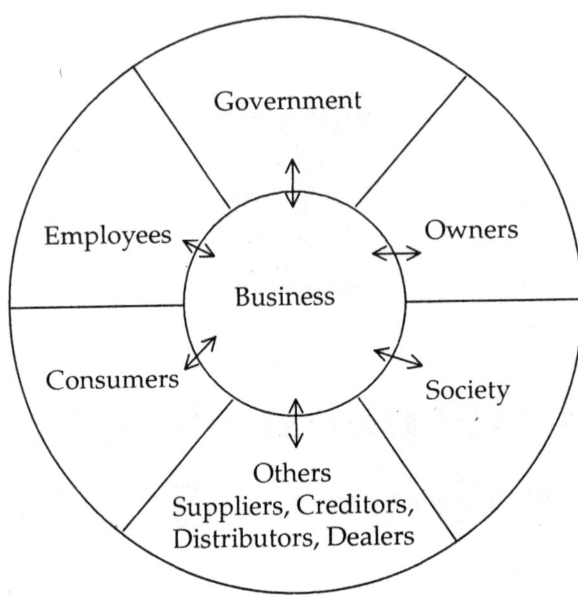

(b) *Salaries for managerial personnel* are to be linked to responsibilities. Ceiling on managerial remuneration by government to be adhered to.

Besides it is to be seen there are not much disparities between wages of employees and salaries of managerial personnel.

(c) *Relationship between employers and employees.* There are various *lapses on the part of employers* which include:

- Unsympathetic treatment to employees by supervisors.
- Favouritism in promotions, etc.
- Lack of communication between management and workers.
- Lack of *appreciation of meritorious achievements* and no condemnation of neglect and lethargy.
- Delay in settling *grievances/disputes* with employees.
- Lapses on part of employees, i.e. indiscipline in carrying out orders.
- Lack of desire by employees to improve efficiency.
- Role of politically inspired trade unions frequent strikes, *gheraos*, etc.

(d) *Industrial legislation*, i.e. laws relating to employees to be followed strictly.

(e) *Welfare of employees*, employer to provide health, safety, working condition and welfare measures for conducive work environment.

EXTERNAL INTEREST GROUPS

1. Responsibility towards Consumers and Community

- The consumer and the community are ultimate judges of business and its products. So it has to be ensured.
- Products meet the needs of consumers.
- Prices are reasonable. There is no hoarding—cornering of products to raise prices.
- After sale service is available.
- Quality and standards (ISI, Agmark) are adhered.
- Consumer associations are to be vigilant and to report falling of standards.

2. Businessmen's Responsibilities towards Government

- Employer has to be law abiding, follow laws relating to trade, factories and labour.
- To pay his dues and taxes fully and honestly.
- Not to purchase political support by unfair means.
- Not to corrupt public servants.
- Avoid adulteration.
- To maintain fair trade practices and avoid hoarding and cornering.

INDIAN SCENE—BUSINESS AS A RESPONSIBLE PERSON

Indian socio-economic environment have lent an added significance to the concept of business as a "responsible person."

(i) Indian government has been committed to socialistic pattern of society, in which private interest is to be subordinated to national considerations.
(ii) The Constitution of India provides for economic and social justice for all, welfare state, laws have been enacted for social justice.
(iii) State financial institutions contribute to a great part of the financial needs of business.
(iv) Emergence and development of professional management is wedded to the fulfilment of socio-economic objectives.
(v) There is growing public awareness and consciousness about the role of business in maintaining environmental protection and cleanliness.
(vi) Growth of trade unions for protection of employee's interests.
(vii) Emergence of consumer protection agencies/forums.

These factors contribute towards corporate social responsibility.

Many large enterprises in India have emphasised their social responsibility in their annual reports, e.g. TISCO, ITC, SAIL, BHEL, ONGC, etc. have developed neighbourhood projects. The Sachar Committee (1978) appreciated that some enlightened business houses are contributing to solve problems of rural development, environment protection, control of pollution and provision of clean water. They are recognising social responsibility as development of corporate ethics.

To conclude, by being more socially responsive, business may avoid further regulations which limit the freedom of business.

It has to be realised that the future of business depends on its *ability and willingness to respond to the changing expectations of society*. Corporations must present themselves as being committed to social causes. A global company has to develop global sensitivity.

The corporations are now doing *'social audit'*, i.e. presenting additional objectives and comprehensive information about organisation's social performance which reflect social responsibilities. Some areas covered in social audit are i.e.:

(a) Social benefits to the staff—various facilities, etc.
(b) Social benefits to the community—local taxes paid to panchayat, municipality, environmental improvements, generation of job potential.
(c) Social benefits to the public—taxes paid and follow the duties toward government.

Box I

Scope of Business Ethics

Ethical issues are there everywhere, at all levels of business activity. Business ethics concern the ground rules of individual company and societal behaviour.

(a) Societal Level

- Concern for poor and down-trodden.
- No discrimination against any particular section or group.
- Concern for clean environment.
- Preservation of scarce resources for posterity.
- Contributing to better quality of life.

(b) Stakeholder's Level

(i) Employees

- Security of job.
- Better working conditions.
- Better recommendation.
- Participative management.
- Welfare facilities.

(ii) Customers

- Better quality of goods.
- Goods and services at reasonably price.
- Not to corner stocks and create securities.
- Not to practice discriminatory pricing.
- Not to make false claims about products in advertisements.

(iii) Shareholders

- Ensure capital appreciation.
- Ensure steady and regular dividends.

- Disclose all relevant information.
- Protect minority shareholders' interests.
- Not to window dress balance sheets.
- Protect interests in times of mergers, amalgamations and takeovers.

(iv) Banks and other Lending Institutions

- Guarantee safety of borrowed funds.
- Prompt repayment of loans.

(v) Government

- Complying with rules and regulations.
- Honesty in paying taxes and other dues.
- Acting as partner in the progress of the country.

CHAPTER

46

Social Responsibility of Business

In this chapter on "Social Responsibility of Business", the following aspects are covered:

1. Introduction
2. Corporate social responsibility: Background.
   2.1 Can business have profit objective only.
3. Meaning of social responsibility of business.
4. Business interest groups.
5. Arguments for social responsibility of business.
6. Arguments against social responsibility of business.
7. How can we strengthen the social responsibility of managers?
8. Social responsibility in Indian scenario.
9. In sum.

1. INTRODUCTION

Present day management responsibility of business are increasingly concerned about the social and ethical issues that their organizations are facing. This is happening throughout the world and India is no exception. Managers manage the organization which is within the society. There are many social issues which impinge on the operation of organizations. Such issues have to be taken into the account by the management.

2. CORPORATE SOCIAL RESPONSIBILITY: BACKGROUND

In the early 20th century; business firms were predominantly concerned with maximizing their profits. In the 1950s, social activists began to question business enterprises' singular objective, of profit maximization. They argued that since business derive their existence from society they have some obligations towards it. The concept of social responsibility became popular after the publication of Howard R. Bowen's Social Responsibilities of Business. Bowen argued that business enterprises should consider the impact of their decisions on society.

Corporate Social Resonsibility has its origin in USA about seven decades ago. It is an obligation of decison-makers to *take actions which protect and improve the welfare of society as a whole along with their own interests.* Such decisions may affect envionment, consumers, and community. It was Peter Drucker who later emphatically argued that management should assume social responsibility. Management should consider the impact of every business policy and action upon society. It has to consider the actions that are likely to promote the public good and to advance the basic beliefs of society, and to contribute to its stability, strength and harmony. He laid emphasis on "Quality of product and customer service."

Later on Sandra Holmes emphasized that in addition to making profit, business should help solve special problems whether or not business creates these problems.

Companies operating in globalised markets are increasingly required to balance the financial and economic considerations of their business with social, community and environmental aspects as well, while building shareholders' value.

2.1 Can business have profit objective only?

The management should consider the earning of profit and performing of social obligations simultaneously.

A business enterprise which is earning profit can serve the society in a better way than an enterprise which is running into losses. Profit objective can't be eliminated as the very survival of the business will be put in danger. A part of the profit can be retained every year and reinvested in productive channels. At the same time, an enterprise is under an obligation not to exploit the customers. It should decrease the cost of production by minimising wastes and delays, and by efficiently using the resources.

To sum up, *earning of profits is necessary for any business enterprise. But it is also the responsibility of management to reconcile the interests of owners, workers, customers and society.*

3. MEANING OF SOCIAL RESPONSIBILITY OF BUSINESS

Social responsibility (SR) means the intelligent and objective concern for the welfare of society that restraints business from destructive activities and leads towards the betterment of human beings. *Corporate social responsibility contends that mangement is responsible to the organisation itself and to all the interest groups with which it interacts.* Other interest groups such as workers, customers, creditors, suppliers, government and society in general are placed essentially equal with shareholders.

4. BUSINESS INTEREST GROUPS

Social responsibility requires identification of various interest groups which may affect the functioning of business. Normally, various groups associated with business are:

Shareholders

The first responsibility of management is towards its shareholders. Management is expected to use the resources effectively and to protect the interest of shareholders.

Workers

Management should treat workers as other wheel of the cart. It should adopt a progressive labour policy. Also, it should pay fair and reasonable wages.

Customers

Management should not mislead the customers by false, misleading and exaggerated advertisement. Also, it should not involve itself in profiteering, hoarding or creating artificial scarcity. Prices should be fair and ensure providing of quality of goods and services.

Creditors/suppliers

There should be healthy and co-operative inter-business relationship. Management should provide accurate and relevant information to creditors and suppliers.

Government

Management should be law-abiding. It should pay all the taxes correct and on time. Business management should not corrupt public servants.

Society

Business should set-up socially desirable standards of living and avoid ostentation wasteful expenditure. It should play a proper role in civic affairs. Business can fulfil its obligations toward society by enhancing the well-being of members of the society.

5. ARGUMENTS FOR SOCIAL RESPONSIBILITY OF BUSINESS

There are several ideas about SR of the business. These arguments run as follows:

(a) Business is a part of society

Business organizations are creatures of society and must respond to social demands. Since business is a sub-system of society, it should contribute to the system as a whole, not only to the sub-system alone.

(b) For Avoidance of government regulations

When a business is unable to fulfil the social roles, it invites more government intervention in the business system. Therefore, in order to avoid government regulation of business, it is preferable to go for social responsibility programmes.

(c) Long-run self-interest business

Business can do better by creating better public image among the various interest groups.

(d) Conscious customers

The customers are well informed. They expect higher quality products at reasonable rates. They don't get fair treatment from business; they will organise themselves and compel business to assume its SRs.

(e) Strong trade unions

The level of education among the workers has been increasing. They understand the need of organizing themselves into unions to advance their economic and social interests. The government has also enacted social security measures due to which it becomes difficult for the business houses to ignore the interests of the workers.

6. ARGUMENT AGAINST SOCIAL RESPONSIBILITY OF BUSINESS

Following are the arguments against social responsibility of business:

(i) Conflicting consideration

A business manager will be guided by two considerations, namely private market mechanism and social responsibilities, which are opposite to each other.

(ii) Responsibility of government

Business should have no relationship with welfare schemes. It is the sole responsibility of the government of the land to adopt schemes and measures for the upliftment of the weaker section of society.

(iii) Inefficiency in the system

There is no substitute for the power of self-interest to get people to act. Any replacement of altruism for self-interest will, therefore, be fatal to efficiency of the system. Managers should manage only in the interest of the shareholders.

The above arguments of classical economists have no weight in practice because modern business cannot be contended merely with enough profits for their growth and stability in economic set-up. The managers must take care of the demands, feelings and attitude of the people and also of those working in the organization.

7. HOW CAN WE STRENGTHEN THE SOCIAL RESPONSIBILITY OF MANAGERS?

There are four options available in this context. These are:

(a) Market regulation, which binds the actions of managers.
(b) Professionalisation of management, which seeks for better information.
(c) Moral management, which incorporates norms and values from outside the market.
(d) Shareholder management, which leaves room for the participation of shareholders.

8. SOCIAL RESPONSIBILITY IN INDIAN SCENARIO

Today managers recognize that since they are managing an economic unit in the society, they have an obligation to the society with regard to their decisions and actions affecting social welfare.

JRD Tata was the first leading businessman to explicitly recognize that business doesn't operate in isolation from society. In 1970, at the instance of JRD Tata, all the major companies in the Tata group started following the concept of social responsibility.

The modern generation of Indian managers show greater concern for social responsibilities of business.

9. IN SUM

Social responsibility means the intelligent and objective concern for the welfare of society that restraints business from destructive activities and leads towards the betterment of human beings. Further the business has SR towards all the interest groups. Business interest groups are: Shareholders, Creditors, Suppliers, Customers, Government and employees. JRD Tata was pioneer in India to accept and inculcate the concept of social responsibility in his business.

CHAPTER

47

Core Moral Responsibilities of Enterprise

According to Peter Pratley (The Essence of Business Ethics), "it is important to define core moral responsibilities at a minimal level. By accepting an outspoken commitment to these responsibilities, TQM can gain a lot. The core moral responsibilities are three-fold.

First of all, the corporation is committed to its original and basic moral core responsibility: that is, *producing goods and services that are functional and safe for the individual consumer*. On top of this perennial cornerstone of business, other core activities now have to be added.

The second moral commitment therefore concerns the larger *environment: environmental core and reduction of resource depletion*.

Finally, the third accepted responsibility refers to *the quality of the corporation itself as a moral community*. At a minimum level this implies the absence of certain abuses.

These three core moral responsibilities for business organisations aim at guaranteeing a minimum of moral excellence. They are linked with an idea of normative entrepreneurial performance and encapsulate what the public may at least expect from an entrepreneur committed to quality management.

These three entrepreneurial responsibilities also imply a redefinition of corporate objectives. It pushes the meaning of the famous separatist expression 'mind your own business' in a quite opposite direction. Corporate mission statements that include these moral responsibilities enlarge the matters for which the public may hold business accountable for by insisting on safe and reliable customer relationships, environmental care and humane working conditions.

The entrepreneur should gain this broader perspective as the corporation commits itself to wider human objectives, especially in relation to our common future. Although industry will go through even more stringent reductions of employee numbers in the future, certain minimum standards of working conditions should be agreed upon by all those committed to quality goods. This statement is a moral appeal for legal means and voluntary covenants to enforce respect for minimum labour rights.

To summarise our discussion:

1. The corporation producing quality products and services accepts specific moral responsibilities. At a minimum level, there are three such corporate responsibilities:
   (a) consumer care, expressed by satisfying demands for ease of use and product safety;
   (b) environmental care; and
   (c) care for minimum working conditions.
2. Corporations should not remain mute about their moral performances and commitments. A balanced presentation of one's corporate response in face of specific moral concerns can create a basis of understanding with one's own employees as well as with the concerned public. Communicate the priorities you have in your commitment to quality management by a sophisticated use of moral talk."

Source: Peter Pratley, The Essence of Business Ethics.

CHAPTER

48

Corporate Ethical Role towards Society

In this chapter, corporation's public policy and its role towards society is covered under following headings:

1. Corporation's ethical role towards society.
2. Contribution of business to society.
3. Establishing of corporate business ethics policies.
4. Company's philosophy on corporate governance.

I. CORPORATION'S ETHICAL ROLE TOWARDS SOCIETY

Some areas of concern are as under:

- *Concern for poor and down-trodden* as a part of social responsibility. Respect for persons and their property.
- *No discrimination* against any particular section or group.
- Concern for *clean environment*.
- Preservation of scarce resources for posterity.
- Contributing to better quality of life by ethical and moral values.
- Fair practices in internal and external policy.
- Besides above concerns, corporation has role towards *stakeholders* such as employees, customers, suppliers, shareholders, banks and lending institutions and the government.

2. CONTRIBUTION OF BUSINESS TO SOCIETY THROUGH

- The core values, such as quality of one's products and services that are functional and safe.
- By providing jobs.
- Usefulness of activities to surrounding community, safeguarding environments.

Thus, to build sound public image through sound business practices, and avoid unethical practices such as, scams, corruption, etc. which tarnish business image. It is quality of corporation itself as a moral community.

3. ESTABLISHING OF CORPORATE BUSINESS ETHICS POLICIES

Corporates to highlight and establish business ethics policies as under:

(a) Values and Commitments

By following certain core values such as honesty, integrity, respect, fairness, purposefulness, trust, responsibility, citizenship and caring.

This ensures ethical treatment of all stakeholders. It is to realise that other person's interests counts.

(b) Laying of Code of Ethics document, laying Policies relating to:

- Payments and gifting.
- Receipt of gifts.
- Political contributions.
- Relating to agents, consultants and representatives, suppliers.

(c) Laying of Business Policy Document containing:

- Fair marketing practice.
- Inside information.
- Financial records and accounting.
- Work ethics.
- Personal conduct.
- Health, safety and environment.
- Quality of goods and services.

(d) Code of Conduct

- For employees.
- Prevention of inside trading, etc.

4. COMPANY'S PHILOSOPHY ON CORPORATE GOVERNANCE

(a) To attain highest level of *transparency, accountability and equity* in all factors of its operations and in all interactions with stakeholders. So as to enhance shareholder's value over sustained period and contribution to society and customers.

(b) Focus on following *principles of corporate governance*:

(i) Recognising the respective *roles and responsibilities of board and management*, such as to provide strategic guidance responsibilities of senior management and their accountability, retain balance of power to avoid individual unfettered power.

(ii) *Having board of appropriate size*, composition to discharge its responsibilities. In addition to non-executive and executive directors to review performance of management competence of directors.

(iii) Safeguarding the integrity of the company's *financial reporting* including role of audit committee.

(iv) *Importance to investor's relations* by holding timely annual general meeting and establishing communication providing information.

(v) *Having a sound system of risk management and internal control*. These include establishing internal audit function, external auditors to review effectiveness, and management to inform investor's changes to company's risk profile.

(vi) Establishing efficient executive remuneration policy.

CHAPTER

49

Value-based Governance in Organisation

In this chapter on "Value-based Governance in Organisation", the following aspects are discussed:

(i) Present scenario of values system in Indian business organisations.
(ii) Guidelines for creation of value-based governance.
(iii) Leadership values.
(iv) To conclude.

When one tries to analyse the current value system that Indians hold, one notices that most of our cultural values are gradually degenerating. Our character has been devalued faster than our rupees. The worse that has happened is that we have started rationalizing and justifying our degraded value system on one or the other pretext. Therefore, there is an indispensable and urgent need for introspection to revive our value system to old glory.

(I) PRESENT SCENARIO OF VALUES SYSTEM IN INDIAN BUSINESS ORGANIZATIONS

In this present turbulent times, a *breakdown in values is noticeable in almost every sphere of life* ranging from family, religion, administration, public life and management of corporate sector. This decline is more obvious in business, industries, public institutions, government departments, voluntary organizations and professional institutions. Owing to the process of privatization, liberalization and globalization intense competition has evolved as basic guidelines for business survival. It is simply a mad-race where each person wants to win over the other, irrespective of the consequences, which leads to *erosion of value system.*

Our whole attitude has become negative, indifferent, fatalistic, escapist, cynical, rigid and argumentive thus what is needed in this hour is not only fulfilling short-term objectives, but also *fulfilment of long-term objectives incorporated with ethical and moral responsibilities by corporate houses,* to survive intense completion. Management should develop human values by setting examples so that they are perceived as role models—the winning combination should include.

(II) GUIDELINES FOR CREATION OF VALUE-BASED GOVERNANCE

Following are some guidelines on how to promote value-based governance through value creation for workforce, customers, investors/share-holders and society. (Figure 1)

FIGURE I

Creation of Value-Based Governance

Satisfied Workforce → Delighted Customers → Happy Shareholders → Happy Society → Satisfied Workforce

1. Value Creation for Workforce

An organisation culture should create a *sense of commitment in the workforce.* They must love their job and should be a dedicated lot and this must be reinforced by the management.

2. Value Creation for Customers

The survival of the organization depends upon the necessary expertise and capability to satisfy global markets. Customers are awakening individually and collectively day-by-day regarding their rights. Growing awareness of needs and rights is changing their behaviour. Customers are becoming increasingly assertive in demanding high quality products and services and they are no more passive onlookers, as they used to be.

3. Value Creation for Investors and Shareholders

Shareholders, investors are the company owners, they have the legitimate right to expect proper return on their investment. So, *fair and ethical treatment should be provided* to them in the following manner:

- The money invested by them should be judiciously used.
- No personal expenditure should form part of the investor's money.

4. Value Creation for Society

Organisation exists within a society and their members are drawn from the society. The organization has it's own values and norms towards society. Thus, business owes it to the society, first on account of consequences of it's own operations and secondly, for being a part of the society in which it operates. Like an individual, a firm should be viewed as a member of the society and accordingly, is expected to behave as a responsible citizen.

- Business organizations are expected to play a leading role in solving some of the major social problems.
- They should not create nuisances.
- Proper measures should be taken for disposal of industrial pollutants.

Thus, social obligations are to be properly discharged by the business organizations.

(III) LEADERSHIP VALUES

Values get transferred from one generation to the other through family, teachers and other members of society. Taking this path of transmission, an individual in an organization perceives his/her superior to be the repository of ethical values. Managers should act as role models for their co-workers. The *value-oriented managers* have to lead their workers with adequate, (i) interpersonal communication and feedback, (ii) teamwork, collaboration and participation for company goals, (iii) share knowledge, (iv) leadership towards the collective success of the whole team, and (v) make employees at ease with receptive and open to suggestions.

So the leadership should try to assess the spirituality quotient (SQ) of the employees, as well as of themselves, in addition to intelligence quotient (IQ) and emotional quotient (EQ) and follow balancing style:

- Positive attitude
- Self-confidence
- Faith
- Strong will-power
- Sense of responsibility
- Empathy.

(IV) TO CONCLUDE

Organisations of tomorrow will crave for self-ordered, self-controlled, self-disciplined and self-motivated employees to survive amidst a dynamic, competitive and changing global economic environment. Employees with commensurate human values to that of organizational values can meet such exacting demands. Such value system can create and sustain perennial satisfaction level and can develop human resources. We have to transform our personality and that of our organization, by *improving following value systems in our organization*:

- Gaining knowledge
- Hard work
- Entrepreneurship
- Regular self-introspection
- Spirit of service
- High goals of integrity

These are the key to organizational excellence.

Source: Amulya Khurana and Bijaya Mishra, Deptt. of Humanities and Social Sciences, IIIT, New Delhi, NIPM, July 2001.

CHAPTER

50

Environmental Ethics

In this chapter on "Environmental Ethics", the following aspects are covered:

1. Gravity of environmental pollution.
2. What is an environment?
3. Environmental pollution in India.
4. New focus in environmental protection.

I. GRAVITY OF ENVIRONMENTAL POLLUTION

Protection of environment is the major issue that confronts business decision-makers.

Problems such as—pollution due to—disposal of toxic waste, eroding of the earth's ozone layer—acid rain and others are serious ecological problems. Causes of these and other threats to environment have their *source in industrial production.* As such the theme of business and environmental ethics has become an essential issue in the field of business ethics.

Some examples of environmental pollution are:

(i) Bhopal Gas Leakage Tragedy

Shortly after midnight on December 3, 1984 outside Bhopal, India, a cloud of deadly methyl isocyanate gas leaked from a pesticide plant owned by the Indian subsidiary of Union Carbide. The choking gas covered the town, quickly killing hundreds—including many children, who were less resistant to the gas than adults—and forcing Bhopal's 6,70,000 inhabitants to flee in panic. By the end of the week more than 2,000 people had died from inhaling the gas, and 1,50,000 more had to be hospitalized for respiratory and eye damage, making Bhopal's 'night of death' the worst industrial disaster in history. Images of stunned families burying or burning their dead and blaming Union Carbide for their agony were boradcast worldwide.

There were immediate repercussions for Union Carbide and for the chemical industy as well. The Indian government accused the plant management of failing to take adequate safety precautions and indicated that it held the parent company ultimately responsible. Lawsuits brought by American lawyers on behalf of the victims asked for billions of dollars in compensatory and punitive damages and threatened to send the company into bankruptcy. Union Carbide's stock price plumetered; it halted production of methyl isocyanate at the one West Virginia plant that produced the chemical in the United States.

Officials in the United States and India called for increased regulation and inspection of chemical processing plants. Many U.S. localities considered passing "right-to-know" laws that would require chemical companies to provide detailed information about hazardous materials to the employees who make them and to residents living near the plants. Several companies countered with voluntary right-to-know programmes to head off public sentiment for government regulation. In the wake of protests against Union Carbide in other parts of the world, some multinational corporations claimed that the Bhopal disaster had chilled the international climate for U.S. business.

Union Carbide, which had earned an above-average record on industrial safety over the decade preceding the disaster, appeared paralyzed by the magnitude of Bhopal's suffering. Corporate Chairman Warren Anderson rushed to India to inspect the site and was briefly arrested by Indian authorities. Union Carbide's one hundred thousand employees observed a moment of silence for the dead and injured; many donated money for disaster relief. Top management spent sleepless nights grappling with the company's crushing problems and its uncertain future. Morale at the company was low; production at many plants temporarily dropped. However, while expressing profound sympathy for the Bhopal victims and promising to make a fair restitution, Union Carbide maintained its essential innocence. "There's no criminal responsibility here", said Anderson.

(ii) Storage Tank Leakage of Pennwalt Corporation

Mr. High, a plant manager at Pennwalt Corporation was at home on vacation, when he got a call on 2.1.1985 that there had been accident at the plant. Mr. High rushed there and found that a storage tank containing sodium chlorate had collapsed and flowed into nearby canal. In less than two hours, his lawyers say, Mr. High surveyed the damage and informed US Coast Guard and Washington State Department of ecology of spill which he estimated at 20,000 gallons of sodium chlorate. But in May 1988, more than 3 years later, Mr. High and Pennwalt Corporation were indicted on charges of negligence. They were also accused of covering up the full extent of spill, which was later found 75,000 gallons. Pennwalt Corporation was fined $ 8 million, while Mr. High was fined $ 650,000 and sent to jail for 9 years.

(iii) Disaster of Super-Tanker Exxon

Another example worth quoting is of environmental disaster of Super Tanker 'Exxon" and here crude oil flowed in sea in Alaska, North America. Marine mammals, fish and other wildlife were killed. Exxon cleaned up operations and spent $ 1.28 billion in its efforts. Exxon

---

Sources: This case was based on material from the following articles: "India's Night of Death", *Times*, December 17, 1984, pp. 22-31; Judith Dobrzynski, William Glaberson, Rosa Kig, William Powell, Jr., and Leslie Helm, "Union Carbide Fights for its Life", *Business Week*, December 24, 1984, pp. 52-56; and Maria Recio and Vicky Cahon, "Bhopal has Americans Demanding the `Right to Know'", *Business Week*, February 18, 1985, pp. 36-37.

proclaimed their clean up a "success", but government of USA was not satisfied and one of the greatest marine disaster in history became an ethical issue for America's largest corporation. Environmentalists continue their attacks on industry.

There are numerous examples of environmental pollutions. So there are many recent cases where corporate organisations and individual managers were prosecuted for environmental crimes. In USA between 1982-89, there were 486 cases. The lawyers say criminal charges should be filed only in instances of deliberate misconduct, not in accidental situations such as Pennwalt Corporation.

Many companies are not aware that all major environmental laws contain criminal enforcement provisions.

The problems of environment have come to the fore in India only during recent years. These have gripped the attention of enlightened people, organised groups, governments, judiciary in India also.

2. WHAT IS AN ENVIRONMENT?

The environment is defined as the totality of man's surroundings. Today's environment may be said to consist of elements each of which is resource. The resources may be grouped into two categories:

(i) *Natural resources*: Land, water, air, fauna and flora, energy and fuels and raw materials, i.e. minerals, and

(ii) *Man-made resources*: The socio-economic structure, cultural heritage, the people.

It is widely recognised now that the quality of environment is fast deteriorating through: Industrial Pollutions—i.e. toxic chemicals, oil spills in the ocean, deforestation.

Air pollution largely caused by automobile exhausts, and other measures, i.e. carbon monoxide, lead, carbon dioxide, sulpher oxide, asbestos.

Water pollution through sewage discharges and drainage from mines, waste composts, chemicals which are toxic for human life, fishes and birds, etc.

Ecology is study of plants, animals, people and institutions in relation to environment. Ecology refers to the inter-relationships between people and fauna (birds and animals).

The flora (plants and trees) and their physical surroundings.

Ecosystem is the totally of-living and non-living elements in the ecological community interacting with one another and the environment.

Partly, the environmental problems may be attributed to negative effects of process of industrialisation and economic development; partly it is also due to poverty and underdevelopment.

Business has, therefore to be concerned with public health, safety, environmental protection.

3. ENVIRONMENTAL PROTECTION IN INDIA

Various steps have been taken such as enactment of laws, establishment of regulatory bodies, semi-judicial authorities. These are as under:

(i) *Legal.* The directive principles of state policy in the Constitution of India lay emphasis on protection of environment. Some laws enacted are as under:
   1. The Air (Prevention and Control of Pollution) Act, 1981, amended in 1988.
   2. The Environment (Protection) Act, 1986.
   3. The Water (Prevention and Control of Pollution) Act, 1974 amended in 1974 and 1988.
   4. The Hazardous Wastes Act, 1989.
   5. The Wildlife Protection Act, 1972.
   6. The Forests (Conservation) Act, 1980 amended in 1988.

(ii) *Regulation.* Administrative orders/policy guidelines have been laid by government. A separate Department of Environment, Government of India was created in 1980.

(iii) Certain regulatory bodies or quasi-judicial authorities have been established such as:
   - National Afforestation and Eco-development Board, and
   - National Wastelands Development Board.

(iv) Manufacturing units have been closed in cities. High Court of Delhi ordered shifting of manufacturing units out of Delhi and closing them. Similarly, Courts have ordered for removal of foundaries from Agra city, and shifting of manufacturing factories from Kanpur.

(v) Various industrial pollution control projects have been started, e.g. Clean Ganga Action Plan, Pushkar Lake Valley, Auroville (T.N.), Tumkar (Karnataka), Gopeshwar in UP, Shivalik Foothills (Punjab).

(vi) Various programmes on environment education, seminars creating awareness and resource management have started.

(vii) Government has also laid (EAP) Environment Action Plan.

All these legal and other steps taken by the Government, central and states have not achieved desired results. The main problem is that there is laxity in the enforcement of the legal provisions. There is lack of coordination between centre and state governments.

4. NEW FOCUS IN ENVIRONMENTAL PROTECTION

(i) Now *more importance to environmental protection* is being given. Social groups, judges are taking initiative. Government is trying to involve NGOs as eyes and ears in terms of grass-root monitoring of environment quality. Government response to environmental concerns is increasing.

(ii) The industry is not only to *obey current environmental laws*, but also to *go beyond them*. To work on solutions to various ecological problems so as to demonstrate, it holds environmental values. Environment laws now a subject for study in courses, research, and to improve equipment, innovate new projects.

(iii) Many companies are not aware that nearly all major laws on pollution control contain criminal enforcement provisions. This *awareness* is making industries to follow statutory provisions seriously.

(iv) Initially, business has been resisting to their role in protection of environment. But now business is *looking for remedial measures* as professionals in industry realise it. This type of resistance was there in consumer protection also in the beginning in the USA.

(iv) Government, business, politicians admit that environment is to be protected gradually, so that industry does not die.

(v) Trust for Environment Education and Community Action, New Delhi (WildwondersIndia@rediffmail.com) is actively involved in conservation movement.

The mission of TEECA is to provide meaningful platform to individuals, students, community groups for interacting and getting real insight into the immediate environment around so that they can have the capacity to know all about the problems and can find solutions to these problems on their own.

CHAPTER

51

Consumer Protection

In this chapter on "Consumer Protection", the following aspects are covered:

1. Consumer—Meaning.
2. Consumerism—Meaning.
3. Rights of consumers.
4. Responsibilities of consumers.
5. Approaches to consumer protection.
6. Laws for consumer protection.

1. CONSUMER—MEANING

Consumer is a person who buys goods or services to be used or consumed by him on his behalf by someone. Goods may include both consumable items or durable consumer goods. While services may be transport, electricity, film shows and like.

The consumers may be exploited in any ways such as:

- Low quality products.
- Wrong price quoted by the sellers, prices are much higher than warranted by the cost of productions.
- Artificially raising prices by forming cartels and adopting restrictive trade practices.
- Unethical advertising. It means making false assertions to the public about goods for sale. Goods offered are different from goods advertised.
- Adulteration.

2. CONSUMERISM—MEANING

Consumerism refers to a movement by consumers to ensure fair and honest (ethical) practices on the part of manufacturers, traders, and dealers and services providers in relation to consumers. The movement may be regarded an attempt by individual consumer activities and consumer associations for creating consumer awareness about the malpractices in the market and finding ways and means to protect their interests.

3. RIGHTS OF CONSUMERS

Consumers have the following rights:

(i) Right to Safety

Consumers have a right to be protected against marketing of goods which are injurious to health and life. We can take precautions to prevent the injury we have a right to complain against the dealer and even claim compensation.

(ii) Right to be Informed

Consumers have the right to be informed about the quantity, quality, purity, standard or grade and price of the goods available so that they can make proper choice before buying any product or service.

(iii) Right to Choose

Every consumer has the right to choose the goods needed from a wide variety of similar goods. Very often dealers and traders try to use pressure tactics to sell goods of poor quality. Sometimes, consumers are also carried away by advertisements on the T.V. These possibilities can be avoided if consumers are conscious of this right.

(iv) Right to be Heard

Consumers have a right to be heard by manufacturers, dealers and advertisers about their opinion on production and marketing decisions.

(v) Right to Seek Redressal

If any consumer has a complaint or grievance due to unfair trade practices like charging higher price, selling of poor quality or unsafe products, lack of regularity in supply of services, etc. or if he has suffered loss or injury due to defective or adulterated products, he has the right to seek redressal. He has a right to get the defective goods replaced or money refunded by the seller or dealer. He also has the right to seek legal remedies in the appropriate courts of law.

(vi) Right to Consumer Education

To prevent market malpractices and exploitation of consumers, consumer awareness and education are essentially required. For this purpose, consumer associations, educational institutions and Government policy-makers are expected to enable consumers to be informed and educated about: (a) the relevant laws which are aimed at preventing unfair trade practice; (b) the ways in which dishonest traders and producers may try to manipulate market practices to deceive consumers; (c) how consumers can protect their own interest; and the procedure to be adopted by consumers while making complaints.

4. RESPONSIBILITIES OF CONSUMERS

(i) Responsibility of Self-help

As a consumer, you are expected to act in a responsible manner to protect yourself from being deceived. An informed consumer can always take care of his interest more than any one else. Also, it is always better to be forewarned and forearmed rather than getting remedies after suffering and loss or injury.

(ii) Proof of Transactions

The second responsibility of every consumer is that the proof of purchase and documents relating to purchase of durable goods should be invariably obtained and preserved. For example, cash memo, guarantee papers, etc.

(iii) File reasonable claim for compensation and avoid unreasonable large claims.

(iv) Use products and services properly during guarantee period thinking product will be replaced.

Consumers can exercise their rights only when they are willing to fulfil their responsibilities.

5. APPROACHES TO CONSUMER PROTECTION

The need for protect interest of consumers arises due to their helpless position and unfair business practices. Some methods are as under:

(a) *Consumers* can regulate and *discipline their own activities* by forming voluntary consumer organisations to check malpractices.

(b) *Manufacturers and traders can spread information* and awareness about the ethical use of their products.

(c) *Manufacturers and traders can self-regulate* and discipline their activities and now not to cheat consumers.

(d) Manufacturers and traders can be *regulated by the government legislation* to take steps against carrying out malpractices. State executives and judiciary role has to become more aggressive.

(e) Consumer's associations have been given status in many laws and they are playing active role.

(f) *Consumer has to be alert*. Self-help is the best help. As such consumers have *to assert their right* and perform their duties.

6. LAWS FOR CONSUMER PROTECTION

Legislation can serve as a potent tool to improve the status of consumers.

There are various laws which protect consumers against different forms of deceit, injury and exploitation. Some laws are mentioned in Box 1. Details of consumer disputes redressal system under the Consumer Protection Act, 1986 are given in Annexure, which provides for (a) compensation and damages to consumer forces not supplying quality product or services, (b) negligence in service by the firm.

Box I

Laws for Protection of Consumers

1. The Agricultural Product (Grading and Marketing) Act, 1937, e.g. get Agmark quality items and businessmen advised to obtain certificates for winning consumers' goodwill.
2. The Bureau of Indian Standards Act, 1986. Certification from BIS for standardisation of quality consumers to look for ISI mark products.
3. The Cigarettes (Regulation, Production, Supply and Distribution) Act, 1975. It requires informing the public about health hazard. For example, "Cigarette smoking is injurious to health" is written on the packets.
4. The Drugs and Cosmetics Act, 1940, to ensure these items are of standard quality, purity and strength and packed in containers giving necessary information about contents of drug.
5. The Drugs and Magic Remedies (Objectionable Advertisements) Act, 1954. The act provides for controlling advertisements of drugs relating to vineral diseases, sexual stimulants, etc. and also to avoid self-medication.
6. The Essential Commodities Act, 1955. This act empowers government to regulate and control of prices, supply, transport, etc. of essential commodities, e.g. coal, drugs, edible oils, petroleum products, milk.
7. The Hire Purchase Act, 1972. It provides essential requirement of hire contract which will then culminate into sale.
8. The Indian Penal Code, 1840. Certain provisions check fraudulent use of false weights or measures, adulteration of drugs, etc.
9. The Prevention of Black Marketing and Maintenance of Supplies of Essential Commodities Act, 1980 to ensure supply to consumers.
10. Prevention of Food Adulteration Act, 1954 to provide for penalties against offences affecting public health (IPC). For example, mixing milk with water, and arrangement for analysis of food articles.
11. The Standards of Weights and Measures Act, 1976:
    - Prohibits non-standards weights and measures;
    - Controller of weights has to exercise checks that weights conform to standards; and
    - Manufacturer has to mention date of package, quantity in package, etc.
12. The Trade and Merchandise Marks Act, 1958:
    - To provide for trade-marks—Bata, Fiat, Birla-Yamaha for generators, Onida for TV.
    - To prevent fraudulent trade-marks of deceptively producing similar products resembling the original items.
13. The Water (Prevention and Control of Pollution) Act, 1974 to prohibit on use of stream or well for disposal of pollution and to check samples.
14. Some recent steps are:
    (i) The Consumer Protection Act, 1986. It lays a three-tier forums for redressal of grievances of consumers:
    - District forums—for loss below 1 lakh.

- State Commission—for loss 1-10 lakhs.
- National Commission.

It is quasi-judicial machinery to provide speedy and simple redress to consumers. A complaint can be in letter form only is adequate, e.g. Complaint of Housing Society v. MTNL. Consumer Protection Council can suggest amendments to the Act.

(ii) Concept of Lok Adalats introduced for speedy and economic redressal of consumer grievances, e.g. MTNL, DESU, Dak and Pension Adalat, etc. They also provide free legal aid.

(iii) Instituting a National Youth Award for Rs. 20,000 on consumer protection.

CHAPTER

52

Quality of Work Life (QWL)

In this chapter on "Quality of Work Life (QWL)", the following aspects are covered:

1. Meaning of quality of work.
2. Components of quality of work.
3. Importance of good worklife quality.
4. Areas of quality of work.
5. Methods to improve QWL.

1. MEANING OF QUALITY OF WORK LIFE

Quality of work life is defined, as the balance between an employee's work demands and outside interests or pressures which entails corporate social responsibility. Most organisations today view QWL as important, but do not formally link it any of their strategic or business plans.

Quality of Working Life is the degree to which members of a work organisation are able to satisfy their personal needs through their experience in the organisation. Its focus is on the problem of creating a human work environment where employees work cooperatively and contribute to organisation objectives. The major indicators of QWL are job involvement, job satisfaction and productivity.

2. COMPONENTS OF QUALITY OF WORK LIFE

The definition of quality of work life involves three major parts:

(a) Occupational health care,
(b) Suitable working time, and
(c) Appropriate salary.

Infact, safe work environment provides the basis for and person to enjoy work. The work should not pose health hazard for the person. Employee satisfaction and quality of work life directly affect a company's ability to serve its customers. QWL requires effective allocation of resources to enhance the productivity and stability of our workforce.

3. IMPORTANCE OF GOOD WORK LIFE QUALITY

- Decrease in absenteeism and turnover.
- Less number of accidents.
- Improved labour relations and job-satisfaction.
- Employee involvement.
- Positive employee attitudes toward their work and the company.
- Increased productivity and intrinsic motivation.
- Enhanced organisational effectiveness and competitive advantage.
- Employees gain a high sense of control over their work.

QWL seeks to create a work commitment in organisations and society at large so as to ensure higher productivity and greater job satisfaction of the employees. It is a process by which an organisation attempts to unleash the creative potential of its personnel by involving them in decisions affecting their work lives. "QWL is a process of work organisations which enables its members at all levels to participate actively and efficiently in shaping the organisation's environment, methods and outcomes. It is a value-based process, which is aimed towards meeting the twin goals of enhanced effectiveness of the organisation and improved quality of life at work for the employees."

4. AREAS OF QUALITY OF WORKING LIFE

Areas of Quality of Working Life are as under:

(a) Compensation

The reward for work should be above a minimum standard for life and should also be equitable.

(b) Health and Safety

The working environment should reduce the adverse effects of pollution that can adversely affect the physical, mental and emotional state of employees.

(c) Job Security

Employees should not have to work under a constant concern for their future stability of work and income.

(d) Job Design

The design of jobs should be capable of meeting the needs of the organisation for production and the individual for satisfying and interesting work.

(e) Social Integration

The elimination of anything that could lead to individuals not identifying with the groups to which they belong. This includes the elimination of discrimination and individualism, whilst encouraging teams and social groups to form.

(f) Protection of Individual Rights

The introduction of specific procedures aimed at guaranteeing the rights of employees at work.

(g) Social Relevance of Work

Initiatives to increase the understanding among employees of the objectives of the organisation and the importance of their part in them.

(h) Respect for Non-work Activities

Respect for the activities that people engage in outside the workplace. The impact of work activities on private life should also be recognised.

5. METHODS TO IMPROVE QWL

In order to improve the quality of working life, the following steps may be followed:

(a) Job Enrichment and Job Enlargement

These attempts to provide a person with exciting, interesting, stimulating and challenging work. In other words, it improves the quality of the jobs. These motivate the employees with higher level needs and overcome problems of monotony in the jobs.

(b) Autonomous Workgroup

Under this, each group of workers is given freedom of decision-making on production methods, distribution of tasks, selection of team members and leaders, work schedules and so on.

(c) Flexibility in Work Schedules

Employees demand more freedom at the workplace, especially in scheduling their work. Among the alternative work schedules capable of enhancing the quality of working life for some employees are:

- *Flexitime.* A system of flexible working hours.
- *Staggered hours.* Different groups of employees begin and end work at different intervals.
- *Compressed work-week.* It involves more hours of work per day for fewer days per week, e.g., five days a week.

(d) Job Redesign

Job redesign based on participative system helps in better job satisfaction.

(e) Opportunity for Growth

Opportunity for growth is important for achievement-oriented employees. If the employees are provided opportunities for their advancement and growth and to develop their personality, they will feel highly motivated. Their commitment to the organisation will also increase.

(f) Employees' Participation

People in organisations have a need for participation in matters affecting their lives. So they want participation in the decision-making process. Employees' participation in the form of suggestion system, management by objectives (MBO), workers' participation in management, etc. provides psychological satisfaction to the employees.

CHAPTER

53

Sexual Harassment at Workplace

In this chapter on "Sexual Harassment at Workplace", the following aspects are covered:

1. Meaning.
2. Definition of sexual harassment.
3. Responsibilities of employers to implement, monitor the guidelines to tackle sexual harassment.
4. Implementation problems.
5. How to meet harassment dilemma?
6. Sexual harassment and laws in India.
7. Who can face sexual harassment?
8. The employer's responsibilities.
9. Effects of sexual harassment on individual and the organisation.
10. Employee's responsibilities.

1. MEANING

Legally, sexual harassment is defined as unwelcome advances, requests for sexual favours and other verbal or physical conduct of a sexual nature.

Most studies confirm that the concept of power is central to sexual harassment. It comes from a superior, a colleague or a subordinate.

In August 1997 judgement of the Supreme Court of India on sexual harassment of working women in the case of *Vishaka* vs. *The State of Rajasthan* has identified sexual harassment as a separate category of legally prohibitive behaviour. The court has laid down guidelines in accordance with international standards to deal with the issue at workplace.

In another case the Supreme Court of India has ruled that sexual harassment at the workplace is a violation of fundamental rights.

2. DEFINITION OF SEXUAL HARASSMENT

According to the orders of the Supreme Court of India sexual harassment is any unwelcome:

(i) Physical contact and advances,
(ii) Demand or request for sexual favours,
(iii) Sexually coloured remarks,
(iv) Display coloured remarks,
(v) Showing pornography, and
(vi) Any other unwelcome physical, verbal or non-verbal conduct of a sexual nature.

Supreme Court has further laid down that:

Actual assault or touch is not required. In such cases, the courts are required to examine the broad possibilities of the case and not get swayed by insignificant discrepancies or narrow technicalities or the dictionary meaning of the expression 'molestation'.

3. RESPONSIBILITIES OF EMPLOYERS TO IMPLEMENT, MONITOR THE GUIDELINES TO TACKLE SEXUAL HARASSMENT

The Supreme Court guidelines lay down certain responsibilities on employers/ management to implement, monitor the procedure in their organisations, public as well as private.

3.1 Procedure for Complaints by Women

The guidelines direct employer's to set-up procedure through which women can make their complaints heard.

A *complaints committee* headed by a woman, and/or of which half the members are women should be deputed to look into complaints of sexual harassment. To prevent undue pressure from within the organisation, the committee should include a third-party representative from an NGO.

All complaints should be handled in confidential manner within a time-bound framework. Annual report should be submitted to the concerned government department.

3.2 Preventive Steps to be taken by Employers

(a) An express prohibition of sexual harassment should be notified, published and circulated.
(b) Amendment of conduct and service rules to include sexual harassment as an offence and provision of appropriate discipline against the offender.
(c) Management also include in S.O. (Standing Orders), personnel manual of their organisation.
(d) Providing such working conditions to ensure there is no hostile environment.

3.3 Awareness of Guidelines

(i) Employees to be allowed to raise sexual harassment issues at workers' meetings.
(ii) Sexual harassment issue to be discussed in employer-employee meetings.
(iii) Rights of women workers to be notified.
(iv) Where such act is offence under IPC, employer to initiate action and complaint.
(v) Complainants or witnesses not to be victimised while dealing cases.
(vi) Employer to assist the employee if sexual harassment takes place by an outsider.

4. IMPLEMENTATION PROBLEMS

Several public and private sector organisations have constituted committees and cells to comply with the Supreme Court guidelines. Experience of implementing guidelines has highlighted some issues:

- It is important that the top management takes serious interest on this issue.
- It is noticed that in many cases recommendations of the committee are ignored and thus denial of justice.
- The usual defence that the harasser puts up is of "inefficiency of complainant or it is conspiracy against him."
- In many cases 'caste factor' is brought in.
- Witnesses do not come forward due to job-careers at stake.
- Too much legalities of evidence, proof from witnesses is asked by the committees.
- If harasser holds a very superior position then it becomes difficult for committee members to secure justice to victim.
- The seat of power becomes tool of misuse, and it could be cloaked as a lure for promotion or increment. Most of the times, divorced, separated or submissive women are the victims.

5. HOW TO MEET HARASSMENT DILEMMA?

It will be relevant to mention views of Nan Demars (You Want To Do What, Which, Where and How To Draw The Line, Simon and Schuster, USA).

"If we remain silent and tolerate harassment, it will continue. I urge you to confront you harassers, document every suspect incident and follow-up conversation. Let it be known that you are taking their inappropriate and unprofessional behaviour seriously. Then, as soon as, you can, try to stop the objectionable behaviour through the use of informal, one to one discussions and incrementally stiffer consequences. When all else fails, resort to formal avenues of protest inside and outside your company."

6. SEXUAL HARASSMENT AND THE LAWS IN INDIA

(i) There are several provisions in IPC (The Indian Penal Code) and include:
   (a) S. 354—Assault or criminal force against a woman with the intent to outrage her modesty.
   (b) S. 509—Words, gesture or act intended to insult the modesty of a woman.
   (c) S. 209—Deals with obscene acts and songs.

(ii) Case can be filed under Rule 5, Schedule 5 of the Industrial Disputes Act, if an employee suffers unfair dismissal or denial of employment benefits as a consequence of her rejection for sexual harassment.

(iii) A civil suit can also be filed for damages under tort laws. The Indecent Representation of Women (Prohibition) Act, 1987 has also potential to be used for such cases.

(iv) In case of a senior IAS officer Rupan Bajaj and KPS Gill in July 1988. Gill was fined by Supreme Court of Rs. 2.5 lakhs in lieu of 3 months' rigorous imprisonment for offences under S. 294 and S. 509 of IPC.

(v) Sexual harassment has been included as misconduct in:
   (a) CCS (Conduct) Rules, 1964, and
   (b) Industrial Employment (Standing Orders) Act, 1946.

(vi) Government is now introducing a legislation incorporating the guidelines of Supreme Court of India.

7. WHO CAN FACE SEXUAL HARASSMENT?

- An individual at the workplace.
- A staffer—from a sweeper to a CEO.
- A non-staffer in any capacity—student, housekeeper, volunteer, on honorarium, maid or consultant.
- Dressed in a sari or suit.
- Working in public or private sector units or non-government organisations.
- Working in the unorganised sector—large or small.
- A person who believes it only happens to others.
- And it could be either gender, male or female.

8. THE EMPLOYER'S RESPONSIBILITIES

- Recognise sexual harassment as a serious offence and include it in the rules and regulations.
- Prevent and punish sexual harassment at the workplace.
- Conduct anti-sexual harassment awareness training for regular and contractual employees as well as for new inductees.
- Formulate an anti-sexual harassment policy, which should:
  - o clearly state the employer's commitment to a safe work environment,
  - o define Sexual Harassment with examples and explicitly term it an offence,
  - o constitute a Complaints Committee as per Supreme Court guidelines,
  - o be aware of the fact that the complainant may delay in lodging a complaint,
  - o ensure confidentiality of the complainant and witnesses,
  - o not punish or harass or transfer the complainant and witnesses for complaining, rather should give the complainant the option to seek transfer of the perpetrator or their own,
  - o make the enquiry procedure time-bound,
  - o provide for maintenance of accurate records of the enquiry procedure, with a copy of it given to both parties,
  - o ensure that the Complaints Committee makes recommendations in their enquiry report, the duty of the employer being implementation of the recommendations, and
  - o ensure that a copy of the enquiry report along with the recommendations is given to both parties.

- Ensure that the equity be conducted as per the law of natural justice.
- Display/distribute the policy/information about the redressal mechanism.
- Prominently display the addresses/contact number of the Complaints Committee members.
- Ensure that third parties or service users such as hotel guests, airline passengers, are aware of the Policy.
- Take prompt action on the complaint even if the complainant does not have eyewitnesses.

9. EFFECTS OF SEXUAL HARASSMENT ON THE INDIVIDUAL

- Physical, emotional and psychological trauma.
- Loss of self-esteem.
- Isolation and ostracism.
- Absenteeism and lowered productivity.
- Loss of job, promotion or job-related activities such as training.
- Suicide and spillover effects into family life.
- Decreased productivity.
- Lowered profitability.
- Valued employees quitting or losing jobs.
- Poor public image.
- Costly court litigation.
- Expensive compensation payouts.
- Unhealthy work atmosphere.
- Strain and mistrust in interpersonal relations.

10. EMPLOYEE'S RESPONSIBILITIES

- Don't blame yourself.
- Don't ignore sexual harassment—it will not go way by itself.
- Recognise the nature of harassment.
- Talk to the perpetrator.
- Talk to others at the workplace or in your family about the harassment and talk with the union, if any.
- Maintain a detailed chronological account of sexual harassment.
- Try and have a witness to the incident.
- Write a letter and/or send your organisation's anti-sexual harassment policy to the harasser by registered post.
- Always retain a copy of the documents/letters sent in connection with your complaint.
- Ensure that the employer formulates an anti-sexual harassment policy and has a redressal mechanism.
- Ask for regular awareness programmes and training to be conducted.
- Approach a women's organisation or call the local helpline or both.
- Lodge a formal complaint without delay.
- Seek counselling.

How an act amounts as sexual harassment or not depends between consenting co-worker? In sexual harassment or in ethics, it is the thought that counts. Gifts are given every where.

CHAPTER

54

Total Quality Management (TQM)

In this chapter on "Total Quality Management (TQM)", the following aspects are covered:

1. Concept of TQM.
2. Steps that identify organisation process towards TQM.
3. Four streams of TQM.
4. Principles of TQM.
5. Key perquisites for implementation of TQM.
6. Quality circles and TQM.

Before we take up the relationship and common features of TQM and OD, it will be appropriate to appreciate the concept of TQM, its features, core values, TQM techniques.

It will be relevent to mention at the outset that as TQMs' emphasis is on creating an organisational culture, that involves extensive participation, an emphasis on teams and teamwork, cooperation between units, generation of valid data, and continuous learning, TQM is highly congruent with OD approaches and values. (French and Bell)

Most companies are interested to improve quality of their products and services through TQM.

TQM approach focuses on *trying to meet customer expectations* or *delighting* the customer. All quality improvement initiatives must begin with an understanding of customer perceptions and needs. TQM is an organisational *strategy* with techniques that deliver *quality products* and/ or *services to customer* and achieves total customer satisfaction. It should be customer, which comes back and not the product.

1. CONCEPT OF TQM

The concept of TQM and what does three *terms total quality management* mean are explained in Figure 1 on next page.

FIGURE I

Concept of TQM

Total	Quality	Management or Control
→ Covers all functional areas. → Covers all employees at all levels. It is employee-centered. → Covers all others— • suppliers, • customers, • who have a stake in the organisation.	→ Conformance to customer's needs expectations, quality service → Fitness for use → Customer satisfaction	→ Effective utilisation of: • men • machines • materials • methods • money • time → Work towards continuous improvement in all spheres and activities of an organisation

TQM is a strategy that is formulated at the top management level and then diffused at all levels. Everyone in the organisation, from CEO to lowest paid workers/clerks are involved in the TQM process.

Under TQM, *not only* the "Customer is King", but so are *internal customers* such as co-workers or other departments. In essence, TQM becomes the *dominant culture* of the organisation. Some *core values* of every one involved in TQM are like:

(i) Make it right for the customer at any cost.
(ii) Customer is always right.
(iii) *Internal* customers are as important as *external* customers.
(iv) Respond to *customer inquiry* or complaint by the end of the day.
(v) Answer the phone bell within *two rings*.
(vi) Not only meet *customer expectations but delight* customers in the process.
(vii) *Team work and cooperation* are important.
(viii) *Every one* is involved in quality effort.
(ix) Respond to every employee's *suggestion* for quality improvement.
(x) Always *strive for continuous improvement*. Never be satisfied with level of quality.

2. STEPS THAT IDENTIFY ORGANISATION PROCESS TOWARDS TQM

Quality is not absolute but continously changing the perception.

(i) Awareness

Every employee *responsible* for continuous improvement and should be *aware* of benefits TQM will bring, e.g. communicate the need for TQM and educate employees.

(ii) Involvement

Organisation to induce sense of belonging in the employees and involve them in every proactive process, e.g. communicate vision, develop supportive culture, develop them.

(iii) Commitment

All employees are committed to satisfy internal and external customers and TQM becomes way of life, e.g. develop teams, goals, recognition systems, promote change, etc.

(iv) Ownership

Good initiative and innovative techinque is recognised which encourages employees to give their best, e.g. recognise achievements, reward success, empower men, etc.

3. FOUR STREAMS OF TQM

TQM goes beyond beating the best by bench marking, it is a process and a means for maintaining the *leadership position* through continuous change, adaptation and improvement (Business Process Re-engineering). TQM is to improve the quality of work of all people at all the functional areas of organisation. It imbibes the philosophy that *there is always a better way of doing things*. It uses ideas of group activity, participation of all, creativity and self-development. TQM consist of four mutually reinforcing interactive streams as shown in Figure

FIGURE 2

Four Steams of the Total Quality Management

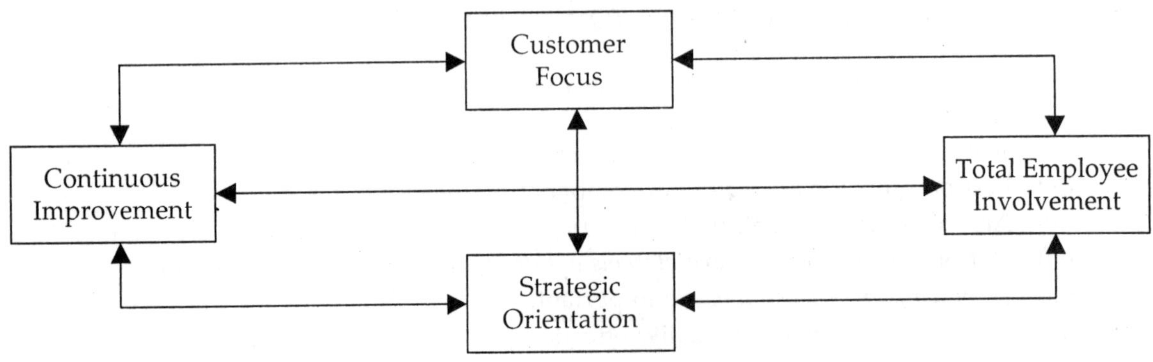

2.

Considering customer focus, continuous improvement, and teamwork as the major constituents of TQM. Dean and Evans (1994) enumerated the principles, practices, and techniques of TQM. Dean and Bowen (1994) have summarised these as in Figure 3 on next page.

4. PRINCIPLES OF TQM

The main principles of TQM are as under: (Figure 3)

FIGURE 3

Principles, Practices and Techniques of Total Quality Management

	Customer Focus	*Continuous Improvement*	*Teamwork*
Principles	Paramount importance of providing products and services that fulfil customer needs; requires organisation-wide focus on customers	Consistent customer satisfaction can be attained only through relentless improvement of processes that create products and services.	Customer focus and continuous improvement are best achieved by collaboration throughout in organization as well as with customers and suppliers.
Practices	Direct customer contact. Collecting information about customer needs. Using information to design and deliver products and services.	Process analysis Re-engineering Problem-solving.	Search for arrangements that benefit all units involved in a process. Formation of various types of teams. Group skills training.
Techniques	Customer surveys and focus groups. Quality function deployment (translates customer information into product specifications).	Flowcharts. Pareto analysis. Statistical process control. Fishbone diagrams.	Organizational development methods such as the nominal group technique. Team-building methods (e.g., role clarification and group feedback).

Source: Dean and Bowen (1994: 395).

- Customer focus.
- *Prevention*: Prevention is better than cure. In the long-run, it is cheaper to stop products defects than trying to find them.
- *Zero Defects*: The ultimate aim is no (zero) defects—or exceptionally low defect levels if a product or service is complicated.
- *Getting Things Right First Time*: Better not to produce at all than produce something defective.
- *Quality Involves Everyone*: Quality is not just the concern of the production or operations department—it involves everyone, including marketing, finance and human resources.
- *Kaizen*: Continuous improvement, i.e. always looking for ways to improve processes to improve quality.
- *Employee Involvement*: Teamwork and joint problem-solving.
- *Leadership*: Manager to provide an inspiring vision, make strategic directions that are understood by all. Manager to instill values that guide subordinates build TQM culture.

5. KEY PERQUISITE FOR IMPLEMENTATION OF TQM

These are as under:

(a) Employees to adhere ethical values.
(b) Maintain integrity with customers.
(c) Trust fosters' participation.
(d) Training of employees for effective job performance.
(e) Team working for problem-solving and share responsibilities.
(f) Communication process to act as an important link with all involved and to get feedback.
(g) Recognition for achievements.

6. QUALITY CIRCLES (QCs) AND TOTAL QUALITY MANAGEMENT (TQM)

Quality circle is a form of group problem-solving, participation at workplace and goal setting with primary focus on maintaining and enhancing product or service quality. Japanese have not only evolved a concept of QC, but practised with amazing results. Dr. Ishikawa conceived the idea of QC. QCs have contributed to removal of defects, improving morale, motivation, and job satisfaction of members. QCs inspire cooperation, teamwork, problem-solving capabilities, safety awareness and cost reduction. These promote harmonious supervisor-worker relationships and leadership development.

Quality circle consist of small teams of workers meeting regularly to pool their ideas and suggestions for improving quality, productivity and efficiency in their own work area. They may meet once a week on company time to solve a particular production problem, or to monitor some change already introduced. The quality circles will have a 'chairman' who is not necessarily the supervisor of the work unit; chairmanship may be rotated amongst the members. Leaders are encouraged to create participation within the group. QCs are found to be more effective where the company has put some resources into training and coaching the participants in problem-solving techniques, running meetings, and so on. Quality circles may be linked together by a co-ordinator/facilitator, or report upwards to a more senior managerial set of QCs.

QCs have been overtaken by a more radical approach called total quality management. This is a 'holistic' approach which fits the OD definition of 'planned whole-organisation change'. Dale and Cooper offer the following comparison of QCs and TQM given in Figure 4.

FIGURE 4

Comparison of QCs and TQM

Feature	*QCs*	*TQM*
• Choice of membership	Voluntary	Compulsory
• Structure	Add-on	Integrated
• Direction	Bottom-up	Top-down
• Scope	In departments	Company-wide
• Aims	Employee relations and work improvements	Quality culture and quality performance

TQM is, therefore, a much broader concept than QCs, and encompasses not only product, service and process quality improvements, but also costs, overall productivity, and the development and involvement of all employees at all levels.

TQM is seen to emphasise problem prevention more than problem-solving. It is customer driven, both internal and external, that is, a customer is anyone, including work colleagues, who receive our individual work output. TQM is more of a long-term organisational strategy than QCs.

Within TQM various emphases are possible, and some writers distinguish between a 'hard' TQM approach which relies heavily on statistical anlaysis, and 'soft' TQM which emphasises teamwork, employee empowerment, open communication, involvement and participation, and skill development. Overall there is probably a shift towards 'soft' TQM.

TQM is a strategy that is formulated at the top management level and then diffused at all levels. Everyone in the organisation, from CEO to lowest paid workers/clerks are involved in the TQM process.

References

Fred Luthans, "Organisational Behaviour", McGraw Hill, Inc., Singapore.

Dean, J.W. Jr., and De Bowen (1994), "Management Theory and Total Quality", *Academy of Management Review*, 19(3): 392-418.

Jagdeep, S. Chhokar, "OD and the Quality Movement" in *OD International and Strategies*, Response Books, A Division of Sage Publications, London.

Bennis, W.G. (1969), Organisation Development: Strategies and Models, Reading, M.A.: Addison-Wesley.

CHAPTER

55

Work-Life Balance

Training and job challenges are viewed by employees as the biggest motivations for joining organisations. These factors are also considered by employer's for attracting and retaining employees. However, due to ever changing work environment, employees have to face new challenges—problems, wide-ranging responsibilities, greater productivity and competitiveness at workplace. These tend to stress and pressure, bringing imbalance in lives of employees.

We shall discuss this topic under following headings:

1. Concept of work-life balance.
2. Its importance.
3. Major factors of change that push emphasis on work-life balance.
4. Corporate strategies to cope work-life balance.
5. Outcomes.

I. CONCEPT OF WORK-LIFE BALANCE

Inspite of landmark improvements in information technology, internet, telecom, travel, scientific research, stress and monotony at workplace continues. Management experts call it as a syndrome of improper work-life balance.

According to Raja Achanta, life is known to be set of pursuits. The list includes: *family, health, wealth, career, social obligations, intellectual* and *spirituality*. A perfectly balanced life for an employee needs a careful adjustment of these quests.

The first two pursuits, i.e. family and health need special attention as these aspects, like glass panes cannot be mended on development of any crack. But the remaining aspects are flexible and provide scope for fixing them. This continuous juggling pulls the employees into a grind and leaves them stressed and stretched. Thus, managing work-life balance is one of the major challenges of new generation of 21st century, as the workplace schedules take its toll on employee's health, relationships and well-being.

2. ITS IMPORTANCE

Importance of work-life balance is being realised both by corporates and employees. With changing times, more and more *employers* are facing the need to adopt the rule, i.e. it is the *productivity* that matters most, *rather than hours spent* by the employees in the office. Employers are making efforts *to be flexible* and trying to face the operational challenges.

Similarly, employees today want to have freedom and live lives their way. They value balance between work and life than ever before.

3. MAJOR FACTORS OF CHANGE THAT PUSH EMPHASIS ON WORK-LIFE BALANCE

These reasons are as under:

(i) Employees in 21st century place *personal life on a higher pedestal* than work-life. The workplace schedules take it toll on employee's health, family relationship and well-being. There are rising divorce rates, spouse relationship problems relating to children and household affairs. Employees expect more life outside work.

(ii) Corporates today function on the principle of empowering employees—which means based on *flexibility and freedom for employees* to take decisions. So employees want from their employer flexi timings, focus on results and overall avoidance of long work hour culture.

(iii) In global organisations the working is becoming *round-the-clock customer service.* This has lead to work-life balance of employees more essential. At the same time technology has added to *the speed* of operation to fight competition and also to meet tougher *deadlines.* Today's world does not go to sleep due to across the globe operations.

(iv) Another factor is rise *in dual* earning couples. Particularly working mothers are major populations (80%) who adversely get affected in balancing jobs performance and family life.

4. CORPORATES STRATEGIES TO COPE WORK-LIFE BALANCE

Corporates have recognised the importance of work-life balance. Some methods adopted by them are to overcome the ill-effects on the overall company performance and individual life.

(i) *Flexi-time* to enjoy flexible hours, this is formulated, by having a core time when the employee presence at work is mandatory, but after these hours, employees can manage their own time accordingly. The scheme works to build trust among employees while also meeting the business needs. This helps in creative work, reducing stress and improving productivity. It helps to balance both personal life and work-life.

(ii) Other flexible arrangements, such as:

- Providing freedom of part-time working, home teleworking, unpaid breaks, job-sharing, parental leave, compressed working week.
- Providing with facilities and services.
- Membership of sport and social clubs and health clubs.
- Leave for career development.
- Employees to develop their own attendance schedules—self-rostering.

- Working long and short days and by accumulating hours of non-working time to use it in future when necessary.
- "Well-being" centers in offices for employees to go and relax.
- Creating employee health management group to prevent and manage workplace stress.

(iii) *New Initiatives by Companies*: These cover yoga, group meditation and exercise, gyms are all taken to energise employees through their natural energy systems and bring fun in their work. Companies are sponsoring sessions like "art of living" for its employees.

Employees are now more conscious that life has four corner stones—family, work, leisure and friends. When planning changes to the structure of one, one has to careful not to make any changes to another area. They learn to relax mind, keep themselves physically, mentally and spiritually fit as possible. They are aware not to hide their feelings as frustration is a major cause of stress. They limit their exposure to stress by cutting back certain commitments and work load.

5. OUTCOMES

All these steps create an atmosphere of trust and communication between management and employees.

Thus balance between work and life is now more critical factor for job satisfaction and motivation. Organizations are interested in rejuvenated and more productive employees. It is involving the hearts and minds of the employees, thus enable them find over all fulfilment and achieve full potential. Thus employees to feel better and perform better. The best kind of creativity is collaborative. One should be continuously open to new and innovative ways to balance family and work. Tailor and customize your strategies to employees' needs. There are positive pay-offs for such efforts, including increased loyalty, money saved and the competitive edge that a loyal, committed work force will provide. One can become a family-friendly manager and keep talent on his team. Two simple strategies can make the manager family-friendly. These are:

(a) *Be flexible*, i.e. think flexibly the next time an employee asks for some need to help child, spouse, old parent. It is more likely that section employees will appreciate (silently). Managers open mindedness and willingness to help a valued employee in time of need long is remembered by employees. At the same time manager can set clear expectations from the employee for results and hold him to those results. As a manager one can no doubt implement some degree of flexibility for the team.

(b) Second is *being supportive*. One can gain more being interested in and supportive to lives of employees outside of work. We quote a small incident mentioned by a receptionist of a company:

"I was so excited about my daughter's singing debut at her high school. She had been taking vocal lessons, had developed a strong, beautiful voice and now was her chance to show it off. She would sing the Star Spangled Banner (without accompaniment) during the all-school pep rally at 1 P.M. My boss was excited for me and said, "No problem," when I asked him if I could go watch her. But here's the best part. Upon my return, with videotape in hand, he asked me how it went and asked if I would show him the tape. It was such a small thing, but meant so much to me. I proudly showed him the video and beamed as he praised my daughter. He showed support in so many ways that day."

There are many ways to show support. Here are some examples:

- Allowing employees' children to come to work with them occasionally, usually to celebrate a special occasion or because of a special need.
- Driving to an employees' house to be with her/his family following a death in the family.
- Accompanying employees to their children's ball games and recitals.
- Inviting an employee and his or her parents, or children to lunch.
- Sending birthday cards or cakes to employees' family members.
- Setting up special e-mail and resource areas on the company intranet for employees' children.
- Work-life balance has become a major challenge for employees and enlightened employer's who want creativity from them.

Work-life balance has become a major challenge for employees and enlightened employer's who want creativity from them.

References

Raja Achanta, "The Work-life Balance", *HRM Review*, March 2004. Gratefully Acknowledged.
S.K. Bhatia, Boost Your Professional Career, Deep & Deep Publications Pvt. Ltd., New Delhi.

PART VIII

GLOBAL VALUES

CHAPTER

56

Ethics in Global Business

In this chapter on "Ethics in Global Business", the following aspects are covered to avoid problems on ethics in global business:

1. Problems on ethical issues in global business.
2. Measures to avoid problems on ethical issues.
   2.1 Acquaintance with ethical codes to guide business worldwide.
   2.2 Environment protection and safety regulations.
   2.3 Discrimination on gender issues.
   2.4 Corruption.
   2.5 Human rights issues in business policies.
   2.6 Protection of employee privacy.
   2.7 Health and safety.

1. PROBLEMS ON ETHICAL ISSUES IN GLOBAL BUSINESS

Many companies are entering global market now. Some companies are experiencing difficulty on ethical norms and adopt some undesirable practices as under:

- Not adhering to labour laws, policies such as paying low wages (exploitative wages), employing child labour, unsafe working conditions, etc.
- Indulge in prevailing corruption.
- Violation of human rights.
- Avoid fair share of govenment taxes.
- Discrimation of women at work place.
- Environmental pollution.
- Not making investment in less developed countries out of enormous profits.
- Violation of copy rights and software laws.
- In this connection also refer to Box 1.

2. MEASURES TO AVOID PROBLEMS ON ETHICAL ISSUES

Measures to avoid problems on ethical issues are explained as under:

2.1 Acquaintance with Ethical Codes to Guide Business Practices

Acquaintance of ethics codes of some countries is required to guide business in worldwide. USA encourages all the business houses to *adopt a corporate mission statement* and *implement voluntary codes of conduct* or *codes of ethics* for doing business globally in upholding and promoting universal standards of human rights in different areas of human rights are given in Figure 1.

FIGURE 1

Areas Adhered to Universal Standards of Human Rights

(i) Provision of a safe and healthy work place.
(ii) Fair employment practices:
  (a) Avoidance of child and forced labour,
  (b) Avoidance of discrimination based on race, gender, national origin or religious beliefs,
  (c) Respect for right of association, and
  (d) Right to organise and bargain collectively.
(iii) Responsible environmental protection.
(iv) Compliance with USA and local laws including prohibiting illicit payments.
(v) Maintenance of corporate culture, which does not allow coercion at work place, but encourages good corporate citizenship and makes contribution to communities in which company operates, where ethical conduct is recognised and valued.

2.2 Environmental Protection and Safety Regulations

Problems such as: *Pollution* due to disposal of toxic waste, eroding of earth's ozone layer, burning of fuel oil, coal and wood has lead to production of carbondioxide. This eroding ozone layer and causing global warming.

- Numerous examples of major *environmental pollutions* such as Bhopal Gas tragedy, 1984, Fire in Bombay High Sea (ONGC), storage tank leakage of Pennwalt Corporation, USA in 1985, destruction of oil tankers in Black Sea in 2007, etc.
- *Water pollutions* are caused due to sewage discharges, drainage from mines, chemicals which are toxic for human life, fishes and birds. These are *caused due to industrial production and human activity*.
- Business and governments world over are concerned with public health, safety regulations and environmental protection.
- Environment of environmental laws which contain criminal enforcement provisions is strictly implemented.
- Standards of product safety and work safety are encouraged.

2.3 Discrimination—Gender Issues

Many barriers for women seeking equal treatment world over exist, such as:

- Glass ceiling or blocked career for women by invisible barriers for reaching to top positions. These activities are gradually removed by countries.
- Sexual harassment at work place, etc. are safeguard by laws.

2.4 Corruption

- Bribes and corruption in international business are common,
- Payoffs have become part of life in award of contracts, and
- To check these practices, certain countries have enacted laws that prohibit their citizens from paying bribes to foreign officials for economic favours.

2.5 Human Rights

- One major ethical dilemma facing firms from democratic nations is whether they should do business in totalitarian countries such as Cuba, Iran, China, Iraq, South Africa and recently Nepal. USA in 1996 decided to decouple human rights issues from trade policy considerations.
- Corporations support and advance *UN's Global Compact (GC) principles* within the company's sphere of influence. Global corporates now advance and support UN's Global Compact principles in their business abroad. It is to commit to ten principles of human rights, labour standards, environment and anti-corruption as part of its strategy, culture and day-to-day operations. Indian MNCs, Bharat Heavy Electricals India (BHEL)—has participated in this programme. For details see BHEL's web site (http://www.bhel.com and also refer Box 2.
- For example, some countries like USA have banned the import of carpets, bangles from India as they allege child labour is used.

2.6 PROTECTION OF EMPLOYEE PRIVACY

Privacy refers to protecting a person's private life, i.e. religious, social beliefs as well as personal life-style, etc. from intrusive actions. Such intrusive actions include five areas which pose ethical dilemmas to employers. (Figure 2)

FIGURE 2

Ethical Issues in Employee's Privacy

(a) Information technology
(b) Aids testing
(c) Whistle blowing
(d) Drug testing
(e) Genetic testing

(a) First relates to *information technology*. Employees are viewed on close-circuit TV, phones are tapped, computer files are read. Thus respect for person in denied.
(b) *Aids* has become a major public health problem. For HR manager the disease raises two issues. Whether a new hire be subject to Aids test? What treatment should be meted out to an employee who is affected with the disease? USA has a legislation that bar job discrimination against people with Aids.
(c) Another area of ethical concern is *whistle blowing*. Employee may feel it obligatory to blow the whistle without following sequence of; actions laid down by company. Employee make organisational misconduct. For example, cases of Enron, World Com, Kellog in India, LG India, Xerox USA, etc. Highway Transport Authority of India.
(d) *Drug testing* may assume an ethical dimension. If the information obtained from drug testing is relevant to the job, subjecting an employee to such a test assumes legitimacy. Where information obtained from drug testing is irrelevant to the job, it amounts to invading an employee's personal life. Such information may also be held against the employee's concerned.
(e) Another dilemma is *genetic testing* which links between one's inherited characteristics and certain illnesses. Genetic testing may be two forms. Genetic screening is used to identify persons who are susceptible to certain genetically-based illness. The goal of screening is to single out individuals who have certain genetic traits. Genetic monitoring is to single out (not people) but harmful substances. Genetic make sense for business as deleting disabled employees means reduction in costs due to illness, absenteeism, health insurance and compensation, etc. Genetic Testing can be held against job-seekers or discriminate against some employees. In addition, it gives way to social stigma to people with genetic defects.

2.7 Health and Safety

Accidents, injuries and illnesses are likely to occur due to industrial hazardous work. Work pressure may cause stress and disorders to eyes and neck such as through repetitive work on computer terminal display.

Issue involved in health and safety is that assessment of risk can be done by qualified person and not by judgement of amount of compensation only as in Bhopal Gas tragedy.

Box I

Areas of Concern and Interest in Not Displaying Ethical Behaviour

Bribery/improper pressure	Substance abuse
Conflict of interest	Whistle-blowing
Receiving and giving gifts	Nepotism
Sexual harassment	Age discrimination
Safety and health practices	Promotion and evaluation favoritism
Privacy and confidentiality	Treatment of the environment
Supplier relations	Use of power and position
Stealing	Copying of software

Box 2

Being Responsible and Ethical is Important!

- Each year more and more companies are taking social responsibility, ethics, and organizational "citizenship" more seriously. Annually, the best public companies, as measured by service to various stake-holder groups (e.g.. customers, employees, general public) are rated by Business Ethics. Some of the comments of managers of these "best" citizen companies' winners are interesting to reflect upon.
- Douglas A. Leatherdale, CEO of St. Paul Companies (#9), a $7.5 billion in revenues insurance company, stated "Corporate responsibility is a deeply rooted tradition in our company and an integral part of our character and reputation."
- Andrew Lock, Vice-President of Human Resources of furniture manufacturer Henry Miller (#7), stated, "We've led the way in creating policies described by others as progressive in including employee recognition programs; gainsharing, adoption of childcare programmes, stock options, and more."
- Dr. A. Wallace Hayes, Vice-President of Corporate Integrity of Gillette (#36), was proud of his company's highest score for its approach to environmental restoration. He stated, "Protecting the environment is part of Gillette's mission and values."
- Being recognized as responsible and ethical indicates a maturing in firms regarding the needs and interest of their stakeholders. St. Paul Companies, Henry Miller, and Gillette are proud to be viewed by their employees and external stakeholders as being concerned and doing something about social responsibility and ethics.

Source: Adapted from, "The 100 Best Corporate Citizens", Business Ethics, May 2001.

CHAPTER

57

Environmental Problems—Global Warming

In this chapter on "Environmental Problems—Global Warming", following aspects are covered:

1. Climate Change—Environmental Problems.
2. Global warming—Concept.
3. Effects of global warming.
4. Efforts to combat global warming.
   4.1 Rio-de-Janerio—Earth Summit (1992).
   4.2 Berlin mandate (1995).
   4.3 Kyoto Protocol (1997).
   4.4 U.N. meet on climate change at Bali (2007).
5. Global warming meet at Bali in summarised form.

1. CLIMATE CHANGE—ENVIRONMENTAL PROBLEMS

Environmental problems like air, water and land pollution or municipal waste disposal exist in every country. The nations have identified the causes for these problems and would continue to deal with them depending upon how severe these are and how serious is commitment for their abatement.

Today, we have a fairly good information about environmental problems. The public being conscious of these problems wants the governments and international agencies to become actively involved in tackling them. The citizens are willing to cooperate in the environmental clean up process because they (especially in developed world) have realised that the risks arising out of environmental damage are real and these pose serious challenge to the lifestyle and their living standards. This consciousness got impetus probably from conservation of nature because it became clear that *resources were being exploited to the extent that they may get depleted and their conservation is one of the ways out*. Resource depletion or exploitation is being carried out both by the individuals and the business corporations, the latter doing it for profit. From conservation attitude, developed a new environmentalism that *emphasised interrelatedness of natural systems*—that there is human-nature relationship and everything in this planet is related and connected to everything else.

Two global environmental problems are:

(i) Global Warming
(ii) Ozone Depletion

In general, *developing countries* are more concerned with *short-term problems* of water resources, air pollution, land degradation, deforestation, etc. The *developed countries*, on the other hand, taking more interest in *global environmental issues* like global warming and ozone depletion. Unless all environmental problems are addressed within an integrated perspective that rakes into account the local and global, there will be little confidence within the developing world that their concerns are being taken into account into the global environmental agenda.

2. GLOBAL WARMING—CONCEPT

Global warming means *gradual increase in world temperatures caused by greenhouse gases (GHGs)*. The main greenhouse gas is carbon dioxide (CO_2); others are nitrous oxide, CFCs (chloroflurocarbons), methane and some organochloride compounds like perflurocarbons (PFCs) and sulphuric fluoride. *GHGs come from various sources, mostly from burning of fossil fuels. These gases trap the sun's rays in the earth's atmosphere causing the temperature to rise resulting in what is known as greenhouse effect or global warming*. The Inter-governmental Panel on Climate Change (IPCC) has estimated that earth's temperature will rise from 1-3 degrees C in the next few decades. It is believed that global warming is leading to extreme weather changes. Hurricanes may be the result of such a change. The Insurance Companies in industrialised countries have stepped in to show their concern as it may be noted that a single hurricane in USA costs 50 billion dollars to global insurance companies.

In view of the serious effects of global warming and subsequent change in climate, Rio conference (1992) in the discussion on climate change *pledged to stabilise GHGs emissions at 1990 level by end of 20th century*.

It may be mentioned that it is not only burning of fossil fuels in power generation, industries, transport and other sources are also responsible for increase in atmospheric temperature. Deforestation also is responsible because the forest cover that existed earlier would have absorbed carbon dioxide.

The theory, according to scientists, is that GHGs which are present in trace amounts trap sun's heat more efficiently by absorbing longer wave length (infrared) radiation from the earth and as concentration of these gases increase, their heat trapping property also increases. Scientists have also indicated that there has been 25% increase in carbon-dioxide concentration during the last 100 years and it is expected that this will double in the next 50 years.

It is simple to assume that rate of concentration of GHGs, particularly CO_2 will depend upon the rate at which consumption of fossil fuels and deforestation proceeds. The developing countries burn fossil fuels at lower rate than industrial world but when the former reach a higher level of development they would also use higher amount of fossil fuels and also their deforestation process may increase, resulting in higher concentration of CO_2 in the atmosphere. Brazil, according to World Watch Institute, is already contributing billions of tons of CO_2 each year through process of deforestation.

Green House Gases (GHGs)

These include Carbon Dioxide (CO_2) (main effect), Methane (CH_4) 20%, Chloroflurocarbons (CFCs) 15%, Nitrous Oxide (NO_2) 5% and Green House Effect is due to them.

3. EFFECTS OF GLOBAL WARMING

Scientists agree that: (i) actual warming has been taking place during the last 100 years; (ii) warming would further raise the temperature of earth by 3-5°C if increase in CO_2 doubles; (iii) if warming continues, coastal areas would see a rise in sea level. If temperature rises further by 3-5°C, sea levels may rise by 0.5 ft. to 5.0 ft. because of melting of mountain glaciers and expansion of oceans. This would result in islands like Maldives getting submerged and many coastal cities getting flooded, forcing the people to leave their original homes. They would be environmental refugees looking for new habitats. Not only rising water levels but there would be other changes due to global warming. These include hot summers for many parts of world which would mean more consumption of electricity. It would also affect agricultural production and ecological balance. (also see Box 1)

4. EFFORTS TO COMBAT GLOBAL WARMING

4.1 Rio-de-Janerio (1992) Earth Summit

At the Earth Summit held at Rio de Janeiro (1992), 153 nations signed the convention on climate change and committed themselves to reduce emissions of CO_2 and other GHGs. Thus there is already agreement among nations that global warming is a serious problem and rather than to wait and watch attitude, steps may be taken towards reducing consumption of fossil fuels by finding out alternative sources of renewable energy better energy management system and to reverse deforestation. It is a documented fact that burning coal produces twice as much CO_2 per unit of heat as natural gas. It is therefore, important to control CO_2 production from burning of coal which can be possible by use of alternative source of energy like solar and wind power. USA with 6% of world population *contributes 25% of world CO_2 emissions*; it has therefore, a greater responsibility in reducing this gas and to evolve new energy strategies.

There is another aspect to the issue of greenhouse gases. Even if effects of CO_2 on global warming are not too great, less use of fossil fuels and alternative sources of energy would not only reduce CO_2 emission but also lessen pollution. It is true that all the strategies to reduce worldwide reduction in CO_2 emission would incur astronomical costs, not billions but trillions of currency, but steps in this direction need to be taken in a phased manner. Following steps have been suggested by experts:

(a) *Cleaning up coal* for which technology exists. This can lead to lesser pollution. Also, conversion of coal to gas is possible. This would further reduce pollution.
(b) *More use of natural gas* than coal because natural gas contains only half the carbon of coal and no sulphur.

(c) *Renewable sources of energy* would ultimately tackle the problem of CO_2 emission and pollution. Wind power and solar energy are obvious choices. But there are other renewable sources like photo voltaic (photo voltaics convert sunlight directly into electricity). These sources produce little or no pollution and involve no safety risks.
(d) *Manufacturing fuel efficient vehicles* is another step.
(e) *Deforestation Reversal.* This is a major step to reduce CO_2 concentration. It is possible to reclaim more land to plant more trees but requires help from social, political and financial institutions.

4.2 Berlin Mandate (1995)

The Mandate launched an *ad hoc* group on the Berlin Mandate (AGBM) 1995 to negotiate a timetable for reductions (See: The Berlin Mandate in Figure 1).

FIGURE 1

The Berlin Mandate

At the first Conference of Parties (CoP 1), held in Berlin from March 26-April 7, 1995.

- The Alliance of Small Island States (AOSIS) urged industrialised nations to cut their carbon dioxide emissions by 20 per cent by the year 2000.
- The UK minister for environment urged a 5-10 per cent cut in greenhouse gas (GHG) emissions by 2010.
- Industrialised countries continued to argue about the stringency of targets.
- India presented a revised form of the AOSIS draft.
- The EU timetable for negotiations by 1997 was adopted.
- It was recognised that existing commitments were not adequate.
- Governments agreed that no new commitments should be introduced for developing countries.
- A restructured Global Environment Facility (GEF) was given another four-year term as the interim financial mechanism.

The Berlin Mandate accepted, for the first time, the need for legally binding targets for industrialised countries. The Mandate recognised that—

- Existing commitments for industrialised nations under FCCC were inadequate,
- New reduction targets and timetables are needed for industrialised countries on the 1990 levels beyond the year 2000, and
- No new commitments should be introduced for developing countries.

An *ad hoc* group on the Berlin Mandate (AGBM) was set-up to negotiate a protocol or another legal instrument with a view to adopting the results at CoP 3 in 1997. CoP 2 was held in Geneva in 1996.

4.3 Kyoto Protocol

CoP 2 decided to hold a conference, CoP 3 in Kyoto in December 1997 to finalise a protocol on GHG emission. At *Kyoto conference, US declared that they would stabilise US emission to 1990 levels by 2010* whereas *EU, G77 and China, demanded reduction by 15% below 1990 level.* USA expected this response and came prepared with a variety of market-based remission trading mechanisms that would help it to take the levels below 1990 levels. These mechanisms were included in Kyoto Protocol. Finally, Kyoto was a big success for US, and a bargain for USA in which trading mechanisms were accepted by other groups. Trading of emissions between nations got into protocol in the last minute, USA signed the protocol. However USA feels that Kyoto would be very expensive for them under the Kyoto accord, 38 industrialised countries have agreed to reduce their emissions of Green House Cases by 2012 to 5.2 percent below the levels in 1990. The issue is not whether CO_2 is a pollutant or nor. In small doses, CO_2 is essential for life on the planet, in large quantities it is a pollutant. So the issue is how much carbon can the US ecosystem absorb. The US is the biggest producer of greenhouse gases in the world producing about a fourth of the total. *The issue is whether the US absorbs all the* CO_2 *it releases.*

4.4 U.N. Meet on Climate Change at Bali in December 2007

Bali roadmap 16-12-2007 will help seal new deal by 2009. Fourteen days of negotiations of 190 countries running deep into midnight on several occasions, finally brought to the understanding. Australia's move to ratify the Kyoto Protocol on Monday would augur well for Indian industry and, at best, would push its case in global negotiations.

It will be to India's advantage. Australia will have to meet reduction targets. They will want to offset some of these targets *by buying carbon credits.* India has generated 21 million carbon credits in 2007 as reported in press on 3.1.2008. This is nearly double compared to what was generated in 2006 (see Box 2). Various organisations are taking proactive measures to adopt environment friendly technologies and have initiated steps to claim carbon credits. The Delhi Metro Rail Corporations (DMRC) is now registered with a United Nations Body for trading in carbon credits (see Box 3). Earth care awards for excellence in climate change are introduced (see Box 4). India Inc will be only too happy to find another market for its growing carbon supply, an official told *Times of India* from Bali.

Finally, the US delegation gave in. It was agreed that developing countries would undertake action on climate change mitigation that *they decide is best for them* and not under any international mandate. But this would be done along with *rich countries passing on cleaner technologies and funding that would help the poor nations* to go greener without hurting their economic development.

> "This three-line sentence, inserted into 'Bali roadmap' has ensured that the world does not throw out the existing UN framework based on principles of equity, which the rich countries had come to Bali wishing to do."

5. GLOBAL WARMING MEETING AT BALI IN SUMMARISED FORM

(i) What was the UN meet at Bali about?

It was the meeting of 190-odd countries that are party to a UN treaty on climate change. The treaty is to push the world towards taking action that *reduces the greenhouse gases* in the atmosphere which cause climate change. While the countries work to reduce these emissions, it also helps countries adapt to the inevitable changes and risks arising out of climate change.

(ii) But why was Bali so much in news?

Under the UN treaty, called the UN Framework Convention on Climate Change, there is an existing deal called the Kyoto Protocol. This protocol demands that the 36 big emitters of greenhouse gases (all industrialized countries) reduce their emissions by a fixed percentage by 2012. Bali was to discuss *what happens after 2012*—what are countries expected to do after the first phase of Kyoto ends in 2012.

(iii) But why would countries have to fight over it for days?

Because at present only the *rich countries, that are responsible for 70%* of the pollution are expected to cut their carbon foot-print. But *these countries wanted that after 2012,* even the *developing countries like India and China,* which are increasing their emissions as they grow *also undertake some kind of emission cuts.* This meant a complete overhaul of the existing UN treaty.

(iv) Why does India and other developing countries oppose such emission cuts?

India believes, and so do most other developing countries, that to cut emissions, which arise out of burning fossil fuels like oil and coal, would put a spanner in India's economic growth. India and most other developing countries contend that if they cut fossil fuel consumption without access to costly high-end technologies, they would suffer economically. Also, they contend, that if the rich countries are the worst polluters, the latter should be held responsible.

(v) What have they decided upon at Bali?

They have decided upon a new set of principles that will, over the *next two years,* help the countries decide a post-2012 deal. By 2009, the world, based on *the 'Bali Roadmap', draw up a new deal, making it clear what's expected of each country.*

(vi) What did India gain at Bali and what did it lose?

Most importantly it has ensured that the existing principles of UN treaty are adhered to, in most parts, in the future too and the meat of the future discussions revolves around what the rich countries have to do in times to come. It has ensured that future negotiations also involve transfer of clean technologies from rich to the poor and developing countries. *It's lost opportunities to gain funding for some actions it already takes reducing greenhouse gases.*

(vii) India has instituted earth care awards for excellence in climate change mitigation and adaptation (see Box 4)

(viii) India, as the first among carbon credit generating countries has started future trading in the commodity. By launching on 21.1.2008 the Multi-Commodity Exchange (MCX). Globally, other carbon credit trading exchanges are the Chicago Climate Exchange and the European Climate Exchange (see Box 5).

References

N.K. Uberoi, Environmental Management, Excel Books, New Delhi.

The Times of India, 2nd January, 2008.

Box 1

Dangerous Aspects of Climate Change

Climate change will hit food, water supplies, creating refugees, create conflicts: UN

Bali

Climate change could heighten tensions and *trigger conflicts* worldwide by worsening water and food shortages and creating new flows of environmental refugees, the United Nations Environment Program said on Monday.

The warning was based on a report prepared by the German Advisory Council on Global Change, which urged nations assembled here for a United Nations climate conference to launch an "ambitious" plan to cut back emissions of carbon dioxide and other global-warming gases.

The UN agency's chief, Achim Steiner, said negotiators should find ways to "climate-proof economies to buffer them against the climatic changes already under way."

The German council's report, which was authored by German and Swiss academics, cited these *potential conflict* areas, among others:

Africa's Sahel region

Climate change is expected to produce water scarcities, drought and crop failures, aggravating social crises in a region already burdened by failing states, such as Somalia, and civil wars, as in Sudan.

The Indian subcontinent

The *shrinking of glaciers* jeopardizes vital water supplies, *changes to the monsoon* may disrupt agriculture, and rising seas threaten millions of people in coastal settlements in Bangladesh. Tides of refugees and hungry populations could further destabilize weak governments in Bangladesh and Pakistan.

China

Heat waves, droughts and rises in sea levels will add to existing environmental stress and present major new problems for an already heavily challenged central government.

Caribbean and Central America

More intense hurricanes could overwhelm government capacities in Island states and impoverished Central American nations.

Appeal

Please reduce your CO_2 emissions and save our locals.

Box 2

India Generates 21m Carbon Credits in 2007

It was a significant and happening year for environment economy. And this is not only in terms of global acknowledgement with the Nobel Peace Prize for climate change movement. India is signing off the year 2007 with over 21 million certified emission reduction (CERs) credits generated by clean development mechanism (CDM) projects during the year. This is nearly double compared to what was generated in 2006, that is over 12 million CERs.

A significant jump in carbon credits generated over the previous year may project a cleaner image of the country's polluting industries, however, experts feel we could have done better.

"Considering the CDM potential in India, this growth rate should have been even more. The major part of the issued CERs have happened from limited sectors (mostly from renewable energy, waste heat recovery, etc.) and in the coming years, we expect wider sectoral coverage and more participation leading to a growth of around 80-100%," said Ernst and Young partner (risk advisory services) Sudipta Das. Given that a majority of CERs are from the first issuance, the industry expects repeat issuance from projects in 2006, 2007 and 2008, next year. This has raised expectations from what the country generates in 2008.

"In the carbon market, the doubling of growth is expected next year too and in further years the growth will be decelerated to reach may be up to 100 million per year of issued CERs in 2012. The clarity on next commitment period, by 2009 can impact the acceleration. And in case commitments in the next period are more stringent, we could reach up to 120 million per year of issued CERs by 2012", said Ram Babu, India MD, CantorCO2e.

Box 3

Metro to Cash in on Carbon Credits

The Delhi Metro Rail Corporation (DMRC) is now registered with a United Nations (UN) body for trading in carbon credits. So Delhi's own world-class metro system will now earn revenue to the tune of Rs. 1.2 crore annually for the environment friendly technologies adopted by it.

Beginning December 29, 2007, Delhi Metro has been registered under the UN Framework Convention on Climate Change (UNFCCC)'s Clean Development Mechanism (CDM)—the first railway project in the world to do so. This will enable DMRC to encash the carbon credits generated through its unique braking system.

"DMRC will now earn Certified Emission Reductions (CERs) for making use of the regenerative braking system in its trains. With this, the corporation can claim 4 lakh CERs for the next 10 years, which translates into a revenue of Rs. 1.2 crore annually" explained spokesperson of DMRC.

The regenerative braking system is environment friendly as it helps control harmful emissions through a unique process. When a train applies brakes, a part of the kinetic energy released is absorbed and routed back to the Over Head Electricity (OHE) lines. This energy is used by the next train on the line, and therefore reduces the overall consumption of electricity on the system by about 30 per cent.

Though the system has been in use on Delhi Metro since its inception, DMRC will now be able to trade the carbon credits earned for money with the registration having come through. "The additional revenue from the sale of CERs will be used to fund additional operational costs for implementing the project, mainly for research and development through which DMRC is looking at developing technologies to further reduce emissions of green house gases and for training of staff to use the new technologies," Dayal added.

The CERs accumulated by Delhi Metro will be bought by Japan Carbon Finance Ltd. who also supported the regenerative braking project. The process for registration with UNFCCC started in September 2006, where M/s Ernst and Young acted as consultants while German technical service provider TUV NORD validated the DMRC project on behalf of UNFCCC.

With the registration having come through, DMRC has already started work to claim carbon credits for the emissions saved by the medal shift of over six lakh commuters daily from buses or cars to the Delhi Metro, since the emissions from these vehicles—when on the road—would have contributed to global warming.

Box 4

Earth Care Awards

For Excellence in Climate Change Mitigation and Adaptation in India

Climate Change is Damaging our World:

(i) Climate change is a serious and long-term challenge that has the potential to affect each and everyone of us. It is one of the biggest issues facing the world today—a global threat no nation can resolve alone.
Today many organizations across the world are joining hands to raise awareness about climate change and taking remedial action to reduce the impact of human-induced climate change.
We believe a combined and sustained effort by corporates and the media can make a major contribution towards making climate change a national priority.

(ii) The JSW—The Times of India Earth Care Awards is one such effort constituted to recognize local and relevant action in tackling challenges posed by climate change. The awards are technically supported by The Energy and Resources Institute (TERI) and Centre for Environment Education (CEE).

(iii) The Earth Care Awards are a Pioneering step taken by JSW and *The Times of India* in response to the increasing need to provide credible and technically-sound leadership to identify and foster actions across several sectors with special reference to mitigation and adaptation imperatives related to climate change and global warming.

(iv) This joint initiative between JSW and *The Times of India* has been fuelled by the incorporation of successful in-house climate change mitigation measures within JSW and the urge to facilitate further action through a mass eco-consciousness movement by engaging the people of the country

Box 5

MCX Kiks-off Carbon Trading

On 21.1.08 India made a silent debut as the first among carbon credit generating countries to launch futures trading in the commodity. Enabling direct trading of an intangible asset like carbon credits, futures trading in carbon credits was launched on 21.1.08 by the Multi Commodity Exchange (MCX), with the first trade taking place at Rs. 1,280 per tonne (about euro 22). Globally, other carbon credit trading exchanges are the Chicago Climate Exchange and the European Climate Exchange.

Joseph Massey DMD, MCX, said, "Launching of carbon credit futures on the Indian trading platform would provide transparency to markets and help producers earn remunerative returns out of environmentally clean projects. Trading in new generation commodities like carbon credits has placed MCX on the global map of innovative exchange for providing global products to the India Industry."

Carbon credits are generated by enterprises in the developing world by using cleaner technologies and, thereby, saving on energy consumption. This consequently reduces their greenhouse gas emissions. For each reduced tonne of carbon dioxide emission, an organisation receives a carbon emission certificate, which it can sell, either immediately or through a futures market, just like any other commodity.

CHAPTER

58

United Nations Global Compact Principles

PARTICIPATION IN THE GLOBAL COMPACT OF THE UNITED NATIONS

Bharat Heavy Electricals Limited (BHEL), has expressed its intent to support and advance United Nation's (UN's) Global Compact (GC) principles within the company's sphere of influence and commit to make the ten principles—on human rights, labour standards, environment and anti-corruption—as part of its strategy, culture and day-to-day operations.

Significantly, BHEL took a lead role in forming the Global Compact Society (GCS)—an apex level forum of Indian Organizations/Institutions, committed to UN's Global Compact Programme. Through this association, BHEL has got a unique opportunity of networking with other corporates and sharing experiences related to social responsibilities, on a global level. At the National Convention, Delhi and the GC Regional Conclave for South Asia Region, Jamshedpur, BHEL actively participated in the conferences and also highlighted its Corporate Social Responsibility (CSR) activities. BHEL's initiatives were appreciated by Mr. Georg Kell, Executive Head, UNGC, besides other dignitaries and participants from India and abroad.

Following is a brief report of how the company has addressed each of the ten principles during 2004-05. This Communication of Progress (CoP), is also available on BHEL's web site (http:www.bhel.com).

These ten principles are covered under four areas:

(a) Human rights,

(b) Labour standards,

(c) Environment, and

(d) Anti-corruption.

(a) Human Rights

(1) Business should support and respect the protection of internationally proclaimed human rights, and

(2) Make sure they are not complicit in human rights abuses.

BHEL practices the above principles in letter and spirit and has framed its policies in consonance with upholding the dignity of its employees.

(b) Labour Standards

(3) Businesses should uphold the freedom of association and the effective recognition of the right to collective bargaining

BHEL has an apex level *bipartite forum* wherein workers are represented by members of recognized unions and the leaders of Central Trade Union Organizations and the Management is represented by Chairman & Managing Director, functional Directors and the Heads of Units.

This forum is used to settle the problems concerning the workers. In addition, BHEL as a true corporate citizen takes pride in labour laws protecting the interests of the working class.

(4) The elimination of all forms of forced and compulsory labour, and

(5) The effective abolition of child labour

BHEL neither practices compulsory labour nor has child labour.

(6) Eliminate discrimination in respect of employment and occupation

BHEL does not discriminate its employees on the basis of factors such as sex, caste, religion, race, etc.

(c) Environment

(7) Businesses should support a precautionary approach to environmental challenges,

(8) Undertake initiatives to promote greater environmental responsibility, and

(9) Encourage the development and diffusion of environmentally friendly technologies

All BHEL Units have been certified to ISO-14000 on Environment Management System and OHSAS-18000 on Occupational Health & Safety, after stringent audits by an international certifying agency.

During the year, all major units of BHEL have achieved 'Zero Effluent Discharge' status. Other major achievements included, rain water harvesting systems in all the townships of the Company, mass afforestation involving the employees and surrounding community besides conservation of natural resources, generation of energy from waste and efficient water management. As part of its commitment towards the society and as a responsible corporate citizen, BHEL is involved in a host of community development programmes in various parts of the country.

- The schools set-up for mentally challenged children in various BHEL Units cater to the aspirations and requirements of the under-privileged children to help them to become self-dependant citizens.

- As a responsible corporate citizen, BHEL has involved itself in the rural development of the villages in the vicinity of its manufacturing plants. The activities include free medical aid, provision for street lights, drinking water and infrastructure support to schools, etc.
- BHEL family has risen in solidarity with the fellow citizens and victims of natural calamities such as flood, tsunami, etc. in various parts of the country by contributing its mite.

  In the area of development and diffusion of environment friendly technology, BHEL is setting up 'Stand Alone' Solar Photovoltaic (SPV) power plants and Solar Power Systems in the rural areas.

(d) Anti-Corruption

(10) Business should work against all forms of corruption, including extortion and bribery

BHEL has initiated a host of 'transparency measures' which will help the Company to avoid corruption. The Company focuses more on the preventive and educative aspects, rather than investigative/punitive ones.

CHAPTER

59

Social Accountability 8000 Certification

MANAGEMENT FOCUS ON ETHICS

Social Accountability 8000 Guidelines

Conducting global business requires organisations to practice sound ethical practices wherever negotiations, business, or transactions occurs. A set of guidelines that emphasize ethical practices in any country is found in the Social Accountability 8000 Certification (SA 8000) Practices. These guidelines were developed by the Council on Economic Priorities Accreditation Agency, which is now referred to as Social Accountability International (www.cepaa.org).

The *guidelines cover* such areas as compensation, disciplinary processes, health and safety, child labour, collective bargaining, and work areas. The *process for obtaining SA 8000* certification is similar to those used for ISO 9000 quality certification. An organisation agrees to an intensive outside team audit and to a series of unannounced inspections by the team of practices, processes, and documents. A certified organisation is provided with written permission to publicize their SA 8000 certification.

In a global marketplace the SA 8000 certification is a *mark of complying with acceptable and ethical practices*. Organisations that have received SA 8000 certification include Disney, Union Bank in Switzerland, Nissan Electric, Mattel, Indian Oil Company, and British Airways.

As long as people pursue economic ends, *business ethics will exist because questions of right and duty* will arise. As the management focus on ethics, "social accountability 80000 guidelines", highlights, companies are interested in exporting their ethics to foreign countries.

The issue of ethics and practicing ethical behaviour took a new meaning with the passing (1991) of "U.S. Sentencing Commission Guidelines". Under the guidelines, companies and managers could be prosecuted and punished even if they did not know about the unethical behaviour. If an organization (non-profits included) could be classified as a business it was subject to the Guidelines.

The U.S. Sentencing Commission Guidelines cover such laws as price fixing, fraud, antitrust violations, civil rights, money laundering, conflict of interest, stolen property, copyrights, and extortion. The Guidelines are intended to not only *bring about compliance*, but also to *encourage preventive steps managers* can take to prevent white-collar crime. If a firm is taking preventive steps to encourage ethnical behaviour or voluntarily disclose illegal activities, the fines imposed are usually much smaller. Fines can be as high as hundreds of millions of dollars. The importance of being in compliance is crucial to managers.

Table 1 illustrates a compliance process that could be important in avoiding stiff fines.

TABLE I

Suggested Steps for Compliance with U.S. Sentencing Guidelines

Steps

1. Establish standards, procedures, and processes to be followed.
2. Executive-level managers are responsible and accountable for overseeing compliance.
3. Be cautious and carry out due diligence to avoid delegating authority to anyone who may have a propensity to engage in illegal activities.
4. Communicate standards and procedures to all employees and agents.
5. Take reasonable steps to achieve compliance, including using monitoring and auditing systems.
6. Enforce standards through fair and prompt disciplinary systems.
7. Evaluate the effectiveness of the systems used.
8. Make alterations in compliance based on evaluation results.

Reference: Thomas N. Duening and John M. Ivancevich, Management Biztantra—An Imprint of Dreamtech Press, New Delhi.

CHAPTER

60

Kind of World Order to Ensure Unity and Peace

We mention here the *preamble to the charter* of the United Nations which highlights the world order to ensure unity and peace among nations. After lapse of six decades when UNO was formed at the end of World War II, some new developments have happened. We can add to UNO preamble, the world *free from terrorism and oppression*. Righteousness and belief in secularism in the heart brings peace to the nation and world.

PREAMBLE

We the People of the United Nations Determined

- to save succeeding generations from the *scourge of war*, which twice in our lifetime has brought untold sorrow to mankind,
- to reaffirm faith in fundamental *human rights*, in the *dignity and worth* of the human person, in the *equal rights* of men and women and of nations large and small,
- to establish conditions under which *justice and respect for the obligations* arising from treaties and other sources of international law can be maintained, and
- to *promote social progress* and better standards of life in larger freedom.

And for these Ends

- to *practice tolerance* and live together in peace with one another as good neighbours,
- to unite our strength to maintain *international peace and security*, and
- to ensure, by the acceptance of principles and the institution of methods, that *armed force shall not be used*, save in the common interest, and

- to *employ international machinery* for the promotion of the economic and social advancement of all peoples.

Have Resolved to Combine our Efforts to Accomplish these Aims

Accordingly, our respective Governments, through representatives assembled in the city of San Francisco, who have exhibited their full powers found to be in good and due form, have agreed to the present Charter of the United Nations and do hereby establish an international organization to be known as the United Nations.

CHAPTER

61

Managing Cultural Diversity

The environment in which managers work today is more dynamic than in the past. The individuals with whom they work in future will be diverse in intents, abilities, values and motivations. Thus, there will be challenges in managing its people and culture diversity in organisations.

In this chapter we shall attempt to summarise our thinking on managing cultural diversity under following headings:

(i) Meaning of cultural diversity.
(ii) Importance of cultural diversity.
(iii) Two aspects of cultural diversity:
  (a) global business operations, and
  (b) work place diversity in organisation.
(iv) Managing cultural diversity.
(v) Advantages of managing cultural diversity.
(vi) To conclude.

(I) MEANING OF CULTURAL DIVERSITY

Culture is "software of the mind", the way people think, act and perceive others and it is shared by societies. Three primary components of culture, relevant to international business are language, religion and attitudes.

Cultural diversity (CD) indicates the characteristics that may make an individual culturally different from another. These differences may be:

(a) Cultural differences involving patterns of life styles, values, beliefs, ideals, practices.
(b) Differences may include race, national origin, language, religion, age, etc.
(c) Differences in views held about the world, codes of social behaviour, communication styles.

(II) IMPORTANCE OF CULTURAL DIVERSITY

1. Cultural diversity is one of the major challenges facing global business organisations, as it is important for success and vitality of the organisation.
2. Management process is increasingly becoming cross-cultural with opening of Indian economy and globalisation. It becomes necessary to have an understanding of various cultures, and the ways to manage the cultural diversity for achieving competitive advantage. This brings one of the major challenges for the MNCs, exporters, tourists, sportsmen, entrepreneurs, artists, diplomats of foreign service, financial experts, researchers, etc. who operate in diverse cultures.
3. It has importance in all activities of life and more so in international business operations, such as:
   - cross-cultural differences in communication can be source of problem due to different meaning and tone of words to different people. So awareness of certain characteristics of other culture reduces misinterpretation and thus in improving communication in business introductions, telephonic conversations and meetings is important.
4. It has implications in all fields of management, such as:
   - in international marketing practices
   - in international advertising
   - in international business negotiations
   - in international human resource management
   - in international practices in industrial relations
   - in international management functions (PODCC)
   - in international developing strategies in global
   - in international organisation structure
   - in international manager's role (MNCs) in global market.

(III) TWO ASPECTS OF CULTURAL DIVERSITY

(a) First Aspect Relates to Global Cultural Diversity

People of one country have common characteristics that differentiate them from people of other countries. This is called international diversity.

Understanding of common characteristics within a particular country is important if we are going to successfully manage in an international business environment.

For example:

- Manager with awareness of national differences knows that British protect their privacy, so Indians would avoid asking British personal questions. In contrast, asking personal questions in India is acceptable. It is sign of showing interest.
- Communication is often difficult with Japanese, Americans value directness. Japanese are more subtle and view directness as not proper.
- Further, Japanese believe in group consensus in decision-making which does not fit well with Americans who are used to making fast decisions.
- In greetings Americans are smiling, firm handshake and eye contact, while Japanese bowing, exchange business cards.

- In U.S.A. women in business have equal rights, opportunities and treated seriously, while in Japan women are not considered for higher management positions. In middle-east women stand to disadvantage.

So MNCs have to develop global strategies to take advantage world-wide by properly managing cultural diversity. This calls for the need to design country specific management practices for each country in which the organisation wants to operate.

(b) Second Aspect Refers to Workforce Diversity in an Organisation

- This aspect looks at differences between people inside the work organisation. The composition of employees is changing to show heterogeneity of whole population. Thus, employee mix is undergoing change and no exclusive population in organisation.
- Workforce is now multi-lingual, multi-racial which have different life-styles, values, beliefs, ideals and practices.
- Even, language, religion, codes of social behaviour, custom, festivals are diverse.
- Workforce includes more women now, older persons. Women require protection against gender discrimination, flexible work schedules, and child care programmes.
- In addition, there are minority workers and disabled individuals.
- Diverse workforce is more educated.
- So the aim is not to remove the differences in cultures, but managers to respond to individual expectations and valuing differences to learn the details of different cultural norms which will help employees to bring out best in them.

(IV) MANAGING CULTURAL DIVERSITY

1. Thus, there is need for preparing managers for foreign assignments through cross-cultural training such as in history, culture, religions, values, political, legal, economy of that country to overcome cultural shock.
2. To develop international business negotiations strategies such as positive overtures, dealing problems and not personalities, emphasis on win-win solutions, create an open and trusting climate, build lasting relationships.
3. To develop second generation organisation structures which (in addition to strategy and structure) take two other aspects:
   (i) Strategic flexibility, and
   (ii) Management process.
4. Train transnational managers with competencies in understanding of:
   (a) Global perspective of world market business environment.
   (b) Knowledge for cultural responsiveness.
   (c) Cross-cultural interaction skills with foreign clients.
   (d) Global strategist to identify unique business opportunities, technologies, etc.
5. Avoiding discrimination in policies, to make a harmonious work place so that all employees benefit from wider range of experiences and ideas. Discrimination can be identified in practices of the organisation, such as racial discrimination in recruitment, employee training and career development opportunities. For example,

wearing of turban by Sikhs in U.K. was discriminated. Differences in job prospects among England's ethnic minorities are now almost as big as differences between them and the majority. White community, according to a Cabinet Office strategy unit study published in March 2003. The Report emphasises that employers still discriminate on basis of ethnicity.

6. To develop policies on sexual harassment, grievance systems and for equal opportunities.
7. Barrier in this change is *mind-set*. It has to be recognised that such as prejudice against other cultural and racial groups, unknown fear of their dominance, avoidance of contact, lack of integration, etc. to be eliminated.
8. In managing diversity, ethics programmes are useful in acknowledging different values and perspectives.
9. To develop organisation culture for valuing differences.
10. HR management systems to be (bias free).
11. Some other steps such as: Involvement of women, cultural differences knowledge to be imparted and accepting for higher career assignments.
12. Education of employees for mind-set about diversity.

(V) ADVANTAGES OF MANAGING CULTURAL DIVERSITY ARE THAT IT CAN IMPROVE ORGANISATIONAL PERFORMANCE

- Groups of people from diverse backgrounds can be more creative and better at problem-solving.
- Companies which manage cultural diversity can develop favourable reputation of good prospective employers of minorities such as Tata, HLL and many more.
- Cultural diversity can get better customers which has a variety of people.
- Organisations which handle multi-culturalism well, create cost advantages over those who do not.
- Ability to manage cultural diversity increases the adaptability and flexibility of management to react to environment changes.
- Belief that people of many different backgrounds can work together and lead to coexistence is now university accepted. In nut shell managers must take positive steps to manage issues of cultural diversity.

Infact, successfully managing cultural diversity can lead to global business advantages. Indian IT sector, which have successful in their global operations, have to be careful in developing cultural sensitivity and preemptive in understanding political and economic environment of the host country.

(VI) TO CONCLUDE

1. Organisations are increasingly becoming multicultural and it is one of its major challenge to have competitive global advantage.
2. Managements have to understand different cultures where they do business and respect each other.
3. Organisations not only to adapt to local culture but also to design practices to suit the culture of each country.

4. Take positive steps:
   - Prepare transnational managers for foreign assignments.
   - Develop HR policies and practices (bias free).
   - Avoid discrimination and provide equal opportunities.
   - Educate employees to change mind-set and prejudice.
   - Develop organisation culture for valuing differences. Open culture develops tolerance for cultures of their employees.
   - To foster mutual adaptation is the only approach works in managing diversity. To make harmonious work place people and employees try to keep "their identity" while on the other hand they are being "homogenised."
   - Top management to support the company's multi-cultural events and encourage employees to attend.
   - Managements must recognise that a heterogenous group will produce better ideas and strategies than homogenous group.
   - A "world culture is a dream." We have to be more realist in taking above steps.

REFERENCE

S.K. Bhatia and Poonam Chaudhary, Managing Cultural Diversity in Globalisation, Deep & Deep Publications Pvt. Ltd., New Delhi.

PART IX

SPECIFIC COURSE REQUIREMENTS

CHAPTER

62

Wisdom Management

ATTRIBUTES OF WISEMEN

Some attributes of wisemen are as under:

(1) Acquiring right intelligence/knowledge leads to wisdom.

(2) Wiseman keeps a perfect balance of body, mind and spiritual aspects.

(a) Body

Wiseman takes care of his body, keeping it fit and healthy and believes it must be kept clean and pure. He takes care of his material comforts (wealth and facilities, etc.). Self knowledge and care does not allow him to indulge in greed and wrong practices.

(b) Mind

Wiseman also is careful to keep his mind up to date of his environment and intellectual pursuits. He has positive thoughts and thinking which are the hallmarks of a wiseman. He influences his followers by love, compassion and high intelligence. He thinks positive in all circumstances and possess purity of thought.

No matter how lofty their station in life may be, wise men are *humble and eager* to learn. They accept correction and try to change when proven wrong. Having discovered the power and beauty of truth, they listen to good counsel. They seek out many advisers and toil in the process of finding information and knowledge. They invest their time, money, and labour in the quest of learning. They enrol in courses of study and *acquire libraries.* As they continually accumulate their knowledge, they both increase their ability to learn and increase the pleasure they get in acquiring it. Indeed, education and learning become a form of recreation for them.

(c) Spiritual

Spiritual man is one attriute of Indian Wisdom Management. Wiseman is in tune with and sensitive to natural impulses, rhythms and currents in life and acts intelligently in the light of this sensitivity. They do not harm others. There is moral purity. They have love for mankind.

Spiritual people respect *all* faiths and religions and have absolutely no difficulty in allowing every man to worship in his own way and in his own place, be it temple, mosque or church. The spiritual personality is not motivated by *Bhaya* (fear), the desire for *Sukha* (happiness) or the wish to escape *Dhuka* (pain or suffering)—the three major forces in life.

One of the oldest definitions of *spiritual living* is given in the Bhagawat Gita—to act without thought of the fruits of action. To act with complete detachment and selflessness because the action is right and necessary. To live selflessly in peace and inner joy/bliss, self-contended.

(3) Honesty

Wise persons are held to the highest standards of conduct which includes ethics, integrity, character, trustworthiness, truthfulness, morality, rightness. They show high consistency between word and deed.

(4) Vision

They have ability to "see into the future" and perceive an improved reality for the community. They have competence of leading through work, action and deed. They communicate their vision and provide direction to follow the vision. They encourage risk taking.

(5) Balance

They are integrated or well-balanced spiritually, mentally, emotionally and physically. This gives good vibrations to others, thereby elevating their spirits in addition to their confidence and passion for excellence.

(6) Self-Learning

They continuously learn of new knowledge and skills and develop cultural awareness and sensitivity, i.e. cultural flexibility.

(7) Self-Confidence

They have self-confidence in order to convince their followers of the rightness of goals and decisions.

(8) Patience

A wise man has patience; he controls his emotions. He quietly ignores an insult. He will not be provoked into a meaningless fight, choosing instead to hold back his anger and to use his intellect to seek peace and reconciliation.

(9) Wisemen Hate Evil

They have no appreciation for senselessness. They look with distaste upon things that are wasteful and destructive.

(10) Differentiate between Right and Wrong

The wise understand the true difference *between right and wrong,* good and evil. They know the real meaning of justice and fair play. They do not judge by appearances only, but they also see with depth. They have insight and foresight, enabling them to perceive both the underlying dynamics of things while accurately anticipating results and consequences. Therefore, they show good judgment and make correct decisions. Wise men are able to successfully perceive ahead because they have faith in the ultimate value of wisdom. And so the wise are law-abiding, heedful of both natural law and social law. They can see far enough ahead to know the benefits of right living.

(11) Self-control and Restrain in Speech

The wise are especially noted by their skill with words. First, they show self-control and restraint in their use of language. Realizing the power of words, they speak with great caution. When they do speak, what they say is true and relevant. Moreover, their words are both dignified and astute.

IN SUM UP

There is no strength like wisdom and there are no great men like the wise. In addition to their love of knowledge and their rejection of evil, wise men, everywhere demonstrate the following common characteristics. They are humble, behaving with cautious reserve and emotional control. Valuing knowledge they actively pursue it in order to live successfully. They eventually develop skill in learning and come to enjoy the process. Their use of words is likewise controlled, knowledgeable and effective.

A man of character expresses all ethical and human values. He is called a wiseman. He has wisdom and wisdom is born of contact with the divine. He has purity of mind/heart, higher consciousness is also called spiritual state of mind and combines in wisdom and values. We can bring about excellence in all work with the help of ethical devotion and spiritual values.

According to Prof. S.A. Sherlekar—"Western model of man and management" could not give rich dividends. It is inadequate in solving all the problems of modern society. Important concepts of Indian Wisdom and thought will enrich Western thought and provide a complete set of ideas for the management of organisations.

In Indian Wisdom, material and spiritual aspects of human existence or life are given equal emphasis and there is very close inter-relationship between worldly life and spiritual life. Both are manifestations or expressions of the divine or pure consciousness.

The holistic approach of Indian Wisdom is needed for modern management to integrate matter/spirit or skills/values or object/subject. Modern management must incorporate Indian ethos to perfect the truncated model of man (stressing only material progress at any cost) and recognise man as a *whole man* to assure wholesome human progress—spiritual as well as material progress—to satisfy the hunger of mind and soul as well as the hunger of physical and vital human being.

Values-based holistic approach to management will assure such all round wholesome human development and prosperity.

REFERENCES

S.A. Sterlekar, *Ethics in Management*, Himalaya Publishing House, Mumbai.
Internet websites.

CHAPTER

63

A Person of Character

1. WHAT IS CHARACTER?

Meaning

What is character? What are the hallmarks of fine character? A man of character strives to practise truth, non-violence, non-stealing, fearlessness and such other vows. He is ready to give up his life, but not truth. He is prepared to die, but will not kill. He is willing to accept suffering, but not inflict it on others. He does not steal, nor takes bribes. He does not waste his time nor that of others, goes on doing his duty fearlessly.

It is in the hands of the students to make good the defects in their character for no one else can do this for them. We must first understand the aim of education. A student who desires to cultivate and build-up character, will learn how to do so from any good book on the subject.

The Lord of creation creates everything in this world as an admixture of good and evil. But a good man selects the good and rejects the evil.

2. ATTRIBUTES OF PERSON OF CHARACTER

(i) Doing One's Duty

Performing one's duty is fundamental concept of work ethic.

It is observing certain discipline, namely, coming to work on time, behaving with respect and dignity with subordinate, colleagues and superiors, staying at work place. During working hours, not wasting time by roaming and chatting, etc. to have strong work orientation. To perform one's job with devotion with initiative and perfection.

One should fulfil one's commitment and be accountable for results. He should be dedicated to hard work. He should protect the interest of the organisation he works for. He should have satisfaction that he is contributing his very best to his organisation.

(ii) Develop Proper Values

Values provide that basic foundation for understanding a person's personality's perceptions and attitudes. Values represent basic convictions or what are right values and those are powerful force affecting attitude and behaviour. Values effect our thoughts, motivation, perceptions and actions. Values guide in our decision-making and resolving conflicts. Values bring *excellence* and perfection in our actions.

Values are internal, deal with internal development of a person, purify mind and heart. The person becomes good in thought, speech and in action, job or work. Thus, values help in *self-development*.

Human values enhance reputation and image of the person.

(iii) Man-making Education

Man-making education can make a man of character, i.e. by strengthening his mind and by which one stands on ones own feet and not swayed by others. Character is formed from the repeated choice of thoughts and action. Make the right choice—we shall have a firm and noble character.

(iv) To Become Good Person

A person becomes good when he actually does good rather than not doing wrong. A good person *has qualities* such as fairness, compassion, courage, integrity, empathy, humility, loyalty and courtesy.

What makes these people good people? They are kind people, and are dependable, stand up for justice, help the needy, make life better for themselves and those around them. Benchmarks can be ethical or legal.

(v) Building a Character Foundation for Society

Everyone has goals for society. To get society in high gear, every member of society needs to understand the role for societal wellness. Setting an example of morality, integrity and character is good place to start. Keep in mind that every person can make a difference.

IN SUM

Focus on character education by building on values of morality, integrity, putting good views news at the front, building right attitude, etc.

Pay special attention to social issues such as, winning war on drugs and smoking, family break-ups, lead by example, etc.

Reference

Bhawan's Journal, March 2000.

CHAPTER

64

Enhancing Your Integrity

(I) IN DAILY PERFORMANCE WE APPLY A STANDARD OF INTEGRITY

- Finding the *right way in gray* areas.
- Creating an *environment* of integrity within our team and company.
- Building *trust among* those for whom we are responsible.

It is in fact near impossible for a person to have enduring success in business without a reputation of trust-worthiness and integrity.

(II) THE NINE INTEGRITY CHARACTERISTICS

1. You know that little things count,
2. You find the white (when others see gray),
3. You create a culture of trust,
4. You keep your word,
5. You care about the greater good,
6. You are honest but modest,
7. You act like you are being watched,
8. You hire integrity, and
9. You stay consistent.

By integrating these steps into your everyday behaviour, you will gain the integrity advantage. These characteristics are explained in detail.

I. You Know that Little Things Count

To have the integrity advantage, you do not lie or cheat on the small things as a result, you are not corrupted by the larger temptations the lure of power, prestige or money. Just as importantly, if you have integrity, you stick to internal code of morality, even at the risk of losing your comfortable place in the world.

2. You Find the White (when others see gray)

To have integrity advantage, you do not make tough decisions alone. You ask questions, receive counsel, reflect, and take a long-term view. In short, you ensure that you never make a *decision that would violate* your internal code of integrity.

3. You Create a Culture of Trust

You help to create the right *work environment*, one that will not test the personal integrity of your employees or co-workers. You reinforce integrity through principles, controls and personal example. And you reward those in your employ who display personal integrity in their actions.

4. You keep your Word

Employees do not follow leaders they do not trust. Employers do not hire people or promote employees they do not trust. Clients do not buy from suppliers they do not trust. To have the integrity advantage, you act with integrity to gain trust.

5. You Care about the Greater Good

You are deeply committed to and take decisions that will benefit the entire organisation to which you belong. You care passionately about your company, products and services, and especially your teammates. Through your work, you gain sense of deeper purpose.

6. You are Honest but Modest

You do not proclaim your virtue or honesty. That is like boasting of your humility. You allow your actions to speak louder than your words.

7. You Act like you are being Watched

You assume your every move is being watched. You ensure that your integrity is passed along to future generations through your example.

8. You Hire Integrity

You hire and surround yourself straight people who have a strong sense of personal integrity. You promote those who demonstrate an ability to be trusted.

9. You Stay Consistent

You have ethical consistency and predictability. Your life demonstrates wholeness and harmony between your values and your actions.

(III) STEPS TO ENHANCE YOUR INTEGRITY

Step I

Assess your integrity using the nine characteristics of integrity rate yourself from 1 to 9 (9 being the highest).

Step II

Get a second feedback and a third. Write down names of few whom you trust and why. Contact these people and seek integrity feedback from them on 9 points about you. Ask them for complete honestly and this will not affect their relations. Information obtained is important. This is a step in the right direction.

Step III

Evaluate ethical health of the organisation in which you participate. The word trustworthy is central what we hope to achieve. Evaluate your organisation on nine characteristics of integrity. Look at little things. Do people you consider to be. Your friends cheat on their taxes and brag about it or steal from their employer. Integrity is as critical in these relationships as in your work organisation.

Step IV

Start an individual revolution. The truth can be achieved if we put some effort. Change requires momentum that momentum has to come from inside of you. For example, I won't use sick leave when I am not sick or I won't lie at work, etc. Focus on the behaviours, at a time, and you will be in your way to making the integrity advantage your advantage.

TO SUM UP

You can take integrity with you. A clergy man reminded a rich miser who was on his death bed that he could not take his riches with him. "Then I am not going", the man replied.

Integrity is one of the few things in life you can take with you, wherever you go, it becomes a part of you and sticks with you through economic downturns, just as it does in the good times. It is something no one can take away from you.

Integrity is truly a competitive advantage—in business and in life. Those people with integrity have one thing in common—they sleep well. Integrity often is its own reward. No one is happy with himself if he is not a good person.

CHAPTER

65

Knowledge Management

WHAT IS KNOWLEDGE MANAGEMENT?

Knowledge Management (KM) is the process through which organisations *generate-value* from their intellectual and knowledge-based assets. Most often, generating value from such assets *involves sharing* them among employees, departments and even with other companies in an effort to devise best practices. It's important to note that the definition says nothing about technology; while KM is often facilitated by IT, technology by itself is not KM. The key to KM is *achieving better business results,* which could come from improved organisational learning. So, KM is *about learning,* learning is the process by which we get knowledge. It helps us to apply knowledge. From the business point, learning is important.

In this chapter we shall discuss following aspects of knowledge management:

1. What Constitutes Intellectual or Knowledge-based Assets?
2. How KM has now made any Information Accessible at a Click?
3. What are Driving Forces for KM?
4. How Companies are Encouraging their Employees to Share Knowledge?
5. How to Build Human Networking into Enterprise?
6. What is the Process of Implementing Knowledge Management?
7. In what ways KM helps a Company?
8. Should KM have a Business Goal?
9. Is KM Static?

1. What Constitutes Intellectual or Knowledge-based Assets?

Not all information is valuable. Therefore, it's up to individual companies to determine what information qualifies as intellectual and knowledge-based assets. In general, however, intellectual and knowledge-based assets fall into one of two categories: *explicit or tacit.* Included among the former, i.e. *explicit* are assets such as patents, trademarks, business plans, marketing research and customer lists. As a general rule of thumb, *explicit knowledge* consists of anything that can be documented, archived and codified, often with the help of IT. Much harder to grasp is the concept of *tacit knowledge*, or the know-how contained in people's heads. The challenge inherent with *tacit knowledge* is figuring out how to recognize, generate, share and manage it. While IT in the form of e-mail, groupware, instant messaging and related technologies can help facilitate the dissemination of tacit knowledge; *identifying tacit knowledge* in the first place is a major hurdle for most organisations.

2. K.M. has now made any Information Accessible at a Click

When L&T's engineering and construction (E&C) business division executed turnkey projects in various corners of the country, problems at the site would mean a flurry of phone calls to locate experts within the company who might be able to solve it. In the process, time, a crucial element in completing projects, would be at a premium. Obviously, communication costs mounted. Not surprising, therefore, that the E&C business division was the first in L&T to embrace knowledge management with its portal KnowNet in late 2000.

Currently, KnowNet helps L&T to not just solve niggling problems at project sites, but also to identify alternative cost-effective solutions on the use of raw materials. Example: While executing a project for a public sector refinery in South India, L&T's engineers felt that the specified material of construction was of a higher grade than required. The result would be higher cost and a longer lead time because the material was more difficult to source. By delving into the learnings of KnowNet, L&T engineers discovered that in three similar projects in the past, a more cost-effective grade of material had been used without any problem. This was double-checked with other contractors who had executed similar projects. As a result of its KnowNet learnings, L&T was able to save nearly Rs. 1 crore on the project. Says K. Venkataramanan, President (operations) of L&T: "KM goes beyond storing information. We are trying to leverage tacit knowledge, which lies in the skill of our people, to deliver results."

Just as L&T uses KM to roll out real-world construction projects at lower cost, infotech major Infosys Technologies, which executes software projects both onshore and offshore, is another pioneer in the use of KM in India. Reason: projects heads and staff tend to be mobile in software. Unless the *learnings from* one project are captured and templated permanently, the speed and quality of execution may suffer. This is simply unaffordable in an era where software vendors are being squeezed on margins by cost-conscious customers.

3. Driving Forces for KM

There are actually two drivers behind the new-found enthusiasm. *One is competition*, and the other is IT. At a fundamental level, companies know that in a *super competitive marketplace* the right knowledge at the right time makes all the difference to performance. With products and services getting commoditised, it is speed and customer and market knowledge, among other things, that gives the edge. It is not enough to have this information in your database somewhere; you need this at the point—and at the instant—when your customer makes a call to the call centre to make a complaint. Companies that can bring deep customer knowledge out of the can and into the heart of day-to-day decision-making cannot do so without adopting KM.

The second *driver for KM is IT push*. Today, there is not a single major international software vendor without a KM-related offering: IBM, Microsoft, Oracle, Siebel, SAP, the works. Not to speak of a whole range of smaller software companies focusing on niche KM areas. From "brainstorming" and collaborative tools to content and document management, from data mining to expert and decision-support systems, from indexing and search engine tools to intelligent agents, every segment in the knowledge management chain has vendor selling solutions or prices of it.

To be sure, KM is not about IT. It is about *creating, recognising, accumulating, sharing and using knowledge to add value to organisations*. When it comes to adding value to corporates, it is organisational knowledge—and not individual knowledge—that matters. This has led to a more formal approach towards managing knowledge, by not just pre-serving information but analysing it and presenting it in a access-friendly format on company intranets.

4. Companies are Encouraging their Employees to Share Knowledge

Many recent entrants are devising ways and means of encouraging their employees to share knowledge. Because employees will only visit the knowledge portal if the information they are looking for is available. In the case of ad agency Lowe, it offers K-Points to employees who contribute to the portal. To encourage usage of the portal, employees who access the information also get points.

5. How to Build Human Networking into Enterprise?

Some steps are as under for sharing KM:

- Working together in *virtual task-focusing teams*, i.e. human networking enterprises.
- Developing *visionary capabilities about the challenges* in our enterprises, through networking or knowledge. Developing data integration strategy and also grow the knowledge-base.
- *Encountering blockades* in transition process by listening and learning from one another.
- Extend virtual task-focusing teams which can *include* suppliers, partners, distributors and customers.
- To practise of *continual learning* and work more in parallel.
- We can share learning to enhance our capabilities in an ongoing process approach advanced by Peter Senge. He has suggested five human values of learning organisations:
  (i) Personal mastery (competencies and skills);
  (ii) Spiritual growth—mental models of values and principles;
  (iii) Shared vision;
  (iv) Team learning and unlearning; and
  (v) Systems thinking.

Thus, we can use the new source of "wealth-creation."

6. Process of Implementing Knowledge Management

Knowledge management is as much *an activity* ("something you do") as it is a *type of system* or technology. That's why it's worthwhile to explore what's involved in implementing KM, or to put it more formally, in *capturing* existing knowledge within an organisation, and then *adapting* that knowledge while capturing new knowledge going forward. Once such knowledge is captured, KM professionals can apply *the processes* of analysis, organisation, assigning relationships and priority rankings between questions and answers.

(a) Document Knowledge

Analyze all possible sources of organisational knowledge to build a taxonomy-of-knowledge-types, and to decide what attributes and values should be associated with each type (let's call an instance of some knowledge type—a specific item of knowledge—a knowledge element). Next, examine all possible sources to uncover existing knowledge elements, and make it possible to discover new knowledge elements.

(b) Share Knowledge

Start by recording all known knowledge elements from documents, communications, and subject matter expert interviews. At each step along the way, include input forms to elicit feedback from KM system users about knowledge elements, element organisation, element search and retrieval, and element relevancy.

(c) Apply Knowledge

This is where *customers and support staff interact with* the knowledge-base to locate and use relevant knowledge. At this stage it is essential to refine the contents of knowledge elements and to adapt the structure of the knowledge-base in response to such interaction. The ability to make and suggest useful relationships between problems and solutions is powerful enough to enlist a strong buy-in from support staff and knowledge management professionals when they see that a dynamic system can improve search results, agent productivity and customer satisfaction. In general, and within the context of customer service systems based on customer contact centers, KM encompasses the broad range of capabilities needed to logically capture, organise, share and use knowledge elements in order to recognize problems and suggest possible solutions to customer service queries.

7. Benefits of an effective KM Programme should help a company do one or more of the following:

- *Foster innovation* by encouraging the free flow of ideas.
- *Improve customer service* by streamlining response time.
- *Boost revenues* by getting products and services to market faster.
- Enhance *employee retention* rates by recognizing the value of employees' knowledge and rewarding them for it.
- *Streamline operations* and reduce costs by eliminating redundant or unnecessary processes.

These are the most examples of strategic benefits. A creative approach to KM can result in improved efficiency, higher productivity and increased revenues in practically any business function. KM to deliver business results.

8. KM must have a Specific Business Goal

A KM programme should not be divorced from a business goal. While sharing best practices is a commendable idea, there must be an underlying business reason to do so. Without a solid business case, KM is a futile exercise.

9. KM is not Static

As with many physical assets, the value of knowledge can erode over time. Since knowledge can get stale fast, the content in a KM programme should be constantly updated, amended and deleted. What's more, the relevance of knowledge at any given time changes, as do the skills of employees. Therefore, there is no endpoint to a KM.

To Conclude

"What is greater than knowledge?" asked the mind.
"A heart that can see and care", whispered the soul.

References

Thirumoothy, Paramasivan, "Knowledge Management Your Key to Develop Competitive Advantage", Jims 8M, Oct.-Dec. 2003.

Prasad, Sangrameshwaran, "Knowledge Management Initiatives", *Indian Management,* May 2003.

Bhatia, S.K., "Knowledge Organisation", *Management of Change and Organisation Development,* Deep & Deep Publications Pvt. Ltd., New Delhi.

Spiritualism and Humanism

In this chapter on "Spiritualism and Humanism", the following aspects are covered:

1. Spirituality.
   1.1 Meaning.
   1.2 Views of personalities.
2. Basic principles and values of spirituality.
   (i) Avoid selfishness.
   (ii) Prayer and meditation.
   (iii) Materialism and the spirituality go-together.
   (iv) Knowledge.
   (v) Self-restraint.
   (vi) Having faith.
   (vii) Spirituality is working for the welfare of every one.
   (viii) Spirituality prepares for facing hardships.
   (ix) Spirituality is our birthright, make sure you seek it.
3. Humanism.
4. Spiritual approach. (Box 1)
5. Liberal legacy of Suffism. (Box 2)

1. SPIRITUALITY

1.1 Meaning

Spirituality is a refined or higher state of the mind. It is really one of the resources of consciousness. It is ability of human beings to view themselves and their own actions. It is ability of "self-consciousness." To be a spiritual person is not to have a particular belief in one or another God. It is the ability to transcend oneself, to see oneself.

I.2 Views of Personality

We give here views of some personalities in spiritual field on the subject.

(i) *Spirituality is about your mind* being happy, feeling free, sharing, and having enthusiasm for life. Spirituality is the essence of any culture or religion in any part of the world. It is self-realisation, self-contentment, love of humanity and mankind. It is establishing truth, justice, love and peace. It is keeping other's interest before own. It is service all around welfare of humanity.

Meditation is a mind without agitation. It improves your perception, observation and expression in life. When you have a better perception of things, life becomes easier. You can accomplish things better.

When you meditate and are relaxed, then you can accomplish things better. Whatever you do with a relaxed state of mind becomes a success.

Each individual is unique. Our life-style, upbringing, etc. influence our growth, so we differ from each other in our capacity to understand. When you meditate, you tap different layers of this growth. Meditation polishes the mind to help imbibe the information available to a person from life itself.

When you meditate, you become eligible to receive. Meditation is a cleansing agent. Meditation is like a shower for the mind. Only right meditation technique and science of living can control minds and lead the man towards the path of enlightenment.

(ii) According to Swami Nikhilananda, spirituality becomes elusive for most people if it is not practical. For *practical spirituality* you have to lead a rational life. Spirituality does not require you to live differently or abnormally. People make a big mistake when they compartmentalise their lives. Most people think practical life has its own set of rules and regulations and spiritual life is not a part of that.

They are wrong, as worldly life or day-to-day life is the outer periphery of spiritual life itself. Everyone does not have to renounce the world to attain spirituality. Swamis and gurus renounce the world only because they want to focus on it more. They are just like scholars who withdraw from everything else to spend more time in research and study. Similarly, some people renounce the world to spend more time contemplating and thinking of God. But ordinary people need not separate spiritual life from worldly life.

You don't have to do something to become spiritual, but whatever you are doing should be done in a spiritual way. If you treat the people you meet as divine and show them the same respect you show a deity at a temple, saying *namaskar* to people itself becomes as spiritual as visiting a temple. So, spirituality is divining each and every moment of your life in your relationships, work, behaviour, beliefs, etc.

2. BASIC PRINCIPLES AND VALUES OF SPIRITUALITY

(i) Avoid Selfishness

There are some *basic principles* and basic values about spirituality such as giving up selfishness. If you work in such a way that you do not think of yourself alone but also of the *welfare of others*, you become spiritual. Spirituality is thinking about and working for the welfare of everyone.

If you do business and think of your profit alone without worrying about the customer, then it's not spirituality. But if you think about the welfare of your customers, and give them proper care, you are spiritual.

Spirituality is about love, and love and selfishness cannot go together.

(ii) Prayer and Meditation

Being spiritual does not mean that you should be praying or meditating all the time. Leading a natural, value-based life is spiritual. Nature is spiritual.

Spirituality is regaining our natural balance and going back to nature. All of us are essentially spiritual. A newborn child is spiritual. Everyone wants to fulfil their desires, but spirituality is about fulfilling your desires without hurting anyone. You do your duty without hurting anyone.

(iii) Materialism and the Spirituality Go Together

Spirituality and materialism are not to be separated. Spirituality should have a touch of materialism and materialism should have a touch of spirituality. By materialism Swami Nikhilananda means practical things. At the Chinmaya Mission, we use computers and air-conditioners as we believe that spirituality does not mean you should be uncomfortable. Similarly, if a material person gives up his business and spends his time praying, it is wrong. A totally materialistic person can be spiritual and a totally spiritual person can be materialistic. Both extremes can go hand in hand.

The last *shloka* of the Bhagavad Gita says where there is Arjuna, there is Krishna. Krishna represents spirituality and Arjuna materialism, and when both go together, there is success and prosperity. So we should not separate worldliness and spirituality.

(iv) Knowledge

To define best conduct, knowledge is essential. Only when you know what to do and what not to do is important. Only when knowledge is applied to conduct, we have the true manifestation of spirituality.

(v) Self-Restraint

Interdependence means interaction. Interaction means the forming of equations. When you strike an equation with anybody there is need *to restrain* one's self-interest so much as to allow the other person's interest also to co-exist. When a balance is struck, it is called sustainable friendship, sustainable environment, sustainable development, etc. depending on the partnership.

(vi) Having Faith

Life has three aspects, the physical, mental and spiritual. Spirituality requires to have faith in the governing power you honour and obey and have personal faith. Spiritual wealth provides faith. It gives love. It brings and expands wisdom. Spiritual wealth leads to happiness because it guides us into loving relationships. Faith gives us security and comfort. Spirituality (faith) reinforces our stand for what is right. Spiritual wealth assures that there is a God who has interest in me, because he created me. Spiritual wealth gives me great peace of mind because my past has been forgiven. Greed, anger cause strife within a person and his dealings with others.

Besides having physical cravings, man also has spiritual aspirations. Man does not *aspire* for just economic and emotional (Artha and Kama) but (Dharma and Moksha) moral and spiritual.

(vii) Spirituality is Working for the Welfare of Everyone

You don't have to do something special to became spiritual, but whatever you are doing should be done in a spiritual way like treat the people you meet as divine and show them the same respect you show to a deity. Spirituality is divining each and every moment of your life: in your relationships, work, behaviour, beliefs, etc. Spirituality is *thinking* about and *working for the welfare* of everyone. If you give your customers, employees proper care, you are spiritual. Spirituality is about love, and love and selfishness cannot go together.

Leading a natural, value-based life and work in the present. Spirituality is about fulfilling your desires without hurting anyone. Only when knowledge is applied to conduct, we have the true manifestation of spirituality. It is necessary to treat every living entity with respect. Conduct is the gateway to self-realisation.

In bringing about a new synthesis of Science and Spirituality in the world of business and building a new universal empire of the spirit, the role of management education is of critical importance. Our management education needs to be inspired by a value system which prizes commitment to the simultaneous pursuit of excellence and social equity, celebration of pluralism and diversity, and acceptance of limits on space and desire in a world of finite resources.

We need entrepreneurs as trustees of society and who pursue the goal of creating more wealth, more as a social obligation to fulfil the national commitment for the removal of poverty, and not merely for the sake of personal enjoyment.

We need professional managers who are intellectually alert, operate on the frontiers of knowledge and are socially involved.

We need national consensus for social and economic regeneration. We should enable our people to lead a life of dignity and self-respect inspired by the humanistic values of civic morality. The task needs a powerful movement for moral regeneration and spiritual awakening of our people. We need human knowledge and education which would lead not merely to assertion of mind over life and matter but to the triumph of the spirit or soul over mind, body and life. India has to lead the world to realise that a bond of spiritual unity links the entire human kind.

Therefore, value-based, holistic and consciousness approach advocated by ancient Indian wisdom becomes essential.

(viii) Spiritually Prepares for Facing Hardships

Hardships are inevitable in life. They often come our way when we least expect them and at a time when we are not prepared to handle them. That is why they usually become stumbling blocks in our lives. But, if we learn to overcome them, they can actually become stepping stones.

Overcoming hardships in life can be likened to athletics, in which victory or defeat is determined by how well an athlete has practised. On the day of the event, the athlete can do nothing more than perform according to his/her existing ability.

Similarly, success or failure in dealing with an adversity depends on how strong we are spiritually when it comes our way. Be it a break-up in relationship, financial loss, disease, failure in getting what one wants or any other disappointment in life, all can be endured with spiritual strength. But lack of strength at the time of problems can break us in spite of all our efforts to overcome them.

Inner strength may not always solve at problem, but it does help us to carry on in life in the midst of hardships. For, it makes us accept the reality no matter how harsh, and to take right decisions at the crucial time. Yet, some of us neglect the spiritual area of our lives and accept defeats.

Given that the spiritual health of our inner selves is of great importance, we need to integrate our spiritual activities with our other daily activities. Activities such as regular prayers to God; dwelling on spiritual truths such as God's love, universal values, and purpose in life; reading scriptures and so on must find a place in our 'busy' schedules. Such activities help us gain spiritual strength and make us conscious of God's presence. It also rejuvenates our trust in Him.

Only if we work out our inner selves in the absence of adversity, will we always be prepared to face and successfully overcome hardships in life. —*Visal Arora*

(ix) Spirituality is Our Birthright, Make Sure You Seek it

Often, people are clueless about spiritual unfoldment. They often dismiss spiritual development by saying that it is not their cup of tea. They may think that spiritual life is meant for monks alone and may avoid seeking God altogether.

From time to time, God sends his emissaries to the world to make spirituality simpler and easier for us to understand. Through their teachings, these gurus make it absolutely clear that everyone is equally entitled to start on the path of spiritual discovery. It is their birthright and they must have it.

Guru Mantra

The aim of human life is to seek God. A person who has attained human life but chooses not to realise God is born in vain. As long as your heart is directed towards God, you cannot be lost in the ocean of worldliness.

Essentially each one of us is spiritual. But we are not conscious of our spiritual nature, because it is asleep deep inside us. It need to be awakened and brought to the surface.

We realise to get to know about spiritual awakening (God), when we realise that there is more to life than just material existence. Strive to awaken our dormant spirituality and keep the spiritual process on track. Seek guidance from a guru. Spirituality will give eternal peace and contentment.

3. HUMANISM

Humanism is a way of life which is democratic. It is concerned with dignity of man, i.e. right of the individual in relation to rights of others. It is personal liberty combined with social responsibility. Humanism is ethical. It is concerned with moral and social problems as mentioned below. It seeks and uses science creatively and not destructively.

(a) Humanism stands for two basic values: first and foremost, *love of fellow-beings* and solidarity and of mankind without distinction of race, caste, creed or nationality; and second, *intellectual integrity* and scientific spirit according to which all beliefs, however firmly held, are liable to modification or rejection in the light of further knowledge and experience.

(b) The consideration of moral and social problems in a scientific spirit.

(c) It is concerned with the preservation and furtherance of moral values in all relations and spheres of life, and with the building up of a better and happier human community.

(d) Humanism is not committed to any views about the existence or non-existence of God.
(e) Humanism regards the *basis of morality* to be a sense of values, which is inherent in human nature, and holds and morality requires no external sanction.
(f) Humanism seeks the *development of individuals* as persons and sees this as inseparable from their free and responsible participation in social relations.
(g) Humanism believes not only in the Understanding Spiritually—Basic Principles and values beliefs between individuals and groups having different views but also in their active co-operation in the advancement of ideals which are common ground between them.

Box I

Spiritual Approach

The spiritual way is to see beyond mere outer appearances and the five senses to an *intuitive perception of the causes behind outer conditions.* Someone with spiritual approach may change and uplift their world by first tranforming and *improving one's own vision.*

Spiritual wisdom gives greater value to all the elements of your life. Inwardly you will gain a greater wealth of peacefulness, faith, love, and spiritual vision. Purify your heart and follow your heart.

One of the main teachings on spirituality is *to look within* and what you seek within yourself. Your innerself is eternal and deeply profound. Look inside awakening.

Spirituality relates more to your *personal search,* to finding greater meaning and purpose in your existence. Looking to love and respect for God, love and respect for your self and everybody.

Spirituality is not same as religion. Religion is the shell, while spirituality is the kernel within that shell. Religion is the train, spirituality, the destination. Spirituality is not just for a chosen few. It is for all who can *live in their higher truth.* You do not have do anything particular to be spiritual. Spirituality inspire you to act with skill, freedom, gratitude and a sense of service. Spirituality is with you wherever you go what spirituality can do for you:

- Spirituality *gives you greater appreciation* for everything in your life.
- Gives you more consciousness of *bigger picture.*
- How to *guide your power.*
- Brings you contentment.
- Is a key to *overcoming sorrow.*
- It *encourageous honesty* and self-acceptance.
- Spirituality helps you to remember that it is all God.

Spiritual Leadership—What does it Take?

True spiritual leadership, with a spirit of humility and service, *will cause people* to follow you because they want to, not because they have to. Genuine humility and spiritual leadership is attractive. People want to follow a person who *serves them and sets an example for them.*

Spiritual leadership insists on humility. *Humility is the attitude* that puts others ahead of you, that considers others more important than yourself. Thinking too highly of yourself prevents you from genuinely caring for others. Humility enables you to serve others wholeheartedly and thereby set an example that others will follow. Spiritual leadership also requires integrity.

Box 2

Liberal Legacy of Sufism

Wrote Amir Khusrau: "One who dies for the love of Truth (God) dies a Sufi (Pure)—and Sufis never die."

Sufi liberalism had other important aspects. While music and dance, dear to the Indian soul, were anathema to the ulema, they were encouraged. Sufi music is full of passionate devotion to God, the unity of body-and-soul and the oneness of mankind. Realising these truths leads to haul or a state of mystic exaltation.

The Sufis incorporated aspects of Hinduism, Buddhism, Judaism and Christianity freely into their teaching. They took concepts such as Moksha from Hinduism and from Buddhism.

The Sufi doctrines of Fana and Baqa (annihilation and subsistence) correspond to Nirvana.

Hasan al-Basri (d.728) the earliest Sufi, disdained both riches and power as the Sufis had no love for worldly pleasures or gains.

The Qadiri order was amongst the most tolerant and progressive Sufi orders and Abd-al-Qadir Jilani, the great saint, emphasized these ten tenets of human behaviour:

- Never swear by God
- Never speak an untruth even in jest
- Never break a promise
- Never curse anyone
- Never harm anyone
- Never accuse anyone of religious infidelity
- Never be a party to anything sinful
- Never impose a burden on others
- Never accept anything from human beings, 'God alone is the giver'
- Look for the good points and not the bad, in others.

Muinuddin Chishti, the saint of Ajmer, never discriminated by religion. On the contrary he encouraged Hindu bairagis to sing their hymns in his presence and also prescribed the dark orange colour of the coarse robes of his devotees. Let us recall this legacy of Sufism that fostered a more humanistic and liberal approach to inter-religious understanding.

Source: Website:

References

Bhanumati Narasimham, *Hindustan Times,* New Delhi, 19.9.2003.
Swami Nikhilananda—Chinmaya Mission, *Hindustan Times,* New Delhi, September 5, 2003.
Tish Malhotra, *Hindustan Times,* 19.9.2003.
Parmarthi Raina, *Hindustan Times,* 29.9.2003.
Professor S.A. Sherlekar, *Ethics in Management,* Himalaya Publishing House, Mumbai.
Vishal Arora, *Hindustan Times,* New Delhi.
Humanism, Memorandum of Association, 1960, Indian Humanism Union.

CHAPTER

67

Understanding Success

1. MEANING OF SUCCESS

Different people have different aim of success:

(a) To some individuals, it may mean *power, fame, money, achievement*, etc.
(b) To some, it is the *talent and the passion* that count in success. (In grid Bergman).
(c) For some, success is *good relationships*, family life, service to others and attain peace of mind.

2. CONCEPT OF SUCCESS

(i) Basically success is *knowing what your values* are and living in a way that is consistent with your values. (Danny Cox)
(ii) The only difference between successful person and unsuccessful person is that successful person *surpasses his goal* and unsuccessful person falls short of his goal. Thus, objective of success is achieving objectives or excellence or surpassing competitor's record or own-self record if that is highest.
(iii) The whole *emphasis is on personality development*, i.e. acquisition of those qualities which will enable on to participate in the struggle for success.

3. PRINCIPLES OF ACHIEVING COMPETITIVE SUCCESS

These are divided into parts as under:

3.1 Basic Attitudinal Traits. Attitude is Core of any Success

- Ambition, to dream, imagination.
- Commitment to win, fire to win, think in terms of success.

- Hard effort to perform at peak.
- Integrity or ethics in success, to observe fairness by following rules.
- Having positive mindset and self-image. Nothing comes without hard struggle.
- Persistence—never to give up attitude, fighting back if unsuccessful and have mental toughness. Have faith in self and God.
- Sense of achievement and pride, sustained enthusiasm. To be passionate in doing things.
- Self-discipline is key to success. To be thankful and grateful.

3.2 For Success in Business

Following aspects are important:

- Having a plan based on shared vision, objectives, goals to achieve in terms of physical, qualitative, financial, i.e. profits, turnover. Plan has to be prepared after forecasting and scanning of environments.
- To have customer focus.
- Building relationship with clients and to be fair to competitors.
- Creativity and innovation is required to be ahead in competition. It is being different from others.
- Diversity and team work.
- Willingness to learn and remain curious in view of rapid changes.
- Cash flow is life blood of business. In competitive environment to be careful about costs and to be economical.
- To identify contingency actions to be taken when things do not go according to plan.
- Appreciate efforts of your employees, colleagues and involve them.

3.3 Overcome Obstacles

These obstacles are as under:

- Ego,
- Fear of failure,
- No plan,
- Lack of formalised goals,
- Lack of priorities, and
- Giving up efforts to achieve goal.

4. ACTION PLAN FOR SUCCESS

To achieve success various steps/stages are involved as under:

Step 1: Dream a vision and be winner

Success is the progressive realisation of worthy goals.

Step 2: Set goals and achieve them

It is putting your dreams into practice. Setting challenging goals to have following features:

S = Specific goals
M = Measureable goals
A = Achievable goals
R = Rational goals
T = Time bound goals

These characteristics can remembered as 'SMART' rule.

Step 3: Persistence and perseverance is vital

- The secret of success is a determination not to fail.
- Success is result of consistent work and right direction towards your goals.
- Great failure is when one gives up trying, when one is just on the verge of success.

Step 4: Determination to succeed

- Success comes from within by control of one's mind. Positive thinking is key to success. One has to be optimist.
- Develop a passion for success and achievement.
- Men are born to succeed not to fail. (Henry Thoreau)
- For success, supreme secret is faith—"can do attitude". Strengthening of self-confidence is essential.

ASAP Model

(a) Aspiration + (s) Strategy + (a) Action + and (p) Passion. ASAP leads to success in life and high career.

Step 5: Have faith in sincere actions and results

Think positive, talk positive, act positive. Infact everything depends on individual to be successful and to be winner.

- Wish you good luck in your endeavours for meaningful career. Having winner's mindset will bring you health, happiness and peace.
- Study success stories of Indian Business Managements such as Mr. Narayana Murthy in Fosys, Mr Ratan Tata of Tata Business Group, Mr. Premji, Wipro, Mrs. Shahnaz Khan and others.

Human Progress

I. MEANING

Progress is an *improvement in the well-beings*. It can be identified with improvement in public life such as service, religious observance, etc.

(i) Progress is more than Economic Growth

Progress means *more than economic growth*. It means a longer life and *better quality of life* for people. It is being happy, feeling free, sharing and having enthusiasm in life. *Spirituality* is the essence of any culture or religion and mankind. It is establishing truth, justice, love and peace. It is keeping other's interest before own. It is *service* welfare of humanity. It is to avoid selfishness. It is self-restraint due to interdependence.

(ii) Spirituality in Life is Important

Life has three aspects, physical, mental and spiritual. Spirituality is having faith in God. Material well-being and spirituality go together. It is working for the welfare of everyone. It is love of human-beings.

(iii) Progress Covers Longer Life Expectancy

A major component of progress is improvement in *life expectancy* rate. It is psychological well-being. It is increasing average caloric consumption of masses.

(iv) Progress is Composite

Progress has many aspects: (a) Professional, (b) Personal growth in maturity and wisdom, and (c) Economic.

(v) Progress involves Responsibility and Empowerment

Progress *comes from responsibility*. By taking responsibility, one can create more results and hence progress.

II. DIMENSIONS OF PROGRESS, I.E. HUMAN PROGRESS INVOLVES

(i) Economic progress,
(ii) Personal progress,
(iii) Social progress,
(iv) Technological progress, and
(v) Environmental progress.

(i) Economic Progress

It is related to scarce resources, their availability, to what extent these are available to maximum number of people. These are like food, clothes, shelter, health, education, per capita income, etc. A good quality of life may cover: *individual's economic progress*, i.e. increase in income, increase in reputation and goodwill, adequate food, etc.

(ii) Personal Progress

Personal progress is in terms of feeling of responsibility, self-awareness, self-esteem recognition of skills/expertise, career aspirations, fitness and health, recognising rights and responsibilities to society at large. Adequate communication skills, problem-solving ability and inter-personal skills contribute to personal progress.

(iii) Social Progress

It is degree of acceptance by the society. It involves more employment opportunities, decrease in poverty, advancement of women, democratic governing systems—Panchayati Raj, access to education, provision of health and welfare measures in the community.

(iv) Technological Progress

To focus on constructive aspects, i.e. welfare of society *versus* human destruction such as atomic bombs, armaments, etc.

(v) Environmental Progress

It involves improvement in drinking water, quality of air, environmentally friendly products, protection of fauna and flora and natural resources, i.e. water, air, forests, decrease in pollution.

III. PROGRESS IS IMPORTANT

Progress is essential for humanity, quality of life, community well-beings, progress of individual, corporations, countries and the world at large. Progress is indicator of what is achieved at large.

Managing Transformation

In this chapter on "Managing Transformation", the following aspects are covered:

1. Meaning of transformation.
2. Need for transformation.
3. Planned change involved in various areas of the organisation.
4. Transformation process.
5. Kurt Lewin's three step model for permanant change in the organisation.
6. Transformation in organisation is visible in different aspects.
7. Strategies for organisational transformation. (See Box 1)

1. MEANING OF TRANSFORMATION

Transformation means bringing a *fundamental* radical change. It is dramatic change, discontinuance with the past. It involves far reaching large scale systems change. Several units of an organisation participate simultaneously in the change process. *Employees* at all levels of the organisation are involved to bring about significant change in the *organisational culture*. Such change resulting from interventions may be different form such as—reduce the layers of the organisation, job titles, duties and responsibilities of employees, and nature of reporting, etc. Relationships may be changed significantly with such changes.

In fact it is to make planned change. It is rediscovery of entire organisation philosophy. Need for transformation has to be realised at all levels including the top-management.

2. NEED FOR TRANSFORMATION

Requirement for change in the organisation may be triggered by various factor/s, such as:

(a) Consumers are growing more demanding and their need have to be met.

(b) Profits now matter more than ever as pressures are mounting from the board of directors which have to be met as they want higher results.
(c) Organisations have to capture the benefits of new technologies and business practices to enjoy these benefits.
(d) As threats are unpredictable, company has to prepare for it, by making company strong enough to absorb shocks.

3. PLANNED CHANGE INVOLVED IN VARIOUS AREAS OF THE ORGANISATION

Planned changes relate to various areas as under:

(a) *Soft aspects*. These aspects are more important, such as mission, vision, purpose, beliefs and values of the people as well as the organisation,
- *Relationships* of people and group working,
- *Development* of people in the organisation for competitive advantage such as their abilities, skills, perceptions, attitudes and performances,
- Organisation culture such as TQM culture to sustain transformation, and
- Learning organisation for enhancing organisational effectiveness.

(b) *Structural changes*, such as in job designs, departmentalisation, authority distribution, line and staff structure, etc.
(c) *Technological changes* in the equipment, information systems, etc., introduction of techniques like TQM, etc. are common in globalisation.
(d) *Hard issues outcomes* are such as profits, prices, cost reduction, market share, and growth projections of business.

4. TRANSFORMATION PROCESS

Organisational change process is a complex process which involves various steps as under and also refer to Box 1:

(a) Diagnosis

- Problem recognition,
- Diagnosis of the problem/problems, and
- Identifying the causes.

(b) Action Plan and Intervention

- Preparing action plan,
- Generating motivation for change, and
- Implementing the change interventions.

(c) Process Maintenance

- Supporting the change and seeking cooperation of various employee groups, and
- Keeping the process of transformation relevant and manageable.

(d) Evaluating the Change and Feedback

The components of organisational transformation process are the diagnostic component, action plan or intervention component, process-maintenance process and evaluation the change. The feedback helps in course correction.

5. KURT LEWIN THREE STEP MODEL FOR PERMANENT CHANGE IN THE ORGANISATION

Three step model for change in the organisation involves change—unfreeze, movement to new state and refreeze. (Figure 1)

FIGURE I

Lewin's Three Step Model for Change

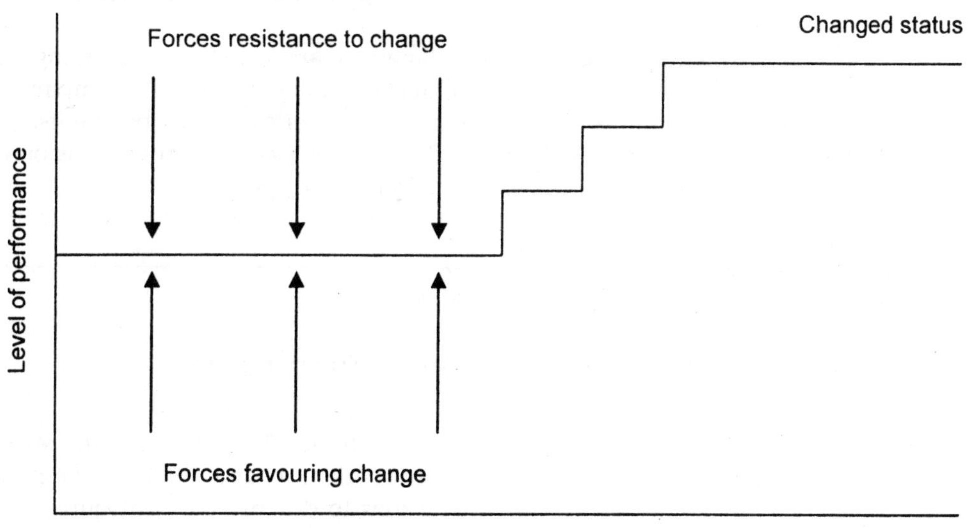

(a) Unfreeze

In this step, employees are educated about the *external and internal* factors that make change imperative. They are told about the benefits that change can bring to them and the organisation. This will motivate employees to welcome change to enjoy the new benefits.

(b) Movement to Change

This involves doing away with old practices and adopting new methods such as installing and operating advanced equipment, new production processes, job duties, etc. This stage involves implementing change.

(c) Refreeze

The third step involves reinforcing change so that the organisation does not revert to old state of things. For example, if the change process involved acquiring new skills, these should be made permanent part of the organisation, repetition and constant reinforcement of new work techniques is essential to sustained change.

This change process is guided and monitored by the top management team (change agent). The employees may be *empowered* to implement change. Edgar Schein reports that three variables are critical to the success of any change in the culture of the organisation. Each stage of change will require extensive involvement by all the stakeholders in the organisation, who are likely to be affected by change

6. TRANSFORMATION IN ORGANISATION IS VISIBLE IN DIFFERENT ASPECTS

Transformed business is known through various benefits:

(i) Everyone stays focussed towards goals. As a result of change, the business becomes a value-producing machine: resources go directly to the activities that deliver the maximum return.

(ii) The company can foresee future. Managers are constantly thinking about what consumers will want tomorrow, next quarter and next year. The company is surprise-proof: always learning, always changing, but never overtaken by events, good or bad.

(iii) Decisions are taken quickly. Integrated business process improve decision-making. As a result, productivity increases. Bureaucracy disappears.

(iv) Innovations introduced bring better customer's satisfaction and long-run profitability.

Box I

Strategies for Organisational Transformation

Organisational transformation strategic plans may involve *radical changes* to the structure, culture and processes of the organisation. This may be in response to competitive pressures, mergers, acquisitions, investment, change of technology, product lines, markets, cost-reduction exercise and decisions to downsize or outsource work. The transformational change may be forced on an organisation by investors or by government decisions. It may be initiated by a new chairman and top management team to turnaround the organisation.

Transformation is advocated as transactional change is merely concerned with the alteration of ways in which the organisation does business and people interact with one another on a day-to-day basis, and 'is effective when what you want is more of what you've already got', 'discontinuous improvement in capability'.

Four strategies for transformational change have been identified by Beckhard (1989):

- *a change in what drives the organisation*—for example, a change from being production-driven to being market-driven would be transformational,
- *a fundamental change in the relationships between or among organisational parts*—for example, decentralisation,
- *a major change in the ways of doing work*—for example, the introduction of new technology such as computer-integrated manufacturing, and

- *a basic, cultural change in norms, values or research systems*—for example, developing a customer-focused culture.

Transformation programmes are *led from the top within the organisation*. They do not rely on an external 'change agent' as did many traditional OD interventions, although specialist external advice might be obtained on aspects of the transformation such as strategic planning, reorganisation or developing new HR processes

(i) Managing the transition

Strategies need to be developed for managing the transition from where the organisation is to where the organisation wants to be. This is the critical part of a transformation programme. It is during the transition period of getting from here to there that change takes place. Transition management starts from a *definition of the future state* and a *diagnosis of the present state*. It is then necessary to define what has to be done to achieve the transformation. This means deciding on the new process systems, procedures, structures, products and markets to be developed. Having defined these, the work can be programmed and the resources required (people, money, equipment and time) can be defined.

The strategic plan for managing the transition should include provisions for *involving people in the process* and for *communicating to them* what is happening, why it is happening and how it will affect them. Clearly the aims are to get as many people as possible *committed to the change*.

(ii) The transformation programme

The eight steps required to transform an organisation have been summed up by Kotter as follows:

(a) Establishing a sense of urgency

- examining market and competitive realities; and
- identifying and discussing crises, potential crises, or major opportunities.

(b) Forming a powerful guiding coalition

- *assembling a group* with enough power to lead the change effort; and
- encouraging the group to work together as a team.

(c) Creating a vision

- creating a vision to help direct the change effort;
- developing strategies for achieving that vision.

(d) Communicating the vision

- using every vehicle possible to communicate the new vision and strategies; and
- teaching new behaviours by the example of the guiding coalition.

(e) Empowering others to act on the vision

- getting rid of obstacles to change;
- changing systems or structures that seriously undermine the vision; and
- encouraging risk-taking and non-traditional ideas, activities and actions.

(f) Planning for and creating short-term wins

- planning for visible performance improvement;
- creating those improvements; and
- recognizing and rewarding employees involved in the improvements.

(g) Consolidating improvements and producing still more change

- using increased credibility to change systems, structures and policies that don't fit the vision;
- hiring, promoting and developing employees who can implement the vision;
- reinvigorating the process with new projects, themes and change agents.

(h) Institutionalizing new approaches

- articulating the connections between the new behaviours and corporate success; and
- developing the means to ensure leadership development and succession.

(iii) Transformation capability required

The development and implementation of transformation strategies *require special capabilities*. As Gratton points out:

Transformation capability depends in part on the ability to create and embed processes that *link business strategy to the behaviours* and performance of individuals and teams. These clusters of processes link *vertically* (to create alignment with short-term business needs), horizontally (to create cohesion), and *temporally* (to transform to meet future business needs).

(iv) The strategic role of HR in organisational transformation

HR can and should play a key strategic role in developing and implementing organisational transition and transformation strategies. It can *provide help and guidance* in analysis and diagnosis, highlighting the people issues that will fundamentally affect the success of the strategy. HR can advise on *resourcing programmes and planning* and implementing the vital training, reward, communications and involvement aspects of the process. It can *anticipate people problems* and deal with them before they become serious. If the programme does involve restructuring and downsizing, HR can advise on how this should be done humanely and with the minimum disruption to people's live.

CHAPTER

70

Organisation and Environment Interface

In this chapter on "Organisation and Environment Interface", the following aspects are covered:

1. Organisation is an open system.
2. Environment forces.
3. General environment.
4. Task environment.
5. Turbulent environment—reasons.
6. Strategies to deal with environment.
   - 6.1 Insulation of organisation from external forces.
   - 6.2 Gaining control over environment.

1. ORGANISATION IS AN OPEN SYSTEM

An organization is an open system that exchanges information, materials and other resources with its environment. It has become essential for modern organizations to understand their external environment and take steps to cope with the changing environment.

Every organization has *two types of environment*, viz., *internal* and *external*. The *internal environment* includes techniques of production, structure, management philosophy, human relations, etc. But *external environment* represents forces outside the organization itself and potentially affect its performance.

The *classical theory* focused on the internal environment of the organization as it treated the organization as a *closed system*. But *system approach* considers organization as an *open system* which has continuous interaction with its external environment for its survival and growth.

2. ENVIRONMENT FORCES

According to S.P. Robbins, "An organization's environment represents anything outside the organization itself. It is composed of those institutions or forces that effect the performance of the organization, but over which the organization has little control." Theoretically, environment forces may be divided into two categories : (i) general environment, and (ii) task environment as shown in Figure 1.

Figure 1

General and Task Environment of Business System

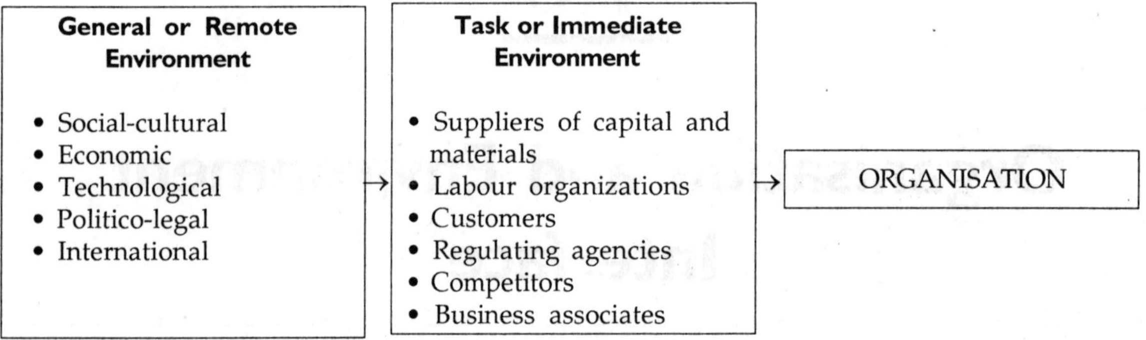

3. GENERAL ENVIRONMENT

It consists of socio-cultural, economic, technological, politico-legal and international forces. These forces are also termed as indirect action elements. The general environment exercises its influence through the task environment.

3.1 Socio-cultural Factors

Sociological factors include : caste structure, mobility of labour, customs and conventions, cultural heritage, etc. All these have a bearing on a business.

Culture refers to the attitudes, beliefs and values that members of a community share in common. The cultural factors may influence the functioning of an enterprise strongly. For instance, in northern parts of India, workers worship their tools on the 'Vishwakarma Day' because of which the factories observe an off-day on this day each year.

3.2 Economic Domain

The economic system of a country may be characterized as capitalist (free enterprise), socialist or mixed.

The Government influences the economic environment of business through economic planning, fiscal policies and budgets, monetary policies, industrial regulations, business laws.

3.3 Technological Domain

Technological environment influences business organizations in terms of investment in technology.

3.4 Politico-Legal Domain

It provides the legal framework within which the business is to function. For instance in India Coca Cola was stopped operations in 1970.

3.5 International Environment

The forces in the international environment may have adverse or favourable impact on the business. For example, the disintegration of U.S.S.R. caused great miseries for the Indian exporters in the early 1960's.

4. TASK ENVIRONMENT

It consists of direct action element in the environment such as shareholders, suppliers, labour organizations, customers, regulating agencies, competitors, and business associates. These are the immediate external forces which have direct influence over the organisation and its management.

4.1 Suppliers

Include those groups which provide capital and materials to the organisation. The shareholders, banks and other financial institutions influence the business polices strategies to a great extent. The suppliers of materials will deal with the business if they are sure about the timely payments against their supplies.

4.2 Labour

The trade unions interact with the management for higher wages and bonus, better service conditions, health facilities, etc. They pressurize for the fulfilment of their demands and even resort to 'go-slow' tactics, strike, gherao, etc.

4.3 Customers

Customer satisfaction is the ultimate aim of all business. It calls for good quality, reasonable price and prompt service of business enterprises and raise their voice against organizations to check on unfair practices.

4.4 Regulating agencies

Such as government departments and other monitoring agencies excise, sales and income tax and quality control departments exercise their controls on business organisations.

4.5 Competitors

The policies and practices of competitors have direct influence on a business unit. If the competitors reduce the price of a product, or improve the quality, the concerned business unit will face the threat of falling sales if it does not take appropriate actions immediately.

4.6 Business associates

It is easier to borrow capital from the business associates during the period of emergency.

5. TURBULENT ENVIRONMENT REASONS

The environment continuously undergoes changes due following factors:

(i) Rapid technological changes.
(ii) Frequent changes in Government economic policies.
(iii) Political uncertainty.
(iv) Social changes, e.g. demand for reservation in jobs for minorities and women.
(v) Changes in fashion and tastes of consumers.
(vi) Labour unrest leading to industrial conflicts.
(vii) Increased competition.

6. STRATEGIES TO DEAL WITH ENVIRONMENT

These are as under :

6.1 Insulation of Organisation from External Forces

Environmental forces are not allowed to penetrate freely into the organisation as it affects its operations. Following strategies are used for minimizing such disruptions:

(i) Buffering

Organizations can buffer themselves by stockpiling resources or warehousing outputs to maintain operations when there are shortages of raw materials or peak demands.

(ii) Smoothing or Levelling

This strategy aims at smoothing the sales throughout the year. During periods of low demand by offering inducements, such as price reductions, to encourage consumers to buy its products.

(iii) Anticipating and Adopting

Changes in environmental conditions, for instance, hotels, and restaurants in popular hill stations can be anticipated during the tourist season and increase their supplies of food, liquor, etc.

(iv) Rationing

It leads to establishing a set of priorities for using organizational scarce resources. For instance, during the summer season, there is a greater demand for milk and thus dairies do not prepare butter, ghee, etc.

6.2 Gaining Control over Environment

To reduce organisation's dependency on the environment and thereby increase its power over the environment. Such strategies are:

(i) Creation of Prestige

By favourable public image of its activities, such as advertisement, publicity.

(ii) Agreements

Agreements with suppliers of materials, banks and financial institutions, labour unions, customers, competitors, etc. will enable the organisation to gain control over the environment.

(iii) Co-optation

Business organizations appoint outside directors on positions of responsibility, the organisation makes them more aware of its problems and attempts to create a common understanding with them to gain support for its action.

(iv) Coalition

A coalition is formed to achieve certain common objectives and those involved in the coalition become allies. A merger combines all resources of the concerned organizations.

(v) Procurement of Key Personnel

By hiring knowledgeable individuals from key organisations and who have knowledge about the operations and policies of competitors.

(vi) Lobbying

For example, the top managers of an organisation may resort to lobbying with some members of the ruling party to regulate the import of certain materials by offering donations.

Stability of the Government is also an important factor from the point of view of growth of business. Businessmen prefer to start new units in those states where there is political stability and where rule of law prevails.

CHAPTER

71

Stress Management

In this chapter on "Stress Management", the following aspects are covered:

1. Meaning of stress.
2. Sources of stress.
3. Nature of the stressors.
   3.1 Environmental stressors.
   3.2 Organisational stressors.
4. Stress coping strategies.
   4.1 Personal strategy.
   4.2 Organisational programmes.

1. MEANING OF STRESS

Randall S. Schuler has stated, "Stress is a dynamic condition in which an individual is confronted with an opportunity, constraint or demand related to what he or she desires and for which the outcome is perceived to be both uncertain and important."

This definition has three features:

(a) *Stress is not necessarily bad in itself.* It also has positive value when it offers potential gain.

(b) *Stress is associated with constraints and demands.* The former prevents you from doing what you desire. The latter refers to the loss of something desired. So when you undergo your annual performance review at work, you feel stress because you confront opportunity, constraints and demands. A good performance review may lead to a promotion, greater responsibilities, and a higher salary. But a poor review may prevent getting the promotion.

(c) *Two conditions are necessary* for potential stress to become actual stress. There must be *uncertainty* over the outcome and the outcome must be *important*. Regardless of the conditions, it is only when there is doubt or uncertainty regarding whether the opportunity will be seized, the constraint removed, or the loss avoided that there is stress. That is, stress is highest for those individuals who perceive that they are uncertain as to whether they will win or lose and lowest for those individuals who think that winning or losing is a certainty. But importance is also critical. If winning or losing is an unimportant outcome, there is no stress. If earning a promotion doesn't hold any importance to a person, he would have no reason to feel stress over having to undergo a performance review.

(d) *Stress is body's reactions, physiological and psychological* to any demand made upon it that requires more of us than usual. Our reception of events, activities stress. It is an individual matter. Certain events may be quite stressful to one person but not to other. Our imagination creates muscular tensions. Thinking process interferes with body. One's mind has substituted physical danger when it is not there. When one sits in an interview, chemicals are produced in the body.

(e) *Stress is not undesirable.* Mild stress actually improves performance. If stress is severe and persists for long period person is not able to cope with anxiety, mention and nervousness. It lowers performance it can be harmful. This is explain in Figure 1.

FIGURE I

Stress and Job Performance Relationship

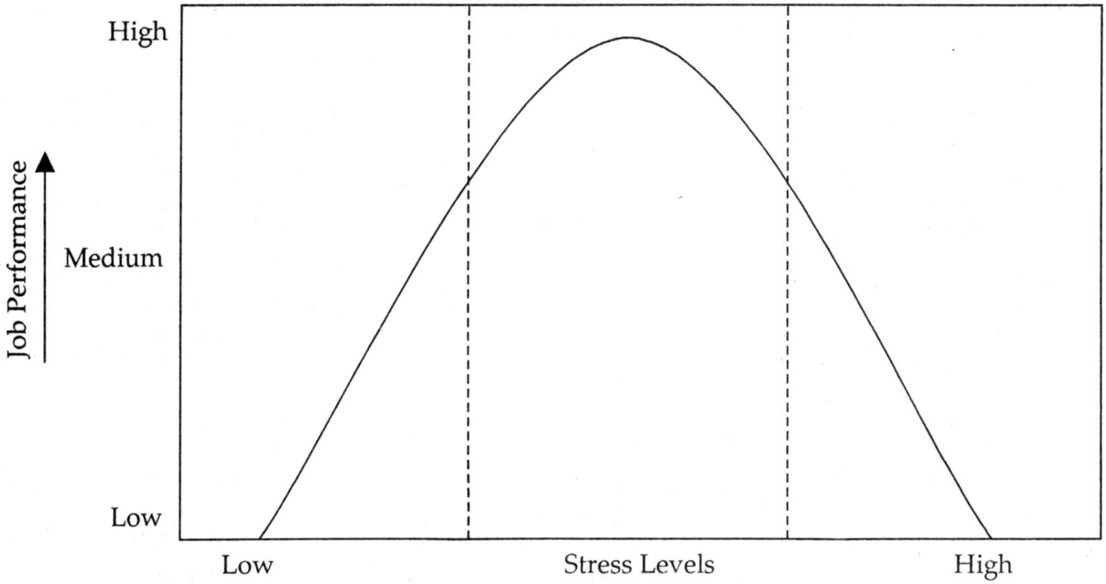

2. SOURCES OF STRESS

The potential stressors in a person's life can be divided into three categories:

(i) Environmental Stressors, which include technical, social, political and economic changes.

(ii) Organisational Stressors, comprises organisational characteristics and conditions, job demands and role characteristics.

(iii) Individual Stressors, which consists of personal characteristics, strengths and weaknesses, personal situation and events and coping efficiency.

A model based on the above classification is shown in Figure 2.

FIGURE 2

Sources of Stress and Consequences

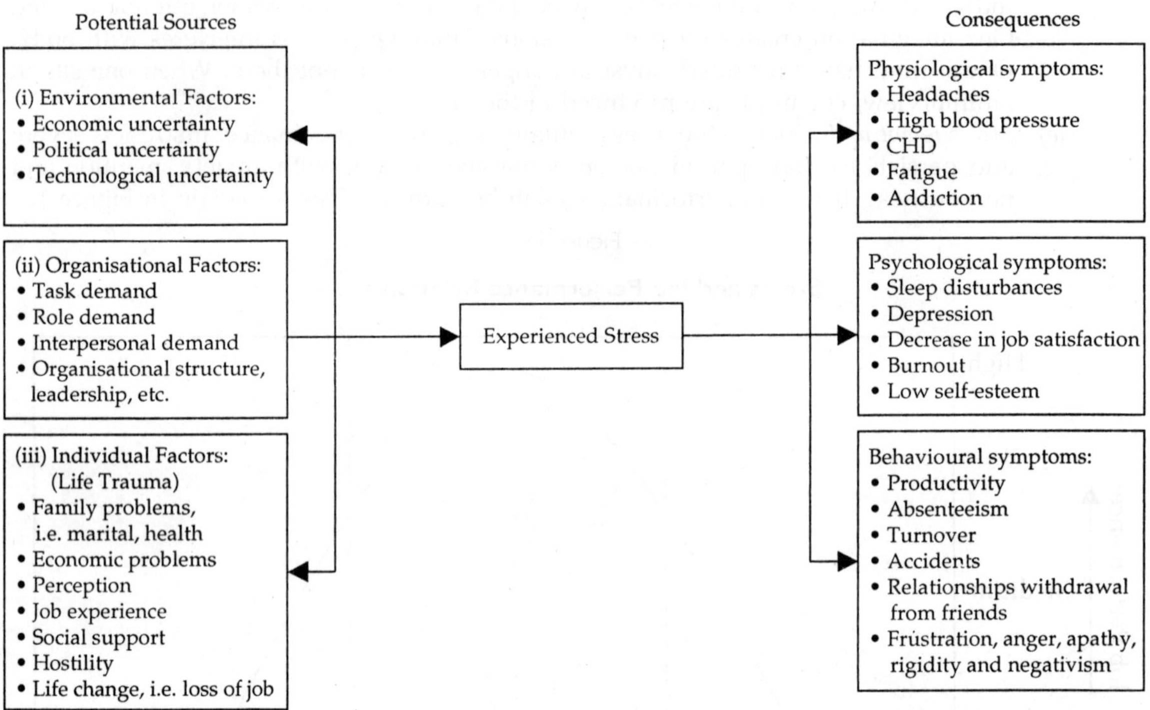

Individuals do not exist in isolation, but are part of an environment, the two most important aspects are the organisational and the non-organisational environment. If both of these environments contain many stressors along with stressors within an individual at the same time, there is likely to be an increased level of stress. Stress levels would also vary according to the degree of interaction between the three types of stressors.

3. NATURE OF THE STRESSORS

3.1 Environmental Stressors

Environmental stressors include:

(a) Economic Changes

Economic changes include inflation or fluctuation in interest rates, which can decrease the purchasing power of individuals and in these circumstances people find it difficult to plan ahead financially. This can create uncertainties in people's lives and result in stress. Similarly, decreasing levels of investment may lead to increasing levels of unemployment, which is another major cause of stress.

(b) Political Changes

Political changes in a country can also cause stress for individuals especially if people are not very clear about what to expect from a new political situation. Sometimes political changes can be so dramatic that the level of uncertainty can create a huge amount of stress for certain groups.

(c) Social Changes

Social changes also cause stress. It was expected that through the "Hong Kong Handover" the long established "American Values" in Hong Kong would change to "Asian Values" in terms of culture, sport and style, which resulted in uncertainties and created a great deal of stress people prior to handover.

(d) Technological Changes

Technological changes are not only part of organisational life but are an inevitable part of daily life, and they have become another environmental stressors. Systems in banking, communication and shopping have become highly dependent on rapidly changing technology and depending on person's acceptance of technology, the facilities provided by such changes can create stress.

3.2 Organisational Stressors

Organisational characteristics and processes can vary dramatically between organisations and, if not designed correctly, can cause stress. Characteristics can be analysed in terms of organisational policies, structure and processes. Some stress-related factors are shown in Figure 3 on next page.

Recent studies have focused on the effects of organisational polities on reviewing stress at work. Life in a highly centralized organisation, where control is concentrated at the top level of the organisation, people at the operating level have little control over their work behaviours and activities and thus becomes a source of stress.

(a) Job Demands and Role Characteristics

Taken together, job-demands and role characteristics constitute another set of stressors in an organisational environment. Job demands include repetitive work, time pressures and deadlines, low skill requirements, responsibility for people and underemployment. Role characteristics are more complicated and consists of:

(i) *Role perception:* Role perception represents an individual's view of how he is supposed to act in a given situation.

(ii) *Role expectation:* Role expectations are defined as how others believe one should act in a given situation. Mismatch between perception and expectation leads to stress.

FIGURE 3

Organisational Characteristics as Stress Factors

Aspects of Organisational Characteristics	*Resulting Stress Situation*
1. *Organisational Policies*:	
• Inequitable performance or inappropriate appraisal • Pay inequities • Idealistic job description	Feelings of unfairness or lack of clarity about personal goals or objectives.
2. *Organisational Structure*:	
• Centralisation of authority of decision-making • Not enough opportunities for growth and advancement • Increased organisational size and lack of participation • Interdependence of organisational units	Lowered feelings of self-efficiency.
3. *Organisational Process*:	
• Poor communication and lack of information • Poor feedback on performance • Ambiguous or conflicting needs • Poor training programmes	Ambiguity and feelings that the worst is about to happen

(iii) *Role conflict*: When an individual is confronted by divergent role expectations, the result is role conflict. It exists when an individual finds that compliance with one role requirement may make compliance difficult with another. This develop stress.

(iv) *Role overload*: Role overload is experienced when an individual or employee is expected to do more than time permits.

(v) *Role ambiguities*: It is created when role expectations are not clearly understood and the employee is not sure what he or she is to do.

(b) Other Organisational Stressors

(i) Air Quality

"Sick building syndrome" is a condition in which an office building or office segment puts polluted air into the worker's environment. This can be caused by solvents in the carpets and furniture, air-conditioning, moths and fungi and so on. If the pollution is bad enough, it can make individual sick and boost stress.

(ii) Excess Noise

Noise pollution can lead to significant work stress and if it is loud enough, can damage one's hearing over long-term. It is loud enough to interfere with one's concentration and raise one's stress level. The sound of people talking and laughing, office printers, computers, ringing phones, faxes and copy machines or meetings going on all combine to raise the stress level.

(iii) Uncomfortable Office Furniture

When an individual is staggering under files, papers and report, the stress level may be compounded if the desk, chair or lighting is not first rate. An individual's own posture is also important. Sitting—especially slouching—puts continuous pressure on lower back muscles and discs.

(iv) Computer Comfort

One of the prime sources for work stress involves the computer—its screen, proper placement of the keyboard and so on.

Organisations go through a cycle. They are established, they grow, become mature, and eventually decline. An organization's life stage, i.e. where it is in this stage cycle—create different problems and pressures for employees. The establishment and decline stages are particularly stress prone. The foundation stage is characterized by a great deal of excitement and uncertainties while the decline stage requires cutbacks, layoffs and different set of uncertainties. Stress tends to be least in maturity where uncertainties are at their lowest ebb. Information technology is particularly facing stress-related problems in a big way and considerable amount is being spent to develop coping strategies.

4. STRESS COPING STRATEGIES

The term 'coping' is used to denote the way of dealing with stress. "It is the process of managing demands (external and internal) that are appraised as taxing or exceeding the resources of the person." People use a combination of three approaches to cope stress.

The first, is *control strategy* to directly anticipate or solve problems, it is to take charge and tackling the problem.

Second is the *escape strategy* which amounts to running a way when they fail to confront.

Thirdly, *symptom management strategy* consists of using methods such as relaxation, meditation, or medication to manage the symptoms of occupational stress.

4.1 Personal Strategy

Basically meeting stress is individual responsibility. He should have accurate information about stress. Some steps are:

- Learn to *recognise its symptoms*. Take symptoms seriously and slow down pace.
- *Change perceptions* which create stress. Do not carry demons in your mind. So minimise stress by changing your attitude. Avoid guilt feeling and share your anxieties. Improve communication and develop relationship of trust and caring of others.
- Learn to *realign goals* which are realistic and attainable. Restructure your job to make it less stressful. Try activities that capture interest and give satisfaction. Pursue some higher values of life.
- Maintain *positive attitude* toward self-development and self-improvement. Overcome stress as it is life long battle avoid obsolescence.
- Practice *relaxation techniques* such as yoga, meditation, biofeedback, intense exercise. Body is a great self-healer such as ability to withstand grief. Play games and avoid competition. Avoid bottling up anger within you.
- Cutback on *excessive hours* of work to overcome burnout. Keep balance between work and home life. Enjoy holidaying.

4.2 Organisational Programmes

The management may pursue the following strategies to reduce job stress:

- Setting clear *objectives* for the organisation. Departments and individuals so as to minimise scope for job conflicts and ambiguity among the employees.
- *Enriching* jobs for the employees.
- Developing *career plans and development* taking into consideration individual capabilities and aspirations, on the one hand, and the organisational requirements, on the other.
- Employee assistance programmes such as engaging of counsellors to guide on matters of career planning and opportunities, tackle alcoholism, drug addiction, etc.
- Training and development programmes.
- Organisation development or transformation programme so as to improve communication, innovation, participation, trust, openness, quality of work life, infact a concept of learning organisation.
- Strengthen process of placement, i.e. matching jobs and individuals and role clarity.
- Compensation to ensure equitable reward system.

CHAPTER

72

IFC Guidelines for Conduct of Projects in Socially and Environmentally Responsible Manner

Following aspects are explained:

1. Equator principles.
2. What is sustainable design and its attributes.
3. Sustainable design criteria.
4. External ratings criteria—LEED.
5. Keys to successful sustainable design.

1. EQUATOR PRINCIPLES

The "Equator Principles" are now the standard in project financing. Since 2003, 31 financial institutions have adopted the "Equator Principles," a voluntary set of guidelines based on International Finance Corporation (IFC) social and environmental policies and procedures that ensure that only projects whose sponsors can demonstrate they will conduct the project in a socially and environmentally responsible manner will be financed. Together, the Equator banks were estimated in 2003 to represent about 75% of the project loan syndication market globally, or $55.1B in project loans.

2. WHAT IS SUSTAINABLE DESIGN?

Sustainable design integrates functional, "green" and community design and construction practices to reduce environmental and human impacts, provide long-term benefits to the community, and reduce project and operational costs. It encompasses the following attributes:

- Optimize worker/occupant use of the site, infrastructure and buildings, and promote occupant health;
- Optimize the nature of the structure, where it is placed on the site, the materials used to build it, and how it is built with an eye to decreasing harmful environmental impacts directly and in the choice of products (e.g. energy efficient) and materials (e.g. recycled content, renewable resources, non-toxic);
- Focus on waste minimization from design through construction and into operations;
- Promote overall site environmental quality and design adaptability over time;
- Optimize the community's relationship with the site, its infrastructure and buildings, seeking to reduce negative impacts and maximize opportunity for community benefits, during and after construction into operations as applicable.

Sustainable design is a growing trend as our customers seek ways to continually improve their environmental and social performance. The US Green Building Council states that buildings in the United States account for 36% of total energy use; 65% of electricity consumption; 30% of raw materials use; and 30% of waste output. The UK Construction Industry sends 30-40% of its construction and demolition waste to landfill—some 24 million tons at a disposal cost of £45 per ton.

3. SUSTAINABLE DESIGN CRITERIA

Sustainable design criteria optimize design and construction performance to reduce project and operating costs, improve energy efficiency and reduce solid waste. In addition, sustainable design considers the human use of sites, infrastructure and buildings seeking to enhance occupant satisfaction, comfort and health. Finally, consideration of community interests and impacts in design and construction helps build public consent for a project.

4. EXTERNAL RATINGS CRITERIA—LEED

Several countries are instituting "green building" programs, including Australia, Canada, China, France, Hong Kong, India, Japan, Spain and the United Kingdom, which came out with the first green building assessment tool called BREEAM (Building Research Establishment Environmental Assessment Method). The United States is experiencing rapid growth in green buildings—over 100 projects have received LEED certification, representing over 158 million square feet. LEED—Leadership in Energy and Environmental design—is a green building rating system developed by the US Green Building Council to establish a common standard of measurement and promote integrated whole-building design concepts. LEED provides a framework for assessing building performance in six areas:

- Site Selection
- Water Efficiency
- Energy and Atmosphere
- Materials and Resources
- Indoor Environmental Quality
- Innovation

LEED also accredits individuals who must pass an exam to demonstrate green building expertise.

5. KEYS TO SUCCESSFUL SUSTAINABLE DESIGN

Sustainable design builds on existing expertise to integrate functional, green and community criteria into design and construction processes. Some attributes of a successful approach to sustainable design are:

- Evaluation of the environmental and human interaction with the site, its infrastructure and buildings.
- Assembling a multi-disciplinary team to integrate selected sustainable design criteria into project processes and plans.
- Engagement with the community on conceptual design to address public interests and seek opportunities to enhance community use and impacts.
- Incorporating efforts to design waste out and consider end of project impacts from the outset to reduce waste and save money.
- Optimizing performance and determining design synergies through the use of simulation modeling.

The Sustainable Checklist provides a process for assessing and integrating design criteria in six areas: site selection, water conservation, energy, materials and resources, occupant health, and community interests.

Reference

Contributed by Neeraj Bhatia, Missuri, Texas, USA.

PART X

ANNEXURES

ANNEXURE I

INSTITUTE OF MANAGEMENT TECHNOLOGY, GHAZIABAD-201001

Syllabus in Business Ethics

Objectives

The course intends to present some broader perspective on basic issues in business ethics which are of relevance to various functions and systems of an organisation.

Contents

1. Ethics and Business: an overview
2. The Ethical Theory
3. Ethical issues related to Employees:
   a. Personnel service contract issues
   b. Privacy and confidentiality issues
   c. Health and Hygiene issue at work place
   d. Employee conduct at work place
4. Ethical issues related to Consumers:
   a. Product liability and safety
   b. Advertising and Marketing (for the business or products or services)
5. Business and Environment
6. Discrimination at workplace
7. The ethical issues related to Finance and Investment
8. Corporate Governance

PART A

1. What are the core values of any society? How business values can be integrated core values.
2. Discuss with suitable examples Socio-Economic character of Business. How business ethics is an integral part of business?
3. What are the major principles of ethical powers to individuals? Discuss and cite some examples also.
4. Discuss the concept of right? What does "Distributive Justice" means? Comment.
5. Discuss, what are the major ancient ethical learning's can be adopted in modern business? Cite some examples of Gandhi's views on ethical business.

PART B

1. What are the major factors to be taken into consideration for classifying the "Socially Responsible Organization"?
2. What are the major ethical issues involved in Multinational's business. Discuss by giving the suitable illustrations.
3. Thomas Aquinas notes two values necessary for a good society, unity and peace. What kind of world systems would be necessary to ensure unity and peace? Can a good society exist in our present interdependent but lawless world?
4. What are the major ethical issues involved in false advertising? Discuss with it's on the society.
5. Discuss the various ethical tests proposed for Corporate Executives. Are these tests essential for checking the ethical attitude of executives?

PART C

1. Discuss the need of structural changes for suitable corporate governance is required in any organization?
2. In your opinion, what should be the Codes for effective Corporate Governance? Discuss.
3. What true security needs would a world order system have to satisfy? How could these be managed at a global level?
4. Carefully examine two advertisements taken from current newspaper or magazines and assess the extent to which they meet what you would consider adequate ethical standards for advertisers. Give suitable reasons for your ethical standards.
5. Write a note by citing suitable examples on current status of Social and Ethical accountability in Indian Business.

PART D

1. Discuss the major ethical issues involved in commercial law of contract? Is "Whistle Blowing" is justified in certain cases? Discuss and cite some examples also?
2. Why trademark is the most ethical issue in marketing practices? Discuss.
3. "Leaders of Industry—managers as well as trade union leaders—should become the vanguard of new culture, the culture of work ethic. Set an example of devotion to duty that will suffuse the entire workforce through layer by layer progression. The, and then only, we and redeem our obligations to stakeholders". In reference to above statement discuss the obligations of business towards stakeholders.
4. What are the various facets of social sciences researches, which may endanger ethics of society? Discuss.
5. What kinds of ethical values are essential for contesting the Lok Sabha Election? Discuss the role ethics in prevailing political parties.

SHORT ANSWER QUESTIONS

1. Ethics and business.
2. Competition and ethics.
3. Socially ethical organization.
4. Individual and Society.

5. Ethics of Multinationals.
6. Ethics is Marketing.
7. Ethical issues in Media.
8. The concept of right.
9. Negative and Positive rights.
10. Sexual Harassments in Workplace.
11. Corporate Governance.
12. Stakeholders of Business.
13. Obligations of Public Enterprises.
14. Scams and Ethical Issues.
15. Ethics of Politics.
16. Distributive Justice.
17. Core Values of Society.
18. Ecological Ethics.
19. Ethics and Computer Piracy.
20. Meaning of "Whistle Blowing".

Case Study I

Ethics and Culture

Bob Simpson is the managing director in the country of West Penguin for Packway Foods, a U.S. food processing company with operations in 12 countries. He buys exotic fruits from the large plantation owners in West Penguin, and Packway Foods has prospered from distributing the rare produce found only is West Penguin as a result of this association. Of course, there are several other companies that are anxious to buy the produce as well, but Bob has lived in West Penguin for many years, and has developed a personal friendship with the half dozen plantation owners who control the entire production of the specialty crops. He is a good friend with General Rafael Oregon, the unofficial leader of the plantation owners. General Oregon also is in charge of the West Penguin military, holds a cabinet post, and has strong ties to the president of the country.

Although several packing companies have approached the growers. General Oregon has, until now, convinced the owners to sell only to Bob, due to their special friendship and long business relationship.

General Oregon called Bob in early November, and mentioned in passing that yet another of Bob's competitors had just been to see him. He had sent her away, and repeated that the growers were quite happy with their arrangement with Packway Foods. Oregon also told Bob that his children were coming home from college over the Christmas holidays. Bob is quite fond of the children, and even helped them obtain scholarships and admission to Florida Stale University. Oregon said he was thinking of buying jet skis for his children as Christmas presents. and he recalled that Bob was a good friend with the local distributor of one of the best brands available. The General wondered if Bob could call his friend and arrange for a special discount for him.

Later that day, Bob thought about Oregon's request. The special arrangement between the growers and Parkway Foods represents perhaps 35 percent of Packway's profits. In fact, it is primarily because of the West Penguin business that Packway has been able to survive and prosper, since they are not nearly as well financed as many of the other large packing companies. Because of this situation, Bob is truly one of the keys to Packway's success and continued financial health.

Oregon had never asked for anything of value for himself in the past. The assistance with the scholarships had only been a question of good contacts and advice. Bob wondered if the General was asking for help in obtaining a discount, or for an expensive gift. He also wondered if this would become a regular feature of their relationship, and if the other growers would follow suit. He especially wondered what to say to his parent company, or even if he should raise the issue, and he also wondered if they would encourage him to go ahead, in spite of the U.S. laws restricting such activities.

Questions

1. Develop an effective negotiation process for management situations with possible legal and ethical implications.
2. What are the major ethical issues involved in this case? Discuss.

CASE STUDY 2

The Five Principles of Ethical Power for Individuals

Purpose: I see myself as being an ethically sound person. I let my conscience be my guide. No matter what happens, I am always able to face the mirror, look myself straight in the eye, and feel good about myself.

Pride: I feel good about myself. I don't need the acceptance of other people to feel important. A balanced self-esteem keeps my ego and my desire to be accepted from influencing my decisions.

Patience: I believe that things will eventually work out well. I don't need everything to happen right now. I am at peace with what comes my way!

Persistence: I stick to my purpose, especially when it seems Inconvenient to do so! My behaviour is consistent with my intentions. As Churchill said, "Never! Never! Naver! Never! Give up!"

Perspective: I take time to enter each day quietly in a mood of reflection. This helps me to get myself focused and allows me to listen to my inner self and to see things more clearly.

Questions

1. Read these five principles of ethical power for individuals. Comment how business is different from these principles.
2. Discuss the significance of these in modern business.

GGS INDRAPRASTHA UNIVERSITY, DELHI

Values and Ethics in Business

Course Objective

The basic objective of this paper is to make the students realize the importance of values and ethics in business. This course endeavors to provide a background to ethics as a prelude to learn the skills of ethical decision-making and, then, to apply those skills to the real and current challenges of the information professions.

Syllabus Contest

UNIT-I

Introduction

Values—Concept, types and formation of values, ethics, values and behaviour, Values of Indian Managers, Ethics, development of ethics, ethical decision-making and decision-making process, relevance of ethics and values in business.

Management of Ethics: Management process and ethics, managerial performance. ethical issues, ethos of Vadanta in management, Hierarchism as an organizational value.

UNIT-II

Corporate Social Responsibility and Consumer Protection

Corporate responsibility of business employees, consumers and community, Corporate Governance, Code of Corporate Governance, Consumerism, unethical issues, in sales, marketing and technology.

UNIT-III

Understanding Progress, Results and Managing Transforming

Progress and Results definition, functions of progress, transformation, need for transformation, process and challenges of transformation.

Understanding Success

Definitions of success, Principles for competitive success, pre-requisites to create blue print for success. Successful stories of business gurus.

UNIT-IV

Knowledge and Wisdom

Meaning of knowledge and wisdom, difference between knowledge and wisdom, knowledge worker *versus* wisdom worker, concept of knowledge management and wisdom management, wisdom-based management.

UNIT-V

Stress Management

Meaning, sources and consequences of stress, stress management and detached involvement.

Concept of Dharma and Karma Yoga

Concept of Karma and kinds of Karma Yoga, Nishkam Karma, and Sakam Karma. Total quality management, Quality of life and quality of work life.

ROHTAK UNIVERSITY

Indian Ethos and Values

UNIT I

Model of management in the Indian socio-political environment; work ethos, Indian heritage in production and consumption; Indian insight into TQM.

UNIT II

Problems relating to stress in corporate management—Indian perspective; teaching ethics; trans-cultural human values in management education.

UNIT III

Relevance of values in management; need for values in global change—Indian perspective; values for managers; holistic approach for managers in decision-making, secular *versus* spiritual values in management.

UNIT IV

Personal growth and lessons from ancient Indian educational system; science and human values.

Annexure II

Committee on Ethics—Rajya Sabha

1. Morality in Politics

Ethics and morality have been the hallmark of public life in India since ancient times. Rulers were expected to observe stricter ethical values and an unethical king was shown no mercy. Ethics and politics, in other words, were inseparable. This ethical and moral legacy was inherited by its national leaders, who demonstrated a high degree of probity and honesty in public life during the freedom struggle led by Mahatma Gandhi, who himself was an embodiment of this tradition. He not only preached morality in public life but also practiced it. He believed that politics without morality is a thing to be avoided.

However, in recent years there is a general feeling that all is not well with the Indian political system, which is functioning under great strain. Concerns are being expressed over the general decline of values in public life.

2. Role of People's Representatives

That there has been general erosion of moral values in all walks of life cannot be denied. Role of people's representatives, who are largely responsible for guiding the system in such a situation, therefore, becomes very critical. Members of Parliament as the people as their role models and the ones who are guiding their destiny look at people's representatives, have, therefore, to be beyond the realm of any kind of suspicion. By and large, the ideological base and the spirit of service which should activate most of them is getting eroded and the kind of elements who are trying to influence the political parties and the political system at large, make everybody think as to how probity in the entire system could be ensured. There may be many ways for ensuring probity in public life, but a self-disciplining mechanism, appears to be the best in an institution like Parliament.

3. Ethics Committee on Rajya Sabha

After lot of deliberations were held in both the houses of Parliament, the Ethics Committee, Rajya Sabha, the first Ethics Committee by any legislature in India was constituted by the Chairman, Rajya Sabha on 4 March by 1997, to oversee the moral and ethical conduct of the Members and to examine the cases referred to it with reference to ethical and other misconduct of Members. It was provided that in all respects of procedure and other matters, the rules applicable to the Committee of Privileges shall apply to the Ethics Committee with such variations and modifications as the Chairman, Rajya Sabha may, from time to time, make.

Setting up of an institution like Ethics Committee was, in fact, a significant event in the history of Indian parliamentary democracy. Such Committees are functioning only in a few countries of the world and with the setting up of this Committee here, India also has joined the group of these select countries.

4. Main Functions of Committee on Ethics of Rajya Sabha

To oversee the moral and ethical conduct of Members and to examine the cases referred to it with reference to ethical and other misconduct of Members.

Besides this, the Committee on Ethics has the following functions, namely:

(a) To oversee the moral and ethical conduct of members;
(b) To prepare a Code of Conduct for members and to suggest amendments or additions to the Code from time to time in the form of reports to the Council.
(c) To examine cases concerning the alleged breach of the Code of Conduct by members as also cases concerning allegations of any other ethical misconduct of members; and
(d) To tender advice to members from time to time on questions involving ethical standards either *suo motu* or on receiving specific requests.

5. Some Recommendations of Committee on Ethics

The Committee has taken a holistic view of the issue and touched upon important aspects of its mandate.

(i) Role of Political Parties

In the first Report, the Ethics Committee expressed its concern about the decline in standard of behaviour in public life and emphasized the need for controlling it. The Committee observed that it was mainly the responsibility of political parties to prevent persons having criminal record entering political process. The Committee was of the view that without the sincerity and the commitment of political parties, probity in public life could not be ensured. The Committee, therefore, urged upon political parties to regulate the conduct of their members. The parameter for the selection of candidates for election by the political parties should be proven standards in public life. This would go a long way in maintaining the credibility of the political system in the estimation of the people. The Committee was happy over the fact that the representatives of the political parties who appeared before the Committee had assured, on behalf of their political parties, their fullest cooperation to the Committee in its endeavour.

(ii) Committee: A Permanent Body

The Committee was against subjecting the Members of Parliament to the disciplinary authority of an agency outside the jurisdiction of the House and, therefore, recommended for making the Ethics Committee a permanent institution in Rajya Sabha.

(iii) Open Ballot for Second Chambers

The Committee also noted the emerging trend of cross-voting by some electors going against their party line, in the elections to Rajya Sabha and the Legislative Councils in States mainly on extraneous considerations. The Committee, therefore, emphasized the need for holding elections to Rajya Sabha and Legislative Councils in States by open ballot, instead of secret ballot with a view to curbing this disturbing trend.

(iv) Need for Electoral Reforms

The Committee also expressed its view on various aspects of electoral reforms such as, revision of ceiling on election expenses, corporate or State funding of political parties and its ramifications, foreign donations to political parties, etc. It emphasized the urgent need for considering these issues in details and suggest suitable measures for minimizing the role of money power in elections.

(v) Code of Conduct for Members

The committee recommended the Framework of a Code of Conduct which prescribes certain do's and don'ts for the Members of Rajya Sabha. The mechanism for investigation of a complaint and suggested penalties for proven unethical conduct or violating the code.

(vi) The ethics committee called upon the legislatures of the states and union territories to set-up ethics committees in their respective houses.

6. Tainted MPs Kicked out, Parliament makes History

On Dec. 23, 2005 Parliamentary history was created when both the Lok Sabha and the Rajya Sabha expelled 11 MPs for misconduct in accepting money for raising questions.

In a precedent-setting decision in over 50 years; the two Houses, acting swiftly on the recommendations of the Committees that went into scam exposed by a sting operation on a news channel, adopted motions for their expulsion which said their conduct was "unethical" and "unbecoming" of MPs and their continuance "untenable".

There was only one case of expulsion for a similar misconduct in 1951 when the Provincial Parliament removed H.G. Mudgal for accepting money from Bombay Bullion traders for doing their work in Parliament. His resignation was not accepted.

In January 2007, the Supreme Court of India has upheld the action of both the Lok Sabha and the Rajya Sabha in expelling the MPs.

Annexure III

Understanding Hinduism

I. Some Features

Hinduism is old time religion over 4000 thousand years. As Hinduism is missing something most of the other major world religions consider as essentials:

(i) *No Founder to start*: Hinduism which claims about 800 million practitioners is unique in that it cannot be traced to any specific individual or historical event. It is seen as eternal and unchanging in its essence. Believers regard it as having existed for ever.

(ii) *Diverse faiths*; the faith, which is as diverse as India itself, is an extraordinary collection of variations and expansions, some ancient, some more recent.

- *Distinctive Core*. This religion places a heavy emphasis on attaining freedom from the perceived world and on eliminating ties to the material plane of existence. For all Hinduisms this is inter-connection.
- Hinduism is an *ongoing, pragmatic, and inspired synthesis*, not the product of any strict ideology or doctrine. This is both its distinction and its greatness. The earliest historical data shows Hinduism expanding and synthesizing the ancient practices of 'competing' cultures. The same features are in place to this very day.

(a) *The Vedic Period*. The Rig Veda, the earliest and among the most revered of the holy scriptures of Hinduism, was developed between 1500 and 1200 B.C.E. There are 1028 Hymns in the Rig Veda. Rig Veda is one of the World's oldest religious scriptures. Between 800 and 300 B.C.E. Further writings were appended to the *Veda*.

(b) Basically *Veda*, a sanskrit word meaning "knowledge", refers to the great collection of early Hindu religious scriptures. The Vedas outline spiritual principles accepted by Hindus as fundamental to their religion. Vedic teachings emphasise the notion of a single supporting reality, manifested in eternal reality. All Hindus embrace the authority of the Vedas.

(c) Collection of *Upanishads* proved to be one of the most influential in the development of Hinduism. The Upanishads are direct accounts of advice from spiritually advanced mystics. The Upanishad sets out the *principle of reincarnation*. The hymns of the Rig Veda appear to incorporate notions of Heaven and Hell, with the virtuous proceeding to Heaven upon death. But around 600 B.C.E., a new trend of thought emerged, one that accepted the principle that a human spirit, in an ongoing quest for perfection, returns and again in varying forms after the death of each physical body. *Freedom from this cycle was seen as a preeminent spiritual goal*. This doctrine is known as reincarnation.

(d) The Upanishads gave rise to masterpieces of human religious thought, the *Bhagvad Gita*. The Bhagvad Gita is an epic poem relating the dialogue between the human prince Arjuna and the beloved Lord Krishna (one of the most important Hindu deities) on the eve of a great battle. In it, Krishna imparts *spiritual wisdom* that reinvigorates the faltering Arjuna. The text emphasizes union with God by means of love, selflessness, and total devotion.

(e) *Vedanta,* one of classical schools of Indian philosophy, gave rise to a number of disciplines, each placing emphasis on the transcendent messages of the Upanishads. This school came into existence around the first century, etc.

2. Hindu Beliefs

Hinduism is a massive religious system, with a glorious profusion of entry points. The following are core beliefs. *Hindus believe* that . . .

(i) *The Vedas* present authoritative and divinely inspired teachings.

(ii) *The doctrine of Karma,* ensures full accountability for every thought, action and word. Hardships and inequalities of this life may be explained by actions and decisions undertaken in previous lives.

(iii) *Moksha.* The doctrine of reincarnation holds that one is trapped by the cycle of life and death until one attains true realisation. The main task of this world is to move beyond all desires so that soul can be released from the cycle of death and rebirth, called *Samara.* Achieving release (Moksha) can take lifetimes, and Hindus believe that the soul goes through many incarnations, rebirth is a sign that the person has not attained enlightenment or release.

(iv) *Family life* and social interaction are *marked by four stages*: The student, the householder, the seekers, and the ascetic. Believers in the last category improve the lot of the world at large through the process of their renunciation.

(v) *Life has four goals*: Righteousness, earthly prosperity, success, and spiritual liberation.

(vi) It promotes the *sanctity of animals,* i.e. cows and peacocks are treated as sacred and Hindus will not permit their slaughter. Cow represents divine and natural goodness and should be protected.

(vii) Hindus believe that there are *four specific Yogas* (disciplines) that can serve as pathways to enlightenment: (a) janana yoga, which summons the power of the mind and emphasizes meditation, (b) bhakti yoga, which encourages the direction of one's love to God, (c) karma yoga, which involves service to others, and (d) raja yoga, which combines elements of all three above into single practice and included the popular discipline of hatha yoga. Hatha yoga is meant to help the practitioner develop complete control over the body.

Social Reality

The system of castes has been a distinctive part of Indian religious and social life for centuries. Operating simultaneously with a caste system has been a broader method of caste-related social ranking. The major classes in this system are: *Brahmins* (a scholarly elite long associated with the priesthood), *kshatriyas* (the ruling and military class), *vaisyas* (merchants and farmers), *sudras* (the peasantry), and beneath the other four designations, the so-called untouchables. Twentieth century reforms began to address the glaring inequities of the system, rendering untouchability illegal.

(viii) Some religions, i.e. Christian, Muslims and Jews regard monotheism (worship of one God) and polytheism (worship of many gods as incompatible. Hinduism is not one of them. The members of the various Hindu sects worship a number of specific deities and follow innumerable rituals in honour of specific gods. Hinduism is an evolving religion, one that has constantly incorporated new practices and outlooks as spiritual needs have demanded.

(ix) Respect for Life and Personal Growth

- The Hindu view of life and death is essential to the day-to-day observance of this faith. Hindus believe that humanity is cast into a long cycle of repetitive incarnation, known as Samsara. Hindus also accept as a transcendent goal one's ultimate escape from that cycle. Spiritual progress, is all about avoiding rebirth.
- For Hindus, each new incarnation offers the opportunity for growth. Believers pursue four life aspirations, each one recognised spiritually valid: pleasure, development of wealth, righteousness and liberation from the cycle of birth, death and rebirth.
- Although Hindus make deliverance from the process of rebirth their highest spiritual goal, they view life itself as sacred.

3. The *Big Three Deities (Trimurti)* or *Avatars* are:

(a) *Brahma* is a personification of the absolute, the creator of the world.

(b) *Vishnu* has many incarnations, of which two are worthy of note here: as Krishna and as Rama. Vishnu is the *preserver* and is seen as a force of transcendent love. Vishnu is the loving protector with four arms. The last hand holds a lotus. It is Vishnu's job to keep the world in running order and protect the innocent.

(c) *Shiva* symbolises the various forms of the *energy* of ultimate. Usually depicted with four arms and surrounded by fire. Shiva is the third supreme god in the Hindu triad. Shiva embodies the *creative force and the ideas of destruction*. Shiva is worshiped in the form of Linga. A conical shaped stone, resting in base called a Yoni. It represents the goddess.

Other Important Deities

(d) *Krishna*, an enormously popular Hindu deity, is an incarnation of Vishnu. He is seen variously as lover, cowherd and military hero. He is the object and source of extraordinary devoted and unfailing love. Krishna combines unsurpassed wisdom with masculine charm and heroic deeds. He is for centuries, *a divine human* for all time.

(e) *Rama* is another incarnation of Vishnu, his story is told in the epic known as the Ramayana.

(f) *Ganesha*: The elephant headed God.

(g) *Hanuman*: Monkey god with the body of man symbolizes perfect devotion.

(h) *Murugan* is the warrior's god of South India. Murugan is usually shown carrying his favourite weapon, a death-dealing spear. He is quick to protect his devotees and generous in granting boons. As northern and southern Indian cultures amalgamated, Murugan became to identified as Skanda, the six headed warrior son of Shiva. Skanda is widely known as Katikeya.

(i) *The sun* is honoured as an important deity by Hindus.

Hindu Goddesses

The Goddesses are still widely worshiped in Hinduism. Goddesses are Avatars in human form:

(i) *Sarasvati* is the goddess of wisdom and divine inspiration.
(ii) *Lakshmi* is the goddess of prosperity and well-being.
(iii) *Durga* and *Kali* are two fierce warriors goddesses. The Kali Avatar will restore righteousness at the end of this world cycle. The future liberator.
(iv) *Lalita* represent pure consciousness and energy.
(v) *Indra* itself is worshiped as goddess.

ANNEXURE IV

A Summary of The Consumer Protection Act

The Act makes it an offence for a supplier (retailer or distributor) to engage in an unfair practice and provides authority for the Director of Consumer Protection to take action before someone has actually suffered a loss as a result of an unfair practice. For example, it is an unfair practice for a supplier to:

- *do or say,* or fail to do or say, anything that may result in a consumer being deceived or misled, such as knowing there is a substantial defect in the product or service, of which the consumer is unaware, or using exaggeration, innuendo or ambiguity.
- *make false claims,* such as a claim that goods or services are available if the supplier has no intention of supplying them or has no reasonable grounds for believing they will be available, or a claim that a price benefit or advantage exists, if it does not,
- *take advantage of a consumer* who is not in a position to protect his or her own interests, such as a consumer's inability to understand the transaction, or including terms or conditions that are harsh or excessively one-sided.
- *exert undue pressure* on a consumer to enter into a transaction, and
- *charge a price* that is grossly above the price being offered for similar products or services.

Remedies

By providing a series of options such as mediation, the Act encourages and provides remedies for consumers and businesses to resolve their own disputes without proceeding to litigation or charges. If these efforts fail, the Act provides for a series of remedies, depending on the severity of the breach. For example, it provides for:

- the *director to take action* on behalf of disadvantaged or vulnerable consumers, including an action where the unfair practice occurred outside Saskatchewan,
- *voluntary agreements* for compliance between a supplier and the director,
- the *court to order* restitution, and
- an application by the director to the *court for an injunction.*

Warranties

Under Part III of the Act, Consumer Products Warranties, retailers are deemed to give minimum warranties, known as statutory warranties, whenever they sell a new or used consumer product. The minimum statutory warranties include:

- the product belongs to the buyer without undisclosed liens or other claims,

- the product is of acceptable quality,
- the product is reasonably durable and fit for the use intended as well as for any specific purpose stated by the retailer,
- the product matches its description and the quality of any samples shown to the consumer, and
- spare parts and repair facilities will be available for a reasonable period of time.

Anyone who buys the product from the original consumer, receives it as a gift or receives it by law is deemed to be given the same warranties by the seller or manufacturer as the original purchaser.

Saskatchewan's legislation also sets out additional warranties and conditions. A seller or manufacturer may make an express warranty, either orally, in writing or through advertising. This warranty relates to the sale or to the quality, quantity, condition, performance, efficiency, use or maintenance of a product. A seller or manufacturer may make an additional written warranty, which is a written warranty to repair, replace or make a refund.

A seller is deemed to adopt any express warranties on labels or packages unless the consumer is told prior to the sale that the seller does not adopt them. A seller does not adopt warranties in advertising produced by the manufacturer, unless he or she expressly or implicitly adopts them.

Retail sellers, in turn, have the right to recover any losses suffered as a result of a consumer's claim against them from the manufacturer.

Unsolicited Goods and Credit Cards

Part IV of the Act, Unsolicited Goods and Credit Cards, provides that when unasked for goods or credit cards are received, the recipient has no legal obligation to the sender to pay for these unsolicited goods, or for any transaction made with the credit card, unless the recipient has first acknowledged in writing that he or she intends to accept the goods or credit card.

Consumer Disputes Redressal System

The Consumer Protection Act was passed by the Parliament in 1986 to protect the interests of consumers. The Act defines legal relationship between consumers and the sellers. It has set-up a framework where the aggrieved consumer can seek redressal under law. He can present his problems in the consumer courts and consumer councils establish for this purpose.

I. What Constitutes a Complaint

Under the act, a complaint means any allegation in writing made by a complaint in regard to one or more of the following:

- One or more defects in goods. The goods hazardous to life and safety, when used, are being offered for sale to public in contravention of provisions of any law for the time being in force.
- Deficiencies in services.
- A trader charging excess price:
  - Fixed by or under any law for the time being in force; or
  - Displayed on goods; or
  - Displayed on any packet containing such good.

2. Where to File a Complaint

A three-tier *consumer disputes redressal system* is provided in the consumer protection Act at the district, State and the National level. These are:

- District forums at the district level.
- State commissions at the state level.
- National Commission at the national level.

If the cost of goods or services and compensation asked for is up to rupees five lakh, then the complaint can be filed in the District Forum which has been notified by the State Government for the district where the cause of action has arisen or where the opposite party resides. A complaint can also be filed at a place where the branch office of the opposite party is located.

If the cost of goods or services and compensation asked for is more than rupees five lakh, but less than rupees twenty lakh the complaint can be filed before the State Commission notified by the State Government or Union Territory concerned.

If the cost of goods or services and compensation asked for exceed rupees twenty lakh then the complaint can be filed before the National Commission at New Delhi.

3. How to File a Complaint

Procedure for filing complaints and seeking redressal are simple.

1. There is no fee for filing a complaint before the District Forum, the State Commission or the National Commission. (A stamp paper is also not required). There should be 3 to 5 copies of the complaint on plain paper.
2. The complainant or his authorized agent can present the complaint in person.
3. The complaint can be sent by post to the appropriate Forum/Commission.
4. A complaint should contain the following information:
    - The name, description and the address of the complainant;
    - The name, description and address of the opposite party or parties, as the case may be, as far as they can be ascertained;
    - The facts relating to complaint and when and where it arose; and
    - Documents, if any, in support of the allegations contained in the complaint.
5. The relief which the complainant is seeking.
6. The complaint should be signed by the complainant or his authorized agent.
7. The complaint is to be filed within two years from the date on which cause of action has arisen.

4. Relief Available to the Consumers

Depending on the nature of relief sought by the consumer and facts, the Redressal Forums may give orders for one or more of the following reliefs:

- Removal of defects from the goods;
- Replacement of goods;

- Refund of the price paid;
- Award of compensation for the loss or injury suffered;
- Removal of defects or deficiencies in the services;
- Discontinuance of unfair trade practices or restrictive trade practices;
- Withdrawal of the hazardous goods from being offered for sale; or
- Award for adequate costs to parties.

5. Procedure for Filing the Appeal

Procedure for filing the appeal is as follows:

(a) Appeal against the decision of a District Forum can be filed before the State Commission within a period of thirty days. Appeal against the decision of a State Commission can be filed before the National Commission within thirty days. Appeal against the orders of the National Commission can be filed before the Supreme Court within a period of thirty days.

(b) There is no fee for filing appeal before the State Commission or the National Commission.

(c) Procedure for filing the appeal is the same as that of complaint, except that the application should be accompanied by the orders of the District/State Commission as the case may be and grounds for filing the appeal should be specified.

6. Speedy Disposal

The thrust of the Act is to provide simple, speedy and inexpensive redressal to consumers' grievances. To ensure speedy disposal of consumers' grievances, the following provisions have been incorporated in the Act and the rules formed thereunder:

(i) It is obligatory for the complainant or their authorized agents and the opposite parties to appear before the Forum/Commission on the date of hearing or any other date to which hearing could be adjourned.

(ii) The National Commission, State Commission and District Forums are required to decide complaints, as far as possible, within a period of three months from the date of notice received by the opposite party where complaint does not require analysis or testing of commodities and within five months if it requires analysis protesting of commodities.

(iii) The National Commission and State Commissions are required to decide the appeal as far as possible, within 90 days from the first date of hearing.

Annexure V

Corporate Social Responsibility—View Point

In almost every country, the role of business is expanding as government's privatise state-run industries and liberalise markets, Corporate Social Responsibility is increasing running business for people, planet and profit.

Concept of CSR Aims to Maximise its Positive Impact on Business

Thanks to the Internet, even small business may find themselves trading internationally. So, how behave, matters to all of us—whether we run our own business, work in one, teach or study business, or seek to influence business behaviour as a public servant or journalist or an NGO. This increasing interest in how business is run is common around the world. Some call it Corporate Social Responsibility—"CSR"— or the Accountable or Stakeholder Corporation; or a commitment to a "triple bottom line" which measures results in terms of People, Profit and Planet; or being a good Corporate Citizen. In essence, we are talking about a business which is seeking to minimise its negative environmental and social impacts and to maximise its positive impacts.

Negative impacts might include a poor work environment (bullying, favouritism, high accident rates, etc.) or undertaking hazardous activities near a residential area. Positive impacts could include incorporating energy efficiency into the design of new products and buildings; reducing excess packaging; ensuring that people of any faith or background are comfortable working in the business.

Thus, CSR is not just about what a company does in the community. This is part of CSR —but only part. You cannot claim to be a responsible business, because you support environmental NGOs if you are an inveterate polluter; or claim to be a responsible business because you provide schools—if you don't help your own staff to learn and upskill. You cannot say you are responsible because you support HIV/AIDS charities if you discriminate against one of your own staff when become HIV+.

Commitment to Ethical Values is CSR

Many businesses—specially smaller firms—seek to be responsible because they believe it is the right thing to do. For them, it is about their personal and organisational values. Other businesses prefer to combine values and value. In other words, they also want to make a business case. Happy Computers is a London-based ICT consultancy founded 16 years ago by Henry Stewart in his spare bedroom. Today it has been ranked in the *Financial Times* 50 Top businesses to work for—and rated first for work-life balance. As a result, Happy have a waiting list of 2000 people wanting to work for them—so they have no recruitment costs and also save on lower staff turnover. BT is a good example of privatisation and liberalisation in action. In the early 1980s, it was a UK state monopoly, just providing fixed line telephones in the UK.

Today, as a plc, it operates in 170 countries on five continents. It has a well-established commitment to corporate responsibility. Over time, they have found that a 10 percent improvement in public perception of BT's CSR leads to a 1 percent improvement in customer satisfaction—if dropped: customer satisfaction would drop 10 percent overnight. They can show environmental cost-savings: £1163 m in the past 10 years in 2005 alone. The company has also found—as many other companies are now doing—that many staff prefer to work for a business whose values they share. Sixty-three percent of employees are more proud to work for BT because of CSR. Thirty percent of their graduate intake say that the CSR reputation affected their decision to work for BT. And the company reckons that worldwide, £2.2 bn of new business they won in 2004-05, had CSR at its core—out of £18.6 bn in total. Now, Happy Computers and BT did not set out on the responsible business journey, in order to achieve these results: they made a genuine commitment—and these results followed. Other business benefits may include wining new business customers and joint venture partners because of alignment of values and outlook.

Businesses that want to get started, might begin by asking themselves and some of their key stakeholders (employees, customers, investors, suppliers, local communities—that is: those affected by the business and/or able to affect the business), what they see as the biggest environmental and social impacts. Whatever your size of business, you can determine to run your business ethically and fairly. On one of my stops in India, I read a front-page newspaper headline about local Tuk-Tuk drivers who were allegedly fiddling their meters to overcharge their customers! Businesses large and small can commit to "reduce, re-use, recycle" when it comes to water, energy and other resources; to encourage staff to volunteer in local community projects such as listening to children read in a local school each week, or talk to them about what it is like to run a business.

Business Organisations Role

Indian business organisations like CII and the Bombay Chamber of Commerce have CSR initiatives to help their members implement Responsible Business initiatives successfully. There is a global interest now in how businesses behave. Ninety-one of the FTSE 100 largest companies now produce a CSR report, as do 69 of the Fortune global top 100 companies and 38 of the Fortune top 50 European companies.

Corporate Social Opportunity to Reinnovative

Corporate Social Responsibility must not be a bolt-on to business operations but be built in to business purpose and strategy. Businesses should not just think of how this commitment can reduce risks—but also how a genuine commitment to Responsible Business can be a source of creativity and innovation—in short, Corporate Social Opportunity rather than Corporate Social Responsibility!

Commitment to Responsible Business as a source of Creativist and Innovation

There are a number of reasons why this might be so. A commitment to responsible business and sustainable development creates more pressure to find new solutions. It makes the business more receptive to 'out-of-the-box' thinking. It makes the company more receptive to approaches from NGOs, governments and academia with ideas for collaboration. A company genuinely practising CSR is more likely to have eclectic and effective stakeholder engagement processes in place—so stakeholders will have better understanding of the company's interests and areas of expertise and where it might be particularly open to new ideas. Outsiders will be more likely to have the company on their radar screen as a potential collaborator and consider it more open to what at first might seem 'zany, crazy ideas'. A company committed to stakeholder engagement will be more likely to have highly accessible and visible contact points that external stakeholders can approach and who in turn can link the external approaches to the most appropriate people inside the business. The company is less likely to have a 'not invented here' mentality—rather, it will engage in 'creative swiping', being open to ideas not just from other businesses but also from other sectors. There will be a corporate culture that is not only willing to work with others but also widely known and respected so that outsiders want to work with it. It is more likely to have the right mindsets for fair and equitable collaboration with other sectors and partners. By understanding sustainability it will be more alert to opportunities as an integral part of keeping costs down and value up.

As I travelled round India, I found examples of businesses—both large and small who are already adopting these principles. The challenge now is to encourage more to do so—and to ensure that these ideas are shared with the next generation of business leaders through MBA and executive management programmes.

Source: David Grayson CBE gave a series of lectures, organised by the British Council, in Delhi, Kolkata, Hyderabad and Mumbai in February 2006. Details can be found on www.britishcouncil.org.in/rights or www.davidgrayson.net

His most recent book: "Corporate Social Opportunity—Seven Steps to Make Corporate Social Opportunity work for your business" is available in the British Council libraries or can be bought from Viva Books, New Delhi.

ANNEXURE VI

An Ethical Approach to Managing Organisational Politics

1. The Reality of Organizational Politics

Politics in organizations is a fact we all have to live with—from the ostensibly harmless gossip in the corridor to the power games of the boardroom. Those who learn how to use it to their advantage are the ones who get ahead.

In simple terms, politics is power in action. But power can be used constructively or negatively.

Unethical Politics

However, when most people are asked their view of politics in the workplace, they think immediately of those who use underhand means, and indulge in other manipulative behaviour—backstabbing, stolen ideas, and 'scapegoating'—to achieve their own goals.

A research report from Roffey Park, published in 2002, found that office politics can reduce organizational productivity, create a lack of trust, increase internal conflict, and lead to greater assistance to change. People who don't get recognized for their performance feel demotivated and have a lower morale.

Why must there be politics in organizations at all, one might wonder. The fact is that organizations are politically complex. The motives underlying politicking are varied. Some have been outlined below:

(a) Conflict over Resources

- Inadequate resources and positions to meet competing demands.
- There are people with different agendas, different values and different goals.
- Departmental budgets and space allocations are limited.
- Job positions and promotions are few, especially at the top, and contenders for these are many.

(b) Ambiguity in Interpretations for Appraisal

Lack of measurable criteria, e.g., what is 'good' performance or 'unsatisfactory' job? Unfair evaluation and preferential treatment in allocating resources lead to perceived inequity and consequent political behaviour.

(c) Incompetence vs. Ambition

People ambitious of top positions, but lacking in competence and professionalism, seek alternate options to gain organizational rewards. They engage in politics to win the confidence of management.

(d) Politics at the Top Management Level

When negative politics is observed at the management level, it filters down the line to the lower levels.

(e) Inadequate or Faulty Systems and Policies

When standards and rules for behaviour are not set, politickers' set their own rules or bend rules to their advantage.

In such a scenario, conflict and competition are inevitable. This creates a potential climate for politics—using power to influence people and situations in one's favour.

Constructive Politics

Politics need not always be negative. It is important at this point to further clarify our understanding of politics. One report describes how politics can be used constructively by "Establishing effective relationships, understanding individual agendas, acting in a principled way, building strong support for constructive ideas, treating everyone fairly, and influencing others rather than directly using power." It is a case of identifying mutual goals and developing win-win strategies that meet the needs of the influencer, other individuals, and the organization.

2. Managing Organizational Politics

How do different people respond to office politics?

(i) The Political Savvy

It is said that one of the abilities of effective managers is political savvy. They accept the inevitability of organizational politics and adjust their attitude and actions so as not to be victimized by unethical politics in the workplace.

By assessing behaviour in a political framework, they can predict the actions of others and use this information to formulate political strategies that will gain advantages for them and their work units.

Political savvy is observed in people with a high emotional intelligence. Thus, those who are more self-aware, have greater self-control are high on empathy and have good communication and social skills. They are known to be more politically astute and better able to handle office politics than those who are not. They are more aware of the political terrain than their less astute colleagues, who, being less wary could be victims of political landmines.

They learn the system, and work round it when they can. To be able to determine the requirements of each situation and each person one faces, and to select just the right approach to make things work not necessarily in a manipulative way, is the nature of a politically savvy person. This helps one move upwards without necessarily compromising one's principles.

The politically astute are skilled at reading the power structures—who the decision-makers are—and then, act upon these. In a situation, where two people of equal caliber are vying for the same position, it is inevitably the one who is more politically astute, bags the post, not necessarily through manipulation, but just by being smart in handling people and situations. Take the case of Subramaniam and Atul.

Case of Subramaniam and Atul

The former, a brilliant financial analyst, lost out to his colleague Atul for the post of Finance Manager. Subramaniam or Subbu (as he was called) was brilliant at Finance, but he was also a very 'keep to myself', 'speak when I'm spoken to' kind of person, more immersed in his work and less aware of what is going on around him. Atul who superseded him was also a good financial analyst and an honest hardworking person, but not in the same league as Subbu. However, Atul had that which Subbu lacked miserably; Atul was 'political savvy'. He was aware of the social and political currents in the organization just as a good cricketer knows the pitch he is going to play on; and like a good cricketer who plays to win and who strategies his game keeping in mind his opponents strategies, so also Atul was playing to win and was capable of adapting his style, tactics and skills to get things done.

Furthermore, he seemed better able to fit in with the organizational culture in a way Subbu didn't. Finally, he was also a friendly and helpful person, good at building relationships. In the process of networking, he made himself and his work visible. Being visible is very important skill and a mark of political savvy. All these contributed to his getting ahead.

Two facts that emerge from this illustration are that it takes more than job-knowledge and competence to get ahead in business. Secondly, you don't have to be a modern day Machiavelli to get ahead. There is a certain ethical know-how to survive and flourish in any organizational climate. It is possible to put one's career on the fast track by practicing positive politics. The one who gets ahead is the one who walks the middle road. He is political astute and realistic about the nature at human organizations, while at the same time believes in ethics and values, and good job performance.

(ii) The Non-Political Person

Most people simply ignore politics. They have a disdain for organizational politics; they don't want to get involved. They simply want to get on with their lives. Furthermore, they naively believe that promotions and compensations should be the inevitable automatic outcome of good and caliber. They are perplexed when this does not happen and feel victimized by the 'system'. For obvious reasons, these people experience low or no job satisfaction compared to their more astute colleagues. It appears that politics in organizations is a fact we all have to live with. "People who ignore it do so at their own peril."

A lot of really good, decent, brilliant people often sabotage their careers because they believe they are above office politics and they can do without it. But the fact is that there is no escaping office politics, as illustrated below in the case of Ramesh, who could not pre-empt a political attack because he was not politically savvy.

The Political Animal

There are many who resort to under-hand means—manipulating the truth, spreading rumors, withholding key information from decision-makers, lobbying on behalf of a particular individual or decision or alternately against it, forming power coalitions, etc. This is politicking in the true sense of the term and is largely in one's own interest at the cost of others. These people are often referred to as political animals—manipulative, self-centered, and incentives.

3. Advantages of Being Politically Savvy

DeLuca says that one of the underlying ideas of being politically savvy is that it involves "moving from a self-interest to an enlightened self-interest perspective"—aligning one's goals with organizational goals. For this very reason, DeLuca observes that a politically savvy person with a good reputation can outmaneuver a *'mach'* because he is recognized for his integrity, and therefore, has a larger following. The *'machs'* on the other hand, are out for themselves, so their net-works are often not that large.

A politically savvy person is more likely to:

(a) Be skilled at steering meetings, negotiating in tough situations, managing conflict and improving an effectiveness, and is therefore, better recognized as leadership material.
(b) Have his ideas accepted as creative and innovative.
(c) Be selected into distinguished, high potential leadership programmes.
(d) Enjoy greater job satisfaction.
(d) Nurture relationships that help his career to blossom.
(e) Pre-empt a political attack.

4. Practical Tips to Develop Political Savvy

For some, the ability to be savvy and astute in managing people comes intuitively. For those who lack the flair, there are many practical ways to develop a positive political environment and use political skills for positive outcomes. Play it straight, but play it smart. The assessment of your performance is not a fully objective process.

All this sounds like common sense, but common sense is not a common thing. That is why so many persons fail to achieve their goals, because they do just what will clearly sabotage their career.

Key Competencies are Success Factors

Develop and leverage key soft skills, especially effective communication skills, to effectively influence outcomes and relationships—

- Be attuned to recognize political games being played.
- Successfully manage your political image.
- Manage your behaviour and impact on the team.
- Understand other people's strengths and weaknesses and work with them.

Develop the ability to bring out the best in people for initiative, good performance, and evidence of improvement—no matter how minimal—through praise and public recognition.

5. Conclusion

Politics is power in action. Power can be used ethically or unethically. Unethical or negative organizational politics hampers creativity, productivity, fairness, motivation, teamwork, and a host of other critical issues. But principled leadership can ensure constructive politics by aligning management practice to corporate values and corporate purpose. In behavioural terms, this means creating systems for open communication, encouraging and fostering an environment in which individuals feel trusted and listened to, rewarding ethical and honest behaviour, and frowning upon or punishing self-serving political behaviour.

I conclude with the words of Linda Holbeche, Director of Research and Strategy, Roffey Park. "The organizational challenge is to create a culture which encourages the use of constructive political behaviour rather than the more negative, self-serving type. For this to work, each individual's agenda must be aligned to the organizational goals."

This is an abstract of an article by Laurainne Theogaraj, Faculty Member, The ICFAI Business School, Bangalore.

Annexure VII

Corporate Social Responsibility—An Indian Experience of ITC

Responding to corporate social responsibility, Indian corporations are conceptualising 'triple bottom line'. The 'triple bottom line' approach has enabled FTC Limited to fulfil its responsibility as a good corporate citizen for the upliftment of all the organs of society. The company has endeavoured to harmonise the balance between the economy, ecology and society in relation to corporate response to issues of sustainable development. These initiatives are mentioned below:

(i) Transforming Rural Poverty to Potential Markets

ITC has recognized rural India both as a buyer and as a seller of agri-products in the form of goods and services. ITC's 'e-Choupal model seeks to address the issues relating to last mile connectivity by leveraging information technology (IT) to build capacity at the grass-root level through empowerment of the small farmer. This model seeks to enhance farm productivity and income by aligning output with market demand through connectivity. Its primary focus revolves around creating markets and servicing such markets commercially. It is observed that co-creation of value through such simultaneous process. This kind of e-infrastructure can also serve as a powerful and effective delivery channel for a host of goods and services, including those related to farm practices, risk management, education and health for rural development and for converting village populations into vibrant economic organizations.

(ii) Promotion of Forest and Wood-based Industry

ITC has a farm forestry project that integrates business purpose with sustainable livelihoods and environment. This has been driven by the realization that India's meagre forest cover has serious implications for the rural poor. The company works with select NGOs and state governments to identify poor tribals with wastelands and organizes them into self-supporting forest user groups. The user group leaders are trained in the best silvicultural practices to grow high quality timber as a viable crop, and other local species that meet domestic fodder, fuel and nutrition requirements. The company provides a comprehensive package of support and extension services to farmers encompassing loans, land development, planting of saplings, plantation maintenance, marketing and funds management. Creating village-level natural resource management committees comprising local farmers has institutionalised this intervention. Substantial employment has been created during pre-monsoon lean periods when agricultural employment is at its lowest. Thus, seasonality-induced migration is stemmed, making viable other social interventions relating to health, nutrition, education, etc. the benefits of this strategic initiative of ITC are much more pervasive. This effort contributes to moisture conservation, groundwater recharge and significant reduction in topsoil losses due to wind and water erosion. With poor households having access to their own woody biomass, the pressure on public forests stands reduced. Such initiatives of the company across the entire value chain have converted the threats to competitiveness and to the quality of social and natural capital into opportunities for a sustainable partnership.

(iii) Women's Empowerment

ITC initiated steps towards economic empowerment of women in order to transform them into powerful agents of social change. Increased income in the hands of rural women means better nutrition, health care and education for their children. ITC's intervention leverages micro-credit and skills training to generate alternate employment opportunities. Since 2001, this initiative of has enabled the establishment of 500 micro-credit groups and the creation of nearly 2000 women entrepreneurs.

(iv) Primary Education

ITC has made initiatives to upgrade school infrastructures, providing books and uniforms, establishment of supplementary learning centres to improve scholastic ability and teacher training programmes. This has made more attractive to children to maximise enrolment and minimize dropouts in the government-supported schools. The opportunities promised by market-based reforms would stand vastly circumscribed in a nation where illiteracy is rampant. ITC's education support programmes are aimed at overcoming the lack of opportunities available to the poor.

(v) Environment, Occupational Health and Safety

ITC invests substantial resources towards sustaining and continuously improving standards of environment, occupational health and safety (EHS) in a bid to attain and exceed international benchmarks. It is well known that the company's various units operate with world-class standards of occupational health and safety and zero lost time accident record during the year. It has set for itself certain key EHS objectives, against which progress is regularly monitored. Over time, the Company seeks to become a carbon positive enterprise, improve the status of being a water positive enterprise and achieve full recycling of solid waste in all its units. Efficiency of resource use through waste reduction continues is considered to be a key thrust area, particularly recycling of solid waste.

There are global pressures to issue reports on non-financial measures of corporate performances which are emanating from a growing bodies of stakeholders including competitors and peers, customers, shareholders, potential investors, the media, employees, and lobby groups. For a number of entities, highly publicized examples of their failure to address non-financial value issues have resulted in significant adverse publicity, payment of heavy penalties, and a negative impact on brand value. As a result, entities are becoming increasingly aware of the need to be accountable for aspects of their performance, not just financial performance, and, moreover, to act responsibly by reporting on it.

Serious corporate governance movement started in 1998 at the instance of Confederation of Indian Industry (CII) and it travelled to the latest 2004-05 listing agreement through various experts' committees. The main corporate governance initiatives in India are as below:

- Desirable Code of Corporate Governance, a voluntary code made by Confederation of Indian Industry (CII) (1998). (see at Annexure XI)
- Kumar Mangalam Birla Committee (2000).
- Naresh Chandra Committee (2002).
- Narayan Murthy Committee (2003).
- New Clause No. 49 of Listing Agreement (Oct. 2004/Dec. 2005). (see at Annexure X)

Annexure VIII

Case Studies

Case Study I

The Non-Plussed MBA Student

Vinod Agashe is an MBA IV semester student at CBSMS and is majoring in HRM. He has a pleasant encounter with Dinesh Singh who is an employee of a private firm located in Bangalore.

Listen to Vinod.

"It was a chance meeting with Mr. Dinesh Singh the other day. He was in a leisurely and conversational mood. Having known that I was a student of HRM, Mr. Singh went on talking about his experience 20 years back.

"Mr. Dinesh Singh was an operator in a public sector undertaking located in Bangalore. He proved his mettle as a draughtsman and was obviously liked by his boss, peers, and subordinates. He served as a draughtsman for 10 long years in the PSU.

"Having come to know the competency of Mr. Dinesh Singh, a private firm (located in Bangalore) wanted to poach on him. Attracted by higher pay and perks, Mr. Singh quit the government-owned organisation.

"The trouble started now. Mr. Vittal, the HR Manager of the private firm insisted on a fitness certificate from a doctor and advised Mr. Dinesh Singh to get one. Mr. Singh went to Dr. Nandish, a general physician, who diagnosed a heart ailment and gave a report accordingly. Mr. Vittal refused to take Mr. Singh in.

"Mr. Singh was on the street. He lost his secured government job. Nor was he acceptable to the firm which made him put in his papers to the government undertaking. He had dependents at home.

"On advice from friends, Mr. Singh consulted Dr. Bharat, a cardiologist and an approved government doctor for several firms in Bangalore. On examination, the doctor certified to the fitness of Mr. Singh but advised him to see him (the doctor) after a couple of months.

"Fitness certificate being produced, Mr. Singh was inducted into the firm. After two months, Mr. Singh promptly met Dr. Bharath who, after a thorough check-up, advised the former to undergo heart surgery.

"Mr. Singh was hospitalised for two months and the entire medical and nursing bill was picked up by his employer.

"Who is right and who is wrong?"

"I am at a loss. Certain questions are bothering me: What ethical issues are involved in this? Was Mr. Singh right? Dr. Nandish wrong? Was Dr. Bharat unscrupulous? Was Mr. Vittal made a fool? Enlighten me."

Case Study 2

Is Process Insurance Enough?

The maintenance, operations, and safety managers of a large chemical company met with the plant manager to discuss safety features that should be designed into the construction of a new process unit for the manufacture of a highly volatile new chemical product. It would be a significant addition to the plant and employ four people per shift.

The safety features under consideration covered all aspects of risk. In total, they would be extremely expensive to instal and maintain. The group deliberated a long time over the probabilities of explosion or fire. They finally agreed that all of the safety devices recommended would prevent the possible hazards, but they were greatly concerned about the cost. Finally, one member of the group said, "Look, it's just not cost-effective to spend the money. What do we have to lose? Our insurance will fully reimburse us for product loss if the unit malfunctions and blows up. It is such a remote possibility that it doesn't make sense to spend the money".

Question

How would you have responded if you had been a member of this group?

Ethical Dilemmas (Experiential Exercise)

Purpose

This activity is designed to illustrate the complexity of ethical decision-making and how people can differ in their views of what is and is not ethical behaviour.

Setting Up the Exercise

Presented below are four situations often encountered in the workplace that pose ethical issues. Read each scenario and place yourself in the position of the respective decision-maker. What would you do? Write your decision for each scenario on a sheet of paper.

(i) The Roundabout Raise

When Joe asks for a raise, his boss praises his work but says the company's rigid budget won't allow any further merit raises for the time being. Instead, the boss suggests that the company "won't look too closely at your expense accounts for a while." Should Joe take this as authorization to pad his expense account on grounds that he is simply getting the same money he deserves through a different route, or not take this roundabout "raise"? Your decision:

(ii) The Faked Degree

Bill has done a sound job for more than a year. Bill's boss learns that he got the job by claiming to have a college degree, although he actually never graduated. Should his boss dismiss him for submitting a fraudulent resume or overlook the false claim since Bill has otherwise proven to be a conscientious and honourable worker, and making an issue of the degree might ruin Bill's career? Your decision:

(iii) Sneaking Phone Calls

Helen discovers that a fellow employee regularly makes about $100 a month worth of personal long-distance telephone calls from an office telephone. Should Helen report the employee to the company or disregard the calls on the grounds that many people make personal calls at the office? Your decision:

(iv) Cover-up Temptation

Bill discovers that the chemical plant he manages is creating slightly more water pollution in a nearby lake than is legally permitted. Revealing the problem will bring considerable unfavourable publicity to the plant, hurt the lakeside town's resort business and create a scare in the community. Solving the problem will cost the company well over $100,000. It is unlikely that outsiders will discover the problem. The violation poses no danger whatever to people. At most, it will endanger a small number of fish. Should Bill reveal the problem despite the cost to his company, or consider the problem as little more than a technicality and disregard it? Your decision:

Compare your responses to those of the general public and the executives. What factors account for any differences in how you responded compared to their decisions?

A Learning Note: This exercise aptly demonstrates the complexities of ethical considerations in decision-making and the source of the complexities: (1) the differing perspectives among individuals concerning what is ethical; (2) their differing interpretations and assessments of situations; and (3) differing goals, needs, and values.

Source: The scenarios were adapted from an article in *The Wall Street Journal*, Dow Jones and Company, Inc., November 5, 1983, pp. 29ff.

Case Study 3

The Five Principles of Ethical Power for Individuals

Purpose

I see myself as being an ethically sound person. I let my conscience be my guide. No matter what happens. I am always able to face the mirror, look myself straight in the eye, and feel good about myself.

Pride

I feel good about myself. I don't need the acceptance or other people to feel important. A balanced self-esteem keeps my ego and my desire to be accepted from influencing my decisions.

Patience

I believe that things will eventually work out well. I don't need everything to happen right now. I am at peace with what comes my way!

Persistence

I stick to my purpose, especially when it seems inconvenient to do so! My behaviour is consistent with my intentions. As Churchill said, Never! Never! Never! Never! Give up!

Perspective

I take time to enter each day quietly in a mood of reflection. This helps me to get myself focused and allows me to listen to my inner self and to see things more clearly.

Questions

1. Read these five principles of ethical power for individuals. Comment how business is different from these principles.
2. Discuss the significance of these in modern business.

Case Study 4

Management Education at the Harvard Business School

Harvard is one of the leading business schools. Yet there is growing concern about whether the school is moving in the right direction. Harvard's mission has been to educate "general managers and business leaders," but recently, over 50 percent of its graduates took job in investment banking and management consulting. Moreover, less than one-fourth of the 2002 MBAs went into manufacturing companies, and of those, most moved into staff, rather than line, positions.

Investment houses and consulting firms are eager to recruit at Harvard, offering attractive starting salaries. While some critics accuse the students of being greedy, many professors supplement their salaries by teaching in corporations, consulting, appearing as expert witnesses, or serving on corporate boards. While consulting can enhance teaching, there is a maximum time officially allowed for outside activities.

The approach to teaching has also changed. The case approach, for which Harvard is famous, used to stress the role of the general manager. While cases are still used, more analytical tools have become increasingly important. For example, the course Business Policy has changed to Competitive Strategy under the leadership of Professor Michael Porter, who, with a background in economic uses concepts and theories in making competitive analyses.

Harvard, once known for developing business leaders, now increasingly educates specialists. Most of the students have shown little interest in joining manufacturing firms. Yet manufacturing may be critical for making the United States competitive.

Questions

1. Do you think Harvard is moving in the right direction?
2. How does Harvard's approach compare with the one used in your school?

Case Study 5

Ethics and Culture

Bob Simpson is the managing director in the country of West Penguin for Packway Foods, a U.S. food processing company with operations in 12 countries. He buys exotic fruits from the large plantation owners in West Penguin, and Packway Foods has prospered from distributing the rare produce found only West Penguin as a result of this association, or there are several other companies that are anxious to buy the produce as well, but Bob has lived in West Penguin for many years, and has developed a personal friendship with the half dozen plantation owners who control the entire production of the specialty crops. He is a good friend with General Rafael Oregon, the unofficial leader of the plantation owners. General Oregon also is in charge of the West Penguin military, holds a cabinet post, and has strong ties to the president of the country.

Although several packing companies have approached the growers, General Oregon has, until now, convinced the owners to sell only to Bob, due to their special friendship and long business relationship.

General Oregon called Bob in early November, and mentioned in passing that yet another of Bob's competitors had just been to see him. He had sent her away, and repeated that the growers were quite happy with their arrangement with Packway Foods. Oregon also told Bob that his children were coming home from college over the Christmas holidays. Bob is quite fond of the children, and even helped them obtain scholarships and admission to Florida State University. Oregon said he was thinking of buying jet skis for his children as Christmas presents, and he recalled that Bob was a good friend with the local distributor of one of the best brands available. The General wondered if Bob could call his friend and arrange for a special discount for him.

Later that day, Bob thought about Oregon's request. The special arrangement between the growers and Packway Foods represents perhaps 35 percent of Packard's profits. In fact, it is primarily because of the West Penguin business that Packway has been able to survive and prosper, since they are not nearly as well financed as many of the other large packing companies. Because of this situation, Bob is truly one of the keys to Packway's success and continued financial health.

Oregon had never asked for anything of value for himself in the past. The assistance with the scholarships had only been a question of good contacts and advice. Bob wondered if the General was asking for help in obtaining a discount, or for an expensive gift. He also wondered if this would become a regular feature of their relationship, and if the other growers would follow suit. He especially wondered what to say to his parent company, or even if he should raise the issue, and he also wondered if they would encourage him to go ahead, in spite of the U.S. laws restricting such activities.

Questions

1. Develop an effective negotiation process for management situations with possible legal and ethical implications.
2. What are the major ethical issues involved in this case? Discuss.

Case Study 6

Pegasus CEO Sets the Tone

Pegasus International Inc. is a leading manufacturer of integrated circuits (chips) and related software for such specialty markets as communications and mass storage, as well as PC-based audio, video, and multimedia. With a focus on innovation, Pegasus is committed to "technology leadership in the new millennium." Its long-standing strategy has been to anticipate changes in existing and emerging growth markets and to have hardware and software solutions ready before the market needs them. The company has also made significant strides in wireless communications.

The systems and products of Pegasus's wireless business have been selling well in its already existing markets in the United States, Japan, and Europe. But, like any company, Pegasus is eager to grow the business. At a strategy session with the Wireless Division, Pegasus CEO Tom Oswald and division managers decide to explore the potential of expanding their business to China.

Initial research indicates that China is likely to develop into a huge market for wireless because its people do not currently have this capability and the government has made spending on wireless a priority. Wireless is really the only choice for China because of the high cost of burying the communications cables necessary in wired systems; further, in underdeveloped countries, copper wires are often stolen and sold on the black market.

Subsequent research does raise one concern for Pegasus wireless managers. They tell Oswald, "We have this problem. China allocates frequencies and makes franchise decisions city-by-city, district-by-district. A 'payoff' is usually required to get licenses."

The CEO says, "A lot of companies are doing business in China right now. How do they get around the problem?"

His managers have done their homework. "We believe most other companies contract with agents to represent them in the country and to get the licenses. What these contractors do is their own business, but apparently it works pretty well because the CEOs of all those companies are able to sign the disclosure statement required by law saying that they know of no instance where they bribed for their business."

"I wonder if paying someone else to do the crime is the same as our doing the crime," Oswald says. "I'm just not very comfortable with the whole question of payoffs. So, let me ask you, if we don't expand into China, how much business will we lose, potentially?"

His Wireless Division Manager responds, "It will be huge not to do business in all the countries expecting payoffs. China alone represents easily $100 million of business per year. It's not life and death, but it is a sizable incremental opportunity for us, not to mention potential Japanese partners who will make significant capital investments. All we have to do is add our already-existing technology. When you consider all that, we have a lot to gain. What will we really lose if our local contractors are forced to make payoffs every now and then?"

Oswald wants his company to succeed, he wants to maximize shareholder value, he wants to keep his job, and he wants to model ethical leadership. He has made an effort to build a corporate culture characterized not only by aggressive R&D and growth but also by integrity, honesty, teamwork, and respect for the individual. As a result, the company enjoys an excellent reputation among its customers and suppliers, employee morale is high, and ethics is a priority at the company.

Questions for Discussion

1. Should Pegasus conclude that doing business in China is a course they will avoid? Explain.
2. How should Oswald proceed?
3. Can U.S. standards of ethical behaviour be applied and complied with in other countries? Why?

Source: Michael L. Hackworth and Thomas Shank, "The case of the Million Dollar Decision," Markkula Center for Applied Ethics, Santa Clara University, July 2001.

Case Study 7

Just a Modest Change in the Records

Jenny Larson was a senior human resources executive reporting to the Vice-President of Employee Relations, of a major company when this incident occurred. One of her responsibilities was administering the psychological assessment programme for, and maintaining the assessment profiles on all senior executives.

The Executive Committee of the Board of Directors asked for a summary profit on each senior executive for succession planning purposes. Jenny felt that to prevent misinterpretation these summaries should be prepared by the consulting firm that had done the original assessments, and therefore she instructed them to do so.

The consulting firm completed the summaries as instructed and forwarded them to the Vice-President of Employee Relations, for review. He then passed them along to Jenny, who was to prepare the final compilation for the Executive Committee. The next week several revised summaries came from the Vice-President. He had made significant changes to the consultants' summaries. On one summary, for example, the Vice-President had changed "promotable" to "not promotable." Jenny was appalled at the changes, and concerned about what to do. The modifications violated her sense of ethics, but she was afraid if she questioned them, she would place her job and her future in jeopardy. The more she thought about it, the more concerned she became. Was it possible someone above the Vice-President level had requested these changes?

Questions

1. What would you have done if you were Jenny? Why?
2. What consequences would you have expected?

Case Study 8

The Dueling Managers

Peter Lee, Operations Manager, and Jan Nelson, Maintenance Manager, both report to Harry Hart, General Manager of Turbo Chemicals. Peter and Jan are about the same age, well-educated and have extensive experience in their respective fields. It would be expected that these two individuals would complement each other and be the answer to every general manager's prayer. Unfortunately, that is not the case.

For some reason, Peter and Jan find it necessary to challenge each other's decisions and ideas anytime they have a mutual problem to solve, and they argue constantly in staff meetings. Recently Jan began to talk to peers in an effort to get them on her side. Peter learning of this, went to Harry Hart and demanded that he call Jan in and tell her to stop. Peter didn't realize Harry Hart was aware of what was happening. Nor did he know Harry had just learned that Peter had deliberately changed a unit turnaround schedule so that it would fall during a period when the maintenance department already had a peak workload.

The matter has been further complicated by the fact that the employees of the two managers have taken sides and joined the fray. Productive work has come to a standstill.

Questions

1. What are the ethics involved in this case?
2. How would you proceed if you were Harry Hart?

Case Study 9

The Dance of the Lemons

When Gregory Samuels joined the Alpha Corporation, he sat down with Linda Jensen, the senior executive to whom he reported, to learn the goals of the organization, and to find out as specifically as possible what was expected of him. As the discussion progressed, Gregory became increasingly ill at ease. Ms. Jensen seemed reluctant to talk in specifics, and avoided sharing confidential information pertinent to Gregory's position.

As the discussion progressed and Gregory's frustration grew, he asked Ms. Jensen about the new assignment his predecessor had been given. "Oh", Ms. Jensen said with a sly grin, "he has joined the Dance of the Lemons." "What do you mean?" asked Gregory. "Well", said Ms. Jensen, "he was not performing effectively, so we moved him to another assignment." "Will he do better there?" asked Gregory. "Who knows?" said Ms. Jensen "but at least he's out of my hair."

"Was there any particular reason why you assigned him to another position, rather than terminate him?" Gregory asked. "Oh, we seldom terminate senior employees, we just move them around the organization hoping we will find a place they will fit. All of us know these moves happen—we call it the Dance of the Lemons."

Sixty days later, after having located another position, Gregory resigned.

Questions

1. Why do you think Gregory resigned?
2. What would you have done under similar circumstances?
3. Does this case involve managerial ethics? Why or why not?

Annexure IX

Ethical Tests/Exercises

I. Five Ethical Decisions: What would you do?

Assume you're a middle manager in a company with about a thousand employees. How would you respond to each of the following situations?

1. A close business associate has asked you for preferential treatment on an upcoming contract and has offered you a generous sum of money for your time and trouble. Do you accept his offer?
2. You have the opportunity to steal $100,000 from your company with absolute certainty that you would not be detected or caught. Would you do it?
3. Your company policy on reimbursement for meals while traveling on company business is that you will be repaid for your out-of-pocket costs, hot to exceed $50 a day. You don't need receipts for these expenses—the company will take your word. When traveling, you tend to eat at fast-food places and rarely spend in excess of $15 a day. Most of your colleagues but in reimbursement requests in the range of $40 to $45 a day regardless of what their actual expenses are. How much would you request for your meal reimbursements?
4. Your kids will be going back to school next week. You have access to your department's office supplies. No one would know if you took any for personal use. Would you take pens, pencils, writing pads, or the like, from the offence and give them to your kids?
5. You've discovered that one of your closest friends at work has stolen a large sum of money from the company. Would you: Do nothing? Go directly to an executive to report the incident before talking about it with the offender? Confront the individual before taking action? Make contact with the individual with the goal of persuading that person to return the money?

2. An Ethics Test

Indicate the degree to which you agree or disagree with each statement.

Ethical Exercise

Strongly Disagree	0	1	2	3	*Strongly Agree*

0 1 2 3

1. Employees should not expect to inform on their peers for wrongdoings. ❑❑❑❑

	0	1	2	3
2. There are times when a manager must overlook contract and safety violations in order to get on with the job.	❑	❑	❑	❑
3. It is not always possible to keep accurate expense account records; therefore, it is sometimes necessary to give approximate figures.	❑	❑	❑	❑
4. There are times when it is necessary to withhold embarrassing information from one's superior.	❑	❑	❑	❑
5. We should do what our managers suggest, though we may have doubts about it being the right thing to do.	❑	❑	❑	❑
6. It is sometimes necessary to conduct personal business on company time.	❑	❑	❑	❑
7. Sometimes it is good psychology to set goals somewhat above normal if it will help to obtain a greater effort from the sales force.	❑	❑	❑	❑
8. I would quote a "hopeful" shipping date in order to get an order.	❑	❑	❑	❑
9. It is proper to use the company 800 line for personal calls as long as it's not in company use.	❑	❑	❑	❑
10. Management must be goal-oriented; therefore, the end justifies the means.	❑	❑	❑	❑
11. If it takes heavy entertainment and twisting a bit of company policy to win a large contract, I would authorize it.	❑	❑	❑	❑
12. Exceptions to company policy and procedures are a way of life.	❑	❑	❑	❑
13. Inventory controls should be designed to report "underages" rather than "overages" in goods received.	❑	❑	❑	❑
14. Occasional use of the company's copier for personal or community activities is acceptable.	❑	❑	❑	❑
15. Taking home company property (pens, tape, paper, etc.) for personal use is an accepted fringe benefit.	❑	❑	❑	❑

3. Answer the following true/false questions

True	*False*	
❑	❑	1. Ethics are of concern only to senior managers.
❑	❑	2. Ethical considerations are vital elements in choosing between people.
❑	❑	3. Performance appraisals require good standards, hard work and open communication between employee and manager.
❑	❑	4. The primary consideration in granting this year's merit increases and bonuses is the amount given last year.
❑	❑	5. It's completely ethical to violate the rights of others if it gets you what you want.
❑	❑	6. If you can't support and endorse your boss, it's time to find another.
❑	❑	7. Employees will generally support a boss who cuts ethical corners.
❑	❑	8. Creating conflict with your peers and involving your employees in interdepartmental disputes is good, competitive fun.
❑	❑	9. If one of your co-workers seems to be better regarded than yourself, be sure to point up his or her shortcomings.
❑	❑	10. Most of us have had little exposure to ethical role models or sound ethical principles.
❑	❑	11. Ethical problems can be solved using sound problem-solving techniques.

True False

❑ ❑ 12. Following the boss's direct orders is a good way to avoid making ethical errors.
❑ ❑ 13. Collaboration with your peers is healthy and ethical when it is done for the right reasons.
❑ ❑ 14. Safety and health are not ethical decisions. They are strictly financial decisions.
❑ ❑ 15. Since you're the boss, you can ethically fire an employee for any reason you choose.
❑ ❑ 16. Managers are often role models for their subordinates.

How would you respond to each of the following situations? Be honest!

❑ ❑ 17. Alter a financial report at your boss's direction?
❑ ❑ 18. Protect a friend and co-worker whose drinking is causing productivity problems in your unit?
❑ ❑ 19. Take credit for work on a report that was prepared by someone else?
❑ ❑ 20. Put off correcting a safety situation because the cost will decrease your division's profitability?
❑ ❑ 21. Change a performance appraisal to reflect more positively on an individual whose advancement is important to your supervisor?

4. How does Your Ethical Behaviour Rate

Below are 15 statements. Identify the frequency of which you do, have clone, or would do these things in the future when employed full time. Place the letter R, O, S, or N on the line before each statement.

R=Regularly; O=Occasionally; S=Seldom; N=Never

______ 1. I come to work late and get paid for it.
______ 2. I leave work early and get paid for it.
______ 3. I take long breaks/lunches and get paid for it.
______ 4. I call in sick to get a day-off when I'm not sick.
______ 5. I use the company phone to make personal long-distance calls.
______ 6. I do personal work on company time.
______ 7. I use the company copier (or personal use).
______ 8. I mail personal things through the company mail.
______ 9. I take home company supplies or merchandise.
______ 10. I give company supplies or merchandise to friends, or allow friends to take them without saving anything.
______ 11. I put in for reimbursement for meals, travel, or other expenses I did not actually eat or make.
______ 12. I use the company car for personal business.
______ 13. I take my spouse/friend out to cat and charge it to the company expense account.
______ 14. I take my spouse/friend on business trips and charge the expense to the company.
______ 15. I accept gifts from customers/suppliers in exchange for giving them business.

5. How Political are You?

To determine your political tendencies, answer the following questions. Check the answer that best represents your behaviour or belief, even if that particular behaviour or belief is not present all the time.

	True	*False*
1. You should make others feel important through an open appreciation of their ideas and work.	❑	❑
2. Because people tend to judge you when they first meet you, always try to make a good first impression.	❑	❑
3. Try to let others do most of the talking, be sympathetic to their problems, and resist telling people they are totally wrong.	❑	❑
4. Praise the good traits of the people you meet and always give people an opportunity to save face if they are wrong or make a mistake.	❑	❑
5. Spreading false rumors, planting misleading information, and backstabbing are necessary, if somewhat unpleasant, methods to deal with your enemies.	❑	❑
6. Sometimes it is necessary to make promises you know you will not or cannot keep.	❑	❑
7. It is important to get along with everybody, even with those who are generally recognized as windbags, abrasive, or constant complainers.	❑	❑
8. It is vital to do favours for others so you can call in these IOUs at times when they will do you the most good.	❑	❑
9. Be willing to compromise, particularly on issues that are minor to you, but major to others.	❑	❑
10. On controversial issues, it is important to delay or avoid your involvement if possible.	❑	❑

6. Learning Moment

Specific Responsibilities: Managers have responsibilities to employees and to stake holders who may have needs that are different. Managers are challenged by attempting to satisfy these needs. In addition, customers, government, and suppliers are also primary stakeholders. What should be obvious is that while employees want fair fringe benefit packages, sound human resource systems, and good treatment, another group such as owners went increased performance and a significant return on the investment. The tug and pull of different responsibilities is complex and difficult.

Questions

Social Responsibility and Business Ethics

Indicate whether the sentence or statement is true or false.

_____ 1. Economist Milton Friedman and others believe that society creates firms to pursue one primary purpose to produce goods and services efficiently and to maximize profits.

_____ 2. Customers and stockholders (owners) are considered external beneficiaries.

______ 3. Many firms choose to meet their governmental reporting obligations by responding promptly to complaints, by providing complete and accurate product information, and by implementing advertising programmes that are completely truthful regarding product performance.

______ 4. From a communications perspective, ethical communication facilitates the individual's ability to make sound choices.

______ 5. Companies that comply with a code of conduct on wages and working conditions will be able to put a label or tag on their clothing that assures consumers that it was made in America.

______ 6. Although ethics are determined from the top of an organization, they must be driven up and across the organization.

Identify time letter of the choice that best completes the statement or answers the question

______ 7. Which of the following is NOT offered by proponents of social responsibility as social obligation as an argument in support of their view?
   a. Businesses are accountable to the owners of the corporation. Therefore, management's sole responsibility is to serve the shareholder's interests by maximizing profits.
   b. Social improvement programs should be determined by law, by public policy, and by the actions and contributions of private individuals.
   c. Society is entitled to more than the mere provision of goods and services.
   d. Allocating business profits to social improvement activities amounts to taxation without representation.

______ 8. Laws and regulations establish the basis for judging product safety, but market and competitive forces often set the standard for
   a. customer preferences.
   b. product quality.
   c. product names.
   d. repeat purchases.

______ 9. The fundamental rights of a stockholder are:
   a. to be guaranteed a profit.
   b. to be insured against losses.
   c. to receive information on which a prudent investment decision can be based.
   d. to have a buyer for the stock should they choose to sell.

______ 10. Wal-Mart and Sears are using ____________ which allow headquarters-based merchandisers to provide store managers in the field with guidance and advice.
   a. videotapes
   b. CD-based training
   c. teleconferencing
   d. monthly inspection

ANNEXURE X

SEBI Code of Corporate Governance

(Incorporation of Clause 49 in the listing agreement)

SEBI had constituted a Committee on Corporate Governance under the Chairmanship of Shri Kumar Mangalam Birla, Member, and SEBI Board to promote and raise the standard of Corporate Governance in aspect of listed companies. The SEBI Board in its meeting held on January 25, 2000 considered the recommendation of the Committee and decided to make the amendments to the listing agreement in pursuance of the decisions of the Board. It is advised that new clause, namely clause 49 of SEBI be incorporated in the listing agreement as under:

Corporate Governance

1. Board of Directors

(a) The company agrees that the board of directors of the company shall have an optimum combination of executive and non-executive directors with not less than fifty percent of the board of directors comprising of non-executive directors. The number of independent directors would depend on whether the Chairman in executive or non-executive. In case of a non-executive chairman at least one-third of board should comprise of independent directors and in case of an executive chairman, at least half of board should comprise of independent directors.

Explanation: For the purpose of this clause the expression 'independent directors' means directors who apart from receiving director's remuneration, do not have any other material pecuniary relationship or transactions with the company, its promoters, its management or its diaries which in judgment of the board may affect independence of judgment of the director

(b) The company agrees that all pecuniary relationship of transactions of the non-executive directors *vis-a-vis* the company should be disclosed in the Annual Report.

2. Audit Committee

(a) The company agrees that a qualified and independent audit committee shall be set-up and that:

(i) The audit committee shall have minimum three members, all being non-executive directors, with the majority of them being independent, and with at least one director having financial and accounting knowledge;

(ii) The chairman of the committee shall be an independent director;

(iii) The chairman shall be present at Annual General Meeting to answer shareholder queries;

(iv) The audit committee should invite such of the executives, as it considers appropriate (and particularly the head of the finance function) to be present at the meeting of the committee, but on occasions it may also meet without the presence of any executives of the company. The finance director, head of internal audit and when required, a representative of the external auditor shall be present as invitees for the meetings of the audit committee; and

(v) The Company Secretary shall act as the secretary to the committee.

(b) The audit committee shall meet at least thrice a year. One meeting shall be held before finalization of annual accounts and one every six months. The quorum shall be either two members or one-third of the members of the audit committee; whichever is higher and minimum of two independent directors.

(c) The audit committee shall have power which should include the following:

(i) To investigate any activity within its terms of reference.

(ii) To seek information from my employee.

(iii) To obtain outside legal or other professional advice.

(iv) To secure attendance of outsiders with relevant expertise, if it considers necessary.

(d) The company agrees that the role of the audit committee shall include the following:

(i) Oversight of the company's financial reporting process and disclosure of its financial information to ensure that the financial statement is correct, sufficient and credible.

(ii) Recommending the appointment and removal of external auditor, fixation of audit fee and also approval for payment for any other services.

(iii) Reviewing with management the annual financial statements before submission to the board focusing primarily on:

- Any changes in accounting policies and practices.
- Major accounting entries based on exercise of judgment by management.
- Qualifications in draft audit report.
- Significant adjustments arising out of audit.
- The going concern assumption.
- Compliance with according standards.
- Compliance with stock exchange and legal requirements concerning financial statements. Any related party transactions, i.e., transactions of the company of material nature, with promoters or the management, their subsidiaries or relatives, etc. that may have potential conflict with the interests of company at large.

(iv) Reviewing with the management, external and internal auditors, the adequacy of internal control systems.

(v) Reviewing the adequacy of internal audit function, including the structure of the internal audit department, staffing and seniority of the official heading the department, reporting structure, coverage and frequency of internal audit.

(vi) Discussing with internal auditors any significant findings and follow up thereon.

(vii) Reviewing the findings of any internal investigations by the internal auditors into matter where there is suspected fraud or irregularity, or a failure of internal control systems of a material nature and reporting the matter to the board.
(viii) Discussing with external ousters before the audit commences, nature and scope of audit as well as have post-audit discussion to ascertain any area of concern.
(ix) Reviewing the company's financial and risk management policies.
(x) To look into the reasons for substantial defaults in the payment to the depositors, debenture holders, shareholders (in case of non-payment of declared dividends) and creditors.

(e) If the company has set-up an audit committee pursuant to provision of the Companies Act, the company agrees that the said audit committee shall have such additional functions features are contained in the Listing Agreement.

3. Remuneration of Directors

(a) The company agrees that the board of directors shall decide the remuneration of non-executive directors.
(b) The company further agrees that the following disclosures on the remuneration of directors shall be made in the section on the corporate governance of the annual report:
(i) All elements of remunerations package of all the directors, i.e. salary, benefits, bonuses, stock options, pension, etc.
(ii) Details of fixed components and performance linked incentives, along with the performance criteria.
(iii) Service contracts, notice period, severance fees.
(iv) Stock option details, if any—and whether issued at a discount as well as the period over which exercisable.

4. Board Procedure

(a) The company agrees that the board meeting shall be held at least four times a year, with a maximum time gap of four months between any two meetings.
(b) The company further agrees that a director shall not be a member in more than 10 committees or act as Chairman of more than five committees across all companies in which he is a director. Furthermore, it should be a mandatory annual requirement for every director to inform the company about the committee positions he occupied in other companies and notify changes as and when they take place.

5. Management

(a) The company agrees that as part of the directors' report or as an additional thereto, a Management Discussion and Analysis report should form part of the annual report to the shareholders. This Management Discussion and Analysis should include discussion on the following matters within the limits set by the company's competitive position:

(i) Industry structure and developments.
(ii) Opportunities and threats.
(iii) Segment-wise or product-wise performance.
(iv) Outlook.
(v) Risk and concerns.
(vi) Internal control systems and their adequacy.
(vii) Discussion on financial performance with respect to operational performance.
(viii) Material developments in Human Resources (Industrial Relations front including number of people employed.

(b) Disclosure must be made by the management to the board relating to all material financial and commercial transactions, where they have personal interest, that may have a potential conflict with the interest of the company at large (for dealing in company shares commercial dealings with bodies, which shareholding of management and their relatives, etc.

6. Shareholder's Interest

(a) The company agrees that in case of the appointment of a new director or reappointment of a director the shareholders must be provided with the following information:
(i) A brief resume of the director;
(ii) Nature of the expertise in specific functional areas; and
(iii) Names of companies in which the person also holds the directorship and the membership of committees of the board.

(b) The company further agrees that information like quarterly results, presentation made by companies to analysts shall be put on company's web-site, or shall be sent in such a form so as to enable the stock exchange on which the company is listed to put in on own web-site.

(c) The company further agrees that a board committee under the chairmanship of a non-executive director shall be formed to specifically look into the redressing of shareholder and investors complaints like transfer of shares, non-receipt of balance sheet, non-receipt of declared dividends, etc. This Committee shall be designated as 'Shareholders/Investors Grievance Committee'.

(d) The company further agrees that to expedite the process of share transfers the board of the company shall delegate the power of share transfer to an officer of a committee or to the registrar and share transfer agents. The delegated authority shall attend to share transfer formalities at least once in a fortnight.

Information to be Placed Before Board of Directors

1. Annual operating plans and budgets and any updates.
2. Capital budget and any updates.
3. Quarterly results for the company and its operating divisions or business segments.
4. Minutes of meetings of audit committee and other committees of the board.

7. Report on Corporate Governance

The company agrees that there shall be a separate section on Corporate governance in the annual reports of company, with a detailed compliance report on Corporate governance. Non-compliance of any mandatory requirement i.e. which is part of the listing agreement with reasons thereof and the extent to which the non-mandatory requirements have been adopted should be specifically highlighted.

8. Compliance

The company agrees that it shall obtain a certificate from the auditors of the company regarding compliance of the conditions of corporate governance as stipulated in the clause and annex the certificate with the directors' report, which is sent annually to all the shareholders of the company. The same certificate shall also be sent to the Stock Exchange along with the annual returns filed by the company.

ANNEXURE XI

CII Code on Corporate Governance

In 1996, CII took a special initiative on Corporate Governance—the first institutional initiate in Indian Industry. The objective was to develop and promote a code for Corporate Governance to be adopted and followed by Indian companies, be those in the Private Sector, the Public Sector, Banks or Financial Institutions, all of which are corporate entities.

This initiative by CII flowed from public concerns regarding the protection of investor's interest, especially the small investor, the promotion of transparency within business and industry; the need to move towards international standards in terms of disclosure of information by the corporate sector and, through all this, to develop a high level of public confidence in business and industry.

A National Task Force was set-up with Mr. Rahul Bajaj, Past President, CII and Chairman and Managing Direction, Bajaj Auto Limited. This Task Force presented the draft guidelines and the code of Corporate Governance in April 1997 at the National Conference and Annual Session of CII.

The important features of CII code are as follows:

1. The key to good corporate governance is a well functioning, informed board of directors. The board should have a core group of excellent, professionally acclaimed non-executive directors, who understand their dual role of appreciating the issues put forward by management, and of honestly discharging their fiduciary responsibilities towards the company's shareholders as well as creditors.
2. The board should meet a minimum of six times a year, preferably at an interval of two months, and each meeting should have agenda items that require at least half a day's discussion.
3. Any listed company with a turnover of Rs. 100 crores and above should have professionally competent, independent, non-executive directors who should constitute:
   (a) At least 30 percent of the board if the Chairman of the company is a non-executive direct, or
   (b) At least 50 percent of the board if the Chairman and Managing Director is the same person.
4. No single person should hold directorship in more than 10 listed companies. As of now, section 275 of the Companies Act allows a person to hold up to 20 directorships.
5. For non-executive directors to play a material role in corporate decision-making and maximizing long-term shareholder values, they need to:
   (a) Become active participants in boards, not passive advisors;
   (b) Have clearly defined responsibilities within the board such as the Audit Committee; and

(c) Know how to read a balance sheet, profit and loss account, cash flow statement financial ratios and have some knowledge of various company laws. This is of course, excludes those who are invited to join board as experts in other fields such as science and technology.

6. To secure better effort from non-executive directors, companies should:
   Pay a commission over and above the sitting fees for the use of the professional inputs. The present commission of 1% of net profits (if the company has a managing director), or 3% (if there is no managing director) is sufficient.
7. While re-appointing members of the board, companies should give the attendance record of the concerned directors (Confederation of Indian Industries). If a director has not been present (absent with or without leave) for 50 percent or more meetings, then this should be explicitly stated in the resolution that is put to vote. As a general practice one should not re-appoint any director who had not had the time to attend even one half of the meetings.
8. Key information that must be reported to, and placed before the board must contain:
   (a) Annual operating plans and budgets, together with up-dated long-term plans.
   (b) Capital budgets, manpower and overhead budgets.
   (c) Quarterly results for the company as a whole and its operating divisions or business segments.
9. Listed companies with either a turnover of over Rs. 100 crores or paid-up capital of Rs. 20 crores should set-up audit Committees within two years.
   Audit Committees should consists of at least three members, all drawn from a company's non-executive directors, who should have adequate knowledge of finance, accounts and basic elements of company law.
10. Under "Additional Shareholder's Information", listed companies should give data on that report:
    High and low monthly averages of share prices in a major Stock Exchange where the company is listed for the reporting year.
11. Major Indian stock exchanges should gradually insist upon a compliance certificate, signed by the CEO and the CFO, which clearly states that:
    (a) The management is responsible for the preparation, integrity and fair presentation of the financial statements and other information in the Annual Report, and which also suggest that the company will continue in business in the course of the following year.
    (b) The accounting policies and principles conform to standard practices, and where they do not, full disclosure has been made of any material departures.
12. For all companies with paid-up capital of Rs. 20 crores or more, the quality and quantity of disclosure that accompanies a GDR issue should be the norm for any domestic issue. Disclosure for domestic issues should be same as that for GDR issues.
13. Government must allow far greater funding to the corporate sector against the security of shares and other paper.
14. It would be desirable for FIs as pure creditors to rewrite their convents to eliminate having nominee directors except:
    (a) In the event of serious and systematic debt default; and
    (b) In case of the debtor company not providing six-monthly or quarterly operational data to the concerned FI(s).

15. If any company goes to more than one credit rating agency, then it must divulge in the prospectus and issue documents the rating of all the agencies that did such an exercise.
16. Companies that default on fixed deposits should not be permitted to:
(a) accept farther deposits and make inter-corporate loans or investments until the default is made good, and
(b) declare dividends until the default is made good.

Annexure XII

Multiple Choice Questions for Online Examinations

Business Ethics and Corporate Governance

Objective four multiple choice questions. Indicate one out of the four given options as correct answer.

1. Which is not statutory machinery for administration under the Companies Act, 1956
   (a) Company Law Board
   (b) Registrar of Companies
   (c) Advisory Committee of the Law Board
   (d) Company Secretary
2. Legislation alone cannot ensure Corporate Governance. What is not required:
   (a) Voluntary codes
   (b) Society values, morals and awakening, their response to corrupt practices
   (c) Role of whistle blowers
   (d) Professional immorality
3. Which factor is not important for quality of Corporate Governance:
   (a) Integrity and commitment of board members
   (b) Adequacy of financial reporting
   (c) Good corporate internal systems and practices
   (d) Preferential allotment of shares to the promoters of company
4. What factor does not damage the Corporate Governance:
   (a) Ineffective board members
   (b) Combining the office of CEO and Chairman
   (c) Boards are big and independent, Directors are not acquainted about company business and problems
   (d) Setting the strategy and direction
5. Which non-financial disclosure is not required by the public limited company:
   (a) Report on relatives of Directors either as employees or board members
   (b) Interest of Director in any contract
   (c) Loan to full time Director for medical expenses
   (d) Loan to non-executive Director for education of family members
6. Financial disclosures required by the public limited company:
   (a) Use of funds raised from public by issuing shares
   (b) Use of funds raised from public by issue of debentures
   (c) Funds raised for are used for that project particular project
   (d) Unclaimed debenture funds after maturity

7. Houses of Parliament disruptions are public wastage of money. What action is not required by the house?
   (a) Evolve a code of conduct for members
   (b) Speaker to be impartial
   (c) Government can exercise arbitrary authority
   (d) Right to raise issue should not be restricted by the Speaker
8. Companies annual reports should give Corporate disclosures:
   (a) Details on the attendance record of Directors on all board meetings
   (b) Loans and advances received by directors
   (c) Number of non-executive directors are more than Executive Directors
   (d) Setting up of Remuneration Committee
9. Which one is not correct?
   (a) Rajya Sabha has ethics committee
   (b) Lok Sabha has ethics committee
   (c) Rajya Sabha can disqualify a member from house for complaints of corruption if allegation is found true after inquiry.
   (d) No member of Parliament has been found guilty of corruption.
10. Is it essential for a candidate for election to parliament to declare:
    (a) Declare his assets and properties
    (b) Give his conduct record of cases against him
    (c) He is convicted of any criminal offence
    (d) Number of spouses is not required
11. Following information must be regularly reported to board:
    (a) Annual operating plans
    (b) Annual budgets
    (c) Internal audit reports
    (d) Annual holiday list
12. To raise the standard of efficiency and good life it is important not to destroy:
    (a) Political corruption
    (b) Business scandals
    (c) Nepotism
    (d) Spiritualism
13. What has not spoiled the good name of our country:
    (a) Profiteering
    (b) Black marketing
    (c) IT work-force
    d) Love of power
14. Which has not much visibility:
    (a) Corporate embeselment
    (b) Political corruption
    (c) Computer piracy
    (d) Chartered Accountants Audit
15. Which factor does not contribute to Corporate Governance:
    (a) Codes of conduct of law-makers
    (b) Values of corporate managers
    (c) Concern of politicians
    (d) Pressure groups and media exposure

16. Which is not only the objective of corporations:
    (a) Maximize profits
    (b) Minimize price for competition
    (c) Bond and stock-holders' interest
    (d) Society's interest
17. Which is not a factor for corporate social responsibility:
    (a) Maximize profits
    (b) Serve as trustees of stakeholders
    (c) Improve quality of life of society
    (d) Solve political problems
18. Which is not a corner-stone in building commercial success of corporation:
    (a) Ethical values
    (b) Integrity and honour
    (c) Corporate image
    (d) Publicity
19. Benefits of ethics programmes are:
    (a) Do for bottom line
    (b) Managerial actions
    (c) Trust in relationships
    (d) Gaining propaganda
20. Ethically oriented managers are:
    (a) More alert
    (b) Stronger in drive
    (c) Bring change in culture
    (d) Smart in making gains
21. Ethical values are hardly inculcated from:
    (a) Parents
    (b) Teachers
    (c) Clubs
    (d) Colleagues
22. Which is not a principle of ethical organisation:
    (a) Fairness of to all stake-holders
    (b) Putting interest of the society ahead of one-self
    (c) Following laws and codes at will
    (d) Behaviour of corporate leaders
23. Corporation must be responsive to:
    (a) Improvement in community quality of life
    (b) Its social power
    (c) Work for social goals
    (d) A politician's pressures
24. Public holds Board of Directors accountable for:
    (a) Environmental protection
    (b) Caring for employees
    (c) Participation in local community welfare schemes
    (d) Banker's action

25. Which is not important committee of Board:
    (a) Audit Committee
    (b) Nomination Committee
    (c) Remuneration Committee
    (d) Works Committee
26. Audit Committee is to provide checks against
    (a) Executive Director
    (b) Quality of financial reporting
    (c) Areas of disagreements between external auditor and management
    (d) Auditors work plan is adequate
27. Which values are not related with morality:
    (a) Competence values
    (b) Modes of behaviour
    (c) Justice
    (d) Socially accepted norms in laws
28. Organization values are related to:
    (a) Attitudes
    (b) Perceptions
    (c) Organization climate/culture
    (d) Global business competition
29. Benefits of organization values are:
    (a) Foster mutual trust and commitment
    (b) Help in achieving greater loyalty
    (c) Ensure optimum results
    (d) Managerial ineffectiveness
30. Values are conveyed in organizations through:
    (a) Formal written instructions
    (b) Stories and legends
    (c) Personal examples of top management team
    (d) Conveying conflicting norms
31. Which term is synonymous with business ethics:
    (a) Socially responsible
    (b) Corporate social responsibility
    (c) The social responsibility of business
    (d) Managerial ethics
32. Ethics of Corporate Governance determines decisions and actions as:
    (a) Right
    (b) Fair
    (c) Just
    (d) Caring special people
33. Which actions of managers are justified as ethical:
    (a) Transfer an officer to satisfy influential members on the Board
    (b) Manipulate profit figures for purpose of trade union negotiations
    (c) To arrange cash payments to an income-tax officer at the instance of the owners.
    (d) Refusal to fiddle with year-end inventories to show higher profit figure to the Board.

34. Which one is not necessary to take decisions based upon moral content
    (a) Sense of responsibility to others
    (b) A test of our character
    (c) Intuitive moral standards and courage
    (d) Personal values are inappropriate as standards for corporate decision.
35. Essence of Corporate Governance is:
    (a) Effective accountability
    (b) Good management
    (c) Codes of conduct
    (d) Transparency
36. Corporate Governance is a system of:
    (a) Structuring, operating and controlling a company
    (b) Good management
    (c) Investing company's finances properly
    (d) Ensuring maximum profits for the share-holder
37. Corporate Governance is not applicable to:
    (a) Private sector only
    (b) Public sector only
    (c) Government
    (d) Both private and public sector
38. The question of Corporate Governance has come up mainly due to:
    (a) Liberalization of economy
    (b) Deregulation of industry and business
    (c) Public demand for better performance
    (d) Protection of stakeholder's interest
39. A Corporation must not be socially responsible for:
    (a) To meet society expectations
    (b) It is in the self-interest of the corporate
    (c) It mitigates pressure and government regulations
    (d) To camouflage Board actions
40. BOD stands for:
    (a) Board of Director
    (b) Board of Directors
    (c) Boards of Decision
    (d) Directors of the Board
41. Which one of the following is not a category of shareholders in India:
    (a) Promoters
    (b) Financial institutions
    (c) Individual investors
    (d) Ministries of Government of India
42. In the private sector who has the firm hold over the companies:
    (a) Individual investors
    (b) Promoters
    (c) Financial institutions
    (d) Customers

43. In the public sector who selects/appoints the board members:
    (a) The PSU concerned
    (b) Controlling administrative ministry
    (c) The BOD
    (d) Financial institutions
44. The head of the BOD is normally called:
    (a) CEO
    (b) President
    (c) Chairman
    (d) Managing Director
45. For effective Corporate Governance CEO of the company:
    (a) Should always head of DOD
    (b) Should never head the DOD
    (c) Be allowed to head the board in some situations
    (d) Should be allowed to appoint the head of the DOD
46. Which one of the following is not a parameter of best boards:
    (a) Accountability of share holders
    (b) Maximization of profits
    (c) Independence of decision-making
    (d) Transparency of disclosures
47. Which one of the following is not a duty of the non-executive directors:
    (a) Duty of care and skill in discharge of their function
    (b) Duty to manage the operational functioning of the company
    (c) Duty to attend board meetings and devote sufficient time and attention to affairs of the company
    (d) Duty not to exceed powers
48. Directors are not liable for:
    (a) Negligence and breach of trust
    (b) Misfeasance
    (c) Complicity in fraud
    (d) Interity
49. The directors appointed by financial institutions on the BOD are called:
    (a) Non-executive directors
    (b) Executive directors
    (c) Nominee directors
    (d) Institutional directors
50. The Companies Act, 1956 came into force on:
    (a) 1 January, 1956
    (b) 1 January, 1957
    (c) 1 April, 1956
    (d) 1 April, 1957
51. SEBI stands for:
    (a) Securities and Exchange Board of India
    (b) Securities and Enterprises Board of India
    (c) Selection of Enterprises Board of India
    (d) Small Exchanges Board of India

52. Cadbury Committee report was published in UK in:
    (a) 1990
    (b) 1980
    (c) 1992
    (d) 1993
53. Cadbury Committee was set-up to address the:
    (a) Problem of good corporate governance
    (b) Financial aspects of corporate governance
    (c) Problem of degeneration of values
    (d) Malpractices in the corporates
54. Which one of the following was not a section of the Cadbury Committee:
    (a) Role of board of directors
    (b) Role of the outside non-executive directors
    (c) Executive directors and their remunerations
    (d) Evaluation of the BOD
55. Who prepared the report titled "Desirable Corporate Governance in India—A Code":
    (a) Government of India
    (b) FICCI
    (c) CII's Task Force
    (d) UTI
56. The above report of code was based on the draft report prepared by:
    (a) Dr. Goswami
    (b) FICCI
    (c) Dr. C.V. Alexander
    (d) Mr. Kumaramangalam
57. Desirable Corporate Governance: A Code (DCGC) recommends that the full board should meet minimum of following items:
    (a) Six times a year
    (b) Once a year
    (c) Twice a year
    (d) Eight times a year
58. A value is a ____________ concept (choose the word most suited to fill the blank):
    (a) Behavioural
    (b) Perceptual
    (c) Management
    (d) Decision
59. Which one of the following is not a major stakeholder in Corporate Governance:
    (a) Employees
    (b) Customers
    (c) Suppliers
    (d) Auditors
60. The ethics of Corporate Governance is the determination of what is right, proper and ________________
    (a) Good
    (b) Pleasing
    (c) Just
    (d) Practical

61. The word"Ethics" is derived from:
   (a) The Greek word "Ethos"
   (b) The French word "Valoir"
   (c) The Latin word "Valeu"
   (d) The Latin word "Vallis"
62. Many managers think of ethics as a question of personal ________________
   (a) Judgement
   (b) Values
   (c) Thinking
   (d) Scruples
63. Ethical issues are truly managerial dilemma because they represent a conflict between an organization economic performance and its:
   (a) Reputation
   (b) Growth
   (c) Social/ethical performance
   (d) Employees job satisfaction
64. Which one of the following is not a method of analysis of an ethical decision:
   (a) Economic analysis
   (b) Legal analysis
   (c) Ethical analysis
   (d) Cost-benefit analysis
65. Feedback cycle (Evaluation of performance) in BOD was advocated by:
   (a) Robert William
   (b) Zander A
   (c) Sir Adrian Cadbury
   (d) Peter F. Drucker
66. Which one of the following is not the essential features of conducting board's performance evaluation
   (a) The directors themselves
   (b) The role of the board
   (c) The working style of the board
   (d) The composition of the board
67. Who should evaluate the performance of the boards as a whole:
   (a) Chairman
   (b) CEO
   (c) Whole Board
   (d) The Promoters and the chairman
68. Who should evaluate the performance of the CEO (when he is not the chairman):
   (a) Chairman
   (b) Whole board
   (c) Whole board (less CEO)
   (d) Promoters
69. Growing demand for Corporate Governance is mainly due to:
   (a) Increasing public scrutiny
   (b) Media's attention
   (c) Critical examination of performance of organizations
   (d) Lack of effectively functioning of Board of Directors

70. What is not guideline for evaluation of CEO?:
    (a) Outcome of tasks based on established standards
    (b) Behavioural aspects
    (c) Specific improvements in planned systems and procedures
    (d) Implementing innovations, and strategic direction to corporation
71. Corporate Governance does not include:
    (a) Accountability
    (b) Transparency
    (c) Controlling
    (d) Autonomy
72. Corporate Governance is a system not to satisfy:
    (a) Creditors
    (b) Shareholders
    (c) Employees
    (d) Politicians
73. Corporate Governance is to ensure that company is managed in the best interest of:
    (a) Customers
    (b) Bankers
    (c) Community
    (d) Individual
74. Many countries have taken measures to improve Corporate Governance by:
    (a) Company laws
    (b) Inheritance laws
    (c) Codes of Corporate Governance
    (d) Ethical norms
75. Corporate Governance is not concerned with:
    (a) Morals
    (b) Values
    (c) Conduct of Management
    (d) Rights
76. Corporate Governance is a subject concerned with fixing:
    (a) Accountability of corporate sector
    (b) Voluntary code of enforcement agencies
    (c) Regulatory agencies
    (d) Media
77. Codes of Corporate Governance are:
    (a) Guidelines
    (b) Essentially to be followed
    (c) Laws to take care
    (d) Have sanction
78. Codes of Corporate Governance do not include:
    (a) Stock Exchange guidelines
    (b) Board must meet six times a year
    (c) Listed companies to have Non-Executive Director
    (d) Director can become member in any number of companies

79. No code has laid that:
    (a) Director not to be considered for re-appointment if does not attend 50% or more meetings.
    (b) All key information must be placed before BOD.
    (c) Audit Committee must be appointed to assist BOD.
    (d) Audit Committee to be avoided from full access to all financial information.
80. Code of Corporate Governance does not include:
    (a) Nominees of Management on Board of Directors can bull doze the Board.
    (b) Members of the Board should have clearly defined responsibilities.
    (c) Creditors should desist from appointing nominee on the Company's Board if its loans are paid on time.
    (d) Companies should accept further deposits if already defaulted on payment of fixed deposits.

REFERENCE

Address by Chairman Y.C. Deveshwar, TC Ltd. at the 96th Annual General Meeting, 27th July, 2007)

Annexure XIII

Ethical Dilemmas—Ethics Challenges

We reproduce here some ethical dilemmas which often confront the people in the organisations or personal lives. These are identified and extracted from Stephen P. Robbins, Timothy A. Judge and Seema Sanghi's, "Organisational Behaviour" for educational exercises.

1. Ethical Dilemma: Is behaviour modification in organisations a form of manipulation?

Two questions: Is OB Mod a form of manipulation? And if it is, is it unethical for managers to manipulate the behaviour of employees.

Critics of OB Mod say that it manipulates employees. They argue that when managers purposely select consequences to control employee behaviour, they rob workers of their individuality and freedom of choice. For instance, an auto parts plant in Delhi reinforces safe working conditions through a game called safety bingo. Every day that the plant has no accidents, employees can draw a number for their bingo card. The first employee to fill a bingo card wins a television set. This program, critics might argue, pressurize employees to behave in ways they might not otherwise engage in. It makes these human beings little different from the seal at the circus who, every time it does its assigned trick, is given a fish by its trainer. Only instead of getting a fish, some employee walks off with a television.

On the question regarding the ethics of manipulation, the answer typically surrounds what the term "manipulation" means to you. Some people believe the term has a negative connotation. To manipulate is to be devious or conniving. Others, however, would argue that manipulation is merely the thoughtful effort to control outcomes. In fact, one can say that "management is manipulation" because it's concerned with planned efforts to get people to do what management wants them to do.

What do you think?

2. Ethical Dilemma: Five ethical decisions: What would you do?

Assume you're a middle manager in a company with about a thousand employees. How would you respond to each of the following situations?

(i) You're negotiating a contract with a potentially very large customer whose representative has hinted that you could almost certainly be assured of getting his business if you gave him and his wife an all-expense-paid cruise to the Mauritius. You know the representative's employer wouldn't approve of such a "payoff," but you have the discretion to authorize such an expenditure. What would you do?

(ii) You have the opportunity to steal INR 100,000 from your company with absolute certainty that you would not be detected or caught. Would you do it?

(iii) Your company policy on reimbursement for meals while traveling on company business is that you will be repaid for your out-of-pocket costs, not to exceed INR 1,000 a day. You don't need receipts for these expenses—the company will take your word. When traveling, you tend to eat at fast-food places and rarely spend in excess of INR 200 a day. Most of your colleagues put in reimbursement requests in the range of INR 500 to INR 600 a day regardless of what their actual expenses are. How much would you request for your meal reimbursements?

(iv) Another executive, who is part of a small planning team in which you're a member, frequently has the smell of alcohol on his breath. You've noticed that his work hasn't been up to standard lately and is hurting your team's performance. This executive happens to be the son-in-law of the company's owner and is held in very high regard by the owner. What would you do?

(v) You have discovered that one of your closest friends at work has stolen a large sum of money from the company. Would you: Do nothing? Go directly to an executive to report the incident before talking about it with the offender? Confront the individual before taking action? Make contact with the individual with the goal of persuading that person to return the money?

3. Ethical Dilemma: Hiring based on genetic data

The Human Genome Project (HGP) began in 1990. Its goal was to identify the approximately 35,000 genes in human DNA and to map out and sequence the 3 billion chemical base pairs that make up human DNA. As the director of the project said, HGP will allow us to read "our own instruction book."

The project was completed in 2003. And now that it's finished, we're faced with a number of ethical issues as to how the information it developed will be used. From an OB perspective, we should be concerned with how genetic information might be used by employers to screen job applicants and employees.

It is now possible for employers to identify predisposed and presymptomatic genetic conditions. People who are predisposed don't have a disease but have an increased likelihood of developing it. Presymptomatic genetic conditions means a person will develop a disease if they live long enough. For instance, there is a gene that predisposes an individual to breast cancer and another that is presymptomatic of Huntington's disease.

There are federal and state laws in the United States that protect individuals against misuse of genetic data. For instance, the Americans with Disabilities Act protects individuals against genetic discrimination in the workplace. But this applies only to organizations with 15 or more employees. And the law doesn't restrict employers from using genetic testing if it's related to job performance.

Employers and insurance companies argue that genetic information is important to limit potential liability for health and life insurance. Critics respond that employees are entitled to their privacy.

Where it's legal, do you think it's ethical for employers to engage in genetic testing with the intent to screen for diseases or potential diseases? Is it permissible, for example, to use a blood test to perform genetic testing on employees without their consent? What about with their consent? Is your answer any different if the genetic information is reasonably related to specific job-performance?

4. Ethical Dilemma: Are CEOs paid too much?

How much is a good Chief Executive worth? Michael Dell, the charismatic hard-driving Chairman of Dell Computers took about INR 11 billion as mix of salary and incentives. That made him probably the highest-paid CEO in the world.

In contrast, in 2001, the higest-paid Indian GEO Dhirubhai Ambani of Reliance Industries took home INR 88.5 million and that's a 75 percent jump in salary, when profits of Reliance Industries rose only by 10 percent to INR 280 billion. Brij Mohan Lal Munjal of Hero Honda, one among the best paid CEOs, in India, took home INR 41.8 million in 2001, while in 2002, the compensation package was INR 75 million. Has the business increased that fold?

Once upon a time, the Companies Act decreed how much a Chairman and Managing Director could be paid. Now the corporate world has been free from these filters and salary cheques are becoming bigger than ever before. Inevitably in India, as in other countries, the biggest winners are CEOs, who are also major stakeholders in their own companies. How do you explain such astronomical pay?

Some say, this represents a classic economic response to a situation in which the demand is great for high-quality top executive talent and the supply is low. Ira Kay, a compensation consultant, says, "It's not fair to compare executives) with hourly workers. Their market is the global market for executives." Other arguments in favour of paying executives millions a year or more are the need to compensate people for the responsibilities and stress that go with such jobs, the motivating potential that seven- and eight-figure annual incomes provide to senior executives and those who might aspire to be, the need to keep the best and the brightest in the corporate world rather than being enticed into investment banking or other high-paying fields, and the influence that senior executives have on company's bottom line.

Contrary to the global argument, executive pay is considerably higher in the United States than in most other countries. The U.S. CEOs are paid more than twice as much as Canadian CEOs, nearly three times as much as British CEOs, and four times as much as German CEOs. This difference is even greater when compared against what average workers make. The U.S. CEOs make 531 times the pay of their average hourly employees. In contrast, the British CEOs made 25 times as much as their workers, Gandhians 21 times as much, and Germans 11 times as much.

Around 300 Indian CEOs are earning salaries of around $200,000, which is what CEOs of mid-sized U.S. companies earn. The ratio of financial and non-financial parameters is 70:30. Stock options are still one of the most popular methods for long-term incentive plans offered to top executives.

According to Narayan Murthy, CEO-Infosys, CEO should be compensated 5 times more than the lowest paid salary of an employee in a company. He is against mandating a ratio but it can be anything between 15 and 25 times the lowest salary.

Anu Aga, Chairman, Thermax, also feels that the excessive flap on CEO emoluments should be cut.

Is high compensation of CEOs a problem? If so, does the blame for the problem lie with CEOs or with the share-holders and boards that knowingly allow the practice? Are CEO's greedy? Are these CEOs acting unethically? What you think?

5. Ethical Dilemma: Workplace romances unethical?

A large percentage of married individuals first met in the workplace. A 2005 survey revealed that 58 percent of all employees have been in an office romance. Given the amount of time people spend at work, this isn't terribly surprising. Yet office romances pose sensitive ethical issues for organizations and employees. What rights and responsibilities do organizations have to regulate the romantic lives of their employees.

Take the case of former General Electric CEO Jack Welch and Suzy Wetlaufer. The two met while Wetlaufer was interviewing Welch for a *Harvard Business Review* article, and Welch was still married. Once their relationship was out in the open, some accused Wetlaufer of being unethical for refusing to disclose the relationship while working on the article. She eventually left journal. Others accused Welch of letting his personal life get in the way of the interest of GE and its share-holders. Some even blamed the scandal for a drop in GE stock.

Welch and Wetlaufer didn't even work for the same company. What about when two people work together in the same work unit? For example, Tasha, an account executive at a Chicago advertising firm, started dating Kevin, one of her account supervisors. Their innocent banter turned into going out for drinks, and then dinner, and soon they were dating. Kevin and Tasha's bosses were in-house competitors. The problem: Sometimes in meetings Kevin would make it seem that Tasha and Kevin were on the same side of important issues even when they weren't. In response, Tasha's boss began to isolate her from key projects. Tasha broke up with Kevin, who then tried to have her fired. Tasha said, "I remember times when I would be there all night photocopying hundreds of pages of my work to show that [Kevin's] allegations (of her incompetence) were unfounded. It was just embarrassing because it became a question of my professional judgment."

These examples show that while workplace romances are personal matters, it's hard to keep them out of the political complexities of organizational life.

Questions

1. Do you think organizations should have policies governing workplace romances? What would such policies stipulate?
2. Do you think romantic relationships would distract two employees from performing their jobs? or why not?
3. Is it ever appropriate for a supervisor to romantically pursue a subordinate under his or her supervision? Why or why not?
4. Some companies like Nike and Southwest Airlines openly try to recruit couples. Do you think this is a good idea? How would you feel working in a department with a "couple?"

6. Ethical Dilemma: Pressure to be a team player

"OK, I admit it. I'm not a team player. I work best when I work alone and am left alone?, says Rahul.

Rahul's employer, an office furniture manufacturer, recently reorganized the unit around teams. All production in the company's factory is now done in teams. And Rahul's design department has been broken up into three design teams.

"I've worked here for 4 years. I'm very good at what I do. And my performance reviews confirms that, I've scored 96 percent or higher on my evaluations every year I've been here. But now everything is changing. I'm expected to be part of our modular-office design team. My evaluations and pay raises are going to depend on how well the team does. And, get this, 50 percent of my evaluation will be on how well I facilitate the performance of the team. I'm really frustrated and demoralized. They hired me for my design skills. They knew I wasn't a social type. Now they're forcing me to be a team player. This doesn't play to my strengths at all."

Is it unethical for Rahul's employer to force him to be a team player? Is his firm breaking an implied contract that it made with him at the time he was hired? Does this employer have any responsibility to provide Rahul with an alternative that would allow him to continue to work independently?

7. Ethical Dilemma: Discrimination against their colleague

Suicide bombers and terrorist attacks have been common-places for decades in much of the Middle East. But not so for North America. The attacks on the World Trade Center and Pentagon buildings on September 11, 2001 opened North American eyes to the reality that terrorism is a worldwide phenomena and that no place is completely safe from terrorist attacks.

Some Americans allowed the actions of a few Arab extremists on September 11th to shape their attitudes toward all Arabs. The result has created new challenges for managers leading diverse groups containing individuals of Middle Eastern backgrounds.

Jeff O'Connell is one of those managers. Jeff oversees a team of five computer chip designers. They work exclusively on defense contracts-designing and building high-powered chips for use by the U.S. military.

Jeff's five person team is a text book example of diversity. They've got a woman from Texas, an African, American from New York, two Russians, and an Arab American who born in California but whose parents both immigrated from Iran. Jeff, himself, was born in Canada but raised in the United States.

In the months following the September 11th attack and again in 2003 following widely publicized suicide bombings at the U.N. building in Baghdad and on a bus in Jerusalem—both killing dozens of innocent people, including children—Jeff became aware that several of his team members were making openly disparaging remarks to Nicholas, their Iranian co-worker. They questioned his Arab friends, his religious practices, and his loyalty to America. Nicholas's colleagues understood little about his Islam religion.

Its illegal in the United States for employers to discriminate. But that doesn't stop employees from discriminating against their colleagues. Jeff sees himself in an ethical dilemma. What, if anything, should he do when he sees team members discriminating against Nicholas because of his ethnicity.

8. Ethical Dilemma: Non-work-related uses of information technology

You work for a company that has no specific policies regarding non-work-related uses of computers and the Internet. They also have no electronic monitoring devices to determine what employees are doing on their computers. Are any of the following actions unethical? Explain your position on each:

(a) Using the company's e-mail system for personal reasons during the workday.
(b) Playing computer games during the workday.
(c) Using your office computer to do Internet shopping during the workday.
(d) Looking for a mate on an Internet dating-service Web site during the workday.
(e) Visiting "adult" Web sites on your office computer during the workday.
(f) All of the above activities conducted before or after normal work hours.
(g) For telecommuters working from home, using a computer and Internet-access line paid for by your employer to visit Internet shopping or dating-service sites during normal working hours.

9. Ethical Dilemma: Do ends justify the means?

The power that comes from being a leader can be used for evil as well as for good. When you assume the benefits of leadership, you also assume ethical burdens. But many highly successful leaders have relied on questionable tactics ends. These include manipulation, verbal attacks, physical intimidation, lying, fear, and control. Consider a few examples:

Bill Clinton successfully led the United States through 8 years of economic expansion. Those close to him were committed and loyal followers. Yet he lied under oath (causing him to lose his law license) and "managed" the truth.

Jeck Welch, former head of General Electric, provided the leadership that made GE the most valuable company in America. He also ruthlessly preached firing the lowest-performing 10 percent of the company's employees every year.

Cisco Systems CEO John Chambers laid off nearly 20 percent of his workforce and commented that the tough times were "likely to be just a speed bump." Tell that to the 17,000 workers he laid off. And yet, Cisco has returned to profitability.

Few U.S. presidents understood foreign relations or made as much progress in building international cooperation than did Richard Nixon. But his accomplishment are largely overshadowed by the meanness, dirty tricks, and duplicity he exhibited during his tenure in the White House.

10. Ethical Dilemma: Ethical leadership or would you work here?

Would you accept a senior leadership position at a major tobacco company like ITC? I've asked that question to students over the years and typically 80 percent or more answers "No."

The content of goals are said to have ethical ramifications. Does that mean that certain types of businesses are inherently unethical? For instance, many students defend their position not to work at a tobacco company because they believe the product the company sells is unhealthy. But where do you draw the line? Would you take a managerial position at ITC? Would your answer be different if the pay was INR 300,000 a month rather than INR 75,000?

Tobacco companies, of course, are not the only firms that produce products that have questionable health consequences. Would you work for United Beneries (TIB) a bravery such as the UB group? The first response from most of my students is "Yes." But many begin to question that response when told that the family lives are less likely to be peaceful. Drivers drive rashly and have a higher chance of causing accidents. So, thousands of people die each year as a result of UB products. Is this a fair conclusion? Does it alter your view of working at UB?

Cookies and ice cream are also products that are hard to argue that these are good for people's health. High in sugar and fats, they contribute to health problems such as obesity, high blood pressure, and high cholesterol. Could you ethically be a manager at Cadburys or Kwality Walls?

What companies, if any, wouldn't you be willing to work for and hold a leadership position in because you find their products or services to be unethical?

11. Ethical Dilemma: Is it unethical to lie and deceive during negotiations?

In Chapter 11, we addressed lying in the context of communication. Here we return to the topic of lying but specifically as it relates to negotiation. We think this issue is important because, for many people, there is no such thing as lying when it comes to negotiating.

It's been said that the whole notion of negotiation is built on ethical quicksand: To succeed, you must deceive. Is this true? Apparently a lot of people think so. For instance, one study found that 28 percent of negotiators lied about a common-interest issue during negotiations, while another study found that 100 percent of negotiators either failed to reveal a problem or actively lied about it during negotiatiors if they were not directly asked about the issue. Why do you think these numbers are so high? The research on negotiation provides numerous examples if when lying gives the negotiator a strategic advantage.

Is it possible for someone to maintain high ethical standards and, at the same time, deal with the daily need to negotiate with bosses, peers, staff, people from other organizations, friends, and even relatives?

We can probably agree that bald-faced lies during negotiation are wrong. At least most ethicists would probably agree. The universal dilemma surrounds the little lies—the omissions, evasions, and concealments that are often necessary to best an opponent.

During negotiations, when is a lie a lie? Is exaggerating benefits, downplaying negatives, ignoring flaws, or saying "I don't know" when in reality you do considered lying? Is declaring that "this is my final offer and non-negotiable" (even when you're posturing) a lie? Is pretending to bend over backward to make meaningful concessions lying? Rather than being considered unethical practices, the use of these "lies" is considered by many as indicator's that a negotiator is strong, smart, and savvy.

When is evasiveness and deception out of bounds? Is it naive to be completely honest and bare your soul during negotiations? Or are the rules of negotiations unique? Any tactic that will improve your chance of winning is acceptable?

12. Ethical Dilemma: Just following orders

In 1996, Betty Vinson took a job as a middle-level accountant for $50,000 a year with a small long-distance company in Jackson, Mississippi. Within 5 years, that long-distance company had grown up to become telecom giant WorldCom.

Hardworking and diligent, Ms. Vinson was promoted to senior manager in WorldCom's corporate accounting division within 2 years. In her new job, she helped compile quarterly results, along with 10 employees who reported to her. Soon after she took the position, Vinson's bosses asked her to make false accounting entries. At first, she said no. But continued pressure led to her finally caving in. Her decision to make the false entries came after the company's chief financial officer assured her that he would assume all responsibility.

Over the course of six quarters, Ms. Vinson made illegal entries to bolster WorldCom's profits at the request of her superiors. At the end of 18 months, she had helped falsify at least $3.7 billion in profits. Of course, the whole scheme unraveled in 2002, in what became the largest fraud case in corporate history.

Ms. Vinson pleaded guilty to two criminal counts of conspiracy and securities fraud, charges that carry a maximum sentence of 15 years in prison. On August 5, 2005, Vinson was sentenced to 5 months in prison and 5 months house arrest. She was also sentenced to 3 years of probation.

What would you have done had you been in Ms. Vinson's job? Is 'just following orders" an acceptable excuse for breaking the law? If your livelihood is on the line, do not say no to a powerful boss? What can organizations do to lessen the chance that employees might capitulate to unethical pressures imposed by their boss?

13. Ethical Dilemma: Is involuntary ethics training unethical?

A lot of companies rely on training as an essential part of their efforts to create an ethical culture. In some cases, this training is short in duration and requires little emotional investment by the employee. For instance, the training might only require regarding a pamphlet describing the company code of ethics, followed by an online quiz to ensure employee understanding. In contrast, some organisations' ethics training is quite lengthy, requiring employees to seriously address their values and principles and to share them with their co-workers. For example, the Boeing Company's training program, called "Questions of Integrity: The Ethics Challenge," is conducted within an employee's work group. Led by their supervisor; employees discuss more than four dozen ethical situations. Each includes four possible ways of dealing with the problem. After the supervisor discusses each situation, employees are asked to choose the best outcome by holding up cards marked A, B, C, or D. Then the supervisor indicates the "ethically correct" answer.

Most of the evidence indicates that for ethics training to be effective, it needs to be intensive and frequently reinforced. Some of the best programs require participants to spend several days a year, every year, engaged in discussions and exercises designed to clarify the organization's ethical expectations.

Is it unethical to ask employees to share their deepest personal values regarding right and wrong with boss and co-workers? Should employees have the right not to participate in ethical training programs that might require them to publicly vocalize their standards, religious principles, or other personal beliefs?

14. Ethical Dilemma: Is it unethical to "shape" your resume?

When does "putting a positive spin" on your accomplishments step over the line to become misrepresentation or lying? Does a resume have to be 100 percent truthful? Apparently, a lot of people don't think so. A recent survey of 2.6 million job applicants found that 44 percent of all resumes contained some lies. To help clarify your ethical views on this issue, consider the following three situations.

Lakshmi left a job for which his title was "credit clerk." When looking for a new job, he describes his previous title as "credit analyst." He thinks it sounds more impressive. Is this retitling of a former job wrong?

About 8 years ago. Eshika took 9 months off between jobs to travel overseas. Afraid that people might consider her unstable or lacking in career motivation, she put down on her resume that she was engaged in "independent consulting activities" during the period. Was she wrong?

Mahadev is 50 years old with an impressive career record. He has graduated from President College, but not clear all the credits for an MBA degree. He is being considered for INR 4.8 million a year vice presidency at another firm. He knows that he has the ability and track record to do the job, but he won't be called for the interview if he admits to not having a management degree. He knows that the probability that anyone would check his college records, at this point in his career, is very low. Should he put on his resume that he completed his degree?

15. Ethical Dilemma: Increasing employee productivity and stress

Mani supervises a staff of 15 people handling back-office functions for a regional brokerage firm in Delhi. With company revenues down, Mani's boss has put increasing pressure on her to improve her department's productivity.

The quickest way for Mani to increase productivity in her department is to lay-off two or three employees and fill the gap by asking the rest of the staff to work harder and put in more time on the job. Since all her employees are on salary, they are not paid for overtime. So, if Mani let three people go and asked her remaining staff to each put in an additional 10 hours a week on the job, she could effectively handle the same workload with 20 percent fewer employees.

As Mani considered this idea, she had mixed feelings. Reducing her staff and asking people to work more hours would please her boss increase job security for those people remaining. On the other hand, she was fearful that she was taking advantage of a weak labour market. Her employees knew that jobs were scarce and would be hard put to find comparable positions elsewhere in the securities industry. The people laid-off would have a tough time finding work. Moreover, she knew that her current staff was unlikely to openly complain about working longer hours for fear that they, too, would be let go. But was it fair to increase the department's productivity on the backs of already hard-working employees? Was it unethical to ask her employees to put in 10 hours more a weak, for no additional money, because the current weak labour market worked to her advantage? If you were Mani, what would you do?

Reference

Stephen P. Robbins, Timothy A. Judge and Seema Sanghi, Organisational Behaviour, Pearson Education, New Delhi. Gratefully acknowledged.

Annexure XIV

Making Marketing Work for CSR in ITC Ltd. (July 2007)

(Environmental Sustainability and Inclusive Growth of Indian Society) ITC Ltd.

1. Financial Performance

The foundations that we have laid over time by investing in R & D, technology and innovation for international competitiveness, supported by a robust governance structure, continue to drive growth in your Company's multiple businesses, providing a strong momentum for a secure future.

You, the shareholders, can draw even greater satisfaction from the fact that these financial results rest on a strong foundation of trust earned by your Company's diverse brands, products and services and the enduring relationships formed with millions of farmers in rural India over several years. It is on this bedrock of trust, competencies, innovation and rural partnerships that we have built our aspiration to be a leader in every business segment we are engaged in.

2. Sustainable and Inclusive Growth

Last year, I had spoken to you on the fundamental pillars of Vision, Values and Vitality that have powered the transformation of your Company over the past decade. I reiterated that envision in a larger societal purpose has always been the hallmark of your Company. Indeed, this 'commitment beyond the market' is a compelling Vision that motivates us to enlarge our contribution to the Indian Society, even as we attain new milestones of excellence in sustainable wealth creation.

We have, over the years, pursued relentless innovation to forge unique business models that synergise long-term shareholder value enhancement with the superordinate purpose of creating greater societal capital. We take pride that your Company is defined by its deeply 'Indian' character that aligns corporate strategy to national priorities.

It is for this reason that we measure our accomplishments not only in terms of financial performance but also by the transformation we have consciously engendered to augment the natural and social capital of the nation. This approach towards achieving Triple Bottom Line benchmarks is key to our resolve to contribute to the national goal of sustainable and inclusive growth. It is my firm belief that business enterprises can and must make a difference towards achieving greater social equity. It is through a fundamental and unwavering commitment to Triple Bottom Line objectives that long-term sustainability of business enterprises can be ensured, unleashing in the process strong drivers that can make national progress more inclusive and equitable.

ITC has received global recognition as an exemplar of Triple Bottom Line performance. For five years in a row, we have achieved and sustained our status as a 'water positive' for organisation. We have also been 'carbon positive' for the last two years. We continue to strive towards achieving a 'zero solid waste' discharge status, having recycled over 90% of solid waste produced during the year. This makes us, to the best of my knowledge, the only business enterprise in the world, of our size and complexity, to accomplish these three dimensions of environmental excellence—an extremely challenging task given the fact we are continuously growing our manufacturing operations.

In addition, through a concerted effort to develop innovative value-chains across our diverse business segments, your Company today is instrumental in creating and sustaining livelihoods for nearly 5 million people, many of whom represent the weakest sections in rural India.

Our deep commitment in ensuring sustainability and competitiveness have given us the confidence to voluntarily publish an annual Sustainability Report with independent reputed third party verification. The 2006 Sustainability Report of your Company, the third in the series, is the first in India and among the top 10 in the world to be presented in accordance with the latest G3 guidelines of the Global Reporting Initiative.

Indeed, these achievements reinforce our commitment in making a meaningful contribution towards sustainable and inclusive growth of the Indian Society.

3. A Social Charter for Business

A few weeks ago, the Hon'ble Prime Minister Dr. Manmohan Singh presented a ten-point 'Social Charter' sharing his vision on the responsibility of corporate for sustainable and inclusive growth. He said, and I quote, "Indian industry must rise to the challenge of making our growth processes both efficient and inclusive. This is our endeavor in Government. It will have to be yours too and I seek your partnership in making a success of this giant national enterprise. If those who are better off do not act in a more socially responsible manner our growth process may be at risk, our polity may become anarchic and our society may get further divided. Invite corporate India to be a partner in making ours a more "humane and just society." Unquote.

To my mind, the Hon'ble Prime Minister's clarion call is not only a responsibility that we, in Indian Business and industry, must commit ourselves to but a crying need that we cannot afford to neglect any longer. While we can justifiably be proud of India's stellar performance in GDP growth, the growing inequity in sharing the fruits of success is indeed a milestone that impedes the nation's true potential. Business Corporation draw heavily on societal resources. Therefore, it is in the enlightened self-interest of business to engage constructively in enlarging its contribution to the broader social and environmental agenda. Competitiveness of firms can be severely threatened by unsustainable environments and a lopsided social structure that creates islands of affluence amidst a sea of poverty. A constructive public-private partnership for socially responsible growth is imperative and must occupy a larger space in the future business strategies of India's corporate sector.

You are indeed aware of the enormous importance of our rural engagement in the future growth of your Company. We have constantly strived to meaningfully blend our social responsibilities with business competitiveness, so that we can continue to create as we enhance the benefits that accrue to rural communities. We recognise that this is the path we must pursue to ensure sustainable and inclusive growth—a philosophy that is central to the vision articulated by Prime Minister's Social Charter for Business.

I take immense pride that the vision enunciated by the Hon'ble Prime Minister echoes the core values that your Company has enshrined in its management philosophy and governance structure. We have indeed been 'practitioners' of this vision for many years now. It gives me immense satisfaction that your Company has executed, on a substantial scale, innovative business strategies which result in 'mainstreaming' the disadvantaged sections in rural India.

4. Various Initiatives/Programmes

Your Company's pioneering e-Choupal initiative today comprises 6,400 choupals transforming the lives of over 3.5 million farmers in 38,500 villages in 9 States of India. We hope to reach out to 10 million farmers in 100,000 villages in the not too distant future. The Social and Farm Forestry Programme of ITC covers 65,000 in over 28 million person days of employment among the disadvantaged. In the process, we have also helped sequester over 2,000 kilotonnes of Carbon Dioxide as a firm commitment to combating climate change. Your Company's Integrated Watershed Development programmes in rural areas cover nearly 27,000 hectares providing critical irrigation to water stressed areas. This year, we have also forged a milestone partnership with the Government of Rajasthan for an integrated watershed development project covering 5,000 hectares. Your Company's initiatives to provide opportunities for non-farm incomes through economic empowerment of women, supplementary education and integrated animal husbandry services continue to make significant strides in rural empowerment.

As a nation, we face today a multi-dimensional challenge to chart a growth path that will transform the lives of almost a third of our billion population who live at the margin. Surely, it is not a task that any single segment of society—be it Government or Responsible Business—can hope to accomplish in isolation. It is true that sustained high rates of GDP growth is one of the surest ways of creating livelihoods for the disadvantaged. However, if such growth impulses do not envision or contain conscious efforts to enhance social value, it is not necessary that high growth rates alone will ensure social equity. In fact, there is a danger that competitive pressures may not actually lead to development and growth in areas that need it the most.

It is important to examine how market drivers can creatively facilitate such long-term investments which have larger societal benefits. Corporates will be able to support a much larger social involvement in their business strategies, if market forces facilitate such investments and returns.

How do we then create a market that will support such corporate action for social development?

5. Mobilising CSR for Economic Growth with Equity

Over the years, progressive organisations have demonstrated several laudable examples of responsible corporate action for social development. Unfortunately, many of these efforts have not been able to reach a level of scale and dimension that can make an impactful difference on a nation as large and diverse as ours. Why is it, that despite possessing rich and diverse managerial capability, a tradition of entrepreneurship, economic resources and the right consciousness, corporates are still unable to participate more meaningful in building natural and social capital?

The reasons are many and complex. These relate to the lack of a conducive external environment as also to organisations' vision, values, leadership and competitive capability. However, if there is one common thread, it is the unassailable fact that markets have failed to reward CSR (Corporate Social Responsibility). They do not adequately provide the drivers required to sustain a level of intensity of long-term engagement necessary to produce results in the vast social fabric. As Prof. David Vogel says, in his recent work titled 'Market for Virtue', and I quote, "CSR is sustainable only if virtue pays-off. The supply of corporate value is both made possible and constrained by the market . . . while there is a place in the business system for responsible firms, the 'market for virtue' is not sufficiently important to make it in the interest of all firms to behave more responsibly."

It is sometimes argued that the 'reputational asset' that CSR attains is an adequate reward in itself, and therefore, does not need any further market incentives. However, at the present stage in India, such a reputational asset has so far not led to any significant consumer support, persuaded sizeable investor interest, or resulted in meaningful preference in Government policies. Therefore, given the ambivalent market response, CSR initiatives, by and large, tend to attempt the minimum, often defined by compliance to regulations, and do not ignite creativity and innovation to accelerate social benefit.

There are also apprehensions amongst many that investing in CSR would put them at a disadvantage *vis-a-vis* their competitors who do not choose to carry such social overheads. Nevertheless, there are worthy exceptions, where organisations have displayed sustained commitment and are certainly the harbingers of social change and an inspiration to others. However, it is only when market forces make CSR a crucial component of shareholder value creation that new competitive forces will emerge in favour of responsible corporate action. It is then that CSR will assume a new dimension—one that is defined by market forces, and not inspired by corporate conscience alone.

I am of the firm belief that private enterprises are well placed to play a much larger role in augmenting natural and social capital. Corporates have create assets and facilities that span the length and breadth of the country, and therefore, constitute the front line of engagement with civil society. The physical presence in communities around their catchments gives them an opportunity to directly engage in synergistic business activities that can create livelihoods and add to preservation of natural capital. More than financial resources, private enterprises possess the more crucial managerial capability to ensure efficient delivery of social projects. In that sense, CSR can lead to optimum utilisation of national resources, given that far higher social benefits will accrue to every unit of incremental cost incurred by the organisation. Thus, given the right market incentives, Indian corporates can significantly add to Government efforts in pursuing growth with equity in constructive public-private partnerships.

The key to corporates sustaining a meaningful strategy for constructive social action therefore lies in the ability to create strong market drivers that incentivise CSR. Civil Regulation, including pressure groups, act as strong drivers to ensure socially responsible action. Government regulation and public policy are also influential drivers. However, these again tend to deliver the bare minimum interventions. Besides, over reliance on regulation can stifle corporate creativity and innovation. A perceptible augmentation of societal capital will take place when market drivers spur innovation and a sense of competition to deliver CSR in ways that positively impact financial results. CSR initiatives then become a part of the balance sheet deliverables, are quantified the market and provide a direct incentive to the company to enhance socially responsible behaviour.

6. Making Markets Work for CSR

Can we, therefore, make markets work for CSR ? Are there compelling market drivers which would give a positive reinforcement to corporates to focus on Triple Bottom Line performance? Can these powerful drivers energise innovation by companies, so that CSR becomes an integral part of the marketing mix and a competitive differentiator?

Fortunately, there is an answer. The most potent force that can trigger a complete rethink of corporate strategy and bring about transformational change lies in the power of consumer franchise. I use the term 'consumer' here in a broader sense to also encompass other market participants including Government—both as a buyer and regulator, Investors, Employees, Job-Seekers and other segments of Civil Society.

6.1 *An enlightened consumer, by exercising a choice in favour of socially responsible enterprises, can unleash a powerful force of incentives.* A 'positive vote' for socially responsible companies, exercised through preference for a company's products and services, would change the context and dimension of meaningful CSR, create strong economic multipliers and enhance shareholder value. The implications of such consumer franchise for business will be wide ranging.

(a) *Consumer preference* will spur a massive movement in corporate innovation to integrate business goals with the building of societal capital.
(b) CSR can also emerge as a distinctive *market differentiator* and help position progressive companies more strongly in the marketplace.
(c) Companies will vie for consumer spend by positioning *CSR as a compelling value proposition.*
(d) Gains would accrue to the company and its shareholders with increasing revenues and goodwill.
(e) Where consumers go, Investors will follow. Investors will increasingly find such *socially responsible companies attractive,* given the larger market gains.
(f) Potential employees would also seek opportunities in such successful companies and the enterprises themselves would be *better positioned in the war for talent.*
(g) Competition amongst CSR exemplars would lead to a perceptible *augmentation of natural and social capital* and this would create a more sustainable future.

Thus, powerful market drivers will emerge to encourage CSR as an integral part of business strategy. In the course of time, stakeholders will build a more enduring relationship with such companies, continuously creating value for the organisation, for its shareholders and the nation.

6.2 Enlisting Consumer Support

The key, therefore, lies in mobilising market participants—the most potent being the consumer—and *enhancing awareness amongst them, so as to empower their decisions.* We will need to ramp up consumer education substantially, so that they are made aware of the power they possess to transform society and bring in enduring social change. Government, Industry and Civil Society will need to join hands in this endeavour to give it more body, scope and reach.

Your Company made a beginning in this direction by creating a high visibility 'cause marketing' campaign involving our popular brands—'Sunfeast' and Aashirvaad'—and highlighted the link with some of our CSR initiatives. It was our endeavour to educate the consumer that with every spend on those brands, they would, in effect, be contributing to the Social Forestry and Watershed initiatives of your Company. You are aware that your Company's 'Classmate' brand contributes significantly towards the education of the underprivileged by earmarking a portion of its proceeds for this cause. I am given to understand that school children actually prefer Classmate products not only for their superior quality, but also for their association with a noble cause. We are command to enhancing these awareness campaigns, and it will be our endeavour to continuously make the consumer aware of the choice that she possesses to support such social programmes by making informed buying decisions.

It is heartening to note that worldwide, consumers are already demonstrating their preference for socially responsible products and services. In 2006, an estimated 1.6 billion worth of Fairtrade products were sold across the world, growing annually by almost 50%. This independent consumer certification mark guarantees that disadvantaged producers are getting a better deal. Today, more than 7 million people—farmers, workers and their families—across 59 developing countries benefit from the international Fairtrade system. In some cases, consumers have also demonstrated that they are willing to pay more for a product or service if it contributes to social good. These are certainly welcome developments although they occupy, as of now, a small proportion of global trade. If these individual efforts of consumers get escalated into collective action, they will certainly have a distinct impact on corporate thinking and action.

Unfortunately, the 'market for virtue' in India is practically non-existent. However, a small beginning has been made. With concerted action from policy-makers and civil society, a significant force can be created by enlightened consumer franchise to *spur industry into innovative thinking for social action.*

India's young demographic profile will also support this trend. In late 2006, a Cone Millennial Cause Study in the US found that, amongst the youth, nearly nine out of ten surveyed stated that they were likely or very likely to switch from one brand to another (price and quality being equal) if the second brand was associated with a good cause. *This goes to indicate that with greater awareness through education and exposure, the future generation will tend to exercise a 'vote' for companies with higher social accountability.* This is now getting to be a worldwide trend, and with increasing connectivity through the Internet, widespread media and new tools for communication, I can see the emergence of a young global community, who share common views, common concerns, and common hopes and aspirations. This is a force that is laying dormant amongst India's confident new young generation, and once unleashed will be a formidable catalyst for change.

6.3 Aligning Forces of Franchise

Given the power of consumer franchise, how do we align forces amongst all the market participants to support a new movement for innovative CSR?

To make 'consumer choice' a compelling market driver we would need to create a supportive institutional framework to facilitate the process of making an informed choice by market participants. Let me briefly elaborate on some of these enablers:

6.3.1 First, the Policy and Institutional Framework.

(i) Market participants would need an effective tool to make an informed choice in favour of a Responsible Corporation. I would *suggest that Government support the development of a 'CSR Sustainability Trustmark', or a series of Trustmarks* defined by Industry segments, which could be displayed on products and services to convey to the consumer that the enterprise follows a strong commitment to building natural and social capital. Voluntary in nature, these Trustmarks, crafted on sound scientific and market principles, will stand for the positive impact a company has made on the environment and the society. The Trustmarks could also be supplemented with Ratings, based on the extent of the individual company's involvement in creating societal capital.

(ii) *The Trustmarks need to be administered by a reputed and independent body or bodies, much like the financial rating agencies.* An institutional framework and appropriate guidelines can be created by a Government-Industry partnership to provide organisational support and credibility.

(iii) *A major impetus can emerge out of Government's consideration to extend fiscal and financial concessions, priority clearance* and other incentives to organisations that attain sustained high ratings. Government and its agencies could also give purchase preferences to suppliers with highly rated Trustmarks.

6.3.2 Second, the role of Industry

(a) *In championing a sincere commitment to a Vision that embraces contribution to Society as a key component of business strategy.*

(b) In moving towards *voluntary disclosure of Triple Bottom Line performance in the Company's Annual Reports*, verified by independent reputed third party organisations.

(c) In making a strong effort *to attain the CSR Sustainability Trustmarks*, and displaying the same on their products and services.

(d) In enlarging the Company's contribution by giving *preference to vendors with a strong CSR and Sustainability orientation.*

(e) In developing a model *code of responsible conduct* by Industry bodies and associations for its members.

(f) In encouraging Modern Retail outlets to develop *special sections that display and sell products with Trustmarks.*

(g) In *support to the creation of Awards* that recognise outstanding Sustainability Performance. This would provide a tremendous reputational asset and incentivise CSR significantly.

(h) In *strengthening reporting on Sustainability* based on guidelines such as the Global Reporting Initiative. I am sure that the Indian operations of multinationals, not listed on Indian bourses, would also want to make such public disclosures and demonstrate their contribution to the Indian Society. I envisage a future where Sustainability Reporting will form an integral part of a firm's public disclosures, and will be valued by stakeholders in equal measure to the established practices of financial reporting.

6.3.3 Third, the Role of Investors

(i) *Investors play a critical role in encouraging social accountability in corporate behaviour.* Globally, there are today hundreds of funds that invest in socially responsible enterprises. These funds rely on Sustainability Indices such as Dow Jones Sustainability World Index, FTSE4Good, Domini 400 Social Index and others to guide investment decisions. These funds have already channeled large amount of investors' savings into companies that have high social brand capital.

(ii) *India has witnessed some welcome developments in this direction in recent years.* The ABN Amro Bank launched a Sustainable Development Fund as India's first Socially Responsible Investing Fund. Recently CRISIL, S&P and KLD have announced that they would develop an Environmental, Social and Corporate Governance (ESG) Index of Indian companies. The Institute of Chartered Accountants of India is also reported to be working on developing a similar evaluation.

(iii) *Individual investors,* while seeking to maximise returns from their portfolio holdings, *could exercise a powerful choice for companies with high Triple Bottom Line performance.*

(iv) Banks and Financial Institutions could ask for voluntary disclosures and *factor the rating in their lending evaluations.*

6.3.4 Fourth, the Role of Civil Society Organisations

(a) Consumer awareness will benefit immensely if *civil society organisations and consumer bodies actively advocate the usage of Trustmarks.* They could also promote awareness amongst constituents to support products and services of companies with higher Sustainability ratings.

(b) *Schools and educational institutions could also promote awareness on responsible corporate behaviour and its association* with the Trustmark ratings on products and services, and design elements in their curriculum to groom citizens of tomorrow as enlightened consumers.

(c) And finally, *the Media,* as one of the most powerful forces of shaping public opinion, *can make a multi-dimensional contribution in this direction.*

It is my strong belief that by aligning such powerful forces, *we will see the emergence of a new consciousness where CSR will transcend from corporate philanthropy to a competitive value proposition.*

7. Your Company has been instrumental in setting up the *CII-ITC Centre of Excellence for Sustainable Development,* which is a unique institution that seeks to address the void in developing requisite capability on Sustainability issues among Indian industry. The Centre endeavours to bring about transformational change in Indian businesses by providing thought leadership, promoting awareness and building capacity. One of the major initiatives of the CII-ITC Centre is to recognise excellence in Sustainability practices by presenting Awards to industry, based on a rigorous process of selection. This attempt to recognise outstanding Sustainability initiatives is designed not only to celebrate individual corporate action, but also to inspire others to follow.

I am convinced that in today's enlightened India, more and more companies will respond to the appeal made by the Hon'ble Prime Minister to forge partnerships for social action, and achieve growth with efficiency and inclusivity. Making markets work for CSR will indeed provide the compelling foundation for such initiatives.

8. Making a Difference

The essence of what I have presented to you today is a considered response to enhancing corporate participation in societal development. Your Company has been at the forefront in providing both thought leadership and action in creating a more secure, sustainable and inclusive future. It is true that no single organ of society will be able to make a significant difference based on their individual action. However, the efforts made by your Company demonstrate that with innovation, commitment and by forging enduring partnerships, we can all make a difference.

Indeed, the challenges seem daunting when we witness the scale of inequity and poverty. The good news is that never before in world history have we possessed so much knowledge, technology and resources to deal with this apparently hopeless situation. *It is indeed heartening to witness a growing corporate consciousness to ensure that the future generations are more secure.* I hope this groundswell of effort will continue to grow and become a committed movement for a better tomorrow.

I firmly believe that Corporates in India have the capability, the vision and the entrepreneurial skill to forge a more prosperous future for the nation, even as they sharpen their competitiveness and grow their businesses globally. Mahatma Gandhi said, and I quote: 'The difference between what we do and what we are capable of doing would suffice to solve most of the world's problems". We need to heed this message to realise our fullest potential.

To be able to stand tall amidst adversity, to live your convictions and know that your actions and beliefs have transformed the lives of millions is at once a humbling and enriching experience. Your Company is indeed privileged to be able to make a difference, and be recognised for the contribution it makes. *Our abiding Vision, the strength of our outstanding human capital, and our commitment to creating enduring value will continue to inspire us as we strive to achieve even greeter success in the future.*

Reference

Address by Chairman Y.C. Deveshwar, TC Ltd. at the 96th Annual General Meeting, 27th July, 2007.

Index